Understanding
Kinetic
Energy

KRISTEN PETERSEN

Cavendish
Square
New York

Published in 2015 by Cavendish Square Publishing, LLC
243 5th Avenue, Suite 136, New York, NY 10016

Copyright © 2015 by Cavendish Square Publishing, LLC

First Edition

This publication represents the opinions and views of the author based on his or her personal experience, knowledge, and research. The information in this book serves as a general
guide only. The author and publisher have used their best efforts in preparing this book
and disclaim liability rising directly or indirectly from the use and application of this book.

CPSIA Compliance Information: Batch #WW15CSQ

All websites were available and accurate when this book was sent to press.

Library of Congress Cataloging-in-Publication Data

Petersen, Kristen.
Understanding kinetic energy / by Kristen Petersen.
p. cm. — (Mastering physics)
Includes index.
ISBN 978-1-5026-0144-5 (hardcover) ISBN 978-1-5026-0147-6 (ebook)
1. Force and energy — Juvenile literature. 2. Dynamics — Juvenile literature. 3. Energy
transfer — Juvenile literature. I. Title.
QC73.4 P484 2015
531.6—d23

Editor: Fletcher Doyle
Senior Copy Editor: Wendy A. Reynolds
Art Director: Jeffrey Talbot
Senior Designer: Amy Greenan
Senior Production Manager: Jennifer Ryder-Talbot
Production Editor: David McNamara
Photo Research by J8 Media

Printed in the United States of America

CONTENTS

INTRODUCTION 4

1 THE BASICS OF MATTER AND ENERGY.... 7

2 THE PHYSICS OF ENERGY 13

3 TYPES OF MECHANICAL ENERGY 21

4 UNDERSTANDING THE LAWS OF ENERGY .. 29

5 GAINING MOMENTUM.............. 37

GLOSSARY 43

FURTHER INFORMATION................ 45

BIBLIOGRAPHY...................... 47

INDEX............................ 48

INTRODUCTION

F rom the complicated systems of nuclear power plants to the simple use of a pulley to make moving heavy objects easier, **physics** helps to explain and understand the world around us, as well as the greater universe. Through physics, we can study **matter, energy,** and motion, and how these three topics are interrelated. Since the days of Sir Isaac Newton, physicists have applied three basic laws of motion to all things, be it throwing a baseball or launching a rocket. Newton's laws help us understand how the planets stay in orbit, as well as how a car's brakes stop it from moving.

Sir Isaac Newton's laws of motion can be used to explain why the planets stay in orbit.

The great value of physics is that its laws and properties apply to all objects, regardless of size. Newton's laws are true for atoms as well as planets and stars. The only place where Newton's laws don't apply is at the subatomic level, for things such as electrons. That is the realm of quantum physics. When you begin to understand and appreciate these laws, you'll gain a deeper understanding of how the world works. After all, the universal application of this information is

Physics can tell you both the amount of spin and the angle of release that will give you the best chance of making a shot in basketball.

used in chemistry, biology, computer science, and engineering, as well as everyday hobbies such as sports, video games, and so much more.

Here is an example using basketball. The higher the arc on your shot, the larger your target area (you can see more of the inside of a cup looking straight down than from the side). However, you must shoot the ball higher to make it come nearly straight down, and the longer it falls the greater its speed. The faster the ball is moving when it hits the rim, the farther it will rebound. According to Creighton University physics professor Gintaras Duda, the perfect three-point shot is released at a 45-degree angle, at just under 20 miles per hour (32 kilometers per hour), with a backspin of two revolutions per second.

Another factor is the soft shot. A ball that comes off the fingertips the correct way will have backspin. A ball with backspin will experience more **friction** when it hits the rim than a ball with no spin. The increased friction will slow the ball, increasing its chances of bouncing into the basket.

This book will help you understand some of the basic concepts of physics, specifically the different types of **mechanical energy**.

All objects in this family's living room are made up of matter, but the television is one of the few that puts energy to work.

ONE

The Basics of Matter and Energy

O ur world, and the entire universe, is made up of both energy and matter. Of the two, matter is easier to understand. All the objects around you are matter. Your television, cell phone, house, family, trees, and the ground are all matter. The planet Earth is matter, as is the moon, the sun, and all the stars you see.

Energy is a harder concept to understand. You cannot always see energy when it is present. Energy is what makes things happen. Imagine what the world would be like without it. Nothing could breathe or move. Plants could not grow. The oceans would never have waves. The sun would not shine. You would not be able to function. Matter without energy would mean that our world would not exist.

Usually you cannot see energy. You only see what it does. You may think that you see energy in the form of gasoline, electrical wires, or batteries, but these really are just substances and objects that have the ability to release energy. What is energy? Scientists define it as the capacity to do **work**. In other words, energy causes change and makes things happen.

Sunflowers grow so that each part faces the sun, thereby maximizing photosynthesis.

ENERGY FROM THE SUN

Most of the energy on Earth comes from one source, the sun. If you stand outside on a sunny day, you can actually see and feel its energy. That is because the sun's energy is released in two primary forms: light and heat. From the food that fuels us to the electricity that powers our television sets and computers, most energy used by humans began as light emitted by the sun.

Although you may feel warm and get a tan after standing outside on a sunny day, your body can convert only some of the sun's rays into usable energy. Flowers, trees, and other plants take care of most of the conversion. Without them, almost all of the sun's energy would flow past Earth and would not cause anything to occur. Every living thing on our planet benefits from the process plants use to convert sun energy into food energy.

TURNING LIGHT INTO ENERGY

Green plants can trap the sun's light energy in a green substance called chlorophyll. As the sun shines on plants, the chlorophyll

Understanding Kinetic Energy

absorbs the light as energy. The word used to describe this process is photosynthesis.

Plants combine light energy with water and carbon dioxide, a gas that is present in the air around us, to make a simple sugar. All green plants, whether or not they taste sweet, contain some form of sugar. Some plants use the sugar to make other kinds of food, such as starches and fats. The food helps to nourish the plants. It also helps to nourish animals, including humans.

Even when we eat meat, we are getting nutrition that once existed in plants. Somewhere along the food chain, an animal got its food from a plant source. A chicken, for example, might eat bugs that ate plants. When we eat chicken, fish, or any kind of meat, we benefit from the food that originally came from a plant source.

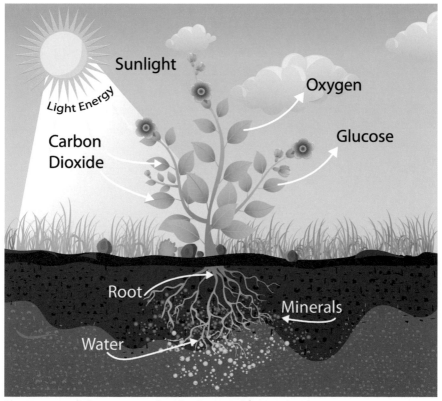

Plants can turn light energy into food for them—and for us.

Renewable and Nonrenewable Energy Sources

Humans and other living things gain energy by eating. Cars, planes, computers, televisions, and most other equipment and machines get most of their energy either directly or indirectly from **fossil fuels**. Just as the energy in food can be traced back to sunlight, so, too, can the energy in fossil fuels. Gasoline, petroleum oil, coal, natural gas, and other forms of energy called fossil fuels get their name from the fact that they developed from the fossilized remains of prehistoric plants and animals.

More than 80 percent of the world's energy, including electricity, comes from fossil fuels. Many large power plants that produce electricity get their energy from coal. Power plants burn coal to create heat energy that boils water to create steam. The steam then rushes through a machine that spins very fast. The spinning produces electricity that wires transport over long distances. When you plug in anything that runs on electricity, you are tapping into this electrical energy.

Fossil fuels take thousands, even millions, of years to form—that's why they're categorized as nonrenewable energy sources. Burning fossil fuels also creates smog and smoke, which may lead to environmental and health problems. The demand for fossil fuels has doubled every twenty years since 1900.

With the need for energy growing, governments and scientists are looking to increase the use of **renewable energy sources** such as solar, hydroelectric, wind, and biofuel.

It takes a long time for plants to turn into fossil fuels, but the wind can be used for energy immediately.

A skier possesses a lot of potential energy at the top of Mont Blanc, one of Europe's tallest peaks.

TWO

The Physics of Energy

When you look at a piece of chicken or a bunch of grapes, or another fuel source such as a battery or a gallon of gas, they might not seem at first glance like a source of energy. After all, you could put all four of those items on a table and they would just sit there, never moving. You need to do something with these objects. You must eat the chicken or grapes, put the battery in a clock, or pour the gas into a lawn mower to harness the energy in them. Until you do something with all of these items, they contain **potential energy**.

At some point, you probably have heard a friend, family member, or even yourself described as having "a lot of potential," usually in reference to ability. This means that the person with potential has not achieved his or her full level of success yet, but that the individual possesses the ability to excel in the future. That is what potential energy is like. Potential energy is the stored energy of an object, which depends on its position, rather than its motion. For this reason, potential energy is also known as the energy of

At the bottom of a jump, the bungee cord holds its maximum elastic potential energy.

position. This stored energy means that the object has the potential to do work. In other words, the stored energy can be released.

To see how potential energy works, try this experiment. Place a rubber band in front of you. Unless you move it, the rubber band will stay where it is. Now, place the rubber band over the tip of your index finger and pull back on it with the thumb and index finger of your other hand. You have just given the rubber band potential energy. As long as you hold the rubber band in that outstretched position, it has the potential to move. Be sure that no one is in front of you and that nothing breakable is in the rubber band's path before you release it.

STRETCHING FOR ENERGY

A rubber band is an example of **elastic potential energy**. This kind of energy can be stored in materials that may be stretched or compressed. Thrill seekers make use of this kind of energy when they jump while tied to a bungee cord. Using special equipment and with the help of professionals, bungee jumpers leap off bridges and other high places. When the jumper reaches the bottom of the jump, potential energy that has built up in the cord will jolt the jumper back up into the air.

Understanding Kinetic Energy

Trampolines also use elastic potential energy. The material stretched out on the trampoline acts like a rubber band. When you come down on it, you give the material stored energy. It then has the potential to bounce you back upward. Springs operate in almost the same way, except they can also be compressed, or squashed down. The compression gives them potential energy.

ENERGY THROUGH CHEMISTRY

Another kind of potential energy is chemical. Until recently, not much was understood about **chemical potential energy.** However, recent advances in the physics of very small particles have enabled scientists to better learn what kind of energy exists on an atomic scale. Bonds between atoms store potential energy. Electrons (tiny subatomic particles that carry a negative electrical charge) and electronic charge differences are what form the bonds. Electrons themselves do not provide any potential energy. Only the bonds between atoms exist as a source of potential energy. Food, batteries, gas, and coal are all examples of chemical potential energy.

When you eat a piece of fruit, for example, your digestive system works on the fruit to break down the nutrients stored within it. If you have not eaten in a while and are active, your body might use this energy right away to help fuel your actions. If not, the fruit's energy could be stored for future use. That is one reason why eating a lot can cause weight gain. Your body stores all of the extra energy as fat, which itself becomes a source of chemical potential energy within your body.

BURNING CALORIES

You probably know that a candy bar has more calories than a small piece of fruit, but do you know exactly what a calorie is? A calorie is a measurement of how much heat energy is contained in food. When we "burn" calories, we are using up the food's energy. Humans burn calories all of the time. Even sitting still reading this book will burn about 100 calories an hour. That is because your body is maintaining its temperature, your heart is beating, you

The Gravity of the Situation

A passenger weighs nothing in a zero gravity aircraft.

Gravity, which is the pull that all objects with **mass** have on each other, provides another form of potential energy. Mass is the amount of matter that a living or nonliving thing has. On Earth, your mass is equal to your weight. If you were to travel to the moon, your mass would stay the same, but your weight would change. That is because on Earth your weight is a measurement of your gravitational attraction to Earth and Earth's gravitational attraction to you. If you weigh 100 pounds (45.36 kilograms) on Earth, you would weigh slightly more than 17.64 pounds (8 kg) on the moon because the effect of the moon's gravity is less than that of Earth's.

When you pick up an object, such as an eraser, you give it **gravitational potential energy**. When you let it go, it will fall to the ground because of gravity. By lifting it up, you give it the potential to move.

Gravitational potential energy is the energy stored within an object due to its vertical position, or height. To determine an object's gravitational energy, three facts must be known: the object's mass, its height, and the acceleration of gravity. On Earth, the acceleration of gravity is equal to 32 feet (9.7 m) per second squared, or

$$32 \text{ ft/s}^2 \ (9.7 \text{ m/s}^2)$$

When these three data points are factored together, a formula is created for calculating gravitational potential energy. The formula is *PE* (gravitational potential energy) = *mgh*, where *m* stands for mass, *g* stands for acceleration of gravity, and *h* stands for height.

are breathing, and other bodily activities are taking place, such as blinking and turning the pages.

Another symbol associated with potential energy is "J." It stands for "joule," which is a unit of measurement in the metric system used to measure work or energy. One joule is equal to the amount of work done when one newton, or 0.225 pounds (0.1 kg) of force, moves an object 1 meter (3.28 feet) in the direction of the force. Since joules are also used to measure all kinds of energy, including heat energy, joules can be used in place of calories. One joule is equal to 0.239 calories.

THE ENERGY OF MOTION

Kinetic energy is the energy that something has when it is in motion. You can often see and feel this energy. If you place a rubber band on a pillow, it will not create much of a dent, but if you shoot the rubber band into the pillow, its force will leave a deeper dent. If you have ever been struck by a rubber band, a baseball, or some other object, you know how strong kinetic energy can be. That is because the potential energy of these objects was released into the kinetic energy of motion.

The formula used to calculate kinetic energy is $KE = (\text{mass} \times \textbf{velocity}^2)/2$, which can also be written as

$$KE = \frac{1}{2}\, mv^2$$

Kinetic energy, then, is equal to one-half the mass of an object times its velocity squared. Velocity, in turn, is speed (distance divided by time) with a direction.

Unlike potential energy, there is only one form of kinetic energy, but different types of motion can exemplify kinetic energy. Three of these types of motion are vibrational, rotational, and translational. **Vibrational kinetic energy** is the energy that something has when it vibrates, which is a form of movement. A drum head or a metal cooking pan that has just been hit, for example, might have a vibrating energy that you can feel.

Musicians give their drums vibrational kinetic energy.

Rotational kinetic energy can be felt if you spin a top on a flat surface. If you feel around the sides of the top without touching it, you might detect a slight breeze. That is air being moved around by the rotational energy created by the spinning top. A similar effect happens when Earth rotates. The atmosphere above Earth can move in response to Earth's circular rotation.

Kinetic and potential energy are closely related, and the category of translational energy is an excellent example of this relationship. When you are not moving, you have potential energy because you can move somewhere else. If you walk over to the kitchen to get a snack, your movement is an example of **translational kinetic energy**. However, once you stop moving, you now have potential energy again (particularly if you eat that snack and it gets you moving!).

The Physics of Energy

THREE

Types of Mechanical Energy

When a top-notch quarterback like New England Patriot Tom Brady throws a pass, it always has the potential to become a touchdown. When the ball leaves Brady's hands, it also has potential and kinetic energy. Both forms of energy fall into the category of mechanical energy. An object derives mechanical energy from both its movement and its relative position. Often, an object simultaneously will have both types of mechanical energy. The spiral movement of the thrown ball is rotational kinetic energy. However, as it travels through the air, it also has potential energy, thanks to gravity.

If you lift this book over your head, you have just given the book mechanical energy through its motion. When it is above the ground, the book has gravitational potential energy.

Pulling back a rubber band is giving the band mechanical energy of motion, but also storing the potential energy that will be released when the rubber band snaps back to its original state.

A quarterback throwing a spiral gives the football rotational kinetic energy, reducing air resistance and maximizing distance.

THE PHYSICS OF WORK

Like the words "potential" and "energy," "work" is one of those
terms that you probably think you know but may not fully
understand. In physics, the word "work" refers to a force that acts
upon an object to cause a displacement, meaning that the object
moves or changes in some way from its original state. Whenever
work occurs, there must be some force, or source of energy, to
initiate the process. When you turn the pages of this book, the
energy derived from food that you ate creates the necessary force.

Force can be defined as power, or energy, exerted on any person
or thing. Force often refers to a push or a pull on something. The
amount of force is used to calculate work. Work equals force times
distance moved, or

$$W = fd$$

Work is measured in foot-pounds or joules. The joule equals
0.7 foot-pounds. Turning book pages does not require much force.
Other activities require more energy. At times, your book bag may
weigh a lot, so you have to use a fair amount of force to lift it up.
If your book bag weighs 25 pounds (11 kg) and you raise it from
a height of 3 feet to 5 feet (0.9 to 1.5 m), you will have done 50
foot-pounds, or 35 joules, of work. That is because the work is equal
to 25 (weight moved) times 2 (feet moved). The force in this case is
equal to the weight of the book bag.

Kinetic energy also sometimes has the ability to transform itself
into potential energy, which can then go back to kinetic energy
to create a continuous cycle. Many gadgets and machines take
advantage of this process because the cycle requires only an initial
force to get things going. Watches, playground swings, and roller
coasters all operate by alternating potential with kinetic energy.

FRICTION AND AIR RESISTANCE

Friction is a force that opposes, or goes against, motion. It occurs
whenever two or more objects with irregular surfaces interact. The

Understanding Kinetic Energy

Roller coasters, such as this one at Busch Gardens in Tampa, Florida, work by rotating potential and kinetic energy.

interaction causes the surfaces to bump, slide, and scrape against each other, which slows down, or stops, motion. Air resistance acts in a similar way. It serves as a frictional force against objects that move through air, such as a pendulum bob or a person on a swing.

Roller coasters make clever use of mechanical energy. Although you can travel at very high speeds on a roller coaster, the cars of most coasters do not have engines. Only an initial force, created by an external engine at the beginning of the ride, sets the kinetic-potential cycle in motion.

At the beginning of a roller-coaster ride, a machine of some kind uses force to pull the coaster car up a hill. A rider sitting in a coaster car at the top of a hill now has gravitational potential energy. The higher the hill, the greater the potential energy will be. The coaster's motion, created by the initial force, and the weight of the ride will then cause the coaster cars and their contents to plummet downward. As the coaster moves, it has kinetic energy. Sometimes this movement will be divided into loops, which can whirl riders around and around in circles. The rotational energy of the loops combines kinetic and potential energy, so the coaster keeps going.

Types of Mechanical Energy

Getting Into the Swing of Things

Energy changes from kinetic to potential as the swing rises.

A pendulum is a suspended object that is free to move between two extremes. Grandfather clocks usually use a pendulum to drive the clock's mechanisms. The height of the pendulum bob above its lowest point determines its potential energy. The central position between swings is its lowest point. As the bob lifts, it has both kinetic and potential energy. When it reaches its highest position above the lowest point, the bob contains only potential energy. At the bob's lowest point when it is about to swing in the other direction, it contains only kinetic energy. This system of mechanical energy causes the clock to do work. The total energy of the pendulum is constant and is just changing back and forth between kinetic and potential energy.

Even a human can act like a pendulum bob. When you sit on a swing, you are at the lowest point of the possible swing arc. To start a swing, potential energy within your body switches to kinetic energy to move you forward and upward. At the highest point of the swing arc, you then become like a pendulum bob at its highest point. In that instant, only potential energy exists if you remain motionless. The potential energy then quickly changes to kinetic energy and you can swing back downward without any effort on your part. If you continued to just sit in the swing without exerting a force, eventually you would stop going back and forth. You do not swing forever because of friction and air resistance.

GRIPPING THE ROAD

If you look at tires on a car, you will see that they have a raised
surface of rubber on them. This surface actually promotes friction.
It helps the car to better grip the road. Whenever the treads wear
down, people have to buy new tires because driving without this
friction can be dangerous. A car without good treads on a wet
surface, for example, could slide and cause a crash. Race car tires

Race cars use bald tires to reduce road friction.

do not have treads. Race car drivers sacrifice safety for speed, and they also drive in a more controlled environment.

If it were possible to design a giant roller coaster across all of the continents, a ride could potentially go on forever converting potential energy into kinetic energy were it not for friction, such as that from the coaster's wheels against the tracks. In fact, imposed friction is what ultimately causes most roller coasters to come to a full stop. Compressed air brakes create friction underneath the cars, and this friction is sufficient to stop the ride's motion.

Your own personal potential energy is often used to make a hand tool work. A screwdriver would sit doing nothing forever, but once you pick it up and start to drive in a screw by turning the screwdriver and the screw clockwise (always remember—lefty loosey, righty tighty!), you turn your potential energy into kinetic energy.

Types of Mechanical Energy

Some of the calories burned during exercise are released as heat.

FOUR

Understanding the Laws of Energy

No matter the system or machine, physicists have discovered and defined laws of energy that are universal. This set of similarities allows physicists to understand machines and energy. A similar situation exists with cars. While there are some differences based on make and model, most automobile engines, tires, and brakes operate the same, allowing mechanics to diagnose problems and repair cars easily. In the same manner, physicists use the laws of energy, particularly the law of **conservation of energy,** to better understand the universe.

THE LAW OF CONSERVATION OF ENERGY

The law of conservation of energy says that there is a fixed amount of energy in the entire universe. This amount can never change. That means energy can never be created or destroyed. We merely change energy from one form to another. For fossil fuels, the amount of energy that plants used to create the potential energy in the fuels equals the sum of all of the forms of energy that are given up when the fuels are burned.

To understand the law of conservation of energy, consider the transformations of energy that occur after you exercise or do some chores around the house. Your body converts food into energy, enabling you to become active. This energy is released as kinetic energy when you move. The amount of energy from the food you eat, however, is not equal to your kinetic energy of movement. A lot of the energy is released as heat, which itself is a form of energy. That is one reason why you feel hot after you run for a while. Your body burns more calories than necessary for your movement and releases the extra energy as heat.

Since heat is energy, heat is conserved, too. For example, at lunchtime, you might place a hot bowl of soup on the table. If you go away for a while to take a phone call, when you return, the soup will be colder than it was before, unless the room was the same temperature as the soup. That is because heat from the soup, released in steam, leaves the soup and is absorbed by air in the room. Since the room is much bigger than the bowl of soup, you likely will not be able to feel any difference in the room's temperature, but the heat energy never completely went away.

Systems have a tendency toward increasing disorder. This tendency is known as entropy, which also may be defined as the degree to which energy within a system is unavailable for conversion into work. When you turn on a light, for example, the electrical energy used to run it results in light and heat. If you have the light on for a while, you can feel the heat if you place your hand next to the light bulb. This heat will be absorbed by the air in the room. Ordered energy, such as the electricity needed to power the light, also

Understanding Kinetic Energy

Penguins huddle to share the heat radiated by their bodies and combat severe cold.

results in this disordered energy, the waste heat that is released in most processes. Physicists are seeking ways to either limit waste heat or to convert it back into ordered energy.

TAKING YOUR TEMPERATURE

When you are sick, you might feel warm if you have a fever. Even when you are healthy and not active, chemical energy in your body is partly released as heat. That is why a normal person has a temperature of 98.6 degrees Fahrenheit (37 degrees Celsius)

A biker must exert extra force to overcome gravity and friction.

The Physics of Riding a Bike

A bike pedaled forward illustrates the **work-energy theorem**. Imagine that you hop on a bike and pedal it forward over a distance of 0.46 meters (18 inches). Recall that energy is often measured in joules. One joule is equal to the amount of energy it takes to lift 0.45 kilograms (1 pound) a distance of 0.23 meters (9 inches). If you weigh 45.36 kilograms (100 lbs.) and your bike weighs 13.61 kilograms (30 lbs.), it would take around 130 joules to move the bike 0.23 meters (9 in). Since you moved forward twice that distance, double that amount of force, or 260 joules, could allow the bike to move forward.

If you have ever tried to bike up a hill, you know that it is not easy. A lot of forces work against you. The force of gravity wants to pull you and your bike down the hill. Friction caused by the hill's irregular surface creates a resistance, or a negative force, against your pedaling. If air is blowing in your face, that, too, can create a negative friction force. If the negative forces in this example add up to 40 joules, then the positive forces would have to be 300 joules for work to equal 260 joules. You would need the extra 40 joules to counteract the negative forces of 40 joules caused by gravity and friction.

If you want to calculate how much work is done by a system, you need to account for numerous factors. Take the example of pedaling a bicycle uphill. The first calculation to make is how much kinetic energy was expended moving from where you started on the bike to where you stopped. This should also consider gravity and friction that you had to overcome while pedaling. If the wind was blowing, you need to consider whether it was with the biker (a positive force helping) or against the biker (hindering). Only when all of this information is considered can the work be calculated.

instead of zero. Although you might not realize it, when you are in a classroom with only nine other students, the ten of you create the amount of heat equal to a blazing fire. You do not feel the heat as you would near a fire because it is dispersed around the classroom.

Work and energy go together. It takes energy to create work, and work will never happen without some kind of force. Also, work can be used to create potential energy. It is possible to figure out how much work has been done by using the work-energy theorem. This theorem states that the net, or total, work performed on an object is equal to the change in the object's kinetic energy. As an equation this is stated as

$$fd = 1/2mv^2$$

where force times distance, equals one-half the product of mass times velocity squared.

Many factors can change an object's kinetic energy. Imagine a football on a sidewalk. It gets kinetic energy if you kick it or throw it. When left alone, however, the football tends to stay put. That tendency to not change without force is called **inertia**.

An English scientist named Sir Isaac Newton (1642–1727) formulated several laws that help explain motion. His first law of motion states that if an object is at rest, it wants to stay that way. If an object is moving, it will keep moving at a constant speed and in a constant direction unless a force changes that.

Forces that act on a kicked soccer ball are the pull of gravity, friction, and air resistance, and they cause the ball to fall back to the ground. If you lessen these factors, any object could travel a great distance. Ice, for example, is smoother than a sidewalk. It lessens the amount of friction. That is why a hockey puck maintains speed as it slides across a rink. Without the walls of the rink, and if more ice were present, the puck could travel an enormous distance.

Understanding Kinetic Energy

This soccer player will have to stay on his toes if he wants to overcome gravity and keep the ball in the air.

This junior hockey player builds momentum as he pulls away from a defender.

FIVE

Gaining Momentum

When considering the energy of a system, **momentum** is another important concept. You've probably heard the term used in day-to-day application, like when a baseball team wins six or seven games in a row, people say the team has "some real momentum." An example closer to the physics definition is when a hockey player barrels down the ice. The heavier the player, and the faster he's skating, the more momentum he has. This is because an object's momentum is calculated with the equation

$$p = mv$$

where p is momentum, m is the mass of the object, and v is the object's velocity. Momentum also takes direction into consideration, so it is considered a vector quantity. So a heavy diesel train engine heading down the tracks at 60 miles per hour (97 kmh) would have more momentum than a lighter engine.

MOMENTUM IN A SYSTEM

Like energy, momentum in a system is conserved—no momentum is gained, and none is lost. What would happen to the football player's momentum if he was running down the field and tackled by a player on the opposing team? At first, you might think that his momentum would be lost, but it really would be redirected toward the player who tackled him. That is why the tackler would feel the force of his impact.

Momentum is conserved in a collision of bumper cars.

As another example, imagine you are sitting in a motionless bumper car at an amusement park. The momentum at this point is zero. Your friend in another car comes at you with ten units of momentum. Upon impact, his momentum would be divided between the two cars. You would move with five units of momentum, and he would move forward with five units.

Understanding Kinetic Energy

If your car is between two other bumper cars, and each of these other cars comes at you from opposite directions, your car would not move. The force of one moving car would cancel out the force of the other moving car because momentum is a vector quantity and the two cars were coming from different directions. The total momentum in this case would be the same as it was at the outset: zero. If you are sitting in your bumper car and your friends both come from the same direction, one after another, you will all move and share in the force of impact.

Energy is passed among the billiard balls in the rack after they are struck by the cue ball.

The game of billiards takes advantage of the **conservation of momentum**. A neat trick based on momentum conservation is demonstrated when a pool player hits a ball toward a row of balls. The momentum of the first moving ball passes through several stationary balls and causes the last one in the row to move forward. Momentum is not lost. It is simply transferred from one ball to another, until finally the last ball in the row moves.

Because momentum has direction, it can transfer at different angles. For example, if a pool player hits a ball toward a V-shaped set of balls, balls from either side of the V will move forward at an equal pace. The momentum of the original ball is shared among them.

Now that you have learned some of the basic laws of energy and momentum, you can use them to your advantage. One day you might decide to become an airline pilot, a professional athlete, an inventor, or a musician. These careers, and more, all involve physics laws.

A strong follow-through on a swing will drive the ball farther.

THE PHYSICS OF ATHLETICS

To hit a baseball or a softball a long distance, you also must lengthen the time of impact. The longer your bat stays in contact with the ball, the greater the distance the ball will travel because more energy will be transferred from the bat to the ball. Great hitters spend countless hours perfecting their swings so they can transfer maximum momentum from their bodies to the ball. One way to increase the time the ball stays on the bat—this applies also to golf—is to follow through on your swing.

Players try to minimize the time the ball stays on the bat when they bunt. They pull the bat back at the moment of contact, imparting less momentum and ensuring the ball doesn't travel too far.

THE PHYSICS OF FLIGHT

Energy and motion laws also help to explain how moving airplanes stay in the sky. In a well-maintained aircraft, passengers can rest easy because a balance of air pressure forces can keep an airplane flying indefinitely, so long as the plane has enough fuel to move in a forward direction.

The next time you travel on an airplane or visit an airport, notice the shape of the airplane's wings. They are slightly curved on the top. The curve causes air above the wing to travel a longer distance than it must travel below the wing, even though air rushes past the plane at an equal rate. So the air above the wing is moving faster than the air below the wing, and fluids (air can be a fluid) that travel faster exert less pressure than fluids at slower speeds. The difference in air pressure created by the wing design gives lift to the lower part of the plane. Air holds the plane above the ground. The wings of birds and the shape of dolphins and whales also often have the curve design that an airplane wing has. This shape gives them lift in air and even in water.

From airplanes to rockets to computers, humans have invented all sorts of objects that operate based on the laws of energy, momentum, and motion. They all release heat as energy. When we use gasoline in cars and planes, or use electricity to run appliances,

Dolphins obtain lift in water or air from the shape of their bodies.

Gaining Momentum

More efficient engines will allow even hybrid cars to go farther on less energy.

we usually turn fossil fuels into heat and other particles, and also create usable energy. That is why the hood of a running car feels warm and exhaust releases from the back. On average, only 25 percent of a car's gasoline actually works to move the car. The other 75 percent turns into heat energy.

An ongoing challenge for both scientists and engineers is improving the energy efficiency of all products, and cars in particular. Advances in biofuel, electric, and hybrid cars are just one way people are trying to reduce their reliance on nonrenewable energy sources. Luckily, the sun provides more than enough energy for the entire human population, as long as we learn to harness that power and potential energy. If we can achieve this, our global society will have all the kinetic energy we need.

GLOSSARY

chemical potential energy The energy stored within atomic bonds in substances.

conservation of energy The physics law that states that there is a fixed amount of energy in the entire universe, and that this amount can never change.

conservation of momentum The physics law that states that the total momentum in a system does not change, even when objects collide.

elastic potential energy Energy that is stored in objects that can be stretched or compressed.

energy The capacity to do work; what causes change and makes things happen.

fossil fuels Gas, coal, petroleum, and other products that are derived from the oily remains of prehistoric plants and animals.

friction A force that opposes motion created by two objects rubbing against each other.

gravitational potential energy Stored energy that comes from gravity, which is the pull that all objects of mass have on each other.

inertia The tendency of an object to remain at rest or in uniform motion in a straight line unless it is acted upon by an external force.

kinetic energy The energy that an object has when it is in motion.

mass The amount of matter that a living or nonliving thing has.

matter Anything that has mass and occupies space.

GLOSSARY

mechanical energy Energy that an object has because of its motion, or its energy stored as a result of the object's position.

momentum A measurement of the amount of inertia and motion that an object has that is equal to an object's mass multiplied by its velocity.

physics The study of matter, energy, and motion.

potential energy The energy that an object has because of its position or because of the arrangement of its parts.

renewable energy sources Solar, wind, water, and other energy sources that are in constant supply.

rotational kinetic energy The kinetic energy of an object rotating around an axis.

translational kinetic energy The energy of an object moving in a straight line.

velocity A measurement of the speed and direction a moving object has.

vibrational kinetic energy The kinetic energy of a vibrating object.

work What occurs when a force that acts upon an object causes a displacement, meaning that the object moves or changes from its original state.

work-energy theorem A physics law that states that the net, or total, work done on an object is equal to the change in the object's kinetic energy.

FURTHER INFORMATION

BOOKS

Bloomfield, Louis. *How Things Work: The Physics of Everyday Life*, 5th ed. New York, NY: Wiley, 2013.

Feynman, Richard. *Six Easy Pieces: Essentials of Physics Explained by Its Most Brilliant Teacher*. New York, NY: Basic Books, 2011.

Feynman, Richard P., and Michael A. Gottlieb. *Tips on Physics: Reflections, Advice, Insights, Practice - A Problem-Solving Supplement to the Feynman Lectures on Physics*. New York, NY: Basic Books, 2013.

Friedhoffer, Robert. *Forces, Energy, and Motion.* (Scientific Magic Series Book 2). New York, NY: Evergreen Books, 2013.

McKinley, Christine. *Physics for Rock Stars: Making the Laws of the Universe Work for You*. New York, NY: Perigee, 2014.

Susskind, Leonard, and George Hrabovsky. *The Theoretical Minimum: What You Need to Know to Start Doing Physics*. New York, NY: Basic Books, 2014.

WEBSITES

About.com's Guide to Physics

physics.about.com/od/physics101thebasics/u/basicconcepts.htm

This website contains a set of basic tutorials about fundamental physics.

Institute of Physics

www.physics.org

This site provides videos, news, experiments and databases that can satisfy the curious mind.

FURTHER INFORMATION

WEBSITES

Brightstorm
www.brightstorm.com/science/physics/

Short online videos provide tutorials meant to sharpen your
knowledge about physics and other branches of science.

The Khan Academy
www.khanacademy.org/science/physics

Get a free education on a wide variety of topics related to physics
from this organization's extensive library of content, including
interactive challenges, assessments, and videos.

The Physics Classroom
www.physicsclassroom.com

This comprehensive tutorial provides instruction for beginning
physics students, and is an outstanding resource for their teachers.

The Physics Hypertextbook
Physics.info

Expand your knowledge of many areas of physics with this free
online textbook that is indexed for easy navigation.

BIBLIOGRAPHY

Asimov, Isaac. *The History of Physics*. New York: Walker and Company, 1966.

Bloomfield, Louis. *How Things Work: The Physics of Everyday Life*. 5th ed. New York: Wiley, 2013.

Farndon, John. *Energy*. New York: Benchmark Books, 2003.

Feynman, Richard. *Six Easy Pieces: Essentials of Physics Explained by Its Most Brilliant Teacher*. New York: Basic Books, 2011.

Gunderson, P. Erik. *The Handy Physics Answer Book*. Farmington Hills, MI: Visible Ink Press, 1999.

Hewitt, Paul G. *Conceptual Physics: A New Introduction to Your Environment*. Boston: Little, Brown and Company, 1974.

Holzner, Steven. *Physics I for Dummies*. Hoboken, NJ: Wiley Publishing, 2011.

Lafferty, Peter. *Force & Motion*. New York: Dorling Kindersley Limited, 1999.

McKinley, Christine. *Physics for Rock Stars: Making the Laws of the Universe Work for You*. New York: Perigee, 2014.

Motz, Lloyd. *The Story of Physics*. New York: Plenum Press, 1989.

"Newton's First Law." The Physics Classroom, www.physicsclassroom.com/class/newtlaws/Lesson-1/Newton-s-First-Law

Susskind, Leonard and George Hrabovsky. *The Theoretical Minimum: What You Need to Know to Start Doing Physics*. New York: Basic Books, 2014.

INDEX

Page numbers in **boldface** are illustrations.

acceleration of gravity, 17
air resistance, **21**, 23, 25, 34

calorie, 15, 17, **28**, 30
chemical potential energy, 15
conservation of energy, 29–30
conservation of momentum, 39

elastic potential energy, 14–15, **14**
entropy, 30

foot-pound, 22
fossil fuels, 10, **11**, 29, 42
friction, 5, 22–23, 25–27, **32**, 33–34

gravitational potential energy, 17, 21, 23

inertia, 34

kinetic energy, 18–19, 21–23, **23**, 25, 27, 30, 33–34, 42

mass, 16, 18, 34, 37
matter, 4, **6**, 7, 17, 29

mechanical energy, 5, 21, 23, 25
momentum, **36**, 37–41, **38**

newton, 18
Newton, Sir Isaac, 4, 34
Newton's law, 4, **4**

photosynthesis, **8**, 9
physics, 4–5, **5**, 15, 22, 37, 39
potential energy, **12**, 13–15, **14**, 17–19, 21–23, 25, 27, 29, 34, 42

renewable energy sources, 10
  biofuel, 10, 42
  hydroelectric, 10
  solar, 10
  wind, 10, **11**, 33
roller coaster, 22–23, **23**, 27
rotational kinetic energy, 19, 21, **21**

translational kinetic energy, 19

velocity, 18, 34, 37
vibrational kinetic energy, 18, **19**

work, 6–7, 14, 18, 22, **23**, 25, 27, 30, 33–34
work-energy theorem, 33–34

Understanding Kinetic Energy

PHASE TRANSITIONS AND CRITICAL PHENOMENA

Cumulative Author, Title and Subject Index
Including Table of Contents, Volumes 1–19

VOLUME 20

PHASE TRANSITIONS AND CRITICAL PHENOMENA

Cumulative Author, Title and Subject Index
Including Table of Contents, Volumes 1–19

Edited by

C. DOMB

Department of Physics, Bar Ilan University, Israel

and

J. L. LEBOWITZ

Department of Mathematics and Physics, Rutgers University,
New Brunswick, New Jersey, USA

VOLUME 20

 ACADEMIC PRESS

A Harcourt Science and Technology Company

San Diego • San Francisco • New York • Boston
London • Sydney • Tokyo

Academic Press
A Harcourt Science and Technology Company
Harcourt Place, 32 Jamestown Road, London NW1 7BY, UK
http://www.academicpress.com

Academic Press
A Harcourt Science and Technology Company
525 B Street, Suite 1900, San Diego, California 92101-4495, USA
http://www.academicpress.com

ISBN 0-12-220320-8

A catalogue record for this book is available from the British Library

Typeset by Mackreth Media Services, Hemel Hempstead
Printed and bound in Great Britain by MPG Books, Bodmin, Cornwall

01 02 03 04 05 MP 9 8 7 6 5 4 3 2 1

Contents for Volume 20

Cumulative Author Index 1
Cumulative Index of Titles 3
Table of Contents, Vols. 1–19 7
Cumulative Subject Index 41

Author Index

Abraham, D.B., **10:**2
Aharony, A., **6:**358, **14:** 4
Alava, M.J., **18:**145
Als-Nielsen, J., **5A:**88

Baker Jr., G.A., **3:**246, **9:**234
Barber, M.N., **8:**146
Betts, D.B., **3:**570
Bhattacharjee, S.M., **13:**236
Binder, K., **5B:**2, **8:**2
Brezin, E., **6:**127
Buckingham, M.J., **2:**2
Burley, D.M., **2:**329

Cardy, J.L., **11:**55
Carlos, S.O., **13:**236
Collins, R., **2:**271

den Nijs, M., **12:**220
Di Castro, C., **6:**508
Diehl, H.W., **10:**76
Dietrich, S., **12:**2
Domb, C. **3:**1, 357
Duxbury, P.M., **18:**145

Emch, G.G., **1:**138
Essam, J.W., **2:**197

Fa Yueh Wu, **1:**332
Forgacs, G., **14:**136

Gaunt, D.S., **3:**181
George, A., **3:**246
Georgii, H.O., **18:**3
Ginibre, J., **1:**111
Gompper, G., **16:**3
Griffiths, R.B., **1:**7

Gunton, J.D., **8:**269
Guttmann, A.J., **3:**181, **13:**3

Häggström, O., **18:**3
Hemmer, P.C., **5B:**108
Hohenberg, P.C., **14:**4

Jasnow, D., **10:**270
Jona-Lasinio, G., **6:**508
Joyce, G.S., **2:**375

Kadanoff, L.P., **5A:**2
Kawasaki, K. **2:**443, **5A:**166
Khorunzhy, A.M., **15:**74
Khoruzhenko, B.A., **15:**74
Knobler, C.M., **9:**164

Lawrie, I.D., **9:**2
Le Guillou, J.C., **6:**127
Lebowitz, J.L., **5B:**108
Lieb, E.H., **1:**332
Lipowsky, R., **14:**136
Luban, M., **5A:**35

Maes, C., **18:**3
Martin, J.L., **3:**97
McCoy, B., **2:**161
Meakin, P., **12:**336
Moukarzel, C.F., **18:**145

Nagle, J.F., **3:**653, **13:**236
Nelson, D.R., **7:**2
Niemeijer, Th., **6:**425
Nienhus, B., **11:**1
Nieuwenhuizen, Th.M., **14:**4

Pastur, L.A., **15:**74

Privman, V., **14**:4

Rieger, H., **18**:145
Runnels, L.K., **2**:305
Rushbrooke, G.S., **3**:246

Sahni, P.S., **8**:269
San Miguel, M., **8**:269
Sarbach, S., **9**:2
Schick, M., **16**:3
Schmittmann, B., **17**:3
Schütz, G.M., **19**:3
Scott, R.L., **9**:164
Selke, W., **15**:2
Shang-Keng Ma, **6**:250
Shcherbina, M.V., **15**:74
Slawny, J., **11**:128
Stanley, E.H., **3**:486
Stell, G., **5B**:205
Stinchcombe, R.B., **7**:152
Syozi, I., **1**:270

Tahir-Kheli, R.A., **5B**:259

Temperley, H.N.V., **1**:227
Thompson, C.J., **1**:177

van Leeuwen, M.J., **6**:425
Vicentini-Missoni, M., **2**:39
Voronel, A.V., **5B**:344

Wallace, D.J., **6**:294
Watson, P.G., **2**:101
Wegner, F.J., **6**:8
Widom, B., **2**:79
Wiegel, F.W., **7**:101
Wiese, K.J., **19**:3
Wilson, K.G., **6**:5
Wood, P.J., **3**:246
Wortis, M., **3**:114

Yang, C.N., **1**:4
Yokoi, C.S.O., **13**:236

Zia, R.K.P., **17**:3
Zinn-Justin, J., **6**:127

Cumulative Index of Titles

Asymptotic Analysis of Coefficients **3**:181
Asymptotic Analysis of Power-Series Expansions **13**:3

Classical Vector Models **3**:486
Closed Form Approximations for Lattice Systems **2**:329
Computer Techniques for Evaluating Lattice Constants **3**:97
Conformal Invariance **11**:55
Conformational Phase Transitions in a Macromolecule: Exactly Solvable Models **7**:101
Correlation Functions and Their Generating Functionals: General Relations with Applications to the Theory of Fluids **5B**:205
Coulomb Gas Formulation of Two-Dimensional Phase Transitions **11**:1
Critical Behaviour at Surfaces **8**:2
Critical Point Statistical Mechanics and Quantum Field Theory **9**:234
Critical Properties of the Spherical Model **2**:375

D-Vector Model or "Universality Hamiltonian": Properties of Isotropically-Interacting D-Dimensional Classical Spins **3**:486
Defect-Mediated Phase Transitions **7**:2
Dependence of Universal Critical Behaviour on Symmetry and Range of Interaction **6**:358
Dilute Magnetism **7**:152
Dilute Quantum Systems **1**:111
Dimer Models on Anistropic Lattices **13**:236

Equilibrium Scaling in Fluids and Magnets **2**:39
Exact Calculations on a Random Ising System **2**:161
Exact Combinatorial Algorithms: Ground States of Disordered Systems **18**:145
Exactly Solvable Models for Many-Body Systems Far from Equilibrium **19**:3

Ferroelectric Models **3**:653
Field Theoretical Approach to Critical Phenomena **6**:127
Field-Theoretic Approach to Critical Behaviour at Surfaces **10**:76
Finite-Size Scaling **8**:146

Generalized Landau Theories **5A**:35
Graph Theory and Embeddings **3**:1

3

Heisenberg Ferromagnet in the Green's Function Approximation **5B:**259
Heisenberg Model **3:**246

Introduction **6:**1
Introductory Note on Phase Transitions and Critical Phenomena **1:**4
Ising Model **3:**357

Kinetics of Ising Models **2:**443

Lattice Gas Theories of Melting **2:**305
Linked Cluster Expansion **3:**114
Low-Temperature Properties of Classical Lattice Systems: Phase Transitions and
     Phase Diagrams **11:**128

Melting and Statistical Geometry of Simple Liquids **2:**271
Mode Coupling and Critical Dynamics **5A:**166
Monte Carlo Investigations of Phase Transitions and Critical Phenomena **5B:**2
Multicritical Points in Fluid Mixtures: Experimental Studies **9:**164

Neutron Scattering and Spatial Correlation near the Critical Point **5A:**88

One-dimensional Models—Short Range Forces **1:**177

Percolation and Cluster Size **2:**197
Polymerized Membranes, a Review **19:**3

Renormalization Group Approach to Critical Phenomena **6:**508
Renormalization Group Theory of Interfaces **10:**270
Renormalization: Theory Ising-like Spin Systems **6:**425
Rigorous Results and Theorems **1:**7

Scaling, Universality and Operator Algebras **5A:**2
Self-Assembling Amphiphilic Systems **16:**3
Spatially Modulated Structures in Systems with Competing Interactions **15:**2
Statistical Mechanics of Driven Diffusive Systems **17:**3
Surface and Size Effects in Lattice Models **2:**101
Surface Structures and Phase Transitions—Exact Results **10:**2
Surface Tension of Fluids **2:**79
Systems with Weak Long-Range Potentials **5B:**108

The $1/n$ Expansion **6:**250
The Behaviour of Interfaces in Ordered and Disordered Systems **14:**136
The C^*-Algebraic Approach to Phase Transitions **1:**138
The Critical State, General Aspects **6:**8
The Domain Wall Theory of Two-Dimensional Commensurate–Incommensurate
     Phase Transitions **12:**220
The Dynamics of First Order Phase Transitions **8:**269
The Growth of Fractal Aggregates and their Fractal Measures **12:**336
The Large-n Limit in Statistical Mechanics and the Spectral Theory of Disordered

Systems **15:**74
The ε-Expansion for Exponents and the Equation of State in Isotropic Systems **6:**294
The Random Geometry of Equilibrium Phases **18:**3
The Renormalization Group—Introduction **6:**5
Theory of Tricritical Points **9:**2
Thermal Measurements and Critical Phenomena in Liquids **5B:**344
Thermodynamics **2:**2
Transformation of Ising Models **1:**270
Two-dimensional Ferroelectric Models **1:**332
Two-dimensional Ising Models **1:**227

Universal Critical-Point Amplitude Relations **14:**4

Wetting Phenomena **12:**2

X–Y Model **3:**570

Phase Transitions and Critical Phenomena
Volume 1

Edited by
C. Domb and M. S. Green

CONTRIBUTORS v
GENERAL PREFACE vii
PREFACE TO VOLUME 1 ix

Introductory Note on Phase Transitions and Critical Phenomena

C. N. Yang

References 4

Rigorous Results and Theorems

R. B. Griffiths

   I. Introduction 7
  II. The Thermodynamic Limit 10
 III. Low Density Expansions 41
 IV. Zeros of the Partition Function 50
  V. Peierls Arguments for the Existence of a Phase Transition 59
 VI. Correlation Inequalities 72
VII. Systems With Continuous Symmetries in One and Two Dimensions 84
VIII. One-dimensional Systems 89
 IX. Miscellaneous Results 94
References 105

Dilute Quantum Systems

J. Ginibre

  I. Introduction 111
 II. Quantum Lattice Systems 115
III. Quantum Continuous Systems 123
Acknowledgements 135
References 135

The C*-Algebraic Approach to Phase Transitions

G. G. Emch

I. Outline 138
II. Introduction 138
III. The *C*-Algebraic Approach 139
IV. One-dimensional Spin-lattices 152
V. Molecular Field Methods 166
VI. Crystallization 170
References 174

One-dimensional Models—Short Range Forces

C. J. Thompson

I. Introduction 177
II. Classical Systems 181
III. Quantum Mechanical Systems 205
References 225

Two-dimensional Ising Models

H. N. V. Temperley

I. Historical Introduction 227
II. Retrospect 236
III. Description of the Method 237
IV. Relationship's with Lieb's Work on "Ice-like" Models 266
References 267

Transformation of Ising Models

I. Syozi

I. Introduction 270
II. Dual Transformation 271
III. Star–Triangle $(Y - \Delta)$ Transformation 278
IV. Limiting Process for Strong or Weak Interaction 285
V. Spontaneous Magnetization 286
VI. Decoration–Iteration Transformation 291
VII. Extended Decoration–Iteration and Star–Triangle Transformations 302
VIII. Appendices 320
Acknowledgements 328
References 329

Two-dimensional Ferroelectric Models

E. H. Lieb and Fa Yueh Wu

I. Introduction	332
II. Ferroelectric Models and Related Problems	333
III. The Thermodynamic Limit for the Ferroelectric Models	345
IV. The Transfer Matrix and its Diagonalization	361
V. Ice Rule Ferroelectric Models on a Square Lattice	384
VI. General Lattice Model on a Square Lattice	450
VII. Other Lattice Models (contributed by R. J. Baxter)	461
VIII. Unsolved Problems	485
Glossary of Principal Symbols	486
References	487
AUTHOR INDEX	491
SUBJECT INDEX	496

Phase Transitions and Critical Phenomena
Volume 2

Edited by
C. Domb and M. S. Green

CONTRIBUTORS	v
GENERAL PREFACE	vii
PREFACE TO VOLUME 2	ix

Thermodynamics

M. J. Buckingham

I. Introduction	2
II. Function–Tangent Contact	10
III. Asymptotic Analysis near the Critical Point	19
IV. Special Cases	31
References	38

Equilibrium Scaling in Fluids and Magnets

M. Vicentini-Missoni

I. Introduction 39
II. Theoretical Basis for Scaling Laws 40
III. Status of the Experiments 61
IV. Empirical Forms of $h(x)$ 63
V. Parametric Representation 69
VI. Conclusion 76
References 77

Surface Tension of Fluids

B. Widom

I. Introduction 79
II. Scaling and Homogenity Conjectures 80
III. Structure of the Interface 86
IV. Critique 93
Acknowledgements 99
References 99

Surface and Size Effects in Lattice Models

P. G. Watson

I. Introduction 101
II. Effect of Modified Arrays on Thermodynamics 105
III. Effect of Modified Arrays on Correlations 140
IV Effect of Finite Size 150
References 159

Exact Calculations on a Random Ising System

B. McCoy

I. Introduction 161
II. The Model 162
III. Specific Heat 164
IV. Spontaneous Magnetization and Spin Correlation Function of the Bulk 184
V. Boundary Magnetization 186
VI. Boundary Spin–Spin Correlation 191
VII. Discussion 193
References 195

Percolation and Cluster Size

J. W. Essam

I. Introduction 197
II. Critical Probabilities 202
III. Numerical Methods for Percolation Functions 226
IV. Critical Exponents 244
V. Dilute Ferromagnetism 249
VI. Related Topics 264
References 269

Melting and Statistical Geometry of Simple Liquids

R. Collins

I. Introduction 271
II. Theoretical Results in Statistical Theory 274
III. Empirical Physical and Computer Models 282
IV. Geometry and Fluid Thermodynamics 290
V. Summary and Conclusions 300
References 301

Lattice Gas Theories of Melting

L. K. Runnels

I. Introduction 305
II. Athermal (Hard Molecules) Systems 308
III. Comparison with the Continuum Model 314
IV. Lattice Models with Square Well Potentials 315
V. Asymmetric Molecules 326
References 327

Closed Form Approximations for Lattice Systems

D. M. Burley

I. Introduction 329
II. Mean Field and Constant Coupling Approximations 333
III. Cluster Variation Method 341
IV. Comparisons 350
V. Further Improvements and Methods 363
References 373

Critical Properties of the Spherical Model

G. S. Joyce

I. Introduction 375
II Basic Results 379
III. Behaviour of the Green's Function $P(z)$ for $z \lesssim 1$ 387
IV Critical Behaviour of Thermodynamic Properties 400
V. Correlation Functions 427
Acknowledgements 440
References 440

Kinetics of Ising Models

K. Kawasaki

I. Introduction 443
II. Master Equation Approach 445
III. Kinetic Ising Models 456
IV. Exactly Solvable Cases 465
V. Approximate Methods 473
VI. Numerical Methods 481
VII. Derivation of Kinetic Ising Models 489
VIII. Applications 491
Appendix A. 493
Appendix B. 496
References 498

AUTHOR INDEX 503
SUBJECT INDEX 511

Phase Transitions and Critical Phenomena
Volume 3

Edited by
C. Domb and M. S. Green

CONTRIBUTORS v
GENERAL PREFACE vii
PREFACE TO VOLUME 3 ix

Graph Theory and Embeddings

C. Domb

I. General Introduction 1
II. Linear Graphs 3
III. Cluster Integral Theory 42
IV. Lattice Constants or Embeddings 57
References 92

Computer Techniques for Evaluating Lattice Constants

J. L. Martin

I. Introduction 97
II. Nature of the Problem 98
III. Canonical Labellings 100
IV. Computer Representation of a Network 103
V. Counting n-clusters on a Crystal Lattice 105
VI. Counting Lattice Constants on a Crystal Lattice 108
References 112

Linked Cluster Expansion

Michael Wortis

I. Introduction 114
II. The Linked-cluster Expansion with Commuting Variables: The Ising Model 120
III. Further Applications and Extensions of the Linked-cluster Expansion 162
Appendix: The Relation of the Free Multiplicities to the Weak Lattice Constants 176
References 178

Asymptotic Analysis of Coefficients

D. S. Gaunt and A. J. Guttmann

I. Introduction 181
II. Ratio Method 187
III. Padé Approximants 202
IV. Method of N Point Fits 219
V. Transformations of Expansion Variables 224
VI. Applications of Darboux's Theorems 232
References 241

Heisenberg Model

G. S. Rushbrooke, George A. Baker, Jr. and P. J. Wood

  I. Introduction 246
 II. Derivation of High Temperature Expansions 253
III. Fuller Details on Special Topics 271
 IV. High Temperature Series Expansions 294
  V. Properties Derived from High Temperature Expansions 301
Appendix I. Basic Mean Reduced Traces 328
Appendix II. Coefficients for $H(s)$ with First and Second Neighbour Interactions. Generalised
   Susceptibility Coefficients for $H(s)$ 341
Appendix III. Coefficients for $H(\infty)$ 344
Appendix IV. Coefficients for $H(\frac{1}{2})$ 346
References 350

Ising Model

C. Domb

  I. Introduction 357
 II. Derivation of Series Expansions 375
III. Critical Behaviour 423
 IV. Miscellaneous Topics 461
  V. Conclusions 476
References 478

D-Vector Model or "Universality Hamiltonian":
Properties of Isotropically-Interacting *D*-Dimensional Classical Spins

H. Eugene Stanley

   I. Introduction 486
  II. Definition of the Universality Hamiltonian 487
 III. Generalizations of the Universality Hamiltonian 492
  IV. Physical Systems Described by the Universality Hamiltonian 502
   V. Scaling Functions for Certain Universal Classes 503
  VI. Crossing Over from One Universal Class to Another 507
 VII. Formalism for Deriving Arbitrary-D Expressions for the Zero-Field Gibbs Potential and the
       Two-Spin Correlation Function 512
VIII. Calculation of the Coefficients in the Zero Field Susceptibility Series 521
  IX. Calculation of the Coefficients in the Zero Field Enthalpy and Specific Heat Series 531
   X. Dependence of Exponents upon D for $d = 3$: A Bilinear Form Hypothesis 537
  XI. Possible Dependencies of Critical Properties upon D for $d = 2$ 543
 XII. Exact Solution of Zero-Field Thermodynamic Properties and Correlation Functions for all
       D when $d = 1$ 551
XIII. Exact Solution of Thermodynamic Properties and Correlation Functions for all
       d when $D = \infty$ 555
 XIV. Dependence of Critical Point Exponents upon D and d for $d > 3$: Hypercubical Lattices 558
  XV. Conclusion and Outlook 559
References 560

X–Y Model

D. D. Betts

I. Introduction 570
II. *X–Y* Model 572
III. Planar Models, Planar Systems and the Universality Hypothesis 579
IV. Zero Field Partition Function 584
V. Susceptibilities and Magnetization Fluctuations 596
VI. Expansions for Fluctuations and Susceptibilities 600
VII. Critical Properties from Analysis of Series 615
VIII. Critical Properties from Scaling Relations 625
IX. Dynamical Properties of the *X–Y* Model 630
X. Two-Dimensional Planar Models 635
XI. Comparison with Experiment 643
XII. Discussions, Conclusions and Outlook 647
References 649

Ferroelectric Models

John F. Nagle

I. Weak Graph Generating Function 653
II. Weak Graph Expansion for Hydrogen Bonded Models 656
III. Applications of the Weak Graph Expansion to Hydrogen-bonded Models 661
References 665

AUTHOR INDEX 667
SUBJECT INDEX 677

Phase Transitions and Critical Phenomena
Volume 5A

Edited by
C. Domb and M. S. Green

CONTRIBUTORS v
GENERAL PREFACE vii
PREFACE TO VOLUMES 5A AND 5B ix

Scaling, Universality and Operator Algebras

Leo P. Kadanoff

Introductory Note 2
I. Critical Points and Thermodynamic Singularities 2
A. The Ising model 3

    B. Other problems 6
    C. Critical singularities 8
    D. The importance of correlation functions 10
    E. Droplet picture of correlation behaviour 10
  II. Mean Field Theory 12
    A. Results 12
    B. Generalizations 15
    C. Failure of mean field theory 15
  III. The Roots of the Theory: Universality 16
    A. Fields and operators 16
    B. Statement of universality hypothesis 17
    C. A simple example 18
    D. Additional universality statements 19
  IV. The Roots of the Theory: Scaling 20
    A. The irrelevance of the length scale 20
    B. A formal description of the length transformation 20
    C. Fixed points 23
    D. Deviations from the fixed point 24
    E. Scaling results for the free energy 25
    F. A simple example of the theory 26
  V. Scale Transformations for Correlation Functions 28
    A. General discussion 28
    B. Formal theory 28
    C. Connections with universality 31
    D. Consequences 31
References 33

Generalized Landau Theories

Marshall Luban

  I. Introduction 35
  II. Uniform Magnetization 38
    A. Generalized Gibbs free energy 38
    B. Molecular field approximation 40
    C. Classical Landau theory 44
  III. Gibbs Free Energy Functional 46
  IV. Classical Landau Functional 49
    A. Thermodynamic properties 49
    B. Ginzburg criterion 54
  V. Generalized Landau Theories 55
    A. Free energy functional 57
    B. Equilibrium properties 58
    C. Josephson inequality 61
    D. Two-dimensional Ising model ($T < T_c$) 63
    E. Superfluid He^4 67
  VI. Time-Dependent Phenomena 71
    A. Landau-Khalatnikov theory 72
    B. Generalized time-dependent Landau theory 73
    C. Applications 75
    D. Propagating modes 78
  VII. Exact Results for Classical Functionals 81
References 83

Neutron Scattering and Spatial Correlation near the Critical Point

Jens Als-Nielsen

I. Introduction 88
II. Theory of Critical Neutron Scattering 89
   A. Scattering cross section and spin correlations 89
   B. Response functions and spin correlations 92
   C. Notation in a uniform presentation of experimental results 95
III. Experimental Methods in Critical Neutron Scattering 97
   A. The three-axis crystal spectrometer 97
   B. The two-axis spectrometer. The quasielastic approximation 99
   C. The resolution of crystal spectrometers 101
IV. Three-Dimensional Ising Systems 105
   A. The order–disorder transition in beta-brass and the Ising model ... 105
   B. Results for beta-brass 109
   C. Comparison, beta-brass and the $3d$-Ising model 118
   D. Other $3d$-Ising systems 118
V. Three-Dimensional Antiferromagnets—$RbMnF_3$, MnF_2, FeF_2 120
   A. Structure, exchange constants, anisotropy 120
   B. The isotropic Heisenberg antiferromagnet $RbMnF_3$ 123
   C. The uniaxial antiferromagnets MnF_2 and FeF_2 129
VI. Three-Dimensional Ferromagnets—EuO, EuS, Fe, Tb 135
   A. The Heisenberg ferromagnets EuO and EuS 136
   B. Critical fluctuations in iron 143
   C. Critical fluctuations in terbium .... 14$
VII. One- and Two-Dimensional Magnetic Systems 147
   A. The one-dimensional antiferromagnet $(CF_3)_4NMnCl_3$ (TMMC) 148
   B. Two-dimensional antiferromagnets of K_2NiF_4 type 153
Acknowledgement 162
References 162

Mode Coupling and Critical Dynamics

Kyozi Kawasaki

I. Introduction 166
II. Long Time Behaviour of Correlation Functions 171
III. Coupling Among Hydrodynamic Modes 175
   A. Thermohydrodynamic derivation 176
   B. Mode coupling expressed as equal time correlations of fluctuations . 179
IV. Transport Coefficients 185
V. Kinetic Equations for Gross Variables 189
   A. Isotropic Heisenberg ferromagnets 199
   B. Isotropic Heisenberg antiferromagnets 205
   C. Single component fluids 208
   D. Binary fluid critical mixtures 213
VI. Time Correlation Functions of Gross Variables 216
VII. Strengths of Mode Coupling, Dynamical Scaling, and Transport Anomalies . 236
   A. Preliminaries 236
   B. Illustrative examples of dynamical scaling 239
   C. Validity of the dynamical scaling hypotheses and transport anomalies . 257
VIII. Dynamical Behaviour near Critical Points 266
   A. Dynamics of order parameters and related variables 267
   B. Critical dynamics not involving order parameters directly 298
   C. Validity of the approximate treatments of kinetic equations 329
IX. Attempts at Microscopic Theories 331
   A. Application of quantum-field theoretical methods 331

    B. Other approaches 335
    X. Related Developments 336
   XI. Concluding Remarks 343
Acknowledgements 344
Appendix A 345
Appendix B 352

AUTHOR INDEX 405
SUBJECT INDEX 413

Phase Transitions and Critical Phenomena
Volume 5B

Edited by
C. Domb and M. S. Green

CONTRIBUTORS   v
GENERAL PREFACE vii
PREFACE TO VOLUMES 5A AND 5B   ix

Monte Carlo Investigations of Phase Transitions and Critical Phenomena

K. Binder

    I. Introduction   2
   II. Descriptions of the Monte Carlo Technique for Spin Systems   6
       A. Master equation approach   6
       B. Accuracy and convergence considerations   16
       C. Monte Carlo calculations with conservation laws   21
       D. Different boundary conditions and their correspondence to physical situations   29
  III. Applications to Static Critical Phenomena   37
       A. Two- and three-dimensional Ising models   37
       B. Two- and three-dimensional classical Heisenberg models   44
       C. Analysis of finite size and rounding effects   53
       D. Spatial inhomogeneities in infinite systems (surfaces, interfaces, impurities)   61
       E. Tricritical points   68
       F. A test of M. E. Fisher's droplet model   70
   IV. Applications to Dynamic Critical Phenomena   73
       A. The single spin-flip kinetic Ising model   74
       B. Comparison of the critical slowing down with other treatments   76
       C. Metastable states and nonequilibrium relaxation   82
       D. Further models   90
    V. Discussion   94
References   96
Addendum 100

Systems with Weak Long-Range Potentials

P. C. Hemmer and J. Lebowitz

I. Introduction 108
  A. The van der Waals–Maxwell theory 108
  B. Rigorous results 110
  C. Metastable states 112
  D. Approximate results 112
II. Rigorous Derivation of van der Waals–Maxwell Theory 113
  A. Preliminaries 113
  B. Statement of main results 116
  C. General bounds 118
  D. Proof of theorem 1 120
  E. Some consequences and extensions of theorem 1 128
  F. Metastability 132
  G. Oscillatory Kac potentials; Gates and Penrose theorem 136
III. Integral Equation Approach 138
  A. Integral equation for the one-dimensional continuum gas 139
  B. Integral equations for the lattice gas 143
  C. The van der Waals limit 145
  D. Expansion for small γ 149
  E. The critical region 153
  F. Correlation functions 157
  G. Mixtures 161
  H. External fields 163
  I. Generalized interactions in one and higher dimensions 166
IV. Systematic Expansions 170
  A. Graph expansion. Introduction 170
  B. Graph expansion. Results 172
  C. The Coulomb interaction 180
  D. Functional integral approach 182
  E. The critical region 186
V. Applications 189
  A. The liquid–gas system 189
  B. The solid–liquid transition 191
  C. Several phase transitions 193
  D. Quantum corrections to the location of the critical point 196
References 198

Correlation Functions and Their Generating Functionals: General Relations with Applications to the Theory of Fluids

G. Stell

I. Introduction 205
II. General Development 208
III. The Decomposition of W_n and Some Expressions Associated with it 216
IV. Results When the Pair Term is Further Decomposed 222
V. The Dyson-equation Form of the Ornstein–Zernike Equation 231
VI. Use of δ-ordering, Γ-ordering; the Core Condition on g_2 (12) and the Mean-spherical Model;
  Nodal Ordering 234
VII. Generalization of the Mean-spherical Approximation and The Self-consistent Γ-ordered
  Scheme to n-particle Functions 239
References 242
Appendix: Critical Behaviour of Approximations and Models for Which the Ornstein–Zernike
  Assumption is Satisfied 246
References to Appendix 258

Heisenberg Ferromagnet in the Green's Function Approximation

R. A. Tahir-Kheli

    I. Introductory Remarks 259
   II. The Random Phase Approximation 260
      A.   The spin-$\frac{1}{2}$ case 260
      B.   The general spin case 265
  III. The Callen Decoupling 277
  IV. Boson Formalism: Extrapolation from Low Temperatures 283
   V. The Intermediate Region 288
      A.   The low-temperature region 294
      B.   The high-temperature region 294
      C.   Temperature close to T_c 297
  VI. Self-consistent Moment Conserving Decoupling Scheme 302
      A.   Series expansion schemes 308
      B.   Results in three dimensions 309
      C.   Near T_c 310
      D.   Results in one dimension 313
      E.   Results in two dimensions 316
 VII. Random, Dilute Ferromagnet: an RPA Coherent Exchange Approximation (RPA–CEA)
      Treatment 317
References 340

Thermal Measurements and Critical Phenomena in Liquids

A. V. Voronel

    I. Isomorphy of Critical Phenomena 344
   II. Experimental Working Conditions with a Liquid 347
      A.   Difficulties of the experiment 349
      B.   Difficulties of interpretation 363
  III. Results of the Measurement of Thermodynamic Properties 365
      A.   Pure liquids 365
      B.   Dilute solution of heptane in ethane 370
      C.   The system ethane/carbon dioxide (liquid–vapour critical line) 375
      D.   The liquid–liquid critical line 378
  IV. Discussion of Results 380
   V. Conclusion 389
References 390
Appendix: Data on Critical Exponents 392

AUTHOR INDEX 395
SUBJECT INDEX 403

Phase Transitions and Critical Phenomena
Volume 6

Edited by
C. Domb and M. S. Green

CONTRIBUTORS v
GENERAL PREFACE vii
PREFACE TO VOLUME 6 ix

The Renormalization Group—Introduction

Kenneth G. Wilson

References 5

The Critical State, General Aspects

F. J. Wegner

  I. Introduction 8
 II. The Renormalization Group 11
    A. Order parameter, critical exponents 11
    B. From discrete to continuous models 14
    C. Scale invariance and basic properties of the renormalization group 17
    D. Definitions and notations 18
    E. Renormalization group equation with smooth momentum cut-off 22
    F. Other renormalization group transformations 27
III. Linearized Theory 29
    A. Fixed point, linearized renormalization group equations 29
    B. Redundant operators 34
    C. Scaling of the free energy 41
    D. Correlation functions in momentum space 45
    E. Correlation functions in coordinate space 49
    F. Trivial (Gaussian) fixed point 54
    G. Comments 60
IV. Nonlinear Theory: The Nontrivial Fixed Point 65
    A. The nonlinear term 65
    B. The nontrivial fixed point in order ε 70
    C. Exponent η 73
    D. Isotropic $\hat{n}$-component model 77
 V. Nonlinear Theory: Homogeneous Systems 80
    A. Scaling fields 80
    B. Invariance properties 85
    C. Universality 88
    D. Coexistence curve 91
    E. Logarithmic anomalies 94
    F. The limit case $y_E = 0$: Phase transitions of infinite order 98
VI. Nonlinear Theory: Correlations 105

    A. Order parameter correlations 105
    B. Recursion equation for correlation functions 107
    C. Correlation functions for finite wave-lengths near T_c 111
    D. Scaling fields for inhomogeneous perturbations, universality of scaling functions 115
References 122

Field Theoretical Approach to Critical Phenomena

E. Brezin, J. C. Le Guillou and J. Zinn-Justin

  I. Introduction 127
    A. Characterization of the static critical behaviour 129
    B. Correlation and thermodynamic scaling 131
 II. Perturbation Theory 132
    A. Perturbation expansion of the partition function 133
    B. Generating functionals for the connected and the one-particle irreducible correlation
        functions 134
    C. Loop expansion 136
    D. Dimensional continuation of Feynman diagrams 139
III. Renormalization Scheme 141
    A. The problem of divergences in local field theories 141
    B. Regularization 143
    C. Renormalization 143
    D. Composite operators 148
    E. Equations of motion 153
    F. Massless theory 156
 IV. Mean Field Theory and the Role of Dimension Four 157
    A. Mean field theory 157
    B. Beyond mean field theory 165
    C. Validity of Landau theory above four dimensions 168
    D. Remark concerning tricritical points 169
    E. Perturbation theory for an arbitrary spin Hamiltonian 169
  V   Critical Phenomena near Dimension Four 170
    A. Renormalization group equations at $T = T_c$ 171
    B. Consequences of the renormalization group equations 174
 VI. Renormalized Theory: Derivation of Scaling Laws Above the Critical Temperature 177
    A. Renormalization at zero momentum 177
    B. Renormalization group equations for the critical theory 181
    C. Expansion around the critical theory 183
    D. Scaling laws above T_c 184
    E. Correlation functions involving S^2 insertions 186
VII. Scaling Laws below the Critical Temperature 188
    A. Equation of state 188
    B. Correlation functions below T_c for Ising-like systems 191
    C. Longitudinal and transverse susceptibilities below T_c for an n-component system 192
VIII. Corrections to Scaling Laws 193
    A. Deviations from scaling in the S^4-theory below four dimensions 193
    B. Logarithmic corrections in four dimensions 195
    C. Deviations from scaling induced by irrelevant even operators 198
    D. Renormalization group equations for the tricritical behaviour 200
 IX. The ε-Expansion: Calculations and Results 202
    A. Calculation of the critical exponents 203
    B. The equation of state 208
    C. The critical spin–spin correlation function for arbitrary magnetization and temperature .. 212
    D. Universal ratios derived from the equation of state 213
    E. Other universal ratios of amplitudes in Ising-like systems 215
  X. Renormalization Group for the n-Vector Model in the Large n-Limit 217
    A. Algebraic method to generate the $1/n$ expansion 218

B.   Existence of the critical theory 219
C.   Fixed point in the large n-limit 220
D.   Results of the calculations in the $1/n$ expansion 220
XI. Discussion of the General n-Vector Model 221
A.   The Hamiltonian density 224
B.   Renormalization group equations 225
C.   Critical exponents 228
D.   Stability conditions 231
E.   Anisotropic corrections to the equation of state for the symmetric fixed point 235
XII. Short Distance Expansions and Critical Phenomena 237
A.   Short-distance expansion of an operator product 238
B.   The renormalization group equation satisfied by the first Wilson coefficient 239
C.   Next-to-leading terms in zero field above T_c 240
D.   Next-to-leading terms in a field or below T_c 241
References 244

The I/n Expansion

Shang-Keng Ma

I. Introduction 250
A.   Simplicity at large n 250
B.   The model and the solution above the critical point 251
C.   Historical note, summary of exponents 255
II. Renormalization Group, Scaling Fields and the Fixed Point 258
A.   Renormalization group 259
B.   Scaling fields 260
C.   RG and scaling fields for $n \to \infty$, critical surface 260
D.   Transformation of the free energy 266
III. Scaling Variables. Scaling Dimensions and Correlation Functions 267
A.   Transformation of random variables, scaling variables 267
B.   Product of scaling variables 270
C.   Correlation functions 270
D.   Discussion 272
IV. Nonzero Magnetization and the Equation of State at $n \to \infty$ 273
A.   Transverse and longitudinal susceptibilities 273
B.   Solution below the critical point and the equation of state 274
V. Calculation of Exponents to $O(1/n)$ 276
A.   Perturbation theory 277
B.   Properties of $\Pi(k)$ and the dressed interaction 278
C.   Evaluation of η and γ 280
D.   Evaluation of α and the Abe–Hikami anomaly 282
E.   Evaluation of $y_{\Delta\tau}$ and $y_{\tau 1}$ 285
F.   Evaluation of y_c, the cubic exponent 287
G.   Results 288
VI. Discussion 288
A.   Other formulations 288
B.   Convergence and extrapolation 289
C.   Long-range force 290
D.   Concluding remarks 291
References 291

The ε-Expansion for Exponents and the Equation of State in Isotropic Systems

D. J. Wallace

Introduction 294
  I. General Formalism 295
    A. The n-component field model 295
    B. Correlation functions 297
    C. Feynman rules 300
  II. The ε-Expansion 304
    A. Résumé 304
    B. Perturbation theory in the critical region 305
    C. The ε-expansion 308
    D. Results for η and γ 314
    E. The irreducible diagram series 320
    F. Notes on evaluation of graphs 322
  III. Equation of State 326
    A. Introduction 326
    B. Setting up the calculation 327
    C. The ε-expansion for the equation of state 333
    D. Parametric models 340
    E. Behaviour near the coexistence curve 343
  IV. Other Perturbations of the Hamiltonian 346
    A. General considerations 346
    B. Scaling variables of the Heisenberg fixed point 348
    C. Calculations and conclusions 350
Acknowledgements 354
References 354

Dependence of Universal Critical Behaviour on Symmetry and Range of Interaction

Amnon Aharony

  I. Introduction 358
  II. The Recursion Relation Approach 359
    A. Reduced Hamiltonian: notations and normalizations 359
    B. Renormalization group iterations 363
    C. The Gaussian model 366
    D. Diagrammatic expansions 371
  III. Spin Anisotropies 376
    A. Crossover to a lower effective spin dimensionality 376
    B. Crossover to mean field behaviour as $n \rightarrow \infty$ (extreme anisotropy) 380
  IV. Long-Range Interactions and Dipolar Systems 382
    A. Isotropic long-range interactions 382
    B. Isotropic dipolar magnets; antiferromagnets 383
    C. Isotropic ferromagnets 387
    D. Anisotropic ferromagnets: XY-like anisotropy 390
    E. Anisotropic Ising-like ferromagnets 392
  V. Generalized "Cubic" Systems: Various Effective Quartic Spin Interactions 394
    A. The competition between Heisenber, Ising and cubic fixed points ... 394
    B. Cubic critical behaviour 398
    C. n coupled m-vector models 402
    D. The random m-component magnet 406
    E. Metamagnetic, bicritical and tetracritical behaviour in antiferromagnets 410
    F. Compressible magnets 413
    G. Systems with larger "spin" dimensionality 416
  VI. Spatial Anisotropies 417

A. Lattice anisotropies 417
      B. Semi-infinite systems 418
VII. Discussion 419
References 421

Renormalization Theory for Ising-like Spin Systems

Th. Niemeijer and J. M. J. van Leeuwen

Introduction 425
    I. Definitions 427
   II. General Theory 434
      A. Eigenvalues and critical exponents 437
      B. Determination of the critical temperature 440
      C. Calculation of the free energy 440
      D. The spontaneous magnetization 447
  III. Correlation Functions 450
      A. Linear weight-factors $P(s', s)$ 451
      B. Simplified treatment of $g(r)$ 453
      C. General discussion of the correlation functions 457
      D. Connection between exponents and eigenvectors 462
  IV. Computational Methods 463
      A. Simple renormalization transformations on finite lattices 465
      B. The cumulant approximation 467
      C. The cluster approximation 470
   V. Applications 473
      A. The triangular lattice 474
      B. The quadratic lattice 484
  VI. Discussion 492
References 499
Appendix A 500
Appendix B 502

Renormalization Group Approach to Critical Phenomena

C. Di Castro and G. Jona-Lasinio

I. Introduction 508
   II. Scaling 511
  III. Block Variables and the Kadanoff–Wilson Approach 514
      A. Block variable transformation 514
      B. Scaling properties at the critical point 516
      C. Linearized group transformation 518
      D. Properties of approach to the critical point 520
  IV. Functional Form of Many-Body Theory 522
      A. Introductory remarks 522
      B. The model 523
      C. Functional equations 526
   V. The Field Theoretic Renormalization Group 528
      A. Group equations 528
      B. Scaling 533
  VI. ε-Expansion and Approximate Treatment of Scaling Variables and Cross-over Effects 537
      A. ε-expansion 537
      B. Scaling variables and cross-over effects 538
  VII. Formal Equivalence of Kadanoff–Wilson and Field Theoretic Re-normalization Groups 540

VIII. Generalized and Non-Linear Transformations 544
References 551
Appendix A. A Connection with Probability Theory 552
Appendix B. Summary of Diagrammatic Expansions 554
Appendix C. Relation to the Callan–Symanzik Equation 555

AUTHOR INDEX 559
SUBJECT INDEX 565

Phase Transitions and Critical Phenomena
Volume 7

Edited by
C. Domb and J. L. Lebowitz

CONTRIBUTORS v
GENERAL PREFACE vii
PREFACE TO VOLUME 7 ix

Defect-mediated Phase Transitions

D. R. Nelson

I. Introduction 2
II. The XY Model and Superfluidity in Two Dimensions 11
III. Dynamic Scaling and Third Sound in Helium Films 31
IV. Statistical Mechanics of Two-dimensional Melting 40
V. Melting Dynamics 66
VI. Anisotropic Melting 74
VII. Line Singularities in Three Dimensions 83
Acknowledgements 93
References 93

Conformational Phase Transitions in a Macromolecule:
Exactly Solvable Models

F. W. Wiegel

I. Introduction 101
II. Adsorption to a Surface 104
III. Helix-Coil Transitions 109
IV. Crystallization by Folding 121
V. Entanglements 131
Acknowledgements 147
References 147

Dilute Magnetism

R. B. Stinchcombe

I. Introduction 152
II. Qualitative Features 154
III. Exact Results and Exactly Soluble Models 174
IV. Monte Carlo and Simulation Results 202
V. Closed Form Approximations 210
VI. Series Expansion Investigations 223
VII. Scaling and Renormalization Group Methods for Dilute Magnets 232
VIII. Selected Experimental Results and Comparison with Theory 262
References 270

AUTHOR INDEX 281
SUBJECT INDEX 290

Phase Transitions and Critical Phenomena
Volume 8

Edited by
C. Domb and J. L. Lebowitz

CONTRIBUTORS v
GENERAL PREFACE vii
PREFACE TO VOLUME 8 ix

Critical Behaviour at Surfaces

K. Binder

I. Introduction 2
II. Mean-field Theory of Surface Critical Behaviour 6
III. Critical Exponents and Scaling Laws 34
IV. Related Phenomena 76
V. Numerical Methods and Their Results 103
VI. Renormalization Group Results 118
VII. Conclusions 134
Acknowledgements 135
References 135
Note added in proof 467

Finite-size Scaling

M. N. Barber

    I. Introduction 146
   II. Preliminaries 148
  III. Finite-size Scaling 158
  IV. Phenomenological Renormalization 171
   V. Extensions of Finite-size Scaling 181
  VI. Exact Calculations 201
 VII. Numerical Tests and Applications 223
VIII. Experimental Tests 250
  IX. Conclusion—Problems and Prospects 257
References 259
Note added in proof 475

The Dynamics of First Order Phase Transitions

J. D. Gunton, M. San Miguel and P. S. Sahni

    I. Introduction 269
   II. Classical Theory of Nucleation 279
  III. Field Theory Models 287
  IV. A Field Theoretic Nucleation Theory 300
   V. Theories of Spinodal Decomposition 319
  VI. Late Stage Growth Theories 333
 VII. Cluster Dynamics 339
VIII. Scaling Theories for Structure Functions 366
  IX. Monte Carlo Studies 374
   X. Studies of Nucleation in Near-critical Fluids 395
  XI. Experimental Studies of Spinodal Decomposition 404
 XII. Tricritical Systems 422
XIII. Special Topics 432
Acknowledgements 455
References 455
Note added in proof 467

AUTHOR INDEX 483
SUBJECT INDEX 497

Phase Transitions and Critical Phenomena
Volume 9

Edited by
C. Domb and J. L. Lebowitz

CONTRIBUTORS v
GENERAL PREFACE vii
PREFACE TO VOLUME 9 ix

Theory of Tricritical Points

I. D. Lawrie and S. Sarbach

I. Introduction 2
II. Scaling Description of Tricritical Behaviour 26
III. Classical Theory 65
IV. The Many-component Limit: An Exactly Soluble Model 96
V. Renormalization-group Theory 113
VI. Concluding Remarks 152
Acknowledgements 155
References 155

Multicritical Points in Fluid Mixtures: Experimental Studies

C. M. Knobler and R. L. Scott

I. Introduction 164
II. History 169
III. Theory 171
IV. Unsymmetrical Tricritical Points in Three-component Systems 180
V. Unsymmetrical Tricritical Points in Four-component Systems 192
VI. Symmetrical Tricritical Points 207
VII. Higher-order Critical Points 225
Acknowledgements 228
References 228

Critical Point Statistical Mechanics and Quantum Field Theory

G. A. Baker, Jr

I. Introduction and Summary 234
II. Constructive Quantum Field Theory 235
III. Continuous Spin Ising Model 281
IV. Renormalization Group Theory of Critical Phenomena 288
V. Quantitative Information about the Critical Point and the Continuum Limit of Field Theory .. 295
References 305
Appendix A: Positivity Hypothesis 309
Appendix B: Detail on Mass Renormalization 310

SUBJECT INDEX 313

Phase Transitions and Critical Phenomena
Volume 10

Edited by
C. Domb and J. L. Lebowitz

CONTRIBUTORS   v
GENERAL PREFACE   vii
PREFACE TO VOLUME 10   ix

Surface Structures and Phase Transitions—Exact Results

D. B. Abraham

    I. Introduction   2
    II. Interfacial Free Energy and Phase Transition in the Ising Ferromagnet   5
    III. Correlation Functions in the Interface—Planar Model   17
    IV. Intrinsic Structure of Interface   23
    V. Results in Three Dimensions   27
    VI. Surface Models   33
    VII. Exactly-solvable Random-surface Models   40
    VIII. Phase Transitions in Surfaces—$d = 2$ 48
    IX. Surface Transitions in Three-dimensional Systems   58
    X. Finite Size Effects for Interfacial Free Energy   62
Acknowledgements   68
References   69

Field-theoretic Approach to Critical Behaviour at Surfaces

H. W. Diehl

    I. Introduction   76
    II. Background, Basic Concepts and Definitions   83
    III. Renormalization Group for the Semi-infinite n-Vector Model   116
    IV. Extensions of the Theory and Related Topics   226
    V. Conclusion Summary and Outlook   256
Acknowledgements   259
Appendix   259
References   260

Renormalization Group Theory of Interfaces

David Jasnow

I. Introduction 270
II. Renormalization Group Background 276
III. Capillary Waves 286
IV. Renormalization Group Studies 297
V. The Low-temperature Approach 336
VI. Interface Dynamics Near Equilibrium 342
VII. Concluding Remarks 357
Acknowledgements 358
References 359

Phase Transitions and Critical Phenomena
Volume 11

Edited by
C. Domb and J. L. Lebowitz

CONTRIBUTORS v
GENERAL PREFACE vii
PREFACE TO VOLUME 11 ix

Coulomb Gas Formulation of Two-dimensional Phase Transitions

B. Nienhus

I. Introduction 1
II. The Coulomb Gas 3
III. Exact Transformations 30
IV. Asymptotic Equivalences 30
V. Conclusions 50
Acknowledgements 51
References 51

Conformal Invariance

J. L. Cardy

I. Introduction 55
II. Scale and Conformal Invariance 60
III. Results for Restricted Geometries 68
IV. Conformal Invariance in Two Dimensions 89
Acknowledgements 132
References 133

Low-temperature Properties of Classical Lattice Systems: Phase Transitions and Phase Diagrams

J. Slawny

I. Introduction 128
II. The Pirogov-Sinai Theory 140
III. Asymptotics of the Phase Diagram 169
IV. Ferromagnetic Systems 183
Acknowledgements 202
References 202

Phase Transitions and Critical Phenomena Volume 12

Edited by
C. Domb and J. L. Lebowitz

CONTRIBUTORS v
GENERAL PREFACE vii
PREFACE TO VOLUME 12 ix

Wetting Phenomena

S. Dietrich

I. Introduction 2
II. General Aspects 9
III. Models with Short-range Interactions 16
IV. Models with Long-range Interactions 41
V. Experiments 93
VI. Models with Several Ground States. 109
VII. Surface-induced Disorder 123
VIII. Melting 137
IX. Wetting Close to Bulk Critical Points 146
X. Non-standard Geometries 155
XI. Disorder. 167
XII. Dynamics 175
XIII. Complex Systems. 188
XIV. Conclusion. 194
Acknowledgements. 195
References (with author index). 195

The Domain Wall Theory of Two-dimensional Commensurate-Incommensurate
Phase Transitions

Marcel den Nijs

Introduction. 220
   I. Cell Spin Models 221
  II. The Fermion Theory for Striped Incommensurate Phases 247
 III. Beyond the Fermion Theory. 286
Acknowledgement 317
Abbreviations 317
References (with author index). 317
Appendix A: The Fermion Hamiltonian of the ANNNI Model. 322
Appendix B: The Fermion Hamiltonian of the Chiral 3-State Potts Model 324
Appendix C: The Disorder Plane in the $p = 2$ Fermion Hamiltonian 325
Appendix D: Urnklapp Operators 327
Appendix E: Higher-order C Solid Phases 329

The Growth of Fractal Aggregates and their Fractal Measures

Paul Meakin

   I. Introduction 336
  II. Diffusion-limited Aggregation (DLA). 360
 III. Experimental Realizations of DLA 386
 IV. The Growth of Fractal Aggregates and Fractal Measures 405
  V. Cluster–Cluster Aggregation. 430
 VI. Summary 469
VII. Recent Developments. 471
Acknowledgements. 477
References (with author index). 477

SUBJECT INDEX 491

Phase Transitions and Critical Phenomena
Volume 13

Edited by
C. Domb and J. L. Lebowitz

CONTRIBUTORS v
GENERAL PREFACE vii
PREFACE TO VOLUME 13 ix

Asymptotic Analysis of Power-Series Expansions

A. J. Guttmann

1. Introduction. 3
2. The ratio method. 16
3. Sequence extrapolation 35
4. Padé approximants 51
5. The rational-approximant method and general inverse Padé approximants. 75
6. Differential approximants. 83
7. Analysis of series in more than one variable. 105
8. Transformations. 120
9. Applications to other areas 130
10. Summary and outlook. 135
11. Programs for series analysis 138
Acknowledgements. 228
References (with author index). 229

Dimer Models on Anisotropic Lattices

John F. Nagle, Carlos S. O. Yokoi and Samendra M. Bhattacharjee

1. Introduction. 236
2. Some two-dimensional dimer models 240
3. Special features of models with K-type transitions 247
4. Mathematical foundations of the transition behaviour. 252
5. Results for thermodynamic properties 260
6. Correlation functions. 271
7. Finite-size effects 273
8. Three-dimensional models 277
9. Application to biomembranes. 280
10. Order parameter, anisotropic field, and application to monolayers 285
11. Application to 2×1 commensurate-incommensurate transitions. 289
12. Concluding remarks 295
References (with author index). 296

SUBJECT INDEX. 299

Phase Transitions and Critical Phenomena
Volume 14

Edited by
C. Domb and J. L. Lebowitz

CONTRIBUTORS v
GENERAL PREFACE. vii
PREFACE TO VOLUME 14. ix

Universal Critical-Point Amplitude Relations

V. Privman, P. C. Hohenberg and A. Aharony

1. Introduction 4
2. Definitions and notation for bulk critical amplitudes. 14
3. Scaling theory 21
4. The renormalization group 32
5. Methods of calculating bulk critical-point amplitudes 41
6. Numerical results for selected models 46
7. Experimental results: statics. 76
8. Experimental results: dynamics. 89
9. Statistics of polymer conformations 92
10. Finite-size systems. 99
11. Concluding remarks. 121
Acknowledgements. 121
References (with author index) 121

The Behaviour of Interfaces in Ordered and Disordered Systems

G. Forgacs, R. Lipowsky and Th. M. Nieuwenhuizen

1. Introduction. 136
2. Interfacial phenomena 138
3. Scaling properties of interfaces. 150
4. Solid-on-solid models of interfaces in pure systems. 220
5. Behaviour of a single interface in the presence of bulk disorder. 256
6. Wetting in the presence of bulk disorder 298
7. Wetting in the presence of surface disorder. 326
Acknowledgements 346
Appendix. Functional renormalization of interface potentials. 346
References (with author index). 354
Note to Chapter 1, added in proof 364

SUBJECT INDEX. 369

Phase Transitions and Critical Phenomena
Volume 15

Edited by
C. Domb and J. L. Lebowitz

CONTRIBUTORS v
GENERAL PREFACE vii
PREFACE TO VOLUME 15 ix

Spatially Modulated Structures in Systems with Competing Interactions

W. Selke

1. Introduction 2
2. Displacement models 7
3. Spin models 29
4. Phenomenological approaches 57
Acknowledgements 65
References (with author index) 65

The Large-*n* Limit in Statistical Mechanics and the Spectral Theory of Disordered Systems

A. M. Khorunzhy, B. A. Khoruzhenko, L. A. Pastur and M. V. Shcherbina

1. Introduction. 74

Part I: Statistical mechanics
2. Preliminary discussion 78
3. Spherical model with uniform spherical field. 88
4. Large-*n* limit of non-translationally invariant n-vector model: main theorems 108
5. Large-*n* limit of disordered *n*-vector model: applications of the main theorems 116
6. Spherical model with a nonuniform spherical field. 137

Part II: Spectral theory
7. Preliminary discussion. 165
8. Wigner model 171
9. Random finite-difference operators 201
Appendix A: The infinite-range limit of the *n*-vector model. 217
Appendix B: Deformed Wigner ensemble (Gaussian random part) 225
Appendix C: Derivation of the moment equations for the deformed Wigner ensemble whose
   random part has finite third moment 227
Appendix D: Derivation of (8.2.10). 229
Appendix E: Diluted matrices 231
Appendix F: Derivation of (9.1.16) 232
Appendix G: Large-interaction-radius model 233
References (with author index). 235

SUBJECT INDEX. 241

Phase Transitions and Critical Phenomena
Volume 16

Edited by
C. Domb and J. L. Lebowitz

GENERAL PREFACE. vii
PREFACE TO VOLUME 16 ix
CONTENTS OF VOLUMES 1–15 xi

Self-Assembling Amphiphilic Systems

G. Gompper and M. Schick

1. The phenomena and approaches to them   3
2. Microscopic models.   22
3. Ginzburg–Landau theory   76
4. The membrane approach.   129
5. Summary and outlook.   164
6. Acknowledgements   166
References   166
Index   177

Phase Transitions and Critical Phenomena
Volume 17

Edited by
C. Domb and J. L. Lebowitz

GENERAL PREFACE   vii
PREFACE TO VOLUME 17   ix
CONTENTS OF VOLUMES 1–16   xi

Statistical Mechanics of Driven Diffusive Systems

B. Schmittmann and R. K. P. Zia

1. Introduction.   3
2. Three perspectives of the standard model   9
3. Long range correlations above criticality   25
4. Critical phenomena   40
5. Physics below criticality.   73
6. Variations of the standard model.   93
7. Related non-equilibrium steady state systems.   170
8. Summary and outlook.   192
9. Acknowledgements   197
References.   198
Index.   215

Phase Transitions and Critical Phenomena
Volume 18

Edited by

C. Domb and J. L. Lebowitz

CONTRIBUTORS v
GENERAL PREFACE vii
PREFACE TO VOLUME 18 ix

The Random Geometry of Equilibrium Phases

H. O. Georgii, O, Häggström and C. Maes

1. Introduction. 3
2. Equilibrium phases 6
3. Some models 14
4. Coupling and stochastic domination 21
5. Percolation. 31
6. Random-cluster representations 47
7. Uniqueness and exponential mixing from non-percolation 72
8. Phase transition and percolation 91
9. Random interactions 112
10. Continuum models 123
References. 129

Exact Combinatorial Algorithms: Ground States of Disordered Systems

M. J. Alava, P. M. Duxbury, C. F. Moukarzel and H. Rieger

1. Overview 145
2. Basics of graphs and algorithms 148
3. Flow algorithms 158
4. Matching algorithms 175

Phase Transitions and Critical Phenomena
Volume 19

Edited by
C. Domb and J. L. Lebowitz

Exactly Solvable Models for Many-Body Systems Far from Equilibrium

G. M. Schütz

1. Introduction	3
1.1 Stochastic dynamics of interacting particle systems	3
1.2 Integrability	4
1.3 Polymers and traffic flow: some notes about modelling	6
1.4 Outlines	13
2. Quantum Hamiltonian formalism for the master equation	17
2.1 The master equation	17
2.2 Expectation values	22
2.3 Many-body systems	23
2.4 Nonstochastic generators	28
3. Integrable stochastic processes	30
3.1 The Ising and Heisenberg spin models	32
3.2 Bethe ansatz	35
3.3 Quantum systems in disguise: some stochastic processes	41
3.4 Algebraic properties in integrable models	50
4. Asymptotic behaviour	53
4.1 The infinite-time limit	53
4.2 Late-time behaviour	59
4.3 Separation of time scales	69
5. Equivalence of stochastic processes	72

Polymerized Membranes, a Review

K. J. Wiese

1. Introduction	3
1.1 Stochastic dynamics of interacting particle systems	3
1.2 Integrability	4
1.3 Polymers and traffic flow: some notes about modelling	6
1.4 Outline	13
2. Quantum Hamiltonian formalism for the master equation	17
2.1 The master equation	17
2.2 Expectation values	22
2.3 Many-body systems	23
2.4 Nonstochastic generators	28
3. Integrable stochastic processes	30
3.1 The Ising and Heisenberg spin models	32
3.2 Bethe ansatz	35
3.3 Quantum systems in disguise: some stochastic processes	41
3.4 Algebraic properties of integrable models	50
4. Asymptotic behaviour	53
4.1 The infinite-time limit	53
4.2 Late-time behaviour	59
4.3 Separation of time scales	69

5. Equivalences of stochastic processes 72
   5.1 Similarity transformations revisited 72
   5.2 Enantiodromy 74
   5.3 First-passage-time and persistence probabilities 75

Cumulative Subject Index

A

A_2BX_4, **15**:59
AB diblock copolymer, **16**:165–66
ABA triblocks, **16**:166
Abe-Hikami anomaly, **6**:282
Abelian symmetry, **7**:4
  phase transitions and, **7**:2
Abelian, groups, **11**:200
Abraham-Newman model, **14**:254–5
Abrikosov lattices, **18**:235–7, **18**:238,
  18:240, **18**:261
Absorbing edge [of interface], **17**:86
Absorbing subset, **19**:56–57
Absorption coefficient, **5B**:381
ACRITH, **13**:53
Actin filaments, **19**:10
Activity, **1**:42, **1**:52, **1**:91, **1**:113, **1**:131,
  1:133, **3**:2, **3**:654
Activity expansion, **3**:370
Adjacency matrix, **3**:14, **3**:16, **3**:42,
  3:103, **3**:104, **3**:589, **3**:590,
  3:603
Adjacency vector, **3**:105, **3**:106, **3**:107
Adler, Moshe and Privman method,
  13:73–75
Admissible arcs, **18**:164, **18**:165
Adsorbate, **12**:5, **12**:7, **12**:15, **12**:16,
  12:22, **12**:59, **12**:78
  interaction, **12**:13, **12**:16, **12**:20,
    12:43, **12**:45, **12**:78, **12**:93,
    12:109, **12**:114–115,
    12:119–122, **12**:139, **12**:147,
    12:149, **12**:167, **12**:169,
    12:172–175
Adsorbed film,
  immobile, **1**:232, **1**:241

Adsorption, **1**:228, **1**:259, **2**:306
  immobile, on crystal surface, **1**:241
Adsorption isotherm, **12**:14, **12**:97,
  12:166
Adsorption operators, **1**:234
Adsorption to a surface, **7**:104–109
Affine connection, **16**:166
n-Alkyl polyglycol ethers (C_iE_j), **16**:5
Aggregation
  annealed site diluted magnets, **7**:156,
    7:174
  antiferromagnets, **7**:161
  ballistic, **12**:436, **12**:439–442, **12**:454,
    12:470
  bonds, **7**:162
  colloidal, **12**:337, **12**:339, **12**:342,
    12:348, **12**:438, **12**:456, **12**:458,
    12:465, **12**:469
  diffusion limited, *see* DLA
  in dilute magnets, **7**:156–162
    cluster-cluster, **12**:337, **12**:348,
      12:350, **12**:358, **12**:430
    kinetics, **12**:350, **12**:357–359,
      12:462–465
  models, **7**:202
Agreement percolation, **18**:91–4,
  18:100–11
Aharonov–Bohm effect,
  entanglements and, **7**:147
Air, **5B**:361
Aisenmann theory, **9**:296
Aizenman–Higuchi theorem, **18**:98
Aizenman–Wehr theorem, **18**:214
Alexander model, **16**:27–8, **16**:58,
  16:58–9
Alexander polynomial, knot theory,
  7:146

Alexander–Orbach conjecture,
    12:351–352
Algebraic decay, **19**:63, **19**:67, **19**:68,
    19:74, **19**:99
ϵ-Algorithm, alternating, **8**:226
Algorithms, complexity of, **18**:149–50,
    18:163
Alloys, **1**:228
    metal-hydrogen, **8**:443–444
    surface enrichment, **8**:14, **8**:94–96
Alloys, binary
    first-order transitions, **8**:289
    lattice models, **8**:5
    phenomenological scaling theory,
        8:370
    spinodal decomposition, experimental
        studies, **8**:404–411
Alloys, critical point, **6**:91
Almost-Markov property *see*
    quasilocality
Aluminium foil, crumpled, fractal
    dimension, **19**:275–276
Aluminium, single alloys, spinodal
    decomposition, experimental
    studies, **8**:404
Amenability, **18**:38
Ammonium halides, **9**:7
Ammonium sulfate
    + benzene, **9**:203
    + ethanol, **9**:203
    + water, **9**:203
Amorphous magnets, **6**:409
Amphiphile–amphiphile interaction,
    16:124
Amphiphile–amphiphile structure
    function, **16**:17, **16**:43, **16**:48,
        16:*49*, **16**:119
Amphiphile bilayers, elastic properties,
    16:127–28
Amphiphilic systems
    membrane approach, **16**:129–64
    microscopic models, **16**:19–20,
        16:22–76, **16**:98, **16**:164
    phenomena of, and approaches to
        them, **16**:3–22
    theoretical approaches, **16**:18–22
Amplitude calculations, **13**:92–94
    ratios, **13**:93–94
Amplitude D, **3**:435, **3**:448

Amplitude fluctuations
    defects and, **7**:7
    Landau theory and, **7**:16–18
Amplitude ratios, **9**:59, **9**:109, **10**:217,
    11:71
Amplitude renormalization, **9**:274
ANALYSE, **13**:150–153
    listing, **13**:198–223
Analysis G-M-L, **6**:508
Analytic continuation, **5B**:133, **6**:309
Analytic correction terms, **14**:38
Analyticity condition, **6**:210
Analyticity, **1**:46, **1**:83
Anderson localization, in random
    system, **8**:250
Anderson model, **15**:166, **15**:187,
    15:201–3, **15**:211
Andrews–Baxter–Forrester models,
    14:252–3
Angle, contact, **12**:4–9, **12**:15, **12**:24,
    12:64, **12**:99, **12**:102, **12**:104–105,
    12:150, **12**:157, **12**:160–163
Angular integrals, **6**:374
Anharmonic fluctuation term, **5A**:82
Anharmonic fluctuations, **5A**:55,
    5A:62
Anharmonic sources, mean
    magnetization and, **6**:16
Anharmonic term, **5A**:61
Anharmonicity of elastic terms, **19**:376
Aniline/cyclohexane mixture, **5A**:309,
    5A:311
Animal, **3**:99
Anisotropic exchange coupling, diluted
    Heisenberg spin systems, transition
    temperatures, coherent potential
    approximation, **7**:218
Anisotropic growth, **17**:77–80
Anisotropic interaction, **3**:557
Anisotropic lattice, **2**:108, **2**:l12, **2**:394,
    2:395, **2**:403, **2**:407
Anisotropic lattices, melting, **7**:79–81
Anisotropic nearest-neighbour
    interactions, **2**:893, **2**:394
Anisotropic rates, *see* Extreme
    anisotropic rates
Anisotropic scaling relations, **15**:61
Anisotropic scaling, melting of smectic-
    A liquid crystals and, **7**:90

Anisotropic structure factors, **17**:42,
  17:*43*
Anisotropy, **5A**:122, **5A**:279, **5A**:281,
  5A:283, **6**:378, **8**:75
  cross-over exponent, **10**:254
  cubic, **6**:231, **6**:272, **6**:526, **9**:7,
    19:430, **19**:431, **19**:433
  cubic, surface, **8**:57
  extreme, **6**:380, **6**:382
  interface tension, **8**:71–72
  planar, **8**:19
  quadratic, **10**:321
  special anisotropic transition, *see*
    Transition
  surface, **8**:19
  terms, **6**:296
  tethered membranes, **19**:375
  uniaxial, **5A**:122, **5A**:129, **9**:2
  uniaxial, surface, **8**:57
  X Y, **6**:390, **8**:19, **8**:76
  see also Strong...; Weak anisotropy
Anisotropy exponent, **17**:42, **17**:44,
  17:51, **17**:52, **17**:54–59, **17**:65,
  17:67, **17**:100–103, **17**:146
Anisotropy measures, **14**:43
Anisotropy of K dimer models, **13**:252,
  13:272–273
Anisotropy parameter, **3**:494, **3**:496,
  3:546
Anisotropy-induced crossover, dilute
  Heisenberg quadratic layer magnet,
  7:268
Annealed bond diluted Ising magnets,
  7:228
  critical concentrations, **7**:199
  critical curve, **7**:200
  two-dimensional, solutions, **7**:198
Annealed bond-diluted magnets
  aggregation, **7**:162
  models, solution, **7**:174, **7**:198
Annealed dilute magnets
  aggregation in, **7**:156–162
  percolation in, **7**:156–162
Annealed dilution, **7**:154–156
Annealed disorder, **7**:152
Annealed disordered systems, **14**:138
Annealed magnets
  critical exponents, renormalization,
    7:162–163

  models, solution, **7**:198–202
Annealed random drive, effects, **17**:94,
  17:149
Annealed site-diluted magnets
  aggregation in, **7**:156
  aggregation of bonds in, **7**:162
  configurations, **7**:162
  models, single cluster, **7**:174
  solution, **7**:202
  percolation and, **7**:161
Annealed site disorder, **7**:154–155
Annihilation operator, **5A**:242, **5A**:252
Annihilation process, **12**:351, **19**:6,
  19:49–50, **19**:72, 195, **19**:210
  see also diffusion limited pair
    annihilation (DLPA); pair
    annihilation; random walk,
    annihilating
Annihilation–creation process, **19**:6,
  19:26–27, **19**:84
Annihilation–exclusion process, **19**:173
Annihilation–fusion process, **19**:206
ANNNH model, **15**:52, **15**:54
ANNNI model (axial next-nearest-
  neighbour Ising), **11**:168,
  12:121–122, **12**:234, **12**:237,
  12:238–240, **12**:251, **12**:288,
  12:298–306, **12**:322–326, **12**:329,
  15:3–4, **15**:23, **15**:27, **15**:30–41,
  15:58, **15**:63
  axial-neighbour interactions, **15**:44
  cubic lattice, **15**:30
  disorder line, **15**:41
  generalized, **15**:45
  generalized soft, **15**:24
  mock, **15**:43–4
  n-vector variants, **15**:52–3
  theoretical analyses, **15**:31
  three-dimensional, **15**:53, **15**:61,
    15:62
  three-dimensional phase diagram,
    15:31–8
  transition lines, **15**:40
  two-dimensional, **15**:44, **15**:65
  two-dimensional brickwork lattice,
    15:44
  two-dimensional phase diagram,
    15:38–41
ANNNI models, **7**:178

Monte Carlo methods, **7:**206
ANNN*XY* model, **15:**52, **15:**62
Anomalous diffusion, **17:**34, **17:**146
Anomalous dimension of the vacuum,
   9:287, **9:**291, **9:**297
Anomalous dimensions, **6:**228, **6:**234
Anomalous tricritical exponents in two
   dimensions, **9:**149
Anomalous tricritical points, **9:**143,
   9:146, **9:**151, **9:**227
Antiferroelectric
Antiferromagnetic energy, **3:**251
Antiferromagnetic lattice, **2:**112
Anticommutation relations, **19:**175,
   19:177, **19:**200, **19:**202
Anticorrelation, **14:**261–2
Anticorrelations, **19:**196–197
Antiferroelectrics, **1:**266, **2:**491–2,
   3:661
Antiferroelectric model, **3:**183
Antiferromagnet, **1:**230, **1:**232, **1:**243,
   1:249, **1:**272, **1:**280, **1:**290, **1:**298,
   1:299, **1:**300, **1:**307, **1:**308, **1:**311,
   1:316, **1:**317, **1:**318, **1:**319, **1:**328,
   3:365, **3:**366, **3:**372, **3:**373, **3:**374,
   3:454, **3:**503, **3:**552, **3:**365, **3:**366,
   3:372, **3:**373, **3:**374, **3:**454, **3:**503,
   3:552, **5A:**276, **5A:**277, **5A:**278,
   5A:316, **5A:**323, **5A:**325, **5B:**5,
   5B:69, **9:**2, **9:**3
  critical behaviour of, **3:**360, **3:**453
  in critical field, **1:**224
  Ising, **3:**363
  isotropic, **5A:**257, **5A:**258, **5A:**260,
   5A:278, **5A:**280, **5A:**294
  K_2NiF, **3:**546
  nickel oxide, **5B:**63
  one-dimensional, **5A:**148–153
  planar, **5A:**280
  singularities of, **3:**373
  super-exchange, **1:**271, **1:**308, **1:**309,
   1:311
  three-dimensional, **5A:**120–135
  two-dimensional, **5A:**153–162
  uniaxial, **5A:**129–135
Antiferromagnetic effects, intrinsic,
   dilute systems with, **7:**173
Antiferromagnetic ground state energy,
   1:220, **1:**224

Antiferromagnetic Heisenberg models,
   coherent potential approximation,
   7:217
Antiferromagnetic Ising model, **14:**50
Antiferromagnetic model, **3:**251, **3:**307
Antiferromagnetic order, **8:**57
  at surface of ferromagnets, **8:**25–27
  parameters, **8:**25
  short-range, **8:**53
  surface, **8:**25, **8:**53
  two-dimensional, **8:**56
Antiferromagnetic order, **17:**139,
   17:142
Antiferromagnetic ordering, **3:**248,
   3:261, **3:**286, **3:**295, **3:**309
Antiferromagnetic picture, **3:**367
Antiferromagnetic structure, **5A:**93
Antiferromagnetic susceptibilities,
   2:355
Antiferromagnetic transition, **5A:**7
Antiferromagnetic transitions, **14:**145
Antiferromagnetism, **1:**228, **3:**363,
   19:32, **19:**156
  spontaneous, **1:**230
Antiferromagnets, **2:**330, **2:**353, **2:**356,
   2:366, **6:**33, **6:**385, **14:**85
  bicritical behaviour, **6:**410
  dilute, **7:**152
    random field effects, **7:**152
  dipolar, **6:**386
  Heisenberg, **8:**56
  metamagnetic behaviour, **6:**410
  optimal configurations, **7:**161
  phase boundaries, dilution and,
   7:270
  tetracritical behaviour, **6:**410
  tricritical point, **8:**26
Antinode, **3:**11
Antiperiodic boundary conditions,
   14:104, **19:**178, **19:**179
Antiphase transition, **1:**94, **1:**95,
   5B:114
Antivortex, **11:**22
Antonoff's rule, **14:**143
AOT, **16:**5, **16:**156
AOT–water–salt mixtures, **16:**117,
   16:*138*
Appell's comparison theorem, **3:**188
Applied stress (AS) percolation, **18:**284

Approximation methods, **19**:5
    see also specific methods, e.g. saddle
        point approximation
Approximation, sharp kink, **12**:53–55
Aqueous amphiphilic solutions *see*
    Water–amphiphile systems
Ar, **2**:57, **2**:58, **2**:59
Argon, **5B**:349, **5B**:359, **5B**:365,
    5B:368, **5B**:370, **5B**:383, **5B**:384,
    5B:385, **5B**:392, **5B**:393
    heat capacity, **5B**:343, **5B**:348
    coexistence curve, **5B**:363
Argon, supercooled, icosahedral
    symmetry, **7**:87–88
Arteca method, **13**:32–33
Articulation, **3**:68
Articulation circle, **5B**:219, **5B**:220,
    5B:224, **5B**:225, **5B**:228
Articulation n-tuples of circles, **5B**:219
Articulation pair, **3**:153, **5B**:229,
    5B:233
Articulation point, **3**:5, **3**:6, **3**:10, **3**:56,
    3:57, **3**:59, **3**:68, **3**:137, **3**:274
Articulation set, **2**:234
Asano contractions, **11**:195
Asanoba lattice, **1**:297, **1**:298
ASEP *see* asymmetric simple exclusion
    process (ASEP)
Ashkin and Teller model, **6**:540
Ashkin Teller, **12**:273–274, **12**:281,
    12:291–293
Ashkin–Teller (1943) model, **11**:2, **11**:3,
    11:26, **11**:35–36, **11**:51, **11**:71,
    11:115
    partition sum, **11**:34
Ashkin–Teller model, **1**:270, **17**:8,
    17:127, **18**:104
Aspect ratios, **14**:118
Assignment problem, **18**:179
Associative and distributive laws, **1**:140
Asymmetric simple exclusion process
    (ASEP), **17**:154, **19**:11, **19**:43,
    19:104–125
    applications, **19**:52
    blockage introduced, **17**:163–164
    boundary conditions, **19**:11, **19**:44
    empty interval probabilities,
        19:237–238
    exact solution, **19**:159

finite size behaviour, **19**:111–114
finite states, **19**:104–110
generalizations, **19**:159
master equation, **19**:114
nearest-neighbour jumps, **19**:43
on a ring, **19**:160
randomness, **19**:160
self-duality, **19**:104–110
self-enantiodromy, **19**:108–110
shocks, **19**:12
stationary distributions, **19**:117
with open boundary conditions,
    17:159–161
with periodic boundary conditions,
    17:155
Asymmetry exponent, **2**:23, **2**:36
Asymmetry parameter, **14**:12
Asymmetry, **2**:25, **2**:29
Asymptotic behaviour, **3**:182, **3**:189,
    10:80
    ASEP, **19**:112, **19**:113
    graphs, **3**:32–40
    nonequilibrium systems, **19**:53–71
    particle systems, **19**:59–69, **19**:481
    scattering amplitude, **19**:101
Asymptotic decay, **5B**:18
Asymptotic expansion, **3**:250
Asymptotic expansions, definition and
    Darhoux's theorem, **13**:15, *see also*
        Power series expansions,
        asymptotic analysis
Asymptotic formula, **3**:312
Asymptotic symmetry, **2**:36
Asymptotic theory, **6**:526
Attenuation coefficient, **5A**:76
Attractive interactions, entanglement
    and, **7**:145
Augmenting path algorithms, **18**:163,
    18:179
Augmenting path theorem, **18**:162,
    18:176-7
Auto-correlation function, **5B**:75, **19**:99,
    19:385
Auto-correlation time, **5B**:80, **5B**:81
Automorphisms of lattices, **18**:8
Axial next-nearest-neighbour Ising
    (ANNNI) model, **16**:27, **16**:56,
    18:197
    see also frustrated magnets

Axial next-nearest-neighbour Ising *see*
    ANNNI
Azeotrope, **5B:**376
    composition, **5B:**378

B

Backbones, **18:**152
Backgammon-pattern configurations,
    17:*113*, **17:**114
Background contributions, **14:**119
Background terms, **14:**40–1
Bak–Sneppen evolution model, **18:**195
Bak–Sneppen model, **17:**186
Baker–Essam model, **9:**24, **9:**25
Baker–Hausdorff formula, **5A:**348,
    5A:350
Balance condition, detailed, **2:**447
Ball and spoke models, **2:**283, **2:**285
Banach space, **1:**112, **1:**120, **1:**133,
    9:291, **15:**175, **15:**176, **15:**190,
    15:225
Band collapse, **19:**215
Band matrices, **15:**188–97
Barber–Hamer algorithm in sequence
    extrapolation, **13:**39–40
    series analysis application **13:**42–48
Barber-pole configurations, **17:**130,
    17:131
Bare-coupling constant, **9:**252, **9:**257,
    9:258, **9:**259, **9:**274
Bare interaction, **6:**280
Bare kernel, **5A:**231
Bare transport coefficient, **5A:**231
Barytropic effect, **5B:**180
Baxter model, **3:**478, **8:**246
Baxter's exact solution, **11:**32
    Potts model, **11:**200
    scaling dimensions, **11:**70
    symmetric eight-model vertex, **11:**70
Baxterization, **19:**50
Baxter–Wu model, **8:**237
BC-SOS Model (Body centred solid-on-
    solid), **12:**278–282, **12:**327–330
BCCD, **15:**39
BCS model, **1:**152, **1:**166
BCS theory of superconductivity, **5A:**2
BCSOS model, **11:**30–32, **11:**34–40,
    11:43, **11:**45

Bead and tether model, **19:**276–277
Becker–Döring nucleation equation
    8:351
Becker–Döring theory, **8:**284–286
BEG (Blume–Emery–Griffiths)
    model, **9:**17, **9:**18, **9:**23, **9:**55
    quenched random impurities, **9:**25
    spin-1 model, **9:**139, **9:**151
Bending elasticity
    experimental values for bilayers,
        16:156
    from Ginzburg–Landau models,
        16:97–115, **16:***104*, **16:***108*
    renormalization of, **16:**136, **16:**147,
        16:149
    within membrane approach,
        16:131–164
Bending rigidity
    crumpling transition, **19:**276–277
    entropic, **19:**258
    flat phase, **19:**268, **19:**271, **19:**272
    fluid membranes, **19:**261–262,
        19:265–267
    self-avoiding membranes, **19:**356
    spectrin in red blood cells, **19:**274
Bending rigidity *see* Bending elasticity
Benzene + sulfur, **9:**218
Berezinski–Kosterlitz–Thouless phase
    transition, **10:**61
Bernoulli percolation, **18:**31–6, **18:**42–4
    bond percolation, **18:**36, **18:**47–8
    site percolation, **18:**32–6
    see also dependent percolation
Bernoullian function, **3:**278
Bessel functions, **19:**64, **19:**98, **19:**121,
    19:169, **19:**170
Beta-brass, **5A:**89, **5A:**105, **5A:**106,
    5A:108, **5A:**109, **5A:**117, **5A:**118,
    5A:140, **5A:**156
    long-range order, **5A:**116
    order-disorder transition, **5A:**105,
        5A:109 118
Bethe ansatz equations (BAE), **19:**40,
    19:110, **19:**111–112
Bethe ansatz methods
    anisotropic Heisenberg chain,
        19:114–117
    asymmetric simple exclusion
        process (ASEP), **19:**111

coordinate, **19**:90
correlations, **19**:51, **19**:99–100
current fluctuation, **19**:158–159
formalism, **19**:24
history, **19**:34
infinite system, **19**:114–117
integrability, **19**:52, **19**:79
polymers, **19**:220, **19**:223
solution, **19**:35–41, **19**:84–88
typical results, **19**:5–6
wave function, **19**:97, **19**:99–100,
    19:101
Bethe ansatz, **1**:439, **1**:450, **1**:461,
    1:462, **1**:471, **1**:479, **14**:110,
    14:112, **14**:303, **14**:307
Bethe approximation, **2**:339, **2**:341,
    2:342, **2**:346, **2**:351, **2**:354, **2**:355,
    2:357, **2**:359, **2**:360, **2**:364, **2**:365,
    2:368, **3**:468, **3**:501, **5B**:40, **5B**:54,
    16:60–6
Bethe lattice
    diluted point to boundary resistance,
        7:197
    diluted Potts model on, **7**:192
    diluted q-state Potts model on, **7**:192
    percolation concentration, **7**:182,
        7:184
    singularities, **7**:180
    solution, **7**:184
Bethe lattice *see* regular tree
Bethe lattice, **2**:198, **2**:206, **2**:241,
    3:400, **3**:528, **14**:66
    decorated, **2**:211
Bethe wave function (ψ), **19**:86, **19**:101,
    19:111, **19**:166, **19**:175
Bethe, Hans, **19**:32, **19**:34
Bethe–Peierls-Weiss approximation,
    5B:4, **5B**:34, **5B**:36, **5B**:318
Bethe–Peierls approximation, **3**:528
Bi-articulation piece, **5B**:224
Bi-critical
    crossover, **9**:102
    point, **9**:11, **9**:16, **9**:164, **9**:223
Biased approximants, **13**:91–92
Biconnected paths, **18**:152
Bicontinuous fluid, **16**:4, **16**:17–8,
    16:62–3, **16**:65–8, **16**:75, **16**:107,
    16:112–13, **16**:125–27, **16**:141–45,
    16:163

Bicritical point, **6**:379, **6**:401, **6**:405,
    6:412, **6**:416, **10**:163, **14**:28, **14**:29,
    14:68–9, **14**:88
Bifurcation point, scaling operator and,
    6:10
Bilayer fluctuations, **16**:115–17
Bilayer structure, **16**:117–21, **16**:123
Bilayers, bending elasticity of, **16**:156
Bilinear form hypothesis, **3**:537, **3**:538
Bilinear property, **19**:212–213
Bilocal operator, **19**:365, **19**:397–399
Binary
    alloy, **1**:187, **1**:190, **5B**:92,
        12:127–128, **12**:178, **12**:187
    fluid mixture, **12**:180–181, **12**:186
    liquid mixtures, **12**:5, **12**:67–92,
        12:104–109, **12**:116, **12**:148,
        12:150, **12**:152, **12**:154–155,
        12:163, **12**:166, **12**:178, **12**:179,
        12:182, **12**:187, **12**:189, **12**:190,
        12:193
Binary
    fluid mixtures, **10**:211, **10**:236
    mixture analogy, **10**:53
Binary alloy dynamics, **5B**:29
Binary fluid critical mixture, **5A**:213,
    5A:255, **5A**:256, **5A**:257, **5A**:258,
    5A:265, **5A**:287, **5A**:289,
    5A:302–310, **5A**:336
    sound attenuation in, **5A**:302
Binary fluid, **5A**:234, **5A**:256, **5A**:290,
    5A:305, **5A**:309, **5A**:326, **5A**:327,
    5A:371, **5A**:372
Binary fluid critical points, **14**:77–82,
    14:89–90
Binary fluid experiments, **14**:365
Binary fluid transitions, **14**:70–1
Binary fluids, **14**:14
Binary liquid, **14**:145
Binary mixed bond disordered
    magnets, phase boundaries, **7**:211
Binary mixture, **5B**:347, **5B**:382
Binary mixtures, **14**:81, **14**:143
    critical point, **6**:91
Binary site randomness, virtual crystal
    approximation, **7**:211
Binder–Stauffer theory, cluster growth,
    8:356–360
Binding centre, **19**:372

Binomial coefficients, **19:**107, **19:**129, **19:**130
Biological systems
  fluid membranes, **19:**257
  growth, **19:**3, **19:**163–164
Biomembranes, dimer models for, **13:**280–285
  degrees of freedom, **13:**280–281
  K-based chain model, **13:**282–283
  order/disorder in, **13:**281
  SQK model, **13:**283–285
    cohesive energy, **13:**284—285
    experimental agreement, **13:**285
  structure, **13:**280
Biopolymerization, **19:**10–12, **19:**43, **19:**104, **19:**148, **19:**220–222
Bipartite graphs, **18:**177–9
Bipartite matching algorithm, **18:**265
Biquadratic exchange
  coupling, **9:**142
  interaction, **9:**17
Bistability, in two-temperature model, **17:**174
BKL (Bicmont, Kuroda and Lebowitz), **11:**167
Bloch equation, **1:**125
Bloch theory, **3:**250
Bloch wall, **12:**236, **12:**238–239, **12:**241–246
Bloch walls, **8:**75, **8:**76, **10:**39, **10:**322
Block spins, **6:**544
Block transformation, **6:**545
  Ising model renormalization group equation and, **6:**29
Block variables transformation, **6:**510, **6:**515
Block variables, **6:**514, **6:**552
Block, **3:**32
Block-spin transformation, **6:**528, **6:**545
Blockage, **19:**160
Blocking probability, **2:**210
Blocking transition, *see Two-species models*
Blocks, **5B:**209
Blossom, **18:**180
Blöte–Hilhorst model, **10:**46, **10:**48
Blue phases, bulk cholesteric, **7:**82
Blume–Capel, **11:**133
Blume Capel model, **9:**17, **9:**20, **9:**141,

9:142, 9:146, 12:72, 12:109, 12:116–118, 12:121, 12:133, 15:50
Emery–Griffiths model, **12:**70, **12:**76, **12:**79
Blume–Emery–Griffiths (BEG) model, **15:**43, **15:**47, **15:**50, **15:**63, **16:**23, **16:**33, **16:**119, **17:**8, **17:**127
BNNNI (biaxial-next-nearest-neighbour Ising) model, **15:**45, **15:**47
Body centred solid-on-solid, *see* BC-SOS
Body-centred cubic (BCC) lattice, **14:**44, **14:**60
Body-centred SOS (BCSOS) model, **14:**224, **14:**252
Bogoliubov inequality, **1:**84, **1:**88, **1:**89
Bogoliubov transformation, **12:**264
Bogoliubov, Parasuik, Hepp and Zimmerman (BPHZ) scheme, **10:**129, **10:**193
Bogoliubov-Tyahlikov theory, **5B:**264, **5B:**265, **5B:**270, **5B:**283
Bogolyubov ansatz, **2:**468, **5A:**171
Bogolyubov inequality, **15:**110, **15:**127, **15:**220, **15:**223
Boltzman statistics, **1:**129, **1:**130, **1:**131, **1:**133, **1:**134, **1:**135
Boltzmann equation, **5A:**190, **5A:**194
Boltzmann weights, **19:**225, **19:**227, **19:**377, 431
Boltzmann–Gibbs distributions, **18:**10
  see also Gibbs distributions, finite volume
Bolzano's theorem, **9:**273
B-bond composite, **5B:**224
Bond concentration, **7:**155
  position space methods, **7:**249
(Bond) cumulant, **3:**263, **3:**266
Bond diluted Heisenberg
  antiferromagnets, two-dimensional, magnon modes, **7:**209
Bond diluted Heisenberg
  ferromagnets, two-dimensional, magnon modes, **7:**209
Bond diluted Ising magnets
  model, critical curve, **7:**254
  simple cubic, bound, **7:**189
  transition temperature, scaling treatment, **7:**254

two-dimensional, critical curve,
    scaling treatment, **7**:254
magnetization, **7**:256
specific heat, **7**:256
spontaneous magnetization, **7**:257
systems, two-dimensional, phase
    boundary, **7**:190
Bond diluted Ising model (BDIM),
    18:113–116, **18**:204
Bond diluted q-state
    Ashkin–Teller–Potts models,
    critical curves, **7**:260
Bond diluted systems, dilute magnets,
    7:156
Bond dilution in disconnecting lattices,
    7:160
Bond disorder, **7**:155, **14**:300–2
Bond disordered Ising magnets, model,
    cluster scaling to one bond, **7**:251
    problems, coherent potential
        approximations, **7**:218
Bond mixed magnets, **7**:156
    percolation concept, **7**:191
Bond model, **5B**:339
Bond orientational order dislocation
    lines in solids and, **7**:85–88
    heavily dislocated solids, **7**:86
Bond percolation, **2**:267, **18**:36, **18**:47–8
    concentrations, **7**:160
    field-theoretic renormalization group
        treatments, **7**:245
    results, **7**:178
    scaling, **7**:252
    two-dimensional, position space
        methods, **7**:249, **7**:250
Bond problem, **2**:199, **2**:203, **2**:206,
    2:211, **2**:213, **2**:221, **2**:222, **2**:223,
    2:225, **2**:227, **2**:229, **2**:230, **2**:235,
    2:236, **2**:241, **2**:242, **2**:243, **2**:245,
    2:257, **2**:268
Bond renormatization, **3**:155
Bond-composite graph, **5B**:224, **5B**:226
Bond-degeneracy factor, **3**:265
Bond-diluted Potts model, **7**:193
Bond-diluted resistor networks, effective
    theory, **7**:221
Bond-disordered magnets, **7**:155
Bond-random Ising model, series
    expansion method, **7**:231

Bond-random quantum transverse Ising
    chain, two-dimensional striped
    random Ising model and, **7**:195
Bond-to-site transformation, **2**:205,
    2:210, **2**:211, **2**:213, **2**:218–9,
    2:243, **2**:245
Bonding, **3**:88, **3**:89, **3**:384
Bonds, **3**:98
Bonds,
    absorbing, **1**:261
    emitting, **1**:261
Boolean models, **18**:124
Border correlation function, **1**:65
Borderline dimensionality, **6**:372
Borderline field, **5A**:24, **5A**:25
Borel methods, **19**:260, **19**:349, **19**:446
Borel summation, **9**:154
Borel–Cantelli lemma, **15**:96, **15**:126,
    15:130, **15**:135, **15**:176, **15**:177,
    15:187
Born approximation, **5A**:90, **10**:213
Born model, **18**:279–80
Born–Bogoliubov–Green–Kirkwood-
    Yvon hierarchy, **5B**:221
Born–Green–Yvon equation, **2**:272,
    2:300
Bose condensation, **1**:33, **6**:10, **6**:60,
    6:61
Bose statistics, **1**:128
Bose–Einstein function, **2**:388
Bose–Einstein statistics, **11**:4
Bose fluid, **3**:488
Bose gas models, **14**:104
Bose gas, **1**:144, **1**:146
    ideal, **1**:33, **1**:50, **2**:379, **2**:409, **2**:410
    interacting, **1**:181
    lattice, **1**:116
Bose model, **2**:42, **2**:43, **2**:44, **2**:48,
    2:74
Bose operators, **1**:234, **1**:235
Bose systems, **1**:33, **14**:364
Bose–Einstein condensation temperature,
    5A:53
Boson field, **6**:294
    Green's functions, **9**:236
    neutral scalar, **9**:235
    quantum field theory, **9**:234–5, **9**:238,
        9:240–1, **9**:288
Boson formalism, **5B**:283, **5B**:330

Boson representation
  renormalized, **5B:**288
Bosons, **1:**20, **1:**32, **1:**50, **1:**51, **1:**95,
  1:129, **6:**528
Bound vortex pairs, **7:**38
Boundaries
  antiphase, curved, motion, **8:**335
  free energy, **8:**13
  magnetization, finite size scaling,
    8:206
Boundary conditions, **5B:**29, **8:**8, **8:**20,
    8:24, **8:**27, **8:**30, **8:**65, **8:**66, **8:**73,
    10:33, **10:**48, **10:**52, **10:**80, **10:**235,
    14:7–9, **14:**100–7, **14:**112–19
  anticyclic, **1:**207, **1:**209
  antiperiodic, **5B:**29, **5B:**32, **8:**149,
    8:213, **11:**77, **11:**118, **19:**178,
    19:179, **19:**213
    ideal Bose gas, **8:**219, **8:**221
    surface free energy, **8:**151
  bulk state, **19:**125
  cyclic, **1:**207, **1:**209, **1:**212, **2:**380,
    10:11, **10:**39
  cylindrical, **10:**14
  Dobrushin, **10:**32, **10:**38
  exclusion interaction, **19:**86,
    19:114–115
  finite systems, **8:**148–150
  fixed spin, **8:**4, **8:**5, **8:**64
  for standard model, **17:**12
    see also Open...; Shifted periodic
    boundary conditions
  free, **1:**76, **5B:**29, **10:**10, **10:**230,
    10:232, **11:**84
  free fermion system, **19:**213
  free edge, **1:**355, **8:**165, **8:**204, **8:**210,
    8:213
  free, periodic and Dirichlet, **9:**242–3,
    9:251–5, **9:**258, **9:**260, **9:**261,
    9:264, **9:**268, **9:**275
  free surface, **8:**149, **8:**219
  Gibbs states, see Gibbs periodic,
    11:85, **11:**95
  Glauber dynamics, **19:**213
  hard wall, **1:**30, **1:**64
  homogeneous, **10:**55
  Minlos-Sinaï, **10:**15
  Neumann, **19:**362
  nonequilibrium systems, **19:**103

open, **19:**89, **19:**125–126,
    19:211–212, **19:**226
  periodic, **1:**18, **1:**89, **1:**217, **1:**358,
    5B:29, **8:**149, **8:**212, **8:**214,
    10:229–30, **10:**232, **10:**235–6,
    19:38–40, **19:**63, **19:**110–114,
    19:178, **19:**179, **19:**182, **19:**194,
    19:213
    finite systems, **8:**164
    surface free energy, **8:**151
  polymers, **19:**220
  reflecting, **19:**66, **19:**67, **19:**104,
    19:105, **19:**111
  renormalized theory, **10:**200
  self-consistent field, **5B:**29
  symmetry-breaking, **10:**9, **10:**18,
    10:65
  thick wall, **1:**29
  thin wall, **1:**29
  toroidal, **10:**13
  twisted, **11:**77
  two-particle, **19:**93
  types, **19:**44
  von Neumann, **8:**219
  wave function, **19:**37
Boundary densities, **19:**96, **19:**151
Boundary effects, **1:**232
  critical behaviour, **19:**361–363
  phase transitions, **19:**52, **19:**103,
    19:104, **19:**126, **19:**143–154,
    19:157
  relaxational behaviour, **19:**98
  reservoir-coupled systems, **19:**88–89
  shock distributions, **19:**120
Boundary fields, **19:**44, **19:**97–98
Boundary free energy, **2:**113, **2:**115,
    2:116, **2:**123, **2:**125, **2:**130
  index of, **2:**115
Boundary index, **2:**130
Boundary of mean-field regime, **14:**191,
    14:197
Boundary operators, **19:**360, **19:**363
Boundary spontaneous magnetization,
  see Spontaneous magnetization
Boundary tension, **1:**229, **2:**170
Boundary terms, master equation,
  19:91
Boundary-induced phase transitions,
  17:159–160

Bounded linear operators, **1**:141, **1**:142, **1**:143, **1**:147
BPW *see* Bethe-Peierls-Weiss approximation
BPZ (Belavin, Polyakov and Zamolodchikov), **11**:56–59, **11**:68, **11**:94, **11**:102–3, **11**:107, **11**:115, **11**:118–9
Braced square net model (BSN), **18**:282–7
Bragg condition, **5A**:102
Bragg glasses, **18**:235, **18**:241, **18**:258–61
Bragg intensity, **5A**:143
Bragg peak, **5A**:154, **5A**:155, **5A**:161
Bragg point, **5A**:104, **5A**:107, **5A**:132, **5A**:135
Bragg reflection satellite peaks, **15**:6
Bragg reflection, **5A**:97, **5A**:102, **5A**:108, **5A**:114, **5A**:116, **5A**:129, **5A**:138
Bragg scattering, **5A**:99, **5A**:101, **5A**:103, **5A**:104, **5A**:113, **5A**:115, **5A**:129, **5A**:135, **5A**:138, **5A**:146
magnetic, **5A**:143
Bragg–Williams critical temperature, **5B**:186, **5B**:187
Bragg–Williams formula, **5B**:184, **5B**:251
Bragg–Williams, **12**:131–136
Bragg–Williams approximation, **1**:82
Bragg–Williams theory, **1**:3, **2**:295, **2**:335
Bra-ket notation, **19**:24, **19**:295, **19**:454
Branch point, **3**:33, **3**:35, **3**:208, **3**:219, **3**:303, **3**:311, **3**:316
Branched polymers, **16**:159
Branching diagram, **3**:79
Branching process, **2**:209
Branching processes, **19**:47, **19**:150–151, **19**:152, **19**:172
Branching ratio, **19**:206
Branching, in synthetic polynucleotides, transitions and, **7**:116–121
Branching–fusion process, **19**:184, **19**:185
Bravais lattices, **15**:48
Brazil nut problem, **17**:183
Brazinski's theta algorithm in sequence

extrapolation, **13**:37–38
series analysis application **13**:42–48
Breadth-first search (BFS) algorithm, **18**:151
Bricmont–Lebowitz–Pfister approach, **10**:23, **10**:25, **10**:26, **10**:27
Bridge points, **2**:3, **2**:4
Bridge, **3**:99, **3**:104, **3**:109
Brillouin scattering, **5A**:307, **5A**:310
Brillouin zone, **5A**:46, **5A**:133, **5A**:138, **6**:27, **6**:296, **6**:361, **6**:362
Broken continuous symmetry, **7**:6
Broken orientational symmetry in crystals, **7**:3
Broken symmetry, **1**:84
Bromine-intercalated graphite, **14**:150
Brownian bridge, **10**:22
Brownian model, **12**:432, **12**:473
Brownian motion, **5A**:190, **5A**:191, **5A**:192, **5A**:340, **14**:99, **19**:9, **19**:23, **19**:65, **19**:411, **19**:439
BST algorithm in sequence extrapolation, **13**:51
series analysis application **13**:42–48
Bubble subgraphs, **6**:323
Bubbles, **6**:217, **6**:278, **14**:152, **14**:153, **19**:431
Bulk
contact exponent, **19**:357–359
correlator, **19**:362
density, **19**:125–128, **19**:138, **19**:139
dynamics, deterministic, **19**:136, **19**:160
equation, **19**:66
Hamiltonian, **19**:90
hopping rate, **19**:145
phases, **19**:126
scheme O (N) system, **19**:425
state, and boundary conditions, **19**:125
Bulk correlation length, **5B**:55, **14**:153
Bulk critical amplitudes, **14**:14–31
Bulk critical-point amplitudes, **14**:41–6
Bulk limit, **14**:7
Bulk properties
effect of interface orientation, **17**:83–87, **17**:92
phase transitions in critical region, **17**:99–103

Bulk surface effects, **10**:77
  correlation length, **10**:84
  critical behaviour, **10**:79
  exponents, **10**:80
  graphs, **10**:129
  magnetic field, **10**:83
  tricritical point, **10**:220
Bulk viscosity, **5A**:265
Bulk with symmetric disorder,
  14:322–3
Burger's vector, **7**:46–49, **7**:54, **7**:70
  dislocations and, **7**:45
Burgers equation, **14**:287–92
  and driven-interface models, **17**:177
  and microscopic nature of shocks,
    17:162, **17**:167
  lattice realization, **19**:104
  one-dimensional, **17**:154
Burgers Vector, **6**:13, **12**:235, **12**:247
Burning algorithm, **18**:152, **18**:188–9,
  18:290
Burton–Keane uniqueness theorem,
  18:43–4
β-function
  derivation, **19**:416, **19**:446
  fixed point, **19**:302, **19**:347, **19**:357,
    19:373, **19**:464, **19**:466
  incomplete, **19**:142
  one loop order, **19**:367, **19**:417,
    19:419, **19**:447
  renormalization, **19**:307, **19**:402,
    19:403, **19**:446, **19**:464
  zeros, **19**:304

C

C_iE_j (*n*-alkyl polyglycol ethers) defined,
  16:5
C_4E_1–decane–water mixtures, **16**:9,
  16:*12*
C_4E_1–octane–water mixtures, **16**:92
C_6E_3–octane–water mixtures, **16**:*94*
C_5E_2–octane–water mixtures, **16**:*94*
C_6E_2–octane–water mixtures, **16**:92
C_6E_3–cyclohexane–water–formamide
  mixtures, **16**:*10*
C_6E_3–decane–water mixtures, **16**:*9*,
  16:*12*
C_8E_3–octane–water mixtures, **16**:92

C_8E_4–octane–water mixtures, **16**:*94*
$C_{10}E_5$–decane–water mixtures, **16**:9,
  16:12
$C_{10}E_5$–octane–water mixtures, **16**:*11*
$C_{12}E_5$, **16**:156
$C_{12}E_5$–octane–water mixtures, **16**:*19*
$C_{12}E_5$–water mixture, **16**:*13*, **16**:72,
  16:76, **16**:120
$C_{12}E_6$, **16**:156
$C_{12}E_6$–decane–water mixtures, **16**:*9*,
  16:*12*, **16**:15
$C_{12}E_8$–water mixtures, **16**:72
C phase, **12**:221–225, **12**:238, **12**:241,
  12:244, **12**:286, **12**:333
$C(\gamma)$-bond function, **5B**:225
C*-algebra, **1**:9, **1**:39, **1**:139, **1**:141,
  1:142
  of quasi-local observables, **1**:142
C-random cluster measures, **18**:60,
  18:62–5
Cactus, **3**:6
  rooted, **3**:30
Caesium manganese fluoride, **5A**:324
Cahn–Allen equation, **17**:80, **17**:176
Cahn–Hilliard equation, **17**:76
Cahn–Hilliard profile, **10**:281–2
Cahn–Hilliard theory, **8**:65–66
Caille exponent, **7**:92
Callan–Symanzik equation, **6**:27, **6**:179,
  6:226, **6**:238, **6**:240, **6**:243, **6**:509,
  6:510, **6**:530, **6**:538, **6**:555, **6**:556,
  6:558
Callan–Symanzik
  equation, **9**:299
  β-function, **9**:293
Callen approximation, **5B**:283, **5B**:288,
  5B:302, **5B**:307
Callen decoupling, **5B**:277, **5B**:278,
  5B:280, **5B**:282, **5B**:283, **5B**:288,
  5B:289, **5B**:300, **5B**:309, **5B**:312
Callen theory, **5B**:281, **5B**:282, **5B**:283
Calorimeter, **5B**:349–352, **5B**:354,
  5B:360, **5B**:362
Canham–Helfrich Hamiltonian,
  19:261–262
Canonical correlation
  of Kubo, **3**:597
Canonical deltahedra, **2**:284, **2**:285,
  2:287, **2**:289, **2**:292

Canonical dimension, **19:**365, **19:**366,
    19:407, **19:**456, **19:**465
Canonical distributions, **19:**62, **19:**108
Canonical ensemble, **5B:**6, **14:**104
Canonical formalism, **1:**114
Canonical labelling, **3:**15, **3:**16, **3:**100,
    3:101, **3:**105, **3:**106, **3:**107, **3:**108,
    3:110
  defined scheme, **3:**105
Canonical matrix, **3:**16
Canonical partition function, **15:**91
Canonical rules, **3:**101
Canterbury approximants, **13:**105,
    13:107–110
  test series performance, **13:**109–110
Capacitated network, **18:**160
Capillary modes, **14:**151
Capillary wave fluctuations, **10:**3, **10:**4,
    10:27, **10:**272–4, **10:**286, **10:**291–3,
    10:295, **10:**302, **10:**304, **10:**309–11,
    10:316–18, **10:**326, **10:**334–5,
    10:367
Capillary waves, **8:**68, **8:**69, **8:**70, **8:**71,
    8:72, **17:**81, **17:**105
  interface delocalization and, **8:**65
  interface roughening transition and,
    8:69–74
  renormalization group treatments,
    7:247
Capillary, **12:**152, **12:**163
  condensation, **12:**156–162,
    12:164–166
  evaporation, **12:**162
  length, **12:**4
  rise, **12:**148, **12:**159, **12:**176
  wave theory, **12:**38, **12:**62–69,
    12:73, **12:**75, **12:**87,
    12:111–115, **12:**125–126,
    12:135–136
Capillary-wave fluctuations, **9:**153
Carbon dioxide
  + ethane, **9:**181
  + ethanol + water, **9:**181, **9:**204
  + methanol + ethane, **9:**181, **9:**182,
    9:183
  + methanol + water, **9:**181, **9:**205,
    9:207
  + nitrobenzene, **9:**184
  + water + methanol + ethanol, **9:**183

Carbon dioxide, **5B:**349, **5B:**352,
    5B:358, **5B:**392, **5B:**393
  azeotropic mixture with ethane,
    5B:358, **5B:**361
  mixture with ethane, **5B:**361
Casimir effect, **10:**81, **10:**230, **10:**236
Catalytic process, **17:**172
Catalytic reactions, **10:**81
Cauchy inequality, **15:**193
Cauchy problem, **15:**164
Cauchy theorem, **3:**33
Cayley relation, **3:**25
Cayley tree configurations, **3:**219
Cayley tree embedding, **3:**442
Cayley tree limit, **3:**38
Cayley tree, **3:**5, **3:**9, **3:**20, **3:**21, **3:**29,
    3:33, **3:**34, **3:**35, **3:**37, **3:**38, **15:**48,
    15:49
  rooted, **3:**21, **3:**24, **3:**27
  rooted free, **3:**25
  rooted labelled, **3:**25
  unrooted, **3:**31
  see regular tree
Cayley trees, **2:**311
CC$_3$ model, **15:**49–50, **15:**58, **15:**65
CCIF$_3$, **2:**63
CE *see* Convex evelope
CEA *see* Coherent exchange
    approximation
Cell spin, **6:**432, **6:**464
  configurations, **6:**426
Cells *see* biological systems
Cells, adsorption in, phase transition and,
    7:109
Celt spin model, **12:**223, **12:**229,
    12:235–237, **12:**246–247
Central limit theorem, **15:**181
Chain bond, **5B:**174, **5B:**234
Chain function, **5B:**223
Chain graph, **5B:**179, **5B:**181, **5B:**187
Chain magnets, transition temperatures,
    experimental, **7:**264
Chain, **3:**92
Chains, one-dimensional, **8:**55
Chaos, **18:**216–17, **18:**230–1,
    18:249–52, **18:**259
Chaotic configurations, **15:**18
Chaotic states, **15:**49
Chaotic structures, **15:**15

Characteristic frequency, **5A**:75, **5A**:246, **5A**:250, **5A**:330, **14**:20, **14**:21, **14**:31, **14**:72

Characteristic function, **2**:385, **2**:391, **19**:321, **19**:361

Characteristic length scale, **5A**:171

Characteristic length, **5A**:242

Characteristic momentum, **6**:2

Characteristic size of oil and water regions, **16**:80

Characteristic temperatures dilute Heisenberg models, **7**:226
dilute Ising models, **7**:226
scaling and, **7**:236

Characteristic velocity, **14**:70

Charge, asymmetry, **11**:17
inversion symmetry, **11**:16
neutrality condition, **11**:5, **11**:18, **11**:19, **11**:106

Charge-charge correlations functions, **7**:20

Chebyshev inequality, **15**:187

Chemical annihilation, **19**:194, **19**:199

Chemical annihilation–creation reaction, **19**:6, **19**:49

Chemical distance, **18**:152

Chemical impurities, **14**:298

Chemical potential gradients (CPGs)
effects, **17**:108–112
in combination with electric fields, **17**:112–118
transverse CPG, interface stability affected, **17**:119–121

Chemical potential, **1**:13, **1**:14, **1**:20, **1**:32, **1**:91, **1**:94, **1**:96, **1**:130, **1**:131, **1**:138, **1**:139, **1**:151, **1**:171, **1**:271, **3**:366, **5B**:209, **5B**:250, **5B**:346, **5B**:360, **14**:14, **19**:156, **19**:373, **19**:412, **19**:413, **19**:414, **19**:421, **19**:423, **19**:428, **19**:457
analyticity, **2**:56
antisymmetry, **2**:56
local, **8**:47

Chemical processes, modelling of, **17**:172

Chemical reactions, diffusion limitation, **19**:6, **19**:194–197, **19**:222–223

Chemical reactions, pattern formation in, **8**:452

Chemisorption, **8**:445–446, **12**:225–226, **12**:232

Chinese postman problem, **18**:225

Chiral clock model, **12**:119–122, **14**:68, **14**:249
exponent, **12**:291–293
melting, **12**:221, **12**:285, **12**:286–291, **12**:293–298, **12**:333

Chiral clock models, **15**:42, **15**:50

Chiral Potts model, **15**:43

Chiral *XY* model, **15**:27

Chirality, **12**:224, **12**:237, **12**:242–244, **12**:246, **12**:288–301

Cholesteric films, two-dimensional, **7**:82

Cholesterics, **7**:74–75

Chromatic polynomial, **3**:86, **3**:87, **3**:90

Chromatic polynomials, **2**:267

Chromium, **5A**:315

Circle of convergence, **3**:184, **3**:205, **3**:234

Circle of meromorphy, **3**:205

Clapeyron equation, **2**:8, **2**:15, **2**:22

Class of code, **3**:409, **3**:411, **3**:417
of configurations, **3**:98

Classical continuum gas, **1**:95

Classical continuum systems, **1**:112, **1**:113, **1**:124

Classical exponents, **9**:55

Classical ferromagnets, **1**:65

Classical fluid, **3**:120, **3**:131, **3**:144, **3**:146, **3**:148, **3**:157, **3**:161
expansion, **3**:138
free energy of, **3**:147

Classical gas, **1**:38, **1**:51, **1**:90, **2**:449

Classical Heisenberg ferromagnet, Monte Carlo method, **7**:207
model, scaling, **7**:259
solution, **7**:182

Classical Heisenberg Ferromagnetic, two-dimensional anisotropic, **11**:166

Classical hydrodynamics near critical point, **5A**:166

Classical Ising magnets, model, solution, **7**:182

Classical lattice gas, **1**:48, **1**:51

Classical lattice system, **1**:12–19, **1**:52, **1**:90, **1**:91, **1**:113, **1**:114

Classical limit, **3**:249, **3**:251, **3**:288, **3**:290
Classical models, **2**:44
Classical planar model, **3**:224, **3**:299, **3**:496, **3**:499
Classical plane rotors, **3**:167
Classical spin systems, **1**:88
Classical systems, one-dimensional, **1**:153
Classical vector model, **3**:72, **3**:87, **3**:89
  D-dimensional, **3**:381
Classical XY model, solution, **7**:182
Clausius–Mossotti formula, **9**:201
Clifford numbers, **1**:250
Clifford operators, **1**:233
Clock models, **11**:23, **11**:24, **11**:28, **11**:201, **12**:118–121, **12**:290, **12**:329
  anti-ferromagnetic, **12**:290, **12**:329
  chiral Potts, **12**:109
  four-state, **11**:33
  symmetry breaking fields and, **7**:27–31
  Z_p model (or p-state), **11**:2, **11**:23, **11**:26
Close-packed lattices, **14**:96
Close-packing density, **1**:36
Close-packing, **1**:183
Closed anisotropic chain, **1**:202
Closed chain, **1**:195
Closed form approximations, **7**:210–223
Closed loop, **6**:278
Closed-form approximation, **2**:9, **2**:308, **2**:330, **2**:364, **5B**:260
Closed-form approximations, **3**:148, **3**:359, **3**:400, **3**:461, **3**:501
  Bethe, **3**:501
  quasichemical, **3**:501
Closure problem, **5B**:221
Cloud point, **8**:274
  location, **8**:396
Cluster algorithms, **18**:67–9
Cluster approximation, **6**:463, **6**:470, **6**:473, **6**:480, **6**:493, **6**:494
Cluster concentration, **5B**:73
Cluster count, **3**:98, **3**:100
Cluster density, **5B**:71
Cluster distribution, **5B**:88
  time-dependent, **5B**:89

Cluster equation
  finite, **3**:84
Cluster expansion method, **2**:366
Cluster expansion, **3**:389
  finite, **3**:396
Cluster expansions, **10**:4, **10**:24, **10**:28
Cluster formation
  dynamical theory, **8**:346
  kinetics, **8**:284
Cluster function, **5B**:175, **5B**:206, **5B**:209, **5B**:211, **5B**:242
Cluster functions, **3**:145
Cluster growth
  Binder–Stauffer theory, **8**:356–360
  Monte Carlo studies, **8**:391–395
Cluster integral theory, **3**:1, **3**:42, **3**:53, **3**:73
Cluster integral, **3**:2, **3**:4, **3**:43, **3**:44, **3**:46, **3**:47, **3**:50, **3**:67, **3**:70, **3**:71, **3**:76, **3**:84, **3**:370, **3**:394, **3**:395
  irreducible, **3**:47, **3**:48, **3**:49, **3**:57, **3**:67, **3**:84, **3**:371
  reducible, **3**:398
Cluster method, **5B**:259
  linked, **3**:607
Cluster methods, **7**:213–215
Cluster models, **8**:342–346
  Monte Carlo studies, **8**:345
Cluster properties, **1**:46, **1**:50, **1**:135, **1**:139, **1**:149, **1**:150, **1**:160, **1**:163, **1**:166
Cluster property, **5B**:216, **9**:274, **9**:275
Cluster shape anisotropy, **14**:43
Cluster shape ratios, **14**:43, **14**:67–8
Cluster size expansion, **3**:71
Cluster size, **18**:35–6
Cluster statistics, Monte Carlo methods, **7**:206
Cluster sum, **3**:395
  irreducible, **3**:403
Cluster theorem, **18**:276
Cluster variation method, **2**:341, **17**:16
  dynamic version, **17**:16–17
Cluster, **3**:99, **3**:103, **3**:106, **3**:107, **3**:370
  connected, **3**:269, **3**:469, **3**:474
  finite, **3**:74
  homogeneous, **3**:398
  inhomogeneous, **3**:401

mean number, **3**:74, **3**:85
null, **3**:86, **3**:89
of *r* labelled points, **3**:81
n-Cluster, **3**:99, **3**:105, **3**:108
counting, **3**:105
Cluster-cluster
　aggregation, **12**:337, **12**:348, **12**:350,
　　　12:358, **12**:430–461, **12**:463,
　　　12:464, **12**:467, **12**:470
　chemically limited, **12**:442, **12**:446,
　　　12:447, **12**:448, **12**:449
　diffusion limited, **12**:442–443,
　　　12:448–453, **12**:456, **12**:459,
　　　12:460, **12**:461, **12**:468–469
　kinetics of cluster-cluster, **12**:454–462
Cluster-cluster interaction process,
　　　5B:5
Clusters, **5B**:5, **5B**:32, **5B**:83, **5B**:84,
　　　5B:85, **5B**:93
　average number, **7**:190
　contour, **8**:340
　dynamics, **8**:339–366
　equilibrium distribution, **8**:342
　fluctuation, **8**:341
　in Ising model, **5B**:95
　linked, **5B**:207
　mathematical, **8**:341–342
Co-existence
　curve, **9**:83, **9**:170, **9**:193, **9**:211,
　　　9:216, **9**:217, **9**:219, **9**:222
　line, **9**:35
　manifolds, three-dimensional, **9**:38
　surfaces, **9**:3, **9**:36, **9**:38, **9**:39, **9**:47,
　　　9:52, **9**:56, **9**:67, **9**:79, **9**:81,
　　　9:100, **9**:102
　three-phase, **9**:14
　two-phase, **9**:14
Co-existence curves, **17**:18, **17**:74–76
　for standard model, **17**:76
　fast rate limit, **17**:152, **17**:*153*
CO_2, **2**:57, **2**:58, **2**:62, **2**:63, **2**:67, **2**:68,
　　　2:72, **2**:73
Coagulation, **19**:47
Coalescence, shocks, **19**:47,
　　　19:117–123, **19**:150–151, **19**:152
Coarse graining procedure, **8**:295
$CoBr_2.6H_2O$, **3**:581
$CoCl_2$, **3**:581
$CoCl_2.6H_2O$, **3**:581

$CoCl_3$, **3**:582
Code
　graphical, **3**:413
　h.c.–p.t., **3**:413
　partial, **3**:417
　s.q., **3**:412
Code method, **3**:360
Code system, algebraic, **3**:413
　diamond-f.c.c., **3**:411
　honeycomb-triangular, **3**:410
Code-balance principle
　complete, **3**:412
Coercive field, **5B**:87
Coexistence curve, **2**:6, **2**:13, **2**:15, **2**:17,
　　　2:18, **2**:19, **2**:22, **2**:23, **2**:26, **2**:28,
　　　2:32, **2**:33, **2**:34, **2**:36, **2**:37, **2**:40,
　　　2:52, **2**:63, **2**:83, **2**:84, **2**:309,
　　　2:310, **2**:410, **2**:431, **2**:432, **5B**:190,
　　　5B:251, **5B**:256, **5B**:257, **5B**:344,
　　　5B:357, **5B**:362, **5B**:365, **5B**:366,
　　　5B:378, **5B**:382, **5B**:384, **6**:10,
　　　6:91–94, **6**:327, **6**:338, **6**:339,
　　　6:343, **6**:345, **8**:68, **10**:77, **10**:323
　asymmetry, **5B**:375, **5B**:384
　essential singularity, **8**:69
　for films of 2,6–lutidine and water,
　　　8:256
　of argon, **5B**:363–383
Coexistence curve exponent β,
　　　5B:392
Coexistence domain, **2**:14
Coexistence line, **19**:134
N-Coloured membranes, **19**:408–434
Coexistent densities, **2**:36
Cofluent hypergeometric function, **9**:277
Coherence distance, **6**:512
Coherence length, **3**:439, **5A**:52, **5A**:57,
　　　16:163
　see Correlation length
Coherence volume, **7**:170
Coherent exchange approximation,
　　　5B:317, **5B**:332
Coherent potential approximation,
　　　5B:319, **5B**:320, **5B**:324
Coherent potential approximation,
　　　7:215–221
　dilute magnetism, **7**:153
Collapse chain, **3**:177
Collapse matrix, **3**:177

Collective mode, **3:**571, **3:**572, **3:**634, **3:**635, **3:**648
Collective oscillatory mode, **3:**633
Collision cross section, **5A:**194
Colouring problem, **3:**655
Combinatorial analysis, **3:**16
Combinatorial factor, **2:**333, **2:**366, **19:**420
Combinatorial method, **2:**105
Commensurability ratios, **15:**5
Commensurate
  melting, **12:**221–224
  incommensurate phase, **12:**240
  transition, **12:**119
Commensurate structures, **15:**2, **15:**6, **15:**11, **15:**31, **15:**34
Commensurate-incommensurate
  transitions, **7:**10, **7:**62–66, **10:**5, **14:**148–50, **14:**190
  Monte Carlo methods, **7:**206
Commensurate-to-incommensurate (CI)
  phase transition, **15:**9–10, **15:**57–9
Communal entropy, **2:**272
Commutation relations, **19:**141, **19:**177
Commutator, **5A:**243, **6:**37
  critical phenomena and, **6:**14
Commuting transfer matrices, **19:**31, **19:**39
Compact phase, **19:**256, **19:**259
Competing (repulsion/attraction]
  interactions, **17:**195–196
Competing [conservation/non-
  conservation] dynamics,
  17:171–173
Competing interaction problem, series
  expansion method, **7:**231
Complete analyticity, **18:**84
Complete matching, **1:**234
Complete set of gross variables, **5A:**171, **5A:**172, **5A:**190, **5A:**208
Complete set of polynomials, **5A:**173
Complete translation group, **1:**173
Complete unbinding, **14:**183
Complete wetting, **14:**141, **14:**142, **14:**183, **14:**298–302
Complex order parameter, **6:**417
Complex systems
  modelling, **19:**6–13
  in nature, **19:**3–4

Complex two-component field model, **6:**526
Complex vector space, **1:**140
Composite graph, **5B:**171, **5B:**172, **5B:**173, **5B:**179, **5B:**224, **5B:**229
Compressibility exponent γ, **5B:**392
Compressibility, **1:**95, **2:**40, **2:**44, **2:**84, **2:**360, **5B:**348
  isothermal, **2:**82, **2:**83
Compressible
  lattices, **9:**30, **9:**152
  magnets, **9:**7
  Ising models, **9:**23
Compressible magnets, **6:**413
Computer algorithm, **3:**107, **3:**108, **3:**110
  summarized, **3:**111
Computer simulation of Gibbs systems, **18:**67–9
Computer simulation, **12:**336, **12:**391
Computer simulations, melting, **7:**53–57
Concavity, **1:**19, **1:**23, **1:**33, **1:**60
Concentration dependencies, percolation model, **7:**234
Concentration expansion method, **7:**224
  quenched site-diluted systems, **7:**228
Concentration fluctuation, **5B:**388
Concentration mode, **5A:**255
Concentration profile, **2:**80
Concentration susceptibility, **9:**108
Concentration, **5B:**360, **5B:**372, **5B:**376, **5B:**382
Condensation phenomena, path integration and, **7:**104
Condensation point, free energy at, singularity, **8:**283
Condensation, classical picture, **8:**280
Condensing gas mixture, **3:**51
Conditional probabilities, **19:**67, **19:**79, **19:**84–85, **19:**86–88
Conductivity
  coherent potential approximations, **7:**219
  effective medium theory, **7:**219, **7:**220
Conductivity, **12:**351, **12:**352, **12:**391, **12:**474

Cones (conical geometry), **11**:86, **11**:88
Confidence limits, **3**:183, **13**:8,
    13:137–138,
    see also Error analysis
Configuration generating function, **3**:26,
    3:27
Configuration space, **19**:394
Configuration sum, analytic evaluation,
    crystallization by folding and,
    7:123–126
Configuration, **3**:26, **3**:98, **18**:7–8
Configurational integral, **3**:43, **3**:54,
    3:70, **3**:71
Configurations
    backgammon-board pattern, **17**:*113*,
       17:114
    barber-pole pattern, **17**:*130*, **17**:131
    for polarized lattice gas, **17**:*136–137*
    during phase separation, **17**:77
    with shifted periodic boundary
       conditions, **17**:*85*, **17**:*87*
Confining tube, **19**:8, **19**:10, **19**:217
Confluent singularities, **3**:500, **13**:7,
    13:138
    differential approximants applied to,
       13:103
    logarithmic, **13**:29–32, **13**:126
    theorem, **13**:31
    Padé approximants for, **13**:61–63
    partial differential approximants
       applied to, **13**:117
    estimation difficulties and, **13**:120
    ratio methods for, **13**:20–21
Confluent singularity, **14**:19, **14**:37–8
Conformal anomaly, **14**:9
Conformal change, **14**:365
Conformal covariance, **6**:51–54
Conformal field theory, **14**:364, **19**:451
Conformal invariance, **6**:10, **10**:187,
    10:201–2, **10**:240, **12**:224, **14**:4,
    14:8, **14**:41, **14**:96–104, **14**:108–13,
    14:115, **14**:120
Conformal mapping of sectors,
    19:311–313
Conformal transformation, **3**:311, **3**:327,
    3:638
Conformal transformations, **11**:56,
    11:64–65, **11**:78, **11**:79, **11**:80
    bootstrap, **11**:103

in two dimensions, **11**:89
Conformational phase transitions in
    macromolecules, exactly solvable
    models, **7**:101–149
Conjugate thermodynamic variables,
    6:513, **6**:526
Connected components and molecules,
    19:319, **19**:320
Connected components, **3**:61, **3**:132
Connected correlation function, **10**:124
Connected linear graphs, **9**:264
Connecting circle, **5B**:212, **5B**:218,
    5B:224, **5B**:226, **5B**:228, **5B**:229
Connective constant, **3**:472
Connectivity percolation problem,
    18:188
Connectivity percolation, **18**:152,
    18:188–90, **18**:289–93
Connectivity theorem, **18**:271–2
Conservation laws, **5B**:10, **19**:31, **19**:32,
    19:35, **19**:99
Conservation of momenta, **6**:373
Conservation of probability, **19**:92–93,
    19:181, **19**:183, **19**:189
Consolute point, **10**:210, **10**:236
Constant coupling approximation, **2**:333,
    2:336, **2**:339, **2**:340, **2**:341, **2**:365,
    2:366, **3**:307, **5B**:318
Constants of motion, **5A**:173
Constrained systems, **9**:102, **9**:152
Contact angle, **10**:53, **10**:55, **14**:142,
    16:93–6, **16**:*94*, **16**:128
Contact exponent, bulk, **19**:357–359
Contact parameter, **2**:11, **2**:12, **2**:16,
    2:17, **2**:18, **2**:19, **2**:23, **2**:24, **2**:31
Containment theorem, **2**:205
Content, **3**:25
Continued fractions, **6**:322
Continuous and discrete time processes,
    19:13–16, **19**:28, **19**:30
Continuous models, large-*n* limit in,
    15:215–17
Continuous
    phase transitions, **9**:208–12
    spin model, **9**:118, **9**:143, **9**:234 (*see
       also* Ising model)
Continuous spin model, **10**:95
Continuous spin variables, **15**:51–7
Continuous symmetry

magnetic systems, two-dimensional, **7**:10
model systems, **7**:11
Continuous symmetry, **1**:84
Continuous wetting transition, **14**:145
Continuum classical gas, hard cores, **1**:25
  in canonical ensemble, **1**:12, **1**:25
  in grand ensemble, **1**:12, **1**:25
Continuum gas, **1**:56
Continuum microscopic models, **16**:32–3
Continuum models, **10**:88, **10**:92, **10**:93, **10**:94, **10**:96, **10**:161
  semi-infinite, **10**:211
Continuum percolation, **18**:123–5
Continuum systems, **1**:41, **1**:52
Contour loops (CLs), **18**:260
Contour map method, **3**:238
Contour map, **3**:240
Contours, **10**:7, **11**:152–3
  contour models, **11**:155–6
  Peierls contours, *see* Peierls
  rarefied ensembles, **11**:157, **11**:166
  renormalized, **11**:168
  with interactions, **11**:167
  with a parameter, **11**:161–2
Contraction
  dipoles, **19**:293–297, **19**:300–301, **19**:352, **19**:353, **19**:360, **19**:382, **19**:462
  divergent, **19**:365
  interaction, **19**:383–384
Convection, **19**:388
Conversion matrix, **3**:62, **3**:63, **3**:67, **3**:74, **3**:77, **3**:176
Convex cost problem, **18**:168–75
Convex cost programming, **18**:182–6
Convex envelope, **5B**:115, **5B**:129
Convex function, **6**:159
Convex function, maximal, **5B**:115
Convexity condition, **1**:103, **2**:21, **2**:25, **2**:26, **2**:46, **2**:250
Convexity inequality, **6**:157
Convexity, **1**:19, **1**:23, **1**:32, **1**:33, **1**:103, **1**:104, **5B**:114
Coordinate space, correlation functions in, **6**:49–54
Coordination number, **3**:127, **15**:74–5

Core condition, **5B**:234, **5B**:236, **5B**:238, **5B**:253
Corner free energy, **14**:116–17
Corner transfer matrix, **11**:88
Corners, **14**:115
Correction amplitudes, **14**:19
Correction coefficients, **14**:39
Correction exponents, **14**:19
Correction function, **3**:453
Correction polynomial, **3**:199, **3**:200, **3**:236, **3**:324, **3**:443
Correction terms critical region, **3**:452
  in equation of state, **3**:361
Correction terms, **2**:402, **2**:403, **2**:417, **14**:38
Correction-to-scaling exponent, **10**:153, **10**:189, **10**:218, **10**:244, **10**:255, **10**:325
Correction-to-scaling, **14**:10, **14**:56–8, **14**:60, **14**:63, **14**:65, **14**:66, **14**:76, **14**:77, **14**:79, **14**:81
Corrections to scaling, **9**:26, **9**:41, **9**:88, **9**:90, **11**:76, **12**:289–290, **12**:293
Correlated bulk disorder, **14**:323–6
Correlated disorder, **14**:295
Correlation behaviour
  droplet picture, **5A**:10–12
Correlation decay, **3**:439
Correlation exponent v, **5B**:41
Correlation exponent, **3**:361
  η, **3**:477
  high temperature, **3**:439
  ν, **3**:477, **3**:496
Correlation factor, **3**:159, **3**:160, **3**:165, **3**:169
  1, *n*-valent, **3**:154
Correlation function coefficients, **3**:514
Correlation function exponents, **3**:321, **3**:542
Correlation function, **2**:104, **2**:117, **2**:119, **2**:143, **2**:250, **2**:252, **2**:297, **2**:427–9, **2**:432, **2**:436, **2**:440, **3**:52, **3**:119, **3**:131, **3**:133, **3**:149, **3**:171, **3**:174, **3**:294, **3**:300, **3**:301, **3**:439, **3**:467, **3**:549, **3**:551, **3**:555, **5B**:43, **5B**:50, **5B**:68, **5B**:74, **5B**:90, **5B**:112, **5B**:120, **5B**:131, **5B**:143, **5B**:157, **5B**:161, **5B**:171, **5B**:175, **5B**:176, **5B**:178, **5B**:179, **5B**:186,

5B:187, **5B**:205, **5B**:224, **5B**:234,
5B:262, **5B**:267, **5B**:295, **5B**:302,
9:113, **9**:130, **9**:252, **9**:258,
9:268, **9**:292
current, **5B**:90
direct, **2**:378, **2**:428–9, **5B**:206
four-point, **11**:67, **11**:100–3, **11**:106,
11:108, **11**:119
Green–Kubo, **2**:444
higher order, **5B**:257
lengths, **9**:203, **9**:285
longitudinal, **5B**:52, **5B**:274
multiple, **3**:471
nearest neighbour, **3**:523
of s.c. classical Heisenberg
ferromagnet, **5B**:51
pair, **2**:92, **2**:98, **2**:116, **2**:142, **2**:144,
2:146, **2**:272
reduced, **5B**:51
residual, **3**:379
s-particle direct, **5B**:210
six-point, **11**:67
spin-spin, **2**:162, **2**:163, **2**:184–8,
2:191, **2**:257, **2**:379, **2**:386,
2:400, **2**:427, **2**:434
three-point, **11**:66, **11**:74, **11**:102,
11:110
transverse, **5B**:274, **5B**:293, **5B**:295,
5B:306
two-point, **11**:19, **11**:84
two-spin, **3**:491, **3**:496, **3**:498, **3**:517,
3:521, **3**:524, **3**:551, **3**:552
XY model, **11**:25
Correlation functions
correlation lengths and, **7**:183
one-dimensional diluted systems,
7:182
quenched models, **7**:179
Correlation functions for dimer models,
13:271–273
anisotropy, **13**:272–273
correlation lengths, **13**:272
Green's functions in, **13**:271–272
Correlation functions, **1**:39, **1**:40, **1**:43,
1:44, **1**:45, **1**:46, **1**:47, **1**:49, **1**:50,
1:63, **1**:76, **1**:82, **1**:91, **1**:97, **1**:111,
1:112, **1**:113, **1**:114, **1**:117, **1**:118,
1:120, **1**:122, **1**:124, **1**:133, **1**:148,
1:150, **1**:195, **1**:195, **1**:204, **1**:213,

1:229, **1**:236, **1**:250, **1**:256, **1**:257,
1:319, **1**:326, **1**:447, **5A**:4, **5A**:10,
5A:28–33, **5A**:64, **6**:48, **6**:106,
6:111–115, **6**:172, **6**:176, **6**:186,
6:191, **6**:192, **6**:240, **6**:252, **6**:256,
6:258, **6**:267–273, **6**:287, **6**:294,
6:297, **6**:300, **6**:302, **6**:304, **6**:331,
6:346, **6**:383, **6**:385, **6**:419, **6**:427,
6:450–463, **6**:512, **6**:515, **6**:517,
6:526, **6**:528, **6**:532, **6**:541, **6**:554,
8:29, **8**:52, **8**:55, **8**:59, **8**:60, **8**:63,
8:74, **14**:4, **15**:218, **16**:41–3, **16**:48,
16:62, **16**:68, **16**:77, **16**:80–1,
16:89–90, **16**:106, **16**:109, **16**:*111*,
16:116–17, **16**:*119*, **16**:*123*, **16**:124,
16:136
analytic properties, **5A**:65, **5A**:66
anisotropic correlation lengths and,
8:28
at surfaces, **8**:34
cluster properties, **1**:46, **1**:50
critical point and, **6**:12
grand canonical, **1**:132
higher-order, **6**:453
in coordinate space, **6**:9, **6**:49–54
large-*n* limit of non-translationally
invariant *n*-vector model,
15:113–16
long-time behaviour, **5A**:171–175
near surfaces, in mean-field limit,
8:27–29
one-particle irreducible, **6**:226
Ornstein–Zernike form, **8**:28
2-point, **6**:51, **6**:112
3-point, **6**:114
recursion equation, **6**:107
scale invariant, **6**:18
scale transformations, **5A**:28
scaling, **8**:43–44
scaling relations, **8**:63
singlet, **1**:41
spin pair, **6**:212, **6**:221, **6**:427
spin-spin connected, **6**:162
triplet, **1**:41
Correlation
functions, **10**:6, **10**:31, **10**:48, **10**:52
inequalities, **10**:27
length, **10**:29, **10**:55–6, **10**:62,
10:221

many-spin, **10**:21
range, **10**:77
Correlation inequalities, **1**:72
Correlation length, **1**:100, **2**:81, **2**:82,
    2:84, **2**:85, **2**:115, **2**:116, **2**:156,
    5B:66, **5B**:67, **5B**:74, **5B**:348,
    5B:388, **6**:3, **6**:48, **6**:127, **6**:215,
    6:216, **8**:8, **8**:15, **8**:21, **8**:23, **8**:24,
    8:29, **8**:30, **8**:33, **8**:35, **8**:39, **8**:41,
    8:44, **8**:46, **8**:50, **8**:57, **8**:60, **8**:72,
    8:74, **16**:42, **16**:80–1, **16**:89–90,
    16:96, **16**:110, **16**:114, **16**:116,
    16:124, **16**:140
  anisotropic, correlation functions and,
    8:28
  antiferromagnetic, **8**:53
  at transition, **7**:233
  bulk, **8**:55
  critical exponents, **7**:172
  concentration and, **7**:165
  correlation functions and, **7**:183
  cross over effects, **7**:169
  diluted chains, **7**:183
  diluted Heisenberg chain magnet,
    7:266
  diluted Heisenberg layer magnet,
    7:267
  diluted Heisenberg model, **7**:269
  diluted Heisenberg quadratic layer
    magnet, **7**:268
  diluted Ising quadratic layer magnet,
    7:266
  diluted isotropic Heisenberg model,
    temperature and, **7**:165
  diluted Potts model, **7**:192
  experimental, **7**:265
  infinite *d*-dimensional spherical
    model, **8**:209
  infinite systems, **8**:151–158, **8**:171
  inverse, **2**:434, **2**:435
  long-wavelength fluctuations, **6**:2
  mean-field theory, **8**:36
  Monte Carlo methods, **7**:204
  one-dimensional diluted systems,
    7:183
  phase boundaries, **7**:165
  quasi-one-dimensional Heisenberg
    system, **7**:265
  surface, **8**:29, **8**:55

  temperature and, **7**:165–168
    dilute Heisenberg magnet, **7**:166
    diluted Ising model, **7**:168
  two-dimensional Ising model, **8**:177
  two-dimensions, **7**:54
  zero-field, **5B**:52
Correlation matrix, **2**:451
Correlation moments, **3**:300
  time-ordered, **3**:170
Correlation, **3**:138, **3**:164, **3**:358, **3**:363,
    3:430, **3**:626, **3**:629, **5B**:108,
    5B:110, **12**:123, **12**:128,
    12:339–341, **12**:473
  below T_c, **5B**:53
  correlation length, (bulk) **12**:157,
    12:177
  critical, **3**:360
  density density, **12**:327, **12**:367,
    12:406, **12**:411, **12**:415–416,
    12:433, **12**:438, **12**:453
  function, **12**:123, **12**:128, **12**:339–341,
    12:473
  higher, **3**:154
  higher order, **3**:130
  length amplitudes, **11**:69
  length, **12**:111–115, **12**:133, **12**:146,
    12:157
  longitudinal, **5B**:50, **5B**:51
  multiple, **3**:378
  of hard-rod mixtures, **5B**:163
  parallel, **12**:177
  3-point, **3**:158
  spin-spin, **3**:375, **3**:635
  time dependent, **3**:648
  transverse, **5B**:50, **5B**:51, **5B**:53
Correlation/correlators
  additive, **19**:313–314
  amplitude, **19**:143
  Bethe ansatz method, **19**:99–100
  calculation, **19**:197–198, **19**:209,
    19:214
  canonical dimension, **19**:456
  and canonical distributions, **19**:108
  decoupling, **19**:222
  density, **19**:108
  derivation, **19**:452
  divergences, **19**:297
  driving effects, **19**:203
  energy–energy, **19**:257, **19**:408

equal time, **19**:140
equations of motion, **19**:164–165
exponential decay, **19**:168
higher order, **19**:96, **19**:164
Laplace transformed, **19**:315–316
large-scale/limit behaviour, **19**:88,
　　19:199, **19**:456
lower order, **19**:165
multipoint, **19**:141
ϕ_4 model, **19**:316
and pair annihilation, **19**:195
and perturbations, **19**:99
polymers, **19**:315, **19**:412
random force field, **19**:390–391
and response function, **19**:383,
　　19:394
static, **19**:377
stationary, **19**:140–141
three point, **19**:117
time derivative, **19**:380
time-delayed, **19**:58, **19**:59, **19**:141
time-dependent, **19**:6, **19**:25, **19**:74,
　　19:84, **19**:91, **19**:136, **19**:141,
　　19:142–143, **19**:174
two-point, **19**:117, **19**:140, **19**:141,
　　19:166
Correlations, **1**:77, **1**:232, **1**:237, **1**:257
anisotropy, free surfaces, **8**:6
antiferromagnetic, **8**:56
fourth order, **1**:257
long-range, **17**:25–40, **17**:93
　　see also Power law decays
Corresponding states law
generalized, **3**:450
Coulomb energy, **19**:283, **19**:285,
　　19:380–381
Coulomb gas (CG) model, **11**:2–51,
　　11:59, **11**:102, **11**:104, **11**:119,
　　14:113, **14**:118
electromagnetic CG, **11**:16
magnetic CG, **11**:14
modified, **11**:105
Coulomb interaction, **1**:38, **5B**:180,
　　5B:181, **5B**:182
Coulomb potential, **19**:283
Coulombic system, **5B**:225
Count, **3**:98
Counterterms, **19**:298, **19**:299, **19**:341,
　　19:382, **19**:383

Counting condition, **18**:272
Counting problem, **2**:331
Counting theorem, **3**:69, **3**:378
chain, **3**:379
Sykes, **3**:379
Counting weight, **3**:380
Coupling constant
dimensionless, **6**:297, **6**:310
effective, **6**:174
Coupling constant, **5A**:23, **14**:32,
　　14:72
Coupling
constant, **19**:302, **19**:342, **19**:366,
　　19:435
canonical dimension, **19**:365, **19**:366,
　　19:465
renormalization, **19**:354, **19**:382,
　　19:420, **19**:447
physical interpretation, **19**:368
renormalized, **19**:301, **19**:302,
　　19:393
Coupling inequality, **18**:22
Coupling, **18**:21–3
optimal, **18**:22–3
Couplings
four-spin, **6**:4
next-nearest-neighbour, **6**:4
strong, problem, **6**:307
renormalization group and, **6**:5
Covariant derivatives, **16**:133
Covering graph, **2**:205, **2**:223
Covering lattice, **2**:206, **2**:218
CPA *see* Coherent potential
approximation
$CrBr_3$, **2**:65, **2**:66, **2**:67, **2**:68, **2**:69, **2**:74,
　　2:75, **2**:76, **3**:506
Creation operators, **1**:208, **5A**:242,
　　5A:252
Critical
adsorption, **10**:207, **10**:213,
　　10:236–7, **12**:42, **12**:112,
　　12:150–154
chiral cross over, **12**:306
dimension, **12**:259–262, **12**:271–283,
　　12:291–293, **12**:327–332,
　　12:358
dynamics, **12**:176, **12**:178
end-point, **10**:271, **10**:326–8, **10**:358,
　　12:43, **12**:54, **12**:81, **12**:90–92

exponents, **10:**111, **10:**112, **12:**65,
    12:146, **12:**148, **12:**173, **12:**184,
    12:225, **12:**227, **12:**253, **12:**255,
    12:258, **12:**271–281
non universal, **12:**114
point Tc, **12:**5, **12:**10, **12:**13, **12:**14,
    12:17, **12:**146–147, **12:**190,
    12:336
radius, **12:**9
renormalized, **12:**168
scaling forms, **10:**204
surface, **12:**6
surface scattering, **10:**202
wall perturbations, **10:**326
wetting, **10:**103–4, **12:**36, **12:**38–40
wetting MFT, **12:**29
Critical amplitude, **2:**400, **2:**413, **2:**433,
    3:183, **3:**188, **3:**194, **3:**211, **3:**212,
    3:213, **3:**216, **3:**235, **3:**424, **3:**429,
    3:431, **3:**432, **3:**435, **3:**441, **3:**452,
    3:460, **3:**571, **3:**615, **3:**616, **3:**620,
    3:625, **3:**627, **3:**628, **3:**629, **3:**645,
    3:646, **3:**647, **3:**648, **5B:**18, **8:**35,
    8:44, **8:**53, **8:**67
criticality of fluids between plates,
    10:230
fourth order fluctuation, **3:**623
isotherm, **3:**435, **3:**448
low temperature, **3:**476
low temperature susceptibility, **3:**441
of magnetization, **5B:**88
of susceptibility, **5B:**88
order parameter, **8:**66
ratios of, **10:**173, **10:**205
$s > \frac{1}{2}$, **3:**432
specific heat, **3:**438, **3:**451
susceptibility derivatives, **3:**437
Critical anomalies, **5A:**168, **5A:**169,
    5A:175, **5A:**187, **5A:**190, **5A:**196,
    5A:202, **5A:**236, **5A:**250, **5A:**260,
    5A:299, **5A:**305, **5A:**311
Critical behaviour, **2:**402, **2:**420, **2:**422,
    2:423–4, **18:**32–5, **18:**37, **18:**195–6
    (see also Multicritical behaviour)
anisotropic, **6:**369
boundary effect, **19:**361–363
N-component spins, **19:**256
cubic, **6:**398, **6:**400
dilute magnets, **7:**242

interfaces, **8:**64–76
Ising-like, **8:**57
isotropic, **6:**400
local, **8:**49
    at defect layers, **8:**74–75
    at surfaces, **8:**76
    critical exponents, **8:**9
    Ising ferromagnets, Landau
        theories, **8:**6–10
lower, defect layers, **8:**65
McCoy–Wu Ising model, **7:**181
modelling, **19:**4
near free surface, **5B:**62
and nonleading terms, **19:**2589
of interface, **5B:**65
of point defect system, **5B:**67
quenched models, **7:**183
random Ising model, **7:**243
randomness and, **7:**169–173
reaction–diffusion systems, **19:**70–71
renormalization group, **19:**5
renormalization group method, **7:**239
series expansion, **7:**223
surfaces, **8:**1–144
    first-order transitions, **8:**33
    mean-field theory, **8:**6–34
tethered membranes, **19:**259
Critical branch (Potts), **9:**151
Critical class, **6:**88
Critical concentration, **1:**313, **1:**314,
    1:315, **1:**319, **2:**198, **2:**199, **2:**250,
    3:473, **5B:**68, **5B:**319, **5B:**334,
    5B:336, **8:**47
annealed bond diluted Ising models,
    7:199
antiferromagnetic, **1:**317
concentration expansion method,
    7:224
dilute Ising model, series expansion
    methods, **7:**227
effective medium condition for, **7:**220
ferromagnetic, **1:**317
for site percolation, quenched models,
    7:179
partial, **1:**319
position space methods, **7:**249
Critical conditions, **7:**175
dilute spin half Ising system, **7:**184
length scaling argument, **7:**237

position space methods, **7:**250
random mixed magnets, **7:**199
Critical consolute point, **2:**84
Critical correlation function, **14:**17
Critical correlation functions,
　renormalization group theory and,
　　7:233
Critical correlation, **5B:**160
Critical curve
　bond annealed Ising model, **7:**199,
　　7:200
　coherent potential approximations,
　　7:218
　dilute Ising magnets, **7:**264
　diluted layer magnets, **7:**258
　dilute XY model, series expansion
　　methods, **7:**231
　quenched site diluted Ising model in
　　transverse field, series expansion
　　methods, **7:**231
　two-dimensional bond diluted Ising
　　model, **7:**254
　position space method, **7:**248
Critical curve, **3:**453
　of antiferromagnet, **3:**453
Critical curves, **2:**354, **2:**355, **2:**357
Critical demixing point, **5B:**liquid-liquid,
　　5B:352
Critical dimension, upper, **17:**61–63,
　　17:94, **17:**100
　phase separators, **19:**364
Critical dimensionality, **8:**57
　lower, **8:**53, **8:**63, **8:**64, **8:**72
Critical droplet, saddle point equation,
　　8:303–307
Critical dynamics, **5A:**171, **5A:**280,
　　5B:94
　finite size scaling, **8:**199
　self-consistent scheme, **5A:**234
Critical end points, **14:**364
Critical end-point
　amplitudes, **9:**86
　lower, **9:**166, **9:**171, **9:**176, **9:**179,
　　9:180, **9:**184
　temperatures, **9:**186, **9:**189, **9:**207
　tie-line, **9:**60
　topology, **9:**85, **9:**100, **9:**148
　upper, **9:**166, **9:**171, **9:**176, **9:**179,
　　9:180, **9:**184

Critical end-points, **9:**5, **9:**9, **9:**14, **9:**15,
　　9:16, **9:**19, **9:**38, **9:**60, **9:**61, **9:**62,
　　9:84, **9:**87, **9:**101, **9:**102, **9:**152,
　　9:164, **9:**166–7, **9:**173, **9:**176,
　　9:177, **9:**183, **9:**192
Critical energy, **3:**427, **3:**620, **3:**622
Critical entropy, **3:**427, **3:**620, **3:**622
Critical equation of state, **3:**360, **3:**435,
　　3:436
Critical equation of state, **5B:**155
Critical exponent ν, **6:**48
Critical exponent α', **5A:**59
Critical exponent α, **5B:**375, **5B:**393
Critical exponent α, **6:**48, **6:**114
Critical exponent β, **5A:**43
Critical exponent β, **5B:**367, **5B:**383,
　　5B:387
Critical exponent β, **6:**48
Critical exponent Δ, **5A:**77, **5A:**78
Critical exponent Φ, **5A:**77
Critical exponent γ, **6:**48, **6:**205
Critical exponent η, **5A:**52
Critical exponent η, **5B:**249
Critical exponent η, **6:**48, **6:**176, **6:**205,
　　6:222, **6:**234
Critical exponent ζ, **5B:**46
Critical exponent, **2:**15, **2:**16, **2:**24,
　　2:25, **2:**27, **2:**28, **2:**29, **2:**30, **2:**31,
　　2:32, **2:**33, **2:**34, **2:**35, **2:**37, **2:**40,
　　2:41, **2:**44, **2:**45, **2:**48, **2:**55, **2:**61,
　　2:68, **2:**70, **2:**76, **2:**85, **2:**86, **2:**103,
　　2:110, **2:**139, **2:**149, **2:**162, **2:**186,
　　2:194, **2:**195, **2:**244, **2:**247,
　　2:251–2, **2:**263, **2:**335, **2:**379,
　　2:400, **2:**401, **2:**407, **2:**426,
　　2:432, **2:**433, **2:**436, **2:**486–7,
　　2:489
　renormalized, **2:**19
Critical exponents (indices), **5A:**8, **5A:**9,
　　5A:15, **5A:**16, **5A:**32, **5A:**45,
　　5A:52, **5A:**53, **5A:**142, **6:**11–14,
　　6:202, **6:**212, **6:**228, **6:**236, **6:**256,
　　6:294, **6:**310, **6:**358, **6:**365, **6:**373,
　　6:433, **6:**436, **6:**437, **6:**511, **6:**512,
　　6:513, **6:**518, **6:**537, **6:**540, **6:**548,
　　7:178, **7:**250
　annealed models, **7:**200
　ε-expansion for, **6:**1
　experimental, **7:**265

in annealed magnets, renormalization, 7:162–163
    scaling relations and, 7:163
Monte Carlo method, 7:203, 7:205
position space methods, 7:254
pure systems, 7:176–177
renormalization, 6:400, 7:201
renormalization group method, 7:233, 7:239
scaling and, 7:235
series expansion, 7:223
Critical exponents
    randomly driven and multi-temperature models, 17:101, 17:103
    standard model
        from simulations, 17:44–46, 17:50
        from theory, 17:65–66, 17:67–71
        relations, 17:54–59
Critical exponents, 3:115, 3:182, 3:183, 3:188, 3:189, 3:191, 3:198, 3:199, 3:200, 3:207, 3:210, 3:211, 3:212, 3:215, 3:221, 3:230, 3:253, 3:305, 3:311, 3:322, 3:325, 3:359, 3:360, 3:424, 3:429, 3:435, 3:439, 3:447, 3:462, 3:464, 3:486, 3:490, 3:492, 3:493, 3:496, 3:497, 3:500, 3:501, 3:502, 3:503, 3:507, 3:511, 3:536, 3:537, 3:538, 3:541, 3:558, 3:571, 3:579, 3:582, 3:583, 3:584, 3:615, 3:616, 3:618, 3:624, 3:625, 3:627, 3:636, 3:640, 3:643, 3:646, 3:647, 3:648, 3:649, 5B:5, 5B:18, 5B:24, 5B:29, 5B:45, 5B:189, 5B:258, 5B:365, 5B:367, 5B:381, 8:22, 8:36, 8:38, 8:50, 8:59, 8:62, 9:2, 9:36, 9:37, 9:44, 9:53, 11:14, 11:35, 11:56, 19:351, 19:421, 19:426
    α, 3:540, 3:620, 3:648, 3:649
    α', 3:440, 3:441
    antiferromagnetic, 3:236
    β, 3:215, 3:216, 3:223, 3:228, 3:229, 3:433, 3:435, 3:540, 3:647
    bulk, 8:42
    correction-to-scaling, 8:171
    crossover, 3:361, 3:464, 3:465, 3:467, 8:36, 8:50, 8:61, 8:64
    δ, 3:361, 3:434, 3:435, 3:446, 3:477
    Δ, 3:446, 3:472, 3:540
    Δ', 3:440, 3:441
    η, 3:439
    exactly solved models, 8:54
    finite size scaling, 8:35–38
    γ, 3:435, 3:441, 3:446, 3:453, 3:460, 3:465, 3:493, 3:495, 3:499, 3:540, 3:556, 3:616, 3:639
    γ', 3:230, 3:440
    γ_2, 3:623
    high temperature, 3:439
    indices, 3:305, 3:319, 3:320, 3:321, 9:288–9, 9:299, 9:305
    interface, 9:165
    interface tension, 8:67
    lines, 9:39, 9:47, 9:52, 9:55, 9:62
    long range force, 3:464
    low temperature, 3:441
    ν, 3:439, 3:472
    of local magnetization near defects, 5B:67
    of relaxation times, 5B:95
    ϕ, 3:542
    physical, 3:221
    points (line of), 11:29, 11:45
    polymerization line, 9:219
    renormalization, 5B:345
    renormalized, 3:474
    scaling laws, 8:34–76, 8:118–123
    scaling relations, 8:47–50
    spontaneous magnetization, 3:360
    static, 5B:95
    surfaces, 8:2, 8:3, 8:49, 8:62, 8:63, 8:64, 9:54, 9:67
    thermodynamic, 3:444
    three-state Potts, 11:42
Critical field, 2:463, 3:459, 8:14
Critical fluctuation, 3:619
Critical fluctuations, 5A:143, 5A:145, 5A:166, 5A:169, 5A:179, 5A:236, 5A:279, 5A:296, 5B:85
    dynamical, 5A:143
    large-scale, 5A:171
Critical frequency of sound, 5B:359
Critical indices, *see* Critical exponents
Critical invariants, 3:450, 3:451

Critical isochore, **2**:44, **2**:47, **2**:51,
  2:52, **2**:54, **2**:55, **2**:56, **2**:64, **2**:72,
  2:77, **5B**:382, **14**:16, **14**:81
Critical isotherm, **2**:40, **2**:43, **2**:44, **2**:45,
  2:49, **2**:54, **2**:61, **2**:62, **2**:75, **2**:408,
  2:410, **2**:417, **2**:418, **3**:187, **3**:323,
  3:434, **3**:435, **3**:447, **3**:448, **3**:451,
  6:328, **6**:335, **6**:338, **6**:512, **14**:17
Critical line, liquid-liquid, **5B**:378,
  5B:384
Critical micelle concentration (cmc),
  16:17, **16**:64–5, **16**:75
Critical mixture shear viscosity, **5A**:168
Critical opalescence, **5A**:88, **5B**:157
Critical parameters, **3**:425, **3**:462
  antiferromagnet, **3**:456, **3**:457, **3**:458
  cristobalite, **3**:462
  equivalent neighbour model, **3**:436
  h.k., **3**:462
  h.p., **3**:462
  h.t., **3**:462
  for $I(s)$ model, **3**:429
Critical phenomena notation, **5A**:95–97
Critical phenomena, **5A**:11, **5A**:12,
  5A:16, **5A**:19, **5A**:20, **5A**:28,
  5A:88, **5A**:168, **5A**:169, **5A**:170,
  5A:188, **5A**:189, **5A**:236, **5A**:267,
  5A:336, **5A**:344, **6**:526, **17**:6–7,
  17:40–73
  field theoretical approach to,
    6:125–247
  renormalization group approach to,
    6:507–558
  scaling theory, **6**:508
  simulation studies, **17**:40–52
  theoretical investigations, **17**:52–73
Critical point exponents, **1**:58, **1**:98,
  1:100, **1**:102, **1**:103
Critical point inequalities, **1**:98
Critical point specification, **13**:91
Critical point, **1**:84, **1**:101, **1**:104, **1**:174,
  1:270, **1**:271, **1**:272, **1**:278, **1**:280,
  1:293, **1**:294, **1**:296, **1**:297, **1**:298,
  1:300, **1**:302, **1**:310, **1**:313, **1**:315,
  1:317, **1**:318, **1**:319, **1**:323, **1**:325,
  3:182, **3**:183, **3**:184, **3**:190, **3**:191,
  3:193, **3**:194, **3**:196, **3**:197, **3**:198,
  3:199, **3**:210, **3**:211, **3**:212, **3**:213,
  3:215, **3**:220, **3**:221, **3**:222, **3**:224,

  3:228, **3**:230, **3**:231, **3**:232, **3**:236,
  3:237, **3**:257, **3**:299, **3**:305, **3**:618,
  3:619, **5A**:2, **5A**:6, **5A**:8, **5A**:10,
  5A:16, **5A**:26, **5A**:31, **5A**:166,
  5A:167, **5A**:168, **5A**:169, **5A**:171,
  5A:176, **5A**:179, **5A**:189, **5A**:208,
  5A:213, **5A**:216, **5A**:266, **5A**:267,
  5A:268, **5A**:297, **5A**:302, **5A**:305,
  5A:312, **5A**:316, **5A**:328, **5A**:329,
  5A:330, **5B**:153, **5B**:387, **6**:251,
  6:516, **6**:518
  antiferromagnetic, **3**:202, **3**:213,
    3:214
  correlation function, **6**:48
  Curie–Weiss, **5B**:183, **5B**:184
  and dynamical behaviour, **5A**:266,
    5A:267
  fluctuations, **5A**:20, **5A**:166
  high temperature, **3**:216
  higher order, **3**:497
  in finite system, distortions,
    8:153–157
  liquid-gas, **5B**:345
  liquid-liquid, **5B**:378, **5B**:388
  perfect wetting near, **8**:83–89
  phenomenological theory, **6**:510
  quantum corrections, **5B**:196
  thermodynamic systems, **6**:511
Critical points, **19**:369, **19**:370
  see also tricritical point
Critical pressure, **14**:14
Critical probability, **2**:201, **2**:202, **2**:211,
  2:216, **2**:218, **2**:220, **2**:222–4,
  2:226, **2**:243–4, **2**:257, **2**:262,
  2:264, **2**:266
Critical properties
  annealed diluted magnets, **7**:162
  dilute magnetism, **7**:152
  random field and, **7**:247
Critical property
  of mixtures, **5B**:163
  van der Waals, **5B**:112, **5B**:160
Critical region, **14**:19
  mean-field description, **3**:114
Critical scaling parameter, **3**:646
Critical singularities, **5A**:8–10
  logarithms, **5A**:8
Critical singularity, phase boundary,
  7:188

Critical slowing down, **2**:489, **5A**:168,
  5A:172, **5B**:16, **5B**:18, **5B**:74,
  5B:82, **5B**:102
Critical speeding up, **5B**:76
Critical state, general aspects, **6**:7–121
Critical surface in parameter space,
  7:240
Critical surface, **3**:467, **3**:468, **3**:497,
  6:260, **6**:265, **6**:266, **6**:267, **6**:271,
  6:530
Critical tangent plane, **2**:13
Critical temperature, **1**:75, **1**:79, **1**:82,
  1:83, **1**:99, **1**:152, **1**:241, **3**:215,
  3:305, **3**:309, **3**:311, **3**:425, **3**:426,
  3:464, **3**:466, **3**:468, **3**:475, **3**:615,
  3:616, **5A**:13, **5A**:52, **6**:160, **6**:369,
  6:373, **6**:436, **6**:440, **6**:482
  antiferromagnetic, **3**:308
  bounds, **1**:115
  ferromagnetic, **3**:308
  film thickness and, **8**:32
  Ising, **3**:472
  mean field, **3**:547
  mean field approximations, **7**:210
  Onsager value, **17**:10, **17**:40
  quenched diluted magnets, **7**:158
  randomly driven and multi-
    temperature models, **17**:103
  shifted, **8**:47
  spontaneous magnetisation, quenched
    models, **7**:179
  standard model, **17**:15, **17**:18, **17**:44
  system with repulsive interactions,
    17:141
  upper bound, **1**:123
Critical temperature shift, **5B**:42
Critical theory, **19**:428
Critical velocity, **5A**:70
Critical wetting, **14**:303–20
Critical-point shift, **14**:120
Criticality, thermodynamics and,
  8:150–153
Cross-over behaviour, **5A**:154
Cross-over exponent ϕ, **6**:243
Cross-over exponents, **6**:229,
  6:366–370, **6**:372, **6**:382, **6**:392,
  6:396, **6**:399, **6**:417, **6**:513
  dipolar, **6**:387, **6**:391
Cross-over function, **6**:420

Cross-over lines, **10**:156
  scaling, **10**:164
  special to ordinary transition,
    10:332
Cross-over point, **6**:366
Cross-over, **6**:232, **6**:358, **6**:365, **6**:369,
  6:370, **6**:379, **6**:387, **6**:399, **6**:419,
  6:538, **6**:539
  to mean field behaviour, **6**:380
  renormalization group and, **6**:3
Crossover behaviour, **3**:511
Crossover effects, **7**:240
  correlation length and, **7**:169
  in quenched dilute magnets,
    7:163–169
  scaling variables, **7**:238
Crossover
  experimental, **9**:12
  exponent, **9**:9, **9**:28, **9**:30, **9**:52, **9**:54,
    9:91
  phenomena, **9**:53, **9**:88
Crossover exponent, **3**:361, **3**:464,
  3:465, **3**:467, **8**:36, **8**:50, **8**:61,
  8:64, **14**:29
Crossover exponents
  dilute Heisenberg quadratic layer
    magnet, **7**:268
  dilute Ising magnets, **7**:238
  position space method, **7**:255
Crossover function, **14**:87
Crossover region, **3**:510, **3**:511
Crossover scaling, **8**:43–44, **8**:61,
  14:28–30, **14**:68
  relations, **8**:23
Crossover temperature, **3**:507, **8**:155
Crossover temperature, dilute
  Heisenberg quadratic layer magnet,
  7:268
Crossover value, **3**:579
Crossover, **3**:486, **3**:507, **14**:19, **19**:66,
  19:116, **19**:197, **19**:199, **19**:218,
  19:305, **19**:407–408
Crumpled phase, **19**:265, **19**:275
Crumpled swollen phase, **19**:257–258,
  19:259
Crumpling transition, **19**:263,
  19:265–267, **19**:273, **19**:276–277,
  19:356
Crystal growth, **5B**:103

Crystal lattice, **3:**98, **3:**104
  n-cluster counting, **3:**105
Crystal spectrometer, **5A:**97
  filter, **5A:**99
  quasielastic approximation, **5A:**99
  resolution, **5A:**101–105
  three-axis, **5A:**97–99, **5A:**103, **5A:**131
  two-axis, **5A:**97, **5A:**99–101, **5A:**123,
    5A:131, **5A:**138
Crystal, hydrogen-bonded, **3:**654
  Perovskite type, **3:**583
Crystalline phases, **1:**172
Crystalline symmetry group, **1:**171
Crystallization point, **5B:**386, **5B:**387
Crystallization, **1:**152, **1:**170
  theory of, **1:**138
Crystallization, by folding, **7:**121–131
Crystallographic group, **1:**174
Crystals
  cubic, surfaces, **8:**13
  growth, in supercooled liquids, **8:**454
CsMnF$_3$, **3:**580
Cu$_3$Au, **12:**128–129, **12:**132–136
Cube, **1:**320, **1:**328
Cubic fields, **9:**66
Cubic lattice, **15:**159–65
Cubic model, **11:**3, **11:**50
  Delta squared model, **11:**133–4,
    11:139, **11:**145, **11:**152, **11:**165,
    11:176
  Phase diagram, **11:**178
  spin-1, **11:**177, **11:**179
  spin-2, **11:**178
  with an infinite spin, **11:**169
  den Nijs formula, **11:**110
Cubic phase, **16:**127
Cubic samples, **14:**105
Cubic symmetry, **5A:**200
Cubic systems, **6:**394
Cumulant approximation, **6:**463, **6:**473,
    6:476
Cumulant correlation, **3:**121, **3:**128,
    3:131, **3:**141, **3:**154, **3:**166, **3:**167
Cumulant decoupling diagram method,
    5B:319
Cumulant expansion, **3:**71, **3:**369, **3:**389,
    6:447, **6:**467, **6:**471, **6:**474, **6:**488,
    6:489, **6:**494
Cumulant function, **3:**265, **19:**204–205

Cumulant method, **3:**253, **3:**254, **3:**258,
    3:261, **3:**264, **3:**268, **3:**290, **3:**390
Cumulant ratio, **14:**100, **14:**101
Cumulant, **3:**45, **3:**54, **3:**131, **3:**254,
    3:260, **3:**262, **3:**265, **3:**268, **3:**472,
    3:519
Cumulant-like expansion, **1:**78
Cumulants, **2:**467, **9:**244, **9:**264
  see Connected correlation functions
Curie point, **3:**185, **3:**186, **3:**300, **3:**310,
    3:313, **3:**316, **5A:**241, **5A:**242,
    5A:270, **5A:**284, **5B:**170, **9:**208
  ferromagnetic, **3:**231
Curie temperature, **1:**272, **2:**350, **3:**183,
    3:186, **3:**248, **3:**251, **3:**307, **3:**309,
    3:358, **3:**359, **5A:**88, **5A:**109,
    5A:132, **5A:**133, **5A:**135, **5A:**144,
    5A:146, **5A:**283, **5A:**284, **19:**32
  paramagnetic, **3:**301, **3:**313
Curie temperatures
  cluster methods, **7:**214
  virtual crystal approximation, **7:**212
Curie–Weiss critical point, **5B:**183,
    5B:184
Curie–Weiss law, **2:**336, **2:**345, **2:**346,
    2:352, **3:**302
Curie–Weiss model, **15:**136
Curie–Weiss–Kac interaction, **15:**156–7
Curie–Weiss–Kac-type infinite-range
  models, **15:**133
Current
  fluctuation, Bethe ansatz methods,
    19:158–159
  maxima and minima, **19:**111, **19:**144,
    19:149–154, **19:**161
  maximal, **19:**133–134, **19:**143,
    19:144, **19:**146, **19:**155, **19:**157
  nonvanishing, **19:**59
  stationary, **19:**66, **19:**104
Current–density relation
  exact results, **19:**148, **19:**150
  and parallel updating, **19:**137–138
  and phase diagram, **19:**144, **19:**153
  point of inflection, **19:**125
  stationary, **19:**111
  traffic models, **19:**155–156, **19:**157
Curvature effects, **10:**237, **10:**240
Curvature tensor, **16:**132
Cut-off, **5A:**172

Cut-point, **3**:68
Cut-set, **3**:68
Cutting bonds, **5B**:233
Cutting circle, **5B**:219, **5B**:225
Cutting plane algorithm, **18**:226–7
Cutting point, **3**:5
Cycle cancelling algorithm, **18**:171
Cycle index, **3**:26, **3**:27, **3**:28, **3**:32, **3**:36
Cyclic boundary condition, **2**:215, **2**:218, **3**:62, **3**:71, **3**:382
  see Boundary
Cyclic boundary, **3**:378
Cyclic determinants, **1**:230, **1**:250
Cyclic group, **3**:26
Cyclic matrix, **1**:263
Cyclohexane-methanol, **12**:86
Cyclomatic number, **2**:234, **3**:9, **3**:10, **3**:11, **3**:34, **3**:39, **3**:41, **3**:61, **3**:68, **3**:86, **3**:89, **3**:472
Cybotactic clusters, **7**:82
Cylinder geometry, **14**:102, **14**:105

D

δ distribution, **19**:452, **19**:463
δ interactions, **19**:371, **19**:372
D-weights, **2**:234, **2**:239
DAG (dysprosium aluminium garnet), **9**:3, **9**:54, **9**:90, **9**:138
Damping constant, **14**:72
Dangerous irrelevant variable, **9**:105, **9**:106, **9**:107, **14**:39
Dangerous irrelevant variables, **10**:171, **10**:257, **10**:321
Dangerously irrelevant operators, **17**:36, **17**:37, **17**:63, **17**:70, **17**:100
Dangling bonds, **7**:222
Dangling ends, **7**:237
Darboux correction term, **3**:443
Darboux form, **3**:424, **3**:429, **3**:430, **3**:431, **3**:435, **3**:452, **3**:453, **3**:454, **3**:455
Darboux second theorem, **3**:234
Darboux theorem, **3**:232, **3**:233, **3**:236, **3**:238
Darboux's theorem, **2**:405, **2**:425
Darboux's theorems, **13**:11–15
  first, **13**:11–13
  second, **13**:13–15

Darboux-type singularity, **2**:388, **2**:423, **2**:425
d-dimensional lattice, **2**:375, **2**:392, **2**:407
Declaunay transformation, **2**:276
De Gennes and Skal-Shklovskii picture, **7**:237, **7**:238
Dead layers, **8**:34
  at magnetic surfaces, **8**:57–59
  Ising models, **8**:58
Debye screening length, **7**:107
Debye shielding length, **5B**:181
Debye–Hückel approximation, **7**:51
Debye–Hückel form, **5B**:181
Debye–Hückel theory, charged plasmas, **7**:25, **7**:26
Debye–Waller factor, **5A**:91, **7**:4, **7**:5
Decimation
  Ising model renormalization group equation and, **6**:29
Decimation transformation, square lattice, **7**:249
Decoagulation, **19**:47
  see also branching
Decorated Ising models, variables, **7**:162
Decorated lattice, **15**:159–65
Decorated mosaic, **2**:218
Decoration, **1**:299, **3**:139, **3**:168
Decoration transformation, **2**:102, **2**:212, **2**:251, **2**:256, **2**:264
Decoupling
  correlators, **19**:222–223
  equations of motion, **19**:164–167
Decoupling procedure, **5B**:279
  Wick, **5B**:279
Deep inelastic electron scattering, **6**:349
Defect fields, finite size scaling, **8**:233
Defect layers, **8**:64, **8**:65, **8**:73
  Ising systems, **8**:34
  local critical behaviour, **8**:74–75
Defect plane, **8**:49
  Ising system, **8**:4
Defects
  free energy, **7**:174
  melting and, **7**:40
  phase transitions and, **7**:1–93
  experiments, **7**:7–11
  theoretical background, **7**:2–7
Defects, in polymers, **19**:8, **19**:9

Definition of dimers, **13**:236
Deformation
    energy, **19**:268
    matrix, **19**:267–268, **19**:278
Deformed harmonic oscillator algebra,
    19:97
Deformed semicircle distribution,
    15:181
Deformed semicircle law, **15**:190,
    15:192
Deformed Wigner ensemble, **15**:168,
    15:169, **15**:181, **15**:224–7
    random part has finite third moment,
        15:227–9
Degeneracy of maximum eigenvalue,
    5B:139
Degree-tuple, **3**:15
Degrees of freedom, **5A**:22
Delocalization, **14**:150, **14**:163,
    14:165–70, **14**:172, **14**:179, **14**:180
Delta squared model, **11**:133–4, **11**:139,
    11:145, **11**:152, **11**:165, **11**:176
    spin-1, **11**:177, **11**:179
    spin-2, **11**:178
    with an infinite spin, **11**:178
Demagnetising effect, **1**:39
Demagnetization tensor, **6**:384
Demagnetizing factor, **2**:61
Demagnetizing field, **8**:29, **8**:30, **8**:31,
    8:33
    extrapolation length and, **8**:32
Dendrite growth, **12**:344–347, **12**:370,
    12:383–384, **12**:388–389, **12**:397,
    12:469, **12**:471
den Nijs formula, **11**:110
"Densities" and "fields", **9**:171–180
Density
    asymptotic behaviour, **19**:53
    correlation function, **19**:93
    decay, **19**:72, **19**:141, **19**:171, **19**:195,
        19:198, **19**:205
    expectation value, **19**:168
    finite, **19**:101, **19**:117
    fluctuations, **19**:167–169, **19**:203–208
    functional theories, **19**:230
    matrix renormalization method
        (DMRG), **19**:71
    nonconstant, **19**:161
    perturbation, local, **19**:59

profile
    constituent profiles, **19**:140,
        19:143
    diffusion limited pair annihilation
        (DLPA), **19**:209
    exact results, **19**:*100*, **19**:128–134,
        19:*132*
    field induced oscillations, **19**:167–169
    Gaussian distribution, **19**:67
    lattice derivative, **19**:130–131
    relaxation, **19**:97
    shape, **19**:134, **19**:143
    single particle, **19**:64
    stationary, **19**:126, **19**:128,
        19:148–149
    TASEP, **19**:139, **19**:149
    thermodynamic limit, **19**:131–134
    time evolution, **19**:62, **19**:99,
        19:117–118, **19**:122
    relaxation, **19**:59–61, **19**:97–99,
        19:165–166, **19**:167, **19**:169,
        19:185
    stationary, **19**:137, **19**:168
    time dependent, **19**:208
Density
    density correlations, **12**:367, **12**:406,
        12:411, **12**:415–416
    profile, **12**:9–10, **12**:20, **12**:46–47,
        12:56, **12**:58, **12**:61–62, **12**:124,
        12:191
Density correlation, **5B**:250
Density expansion, **3**:370, **3**:389, **3**:405
Density fluctuations, **2**:81, **2**:83, **5A**:304
Density matrix, **1**:129, **1**:130, **1**:131,
    1:143, **1**:145, **2**:337, **3**:630, **6**:170
Density of degrees of freedom, **6**:364
Density of states
    coherent potential approximation,
        7:217
    diluted Heisenberg antiferromagnets,
        7:209
    1–magnon, **7**:209
    spin wave, calculations, **7**:209
Density of states, **5B**:319, **5B**:330,
    15:166–9, **15**:181
Density profile, **2**:62, **2**:91, **2**:93, **2**:95,
    5B:108, **14**:316
Density series, **3**:409
Density variables, **6**:527

Density, **1**:35, **1**:138, **1**:189, **3**:366,
    3:371, **5B**:360, **5B**:382, **5B**:387,
    14:14, **14**:18
Density-height profiles, **2**:63
Dependent percolation, **18**:37–42
    Ising model, **18**:39–41, **18**:65–6
    see also Bernoulli percolation;
    random-cluster model
Depinning, **12**:171, **14**:228–44
Depolarising effect, **1**:39
Depolarizing field, **8**:30, **8**:31
Deposition processes, **12**:384
Depth first search algorithm, **18**:152
Desorption walls, **12**:241, **12**:244
Destination site, **3**:109, **3**:110
Detailed balance condition, **5B**:8, **5B**:73
Detailed balance equation, **5B**:15,
    5B:95
Detailed balance, **2**:493, **2**:495–6,
    19:57–59, **19**:62, **19**:103,
    19:104–105, **19**:110
Determinant representation, **19**:158,
    19:159
Developable surface, **2**:38
Deviation wavevector, **5A**:93
Devil's staircase, **12**:261–262, **12**:316,
    12:330–331, **15**:6, **15**:18, **15**:24,
    15:25, **15**:36
Dewetting, **12**:15, **12**:18, **12**:88,
    12:95–97, **12**:150, **12**:160
Diagonal representation, **1**:210
Diagram equation, **5A**:228
Diagrammatic expansions, **6**:371, **6**:510,
    6:554
Diagrams
    connected, **6**:154, **6**:155
    one-loop, **6**:144
    two-loop, **6**:145
Diamagnetic effect, **5A**:40
Diamagnetism, **1**:104
Dielectric breakdown, **12**:337,
    12:384–386, **12**:396
    trees, **12**:402–403, **12**:426–427,
    12:471
Difference correlation, **14**:155, **14**:156,
    14:168
Differential approximants, **13**:83–104,
    see also Partial diffential
    approximants

amplitude calculations, **13**:92–94
applications, **13**:96–104
    confluent singularities, **13**:103
    Ising model, three-dimensional,
        13:87, **13**:97
    Ising model, two-dimensional,
        13:96–97
    test series, **13**:97, **13**:100–103
biased, **13**:91–92
convergence theorems new results,
    13:103–104
development, **13**:4
invariance properties, **13**:95–96
and other methods, **13**:94–95
as Padé approximant generalization
    inhomogeneous, **13**:85–86
    multidemensional, **13**:106
    natural, **13**:84–85
practical difficulty, **13**:90
recurrence-relation method, **13**:83–84
singular behaviour, **13**:89–90
Differential cross section, **5A**:89
Differential renormalization group
    equations, **7**:21
Diffraction peaks, **12**:225, **12**:268–271
    pitch, **12**:267–271
Diffusion coefficient, **5A**:260, **5B**:347,
    5B:389, **14**:227, **15**:211, **16**:17–8,
    16:*18*, **16**:138
Diffusion
    coefficient, **19**:23, **19**:82–83, **19**:124,
        19:148, **19**:169
    collective, **19**:116
    constant, **19**:60, **19**:116, **19**:149,
        19:197
    discrete-time dynamics, **19**:97
    in inhomogeneous media, **19**:42
    limitation, **19**:4
    master equation, **19**:63
    perturbation, **19**:124
    propagator, probability conserving,
        19:314
    of reconstituting dimers, **19**:101
    shocks, **19**:117–123
    tracer, **19**:44–45
Diffusion constant, **5A**:265, **5B**:90, **14**:71
Diffusion, **2**:461, **2**:492, **5A**:266,
    5A:271, **5A**:288, **5B**:357, **5B**:358,
    12:68

Diffusion, one-dimensional, on lattice,
    8:319
Diffusion-limited annihilation,
    19:49–50, **19**:195
Diffusion-limited branching–fusion,
    19:74, **19**:167
Diffusion-limited chemical reactions,
    19:6, **19**:194–197, **19**:222–223
Diffusion-limited fusion, **19**:163,
    19:164, **19**:168–169, **19**:181
Diffusion-limited pair annihilation
    (DLPA), **19**:49–50, **19**:193–210
    density, **19**:205, **19**:209
    and DLFPA, **19**:77
    dynamics, **19**:193–211
    and Glauber dynamics, **19**:74,
        19:163
    Hamiltonian, **19**:73, **19**:181
    local properties, **19**:208–210
Diffusion-limited pair
    annihilation–creation, **19**:74,
    19:176
Diffusionless random sequential
    absorption process, **19**:167
Diffusive mixing/spreading, **19**:61,
    19:149, **19**:176, **19**:208, **19**:259
Digamma-function, **14**:111
Dihedral group, **3**:26, **3**:30
Dijkstra's algorithm, **18**:154–6, **18**:172
Dilatation factor, **7**:250
Dilatation, **6**:37
    homogeneity parameter and, **7**:235
    parameter, **6**:174
    transformation, **6**:22, **6**:64
    transformation of parameters and,
        7:239
Dilation operator, **19**:321
Dilute anisotropic Heisenberg model,
    position space methods, **7**:248
Dilute antiferromagnets coherent
    potential approximation, **7**:216
    in magnetic field, position space
        methods, **7**:258
    supersymmetry, **7**:247
    uniform field, **7**:173
Dilute chain Ising magnets, position
    space methods, **7**:248
Dilute continuous symmetry magnets,
    crossover exponent, **7**:238

Dilute droplet phase, **16**:107, **16**:120,
    16:*141*, **16**:144
Dilute ferromagnet, **5B**:260, **5B**:319,
    5B:335
Dilute ferromagnets
    coherent potential approximation,
        7:216
    dynamic response, moment method,
        7:223
Dilute frustrated Ising systems, Monte
    Carlo methods, **7**:207
Dilute gas, **5A**:336, **5A**:338, **5A**:340,
    5A:343
Dilute Heisenberg antiferromagnets,
    coherent potential approximation,
        7:217
Dilute Heisenberg chains, transverse
    dynamics, **7**:198
Dilute Heisenberg ferromagnets coherent
    potential approximation, **7**:217
    excitations, coherent potential
        approximation, **7**:217
    spin wave properties, **7**:207
Dilute Heisenberg layer magnet
    correlation length, **7**:267
    dynamic properties, **7**:268
Dilute Heisenberg magnets
    correlation length, temperature and,
        7:166
    characteristic temperatures, **7**:226
    series expansion methods,
        7:229–230
    static critical phenomena, scaling
        methods, **7**:259
    static crossover experiment, **7**:259
    spin wave specific heat, **7**:198
Dilute Heisenberg quadratic layer
    magnet, correlation length,
        7:268
Dilute Heisenberg systems, **14**:88–9
Dilute Ising chains, crossover functions,
    7:198
Dilute Ising ferromagnets, critical
    slowing down, Monte Carlo
    methods, **7**:207
Dilute Ising magnets
    crossover exponent, **7**:238
    exactly soluble, phase boundary,
        7:190

models, characteristic temperatures, **7**:226
  in transverse field, coherent potential approximations, **7**:218
  mean field theory, **7**:215
  percolation point, **7**:190
  position space methods, **7**:248
  scaling, phase diagram, **7**:253
  series expansion methods, **7**:227–229
  thermal and percolative features, **7**:253
  transition temperatures, **7**:236
  thermal percolation crossover, **7**:242
  three-dimensional, phase diagram, **7**:164
  transition temperatures, experimental, **7**:264
  two-dimensional, experimental, **7**:268–270
Dilute Ising model, **9**:23
Dilute Ising systems, **14**:89
Dilute isotropic Heisenberg model, position space methods, **7**:248
Dilute isotropic *n*-vector models, thermal percolation crossover, **7**:194
Dilute layer Ising magnets, position space methods, **7**:248
Dilute magnet, **1**:266
Dilute magnetic alloys, **2**:372
Dilute magnetic systems, **14**:30, **14**:63–4
Dilute magnetism, **7**:151–280
  experimental results, **7**:262–270
  theoretical, **7**:153
Dilute magnets
  dynamic exponent, position space method, **7**:251
  dynamic properties, experimental, **7**:268
  experiments, **7**:153
  field-theoretic renormalization group treatments, **7**:242–247
  Heisenberg, **7**:153
  homogeneity, **7**:232–238
  Ising, **7**:153
  phase diagram, real space calculation, **7**:248
  position space methods, **7**:247–262

pure system, **7**:153
qualitative features, **7**:153–173
renormalization group methods, **7**:232–262
scaling, **7**:232–262
spin waves stiffness, position space methods, **7**:251
thermal behaviour, at percolation threshold, **7**:169
transition temperature, **7**:270
XY, **7**:153
Dilute *n*-vector models, thermal behaviour, near percolation threshold, **7**:194
Dilute quantum systems, **7**:270
Dilute resistor networks, percolative conductivity, **7**:196, **7**:208
Dilute spin half Heisenberg model, three dimensional, phase diagram, **7**:259
Dilute spin half Ising system, critical condition, **7**:184
Dilute weakly coupled chain systems, position space methods, **7**:258
Dilute XY model, series expansion methods, **7**:230–231
Diluted anisotropic Heisenberg antiferromagnets
  paramagnetic phases, coherent potential approximation, **7**:217
  spin flop phases, coherent potential approximation, **7**:217
Diluted anisotropic Heisenberg ferromagnets, excitations, moment calculations, **7**:223
Diluted anisotropic Heisenberg model, position space methods, **7**:248
Diluted anti-ferromagnets in a field (DAFF), **18**:197, **18**:207–12, **18**:216–21
  see also random-field Ising magnets (RFIM)
Diluted bond disordered magnets, phase boundaries, **7**:211
Diluted classical Heisenberg model, position space methods, **7**:248
Diluted ferromagnets, dynamics, exact results, **7**:196–198
Diluted Heisenberg antiferromagnets
  spin wave properties, **7**:207

two-dimensional, density of states,
  7:209
Diluted Heisenberg chain magnet,
  correlation length, **7**:266
Diluted Heisenberg ferromagnets cluster
  methods, **7**:215
  coherent potential approximation,
    7:217, **7**:218
  moment calculations, **7**:222
  spin wave dynamics, coherent
    potential approximations, **7**:219
  spin wave stiffness, **7**:196, **7**:197,
    7:208
Diluted Heisenberg layer magnet
  dynamic properties, **7**:269
  Monte Carlo methods, **7**:209
Diluted Heisenberg magnets crossover
  from percolation to thermal
  behaviour, **7**:235–236
Diluted Heisenberg
  models, **7**:193
    two-dimensional, correlation length,
      7:269
  phase diagrams, **7**:166
  renormalization group description,
    7:241
  spin wave dynamic models, **7**:196
  spin wave stiffness, **7**:208
  thermal percolation crossover, **7**:242
  three-dimensional, experimental,
    7:264
    Monte Carlo methods, **7**:204
  two-dimensional, experimental, **7**:264
    Monte Carlo methods, **7**:204
Diluted Heisenberg spin systems with
  anisotropic exchange couplings,
  transition temperature, coherent
  potential approximations,
  7:217–218
Diluted Ising chains, Glauber dynamics,
  7:197
Diluted Ising ferromagnets, cluster
  methods, **7**:214
Diluted Ising layer magnet, correlation
  length, **7**:267
Diluted Ising magnets
  crossover from percolation to thermal
    behaviour, **7**:235–236
  Glauber dynamics, **7**:207

model, bounds, **7**:189
  correlation length versus
    temperature for, **7**:168
  solutions, **7**:185–190
  three-dimensional, smeared
    transitions, **7**:265
  transition temperature, scaling
    calculation, **7**:255
  two-dimensional, smeared transitions,
    7:265
Diluted Ising quadratic layer magnet,
  correlation length, **7**:266
Diluted isotropic Heisenberg model,
  three-dimensional, phase diagram,
  7:164
Diluted layer magnets
  critical curves, **7**:258
  position space method, **7**:258
Diluted matrices, **15**:231
Diluted Potts models, **7**:173
  correlation length, **7**:192
  position space methods, **7**:248,
    7:260
Diluted random matrices, **15**:188–97
Diluted resistor network, conductivity,
  7:219
Diluted spin half Heisenberg magnet,
  three-dimensional, critical curve,
  7:260
Diluted transverse Ising model
  position space methods, **7**:261
  transition temperature, **7**:270
  two-dimensional, percolation
    behaviour, **7**:195
Diluted uniaxially anisotropic
  Heisenberg model, position space
  methods, **7**:261
Diluted XY model, **7**:193
  position space methods, **7**:248
  three-dimensional, phase boundary,
    7:164
Diluted zero temperature Heisenberg
  models, dynamics, **7**:209
Dimensional analysis, **6**:177, **6**:189,
  6:348, **6**:517, **10**:97
  characteristic length and, **6**:2
  regularization, **10**:80, **10**:119, **10**:125,
    10:133, **10**:134, **10**:141, **10**:143,
    10:147, **10**:158, **10**:214

renormalization, **10:**125, **10:**126,
  10:131, **10:**135, **10:**151, **10:**178,
  10:183
Dimensional arguments, **6:**418
Dimensional crossover
  diluted layer magnets, **7:**258
  position space methods, **7:**248
d-dimensional hypercubic lattice,
  5B:252
Dimensional regularization parameter,
  19:399
Dimensionality < 4, **5A:**16
Dimensionality > 4, **5A:**54
Dimensionality d of space, **15:**74–5
Dimensionality of space, d, **6:**358
Dimensionality, **5A:**8, **5A:**17, **5A:**20,
  7:170
Dimensionless variables, **6:**530, **6:**531,
  14:47
Dimensions
  E, **6:**511
  ϕ, **6:**511
Dimer coverings, **1:**259
Dimer generation function,
  on hexagonal lattice, **1:**444
Dimer models on anisotropic lattices,
  13:235–297
  for biomembranes, **13:**280–285
  bond energies, **13:**238
  correlation functions, **13:**271–273
  finite size effects, **13:**273–277
  K models, thermal behaviour,
    13:236
  for monolayers, **13:**285–287
  monomer-dimer basic model, **13:**237
  order parameters, **13:**285–286
  partition function, **13:**238
  thermodynamic properties,
    13:260–270
  three dimensional, **13:**277–280
  transitions, *see also* K-lype transitions,
    Onsager-type transitions
  behaviour **13:**252–260
  commensurate-incommensurate,
    13:289–294
  and specific heat, **13:**236
  two-dimensional, **13:**240–247, *see
    also* K dimer models, 3–12/1,
    13:244,

4–8/1, **13:**244–245, **13:**251,
  13:266,
4–8/2, **13:**245, **13:**249–250,
  13:251, **13:**266–269,
  13:292–293,
4–8/4, **13:**246–247, **13:**269–270,
  4–8s/2/1, **13:**245–246
  SQK models, **13:**243–244, **13:**249,
    13:270, **13:**283–285
  VH models, **13:**241–243, **13:**251–252,
    13:260–265
Dimer models, **11:**3
Dimer problem, **1:**233, **1:**234, **1:**236,
  1:259, **1:**260, **1:**263
Dimer technique, **3:**661
Dimer, **1:**233
  external, **1:**261
  internal, **1:**261
Dipolar behaviour, **6:**387
Dipolar field, **5A:**91
Dipolar forces, **8:**6
Dipolar interaction, **3:**283
Dipolar interactions, **8:**29, **8:**32
Dipolar Ising model, **14:**40, **14:**63
Dipolar Ising systems, **14:**88
Dipolar parameter, **6:**391
Dipolar systems, **6:**358, **6:**382–394,
  8:29–33
Dipolar systems, critical properties,
  17:102
Dipoles
  approaching boundary, **19:**363
  bilocal operators, **19:**282
  coincidence, **19:**381
  contraction, **19:**293–294, **19:**295,
    19:297, **19:**300–301, **19:**352,
    19:353, **19:**360, **19:**382, **19:**462
  Coulomb energy, **19:**283–285
  MOPE approach, **19:**291–292, **19:**418
  replacement, **19:**299
Dirac function, **1:**126
Dirac operators, **1:**255, **1:**257, **1:**258
Dirac sea, **19:**40
Dirac units, **1:**250
Dirac–Hilbert space notation, **19:**19
Direct interaction, **14:**186
Direct neighbours, **2:**275, **2:**278
Directed cycles, **18:**154
Directed percolation, **11:**60

Directed percolation, **17**:172
Directed polymer in random media
(DPRM), **18**:187, **18**:190–5,
18:204–7, **18**:234, **18**:237,
18:241–6
Directed polymers, **14**:298, **14**:318
Dirichet region, **2**:275
Dirichlet boundary condition, **10**:176,
10:197, **10**:200, **10**:212, **10**:226,
10:235, **10**:238, **10**:240, **10**:244
Dirichlet polygons, **7**:40
Dirichlet series, **11**:170, **11**:172
Disagreement percolation, **18**:73–8,
18:121–3
Disclinations
elastic constants and, **7**:48
hexatics, **7**:72
melting and, **7**:46–47
of layered materials and, **7**:77
unbinding temperature, **7**:74
unbinding transition, dynamics and,
7:71–74
elastic constants and, **7**:48
free energy, **7**:51
fugacity, **7**:93
in melting, **7**:46, **7**:54
in solids, bond orientational order
and, **7**:85–88
in two-dimensional crystals, phase
transition and, **7**:7
loops, melting of smectic-A liquid
crystals and, **7**:90
melting and, **7**:45
of layered materials and, **7**:77
on periodic substrates, melting and,
7:59
two-dimensional melting and, **7**:18
unbinding transition, dynamics,
7:69–71
layered materials, **7**:78
Discontinuities, **19**:435, **19**:437
Discontinuity fixed points, **9**:139
Discontinuous unbinding transition,
14:184
Discontinuous wetting transition,
14:144
Discrete Gaussian, *see* Gaussian
Discrete nonlinear mappings, **15**:49
Discrete spin variables, **15**:42–51

Discrete time systems, **19**:52, **19**:69–70,
19:97
Discrete variables
mean magnetization and, **6**:16
Discrete-vector models, **16**:59
Disjoining pressure, **14**:181
Dislocation
core size, **12**:290
core energy, **12**:235, **12**:315
Dislocation-mediated-melting, **12**:232
Disorder
averaging over, **19**:259
correction, **19**:402
correlation, **19**:388, **19**:392
–disorder contraction, **19**:399
environment, **19**:77, **19**:388–408
interaction, time ordered, **19**:392
intrinsic, **19**:278–279
isotropic, **19**:*389*
nonpotential (transverse), **19**:388,
19:389, **19**:395, **19**:407
quenched, **19**:259, **19**:389
renormalization, **19**:397–399
static, **19**:389
topological, **19**:42
Disorder line, **16**:35, **16**:47–8, **16**:54–5,
16:*56*, **16**:75, **16**:80–1, **16**:89,
16:91–3, **16**:*106*, **16**:111
Disorder of chemical origin, **14**:332–41
Disorder temperature, **1**:348
Disorder variables
dilute magnets, **7**:154, **7**:155
Disorder-driven crossover, **14**:339–41
Disorder-induced roughness, **14**:264,
14:273
Disordered elastic media, **18**:241,
18:252–64
Disordered flux arrays, **18**:235–41
Disordered Heisenberg magnets,
coherent potential approximation,
7:216
Disordered Ising systems, **14**:30
Disordered systems, **15**:166, **18**:112–23
Disordered-incommensurate transition,
15:65
Dispersion integral, **19**:435
Dispersion relation, **5B**:311, **19**:67,
19:115
Displacement models, **15**:7–29

Displacement vector, **19**:268
Displacive ferroelectrics, **3**:647, **3**:649
Displacive phase transition, **3**:583
Displacive transition, **3**:488, **3**:646
Distance geometry, **19**:309
Distance labels, **18**:153
Distant neighbour interaction, **3**:462
Distribution function of the order
    parameter, **14**:312–13
Distribution function, **5B**:157
    cavity-cavity, **5B**:240
    particle-cavity, **5B**:240
Divergences
    bilocal operators, **19**:397–399
    local, **19**:282–284, **19**:380–381,
        19:395–396
    overlapping, **19**:324
Divergencies in local field theories,
    6:141
DLA (diffusion limited aggregation),
    12:341, **12**:343–344, **12**:357,
    12:359, **12**:360–386, **12**:392–408,
    12:419, **12**:423–430, **12**:439,
    12:453, **12**:455, **12**:458, **12**:461,
    12:468–476
    noise reduced model, **12**:374–375,
        12:471
DLPA *see* diffusion-limited pair
    annihilation (DLPA)
DNA
    double-stranded, homogeneous,
        order of transition, **7**:110–116
    melting profile, **7**:110
    non-self-entangled, **7**:133
    entanglement, **7**:134
        topology, **7**:147
    heterogeneous, helix-coil transitions,
        7:110
    non-entangled configurations, **7**:133
    single-stranded, nucleotides, sequence,
        7:110
DNA
    dynamics, **19**:215–220
    gel electrophoresis, **19**:8
    relaxation, **19**:217–219
    reptation, **19**:10
    structure, **19**:375
DO (disordered phase), **12**:110–118,
    12:123–124, **12**:131

line, **12**:253, **12**:270, **12**:298,
    12:299–306, **12**:325–327
Dobrushin boundary conditions, *see*
    Boundary conditions
Dobrushin's uniqueness condition,
    18:77–8
Dobrushin–Lanford–Ruelle (DLR)
    states, **18**:10–11
    see also Gibbs measures
Domain of attraction, **6**:553
Domain
    of attraction, large, **19**:389
    growth, **19**:47, **19**:389
    statistics, **19**:214
    wall
        in ASEP, **19**:105, **19**:117
        diffusion, **19**:149, **19**:171
        driving, **19**:185, **19**:187
        duality, **19**:74, **19**:79, **19**:81,
            19:163, **19**:176, **19**:179,
            19:188–191, **19**:210–211
        dynamics, **19**:134–136
        fluctuations, **19**:141–143,
            19:148–149
        hopping, **19**:188
        motion, **19**:145
        random walk, **19**:122, **19**:135,
            19:143, **19**:148
        as shock, **19**:144–145
        and spin–spin interaction, **19**:36,
            19:47
        stability, **19**:124–125
        types, **19**:146
Domain splitting and merging, **17**:87–90
    critical angle, **17**:89
Domain wall renormalization group
    (DWRG), **18**:232, **18**:248,
    18:249–50
Domain wall, **10**:13, **10**:14, **10**:30,
    10:49, **10**:272, **10**:319, **10**:326,
    10:358, **14**:138
Domain walls
    and 4–8/2/1 model behaviour, **13**:268
    in commensurate-incommensurate,
        transitions, **13**:290–291
    K models, **13**:291, **13**:292–294
    density, **13**:286
    perturbations, **13**:248
    4–8/2/1 dimer model, **13**:249–250

Domain walls, **11**:37, **11**:40–41, **11**:44,
    11:48, **12**:124, **12**:221, **15**:9,
    15:29
  direction, **12**:229–230
  dislocations, **12**:220
  energy, **12**:227, **12**:235, **12**:250
  entropies, **12**:220, **12**:237
  interactions, **12**:250, **12**:258
  width, **12**:226–233
Domains, **8**:72
  equilibrium shape, **8**:72
  growth, Lifshitz–Slyozov prediction,
    8:355
  structure, **8**:30
  walls, **8**:30
Dominant *(n-m)* isotropy, **6**:378
Double critical point, **9**:227
Double cross, **3**:259
Double diamond phase, **16**:1*45*
Double poles, two-loop diagrams,
    19:345–346
Double ϵ-expansion, **19**:364–368
Dressed interaction, **6**:278, **6**:279
Drift
  diffusion-limited annihilation, **19**:195
  distance, **19**:149
  and hard-core interaction, **19**:104
  velocity, **19**:23, **19**:60, **19**:116,
    19:146–147, **19**:215, **19**:216,
    19:217, **19**:403
Drifting fixed point, **14**:207–8
Driven-interface models, **17**:175–179
Driving process, effects, **19**:195, **19**:199,
    19:203
Drop, **12**:4–6, **12**:15
  sessile, **12**:2–4
Droplet condensation model, **1**:86
Droplet model, **2**:96, **2**:444, **3**:435,
    3:440, **3**:469, **3**:477, **5B**:70, **5B**:71,
    5B:88, **5B**:95, **5B**:103, **9**:25, **9**:289
  classical, **8**:279–284, **8**:342
  Fisher, **8**:342
Droplet picture, **5A**:10, **5A**:11
Droplet, **12**:229, **12**:232, **12**:244,
    12:248, **12**:295, **12**:310
Droplets
  boundaries at criticality, **19**:429–430
  energy cost, **19**:431
  instanton behaviour, **19**:441–442

  nature, **19**:260
  spin, **19**:431
Droplets, **5A**:12, **5A**:167, **8**:69, **14**:142
  growth, in binary fluids, **8**:416
  liquid, **8**:72
Drumhead model, **10**:290–1, **10**:293,
    10:295–7, **10**:309, **10**:336, **10**:339,
    10:356
  lattice, **10**:341
  Potts models, **10**:342
Dry spreading, **14**:143
Drying, **12**:13
  transition, **12**:7, **12**:57
Dual lattice, **2**:115, **2**:116
Dual linear programming problem,
    18:183
Dual parameter, **1**:272, **1**:275, **1**:296
Dual relation, **1**:278
Dual string model, **11**:56
Dual transformation, **10**:39
Duality argument, **3**:663
Duality relation, **3**:661
Duality transformation in
    renormalization group, **6**:13
Duality transformation, **2**:108
d-weights, **2**:231, **2**:232–4, **2**:239
Duality transformations, **12**:328
Duality, **3**:662, **14**:41
Duality, domain wall, **19**:74, **19**:79,
    19:81, **19**:163, **19**:176, **19**:179,
    19:188–191, **19**:210–211
Duality, position space methods, **7**:248
Dumbell, **3**:11, **3**:70l, **11**:12
Dynamic critical behaviour, **10**:245
  dynamical interfacial phenomena,
    10:358
  dynamical scaling, **10**:345
Dynamic critical phenomena, **5B**:4,
    5B:73, **5B**:103, **11**:79
Dynamic evolution, **5B**:24
Dynamic functional, **17**:6, **17**:35, **17**:60
  randomly driven and multi-
    temperature models, **17**:103
  standard model, **17**:35, **17**:61, **17**:62
Dynamic matrix ansatz, **19**:89–95,
    19:99, **19**:101
Dynamic mean-field theory, **17**:5,
    17:16–19, **17**:141
Dynamic model, **5B**:15

Dynamic response, moment calculations, **7:**222–223
Dynamic scaling forms, relaxation times, **7:**198
Dynamic scaling hypothesis, **5B:**75, **5B:**80, **5B:**81, **5B:**85, **5B:**86
Dynamic scaling theory, **3:**633
Dynamic scaling, **5B:**380, **7:**33–36, **17:**78
   diluted ferromagnets, exact results, **7:**196–198
   disclination unbinding transition, **7:**71–74
   finite size scaling and, **8:**198–201
   in helium films, **7:**31–39
Dynamic shear viscosity, **7:**71
Dynamic stochastic model, **5B:**6
Dynamic structure factor, **15:**14
Dynamic susceptibility, **5B:**22, **5B:**23, **5B:**82, **5B:**90
Dynamical amplitudes, **14:**21, **14:**31
Dynamical equations, **19:**5
Dynamical exponent, **14:**21, **19:**65, **19:**158, **19:**385, **19:**387, **19:**389, **19:**403
Dynamical properties, **14:**75
Dynamical RG, **14:**46
Dynamical scaling, **2:**488, **5A:**101, **5A:**128, **5A:**234, **5A:**236, **5A:**239–256, **5A:**257, **5A:**259, **5A:**260, **5A:**262, **5A:**263, **5A:**265, **5A:**278, **5A:**298, **5A:**313, **5A:**325, **19:**63–65
Dynamical scaling function, **5A:**145
Dynamical scaling hypothesis, **5A:**170, **5A:**281
Dynamical scaling predictions, **5A:**144
Dynamical structure function, **19:**59–61
Dynamics of phase transitions, **2:**445
Dynamics, **14:**19–21, **14:**30–1, **14:**46, **14:**69–75, **14:**89–92, **14:**365
   first-order phase transitions, **8:**267–465
   stochastic, **19:**3–4, **19:**14
   ultraslow, **19:**389
Dyson equation, **3:**175, **5A:**228, **5B:**206, **5B:**231, **6:**554, **7:**216
   many-body, **3:**139

Dyson–Schwinger equation, **19:**69–70, **19:**166, **19:**308
Dysprosium aluminium garnet, **2:**195, **5A:**119, **5A:**120
Dzialoshinsky–Moriya interaction, **3:**579, **3:**581, **3:**582

E

Earthquake models, **17:**186
Easy access systems, exponential low temperature dependents, **7:**167
Easy axes, **6:**400, **6:**401
Easy axis antiferromagnet, **5A:**258, **5A:**259, **5A:**280, **5A:**281
Easy axis ferromagnet, **5A:**258, **5A:**259, **5A:**279, **5A:**280, **5A:**298
Easy axis of magnetization, **5A:**10
Easy plane of magnetization, **5A:**10
Easy-axis anisotrophy, **10:**255
Eddington numbers, **1:**250
Edge boundaries, **10:**3, **10:**4, **10:**237
   free energy, **10:**237
   operator, **10:**239
Edge disjoint, **3:**61
Edge perimeter, **3:**82
   full, **3:**83
Edge permutation group, **3:**27, **3:**28
Edmonds' algorithm, **18:**180–1, **18:**233
Edmonds' theorem, **18:**181
Edwards model, **19:**279, **19:**314, **19:**434, **19:**436, **19:**439–441, **19:***450*
Edwards–Anderson Ising spin glass
   position space methods, **7:**247
   three-dimensional, position space methods, **7:**248
   two-dimensional, position space methods, **7:**248
Edwards–Anderson model, **18:**221–3, **18:**228
Edwards–Anderson order parameter, **15:**82, **15:**100, **15:**102–4, **15:**133, **15:**134
Edwards–Anderson spin glass model
   Monte Carlo methods, **7:**207
   series expansion methods, **7:**232
Edwards–Sokal coupling, **18:**48–9, **18:**53, **18:**58–9

Edwards–Wilkinson universality, **19:**235
Effective exponent, **5B:**39, **5B:**40, **5B:**48, **5B:**80, **9:**53, **9:**54, **9:**88, **9:**89, **9:**90
Effective exponents, **8:**53
Effective field boundary condition, **5B:**4, **5B:**44
Effective field boundary, **5B:**64
Effective field theory, **19:**378
Effective Hamiltonian, **14:**150, **14:**153, **14:**154, **14:**177, **14:**185–7, **19:**269, **19:**270, **19:**279, **19:**436
Effective medium approximation, **7:**215–221
Effective medium theory, bond-diluted resistor networks, **7:**221
Effective potential, **15:**18
Effective range, **5B:**112
Effective surface field, **5B:**34
Effective system, **19:**6
Effective-field approximation, **3:**150, **3:**163
Ehrenfest urn model, **2:**460
Eigenexponents, **14:**10
Eigenoperators, **6:**31, **6:**32, **6:**34, **6:**36, **6:**38, **6:**40, **6:**45, **6:**54, **6:**67, **6:**82, **6:**96, **6:**110, **6:**365, **14:**33
  complete set, **6:**56
  RG transformation linearized around a fixed point, **6:**9
  translational invariant, **6:**55, **6:**59
Eigenperturbations, **14:**208–11
Eigenstates, **19:**31, **19:**39, **19:**90
Eigenvalue exponents, **9:**144
Eigenvalue spectrum, **5B:**142
Eigenvalues, **6:**32, **6:**365, **6:**437, **6:**482, **6:**519, **6:**547
  irrelevant, **6:**461
  marginal, **6:**434
  relevant, **6:**438, **6:**440
Eigenvectors, **6:**519, **6:**520, **19:**54, **19:**90
Eight vertex configuration, **3:**659
Eight vertex model, **3:**579, **3:**583, **19:**5, **19:**52, **19:**160
Eight vertex problem, **1:**451
  equivalence with Ising problem, **1:**466

Eight-vertex (8V) (symmetric) model, **11:**2, **11:**3, **11:**30, **11:**32, **11:**115
Eight-vertex model, **8:**229, **9:**23, **12:**252, **12:**273, **12:**281, **12:**291–293, **12:**299, **12:**304
Einstein formula, **5B:**91
Einstein relation, **19:**215
Elastic constants, **7:**50
Elastic energy, **19:**371
Elastic force, polymers, entanglement, **7:**144
Elastic free energy, **16:**97, **16:**134–35, **16:**137, **16:**140, **16:**149
Elastic glasses, **18:**234–5, **18:**239–41, **18:**252–5, **18:**258–64
Elastic interactions, **10:**257
Elastic manifolds *see* polymers
Elastic terms, anharmonicity, **19:**376
Elastic-free energy, **7:**45
  functional, **7:**4
Elasticity, polymers, entanglement and, **7:**134
Elasticity, renormalization, **19:**401, **19:**404, **19:**405
'Electric' field, **17:**11
Electric field, **19:**104, **19:**167, **19:**217
Electric quadrupole component, **12:**223
Electrical resistance anomaly, **14:**86
Electrochemical deposition processes, **12:**387–391
Electrolyte, **12:**189
Electron diffraction, low energy, **8:**3
Electron paramagnetic resonance, **5A:**320–324
Electron, motion, **19:**167
Electron-hole condensation, in series conductors, **8:**441–443
Electron-spin resonance, **14:**92
Electronic orbital motion, **5A:**91
Electrostatic forces, conformational phase transitions in macromolecules and, **7:**102
Electrostatic interaction energy adsorption of macromolecules to surfaces and, **7:**107
Electrostatic interactions, **16:**98
Electrostatic repulsion, **16:**155
Elementary graphs, **2:**232

Elementary particle physics, **6**:4
 characteristic length and, **6**:2
Ellipsometry, **12**:141, **12**:153
Embedding, **3**:3, **3**:57, **3**:59, **3**:61, **3**:65,
 3:66, **3**:72, **3**:73, **3**:97, **3**:98, **3**:105,
 3:108, **3**:109, **3**:110, **3**:117, **3**:176,
 3:287, **3**:375
 computer counting, **3**:97, **3**:98
 computer representation, **3**:105
 connected graph, **3**:73
 free, **3**:117, **3**:176, **3**:177
 low-temperature count, **3**:100
 strong, **3**:59, **3**:61, **3**:63, **3**:78, **3**:117,
  3:411
 in symmetry system, **3**:98
 weak, **3**:59, **3**:61, **3**:63, **3**:67, **3**:72,
  3:117, **3**:134, **3**:176, **3**:177,
  3:269, **3**:270
Emission operators, **1**:234
Empty interval probabilities, **19**:167,
 19:173, **19**:181, **19**:184, **19**:212,
 19:237–238
Emulsification failure, **16**:144
Enantiodromy, **19**:74–75, **19**:81n, **19**:82,
 19:162–164, **19**:173
Energetic approximation, **3**:453, **3**:456
 to susceptibility, **3**:453
Energy balance, **14**:258–60
Energy
 barriers, random, **19**:42
 –energy correlation function, **19**:257,
  19:408
 expression, integral representation,
  19:86
 function, Ising model, **19**:48
 gap
  finite, **19**:67–68
  free fermion systems, **19**:191–192,
   19:193
  limit behaviour, **19**:69, **19**:193
  and relaxation time, **19**:171
  volume independent, **19**:110,
   19:111
Energy correlation function, **6**:516
Energy correlation time, **5B**:79
Energy density correlation function,
 5A:81
Energy density, **6**:272
Energy density, local, **8**:49

Energy fluctuation density, **6**:526
Energy fluctuations, **5A**:312
Energy gap function, **5A**:36
Energy gap, **14**:106
Energy operator, **6**:369
Energy relaxation time, **5B**:79
Energy relaxation, **2**:489
Energy representation, **2**:14
Energy, **3**:232, **3**:314, **3**:637
 exchange, **3**:247
 reduced, **3**:379
Energy-energy correlation, **6**:114, **6**:183,
 6:187, **6**:192, **6**:197, **6**:462
Energy-energy correlations, **1**:105
Energy-momentum tensor, **11**:56
Ensembles, **1**:11
 canonical, **1**:11, **1**:12, **1**:36, **1**:37,
  1:63, **1**:64, **1**:360
 grand canonical, **1**:11, **1**:12, **1**:36,
  1:37, **1**:43
 microcanonical, **1**:11, **1**:12, **1**:37
 thermodynamic equivalence, **1**:36
Entangled configurations, **7**:142
Entanglement classes,
 macromolecules, **7**:134
Entanglement index, **7**:136, **7**:142,
 7:143
Entanglements
 Aharonov–Bohm effect and, **7**:147
 macromolecules, **7**:131–147
  with continuous curve, **7**:134–138
 polymers, topology, **7**:147
 with straight line, **7**:138–45
Enthalpy coefficients, **3**:536
Enthalpy series, **3**:528
Enthalpy, **3**:534, **3**:552, **5A**:377
 magnetic, **3**:551
 reduced, **3**:523
Entropic repulsion, **10**:59, **10**:60, **10**:67
Entropy breathing, **12**:226, **12**:237,
  12:307–315
 dislocation, **12**:307
 meander, **12**:220, **12**:237, **12**:255,
  12:258, **12**:271, **12**:282, **12**:307,
  12:311, **12**:314–316
Entropy change, **3**:314
Entropy density, **5A**:181, **5A**:183, **6**:272
Entropy mode, **5A**:250, **5A**:253,
 5A:254, **5A**:256

Entropy of fusion, **5B:**193
Entropy of mixing, **16:**17, **16:**72, **16:**147
Entropy representation, **2:**14, **2:**111
Entropy surface, **2:**2, **2:**5, **2:**7, **2:**10, **2:**12 primitive, **2:**4, **2:**6
Entropy, **1:**33, **1:**35, **1:**78, **1:**101, **1:**178, **1:**180, **1:**199, **1:**200, **1:**224, **1:**225, **1:**231, **1:**249, **3:**551, **3:**553, **3:**584, **3:**595, **3:**621, **5A:**180, **5A:**250, **5A:**253, **5A:**254, **5A:**256, **5A:**260, **5A:**330, **5A:**337, **5A:**354, **14:**265–7
Landau Hamiltonian and, **6:**16
maximum-entropy principle, **17:**18
residual, **1:**266
Entropy, K dimer model, **13:**287
Entry parameter, **3:**383
Epidemic, **2:**199
Epidemics, **17:**172
Epsilon algorithm in sequence extrapolation, **13:**36–37
Equal areas condition, **2:**90
Equation of motion, **14:**20
Equation of state, **1:**11, **2:**40, **2:**41, **2:**45, **2:**46, **2:**49, **2:**61, **2:**63, **2:**65, **2:**70, **2:**71, **2:**72, **2:**73, **2:**74, **2:**75, **2:**76, **5B:**168, **5B:**178, **5B:**189, **5B:**191, **5B:**193, **5B:**194, **5B:**195, **5B:**370, **6:**161, **6:**188, **6:**202, **6:**208, **6:**213, **6:**216, **6:**221, **6:**236, **6:**237, **6:**256; 273–276, **6:**295, **6:**297, **6:**326, **6:**329, **6:**330, **6:**332, **6:**333, **6:**334, **6:**335, **6:**336, **6:**337, **6:**339, **6:**340, **6:**341, **6:**342, **6:**383, **6:**535, **8:**66, **8:**67, **9:**129, **9:**130, **9:**131, **9:**133, **9:**137, **14:**4, **14:**15, **14:**21, **14:**47, **14:**51, **14:**77, **14:**81, **14:**85–7
anisotropic corrections, **6:**235
critical, **2:**211, **2:**379, **2:**407–9, **2:**411–2, **2:**414, **2:**417, **2:**421, **2:**424
dipolar, **6:**389
ε-expansion for, **6:**1, **6:**293–354
homogeneous, **3:**444
in critical region, **3:**435, **3:**444, **3:**450
magnetic, **3:**400, **3:**402, **6:**131
mean field, **3:**445, **3:**447
Padé virial, **5B:**191
scaling, **2:**55, **3:**452

Equations of motion, **6:**153-157
calculations, **19:**464
consequences, **19:**305, **19:**466
decoupling, **19:**164–167, **19:**169
free fermion model, **19:**184, **19:**187, **19:**213–214
Glauber dynamics, **19:**187
and global rescaling, **19:**305–307
for magnetization, **19:**187
Pauli matrices, **19:**182
solving, **19:**141
for time-dependent operators, **19:**198
for vacancy strings, **19:**169
Equilibrium distribution, **5B:**14, **5B:**20, **19:**54, **19:**104–105, **19:**117
systems, **19:**4, **19:**57–58
Equilibrium mass fraction, **5A:**182
Equilibrium order parameter, **5A:**50
Equilibrium problem, **3:**473
Equilibrium properties, **5A:**58
Equilibrium state, canonical, **1:**139, **1:**144, **1:**146, **1:**156, **1:**157
grand canonical, **1:**143, **1:**144, **1:**151, **1:**170
Equivalence class, **1:**143
Equivalence, **19:**72–74
Equivalent neighbour model, **3:**286, **3:**306, **3:**321, **3:**463, **3:**497
$Er^1_2Na^1_2MoO_4$, **3:**581
Ergodic average, **1:**148
Ergodic measures, law of large numbers, **18:**14
Ergodic system, **2:**473
Ergodicity property, **15:**88–9
Ergodicity, **1:**139, **1:**150, **5B:**7, **5B:**21, **19:**54–57
Error analysis
for Padé approximants, **13:**57–59
for ratio method, **13:**34
for sequence extrapolation, **13:**36, *see also* Confidence limits
Error estimates, **3:**183
Error function, **19:**88
$ErVO_4$, **3:**581
Escher, M C, **17:**12
Essential singularities, **10:**305
Essential singularity, **5B:**133, **7:**50, **7:**180, **8:**74, **12:**15, **12:**153, **12:**303, **12:**330

coexistence curve, **8**:69
first-order phase transition, **8**:316–319
in percolation problems, **8**:449–451
interface free energy, **8**:73
specific heat, **7**:22
Ethane, **5A**:327, **5B**:349, **5B**:356,
　　5B:357, **5B**:358, **5B**:365, **5B**:367,
　　5B:371, **5B**:372, **5B**:373, **5B**:377,
　　5B:385
　+ ethanol, **9**:184
　+ n-eicosane, **9**:188, **9**:189
　+ n-heptadecane, **9**:190
　　+ n-hexadecane + n-eicosane,
　　　9:183, **9**:188, **9**:190
　　+ n-nonadecane, **9**:188, **9**:189
　　+ nonadecane + eicosane, **9**:188
　　+ n-octadecane, **9**:189, **9**:190
Ethane/carbon dioxide system, **5B**:375,
　　5B:377
　azeotropic, **5B**:358, **5B**:361
Ethanol + benzene, **9**:203
Euclidean field theory, S-matrix, **6**:524
Euclidean group, **1**:170, **1**:171
Euclidean invariant, **1**:151, **1**:170, **1**:171,
　　1:173
Euclidean matching problem, **18**:197,
　　18:233–4
Euclidean symmetry, **1**:152
Euctidean
　boson field theory, **9**:281
　free field theory, **9**:241–8
　random field theory, **9**:258
Euler characteristic, **16**:112, **16**:113,
　　16:133
Euler equation, **5A**:48, **5A**:50, **5A**:58,
　　5A:67, **6**:311
Euler relation, **1**:277
Euler transformation, **3**:205, **3**:225,
　　3:231, **3**:526, **3**:633
Euler transformations, **13**:121
　and Padé approximants, **13**:55
Euler
　β-function, **19**:301
　Γ function, **19**:444
Euler's law (of edges), **2**:213, **2**:265
Euler's relation, **11**:37
Euler's theorem, **2**:277, **2**:282
Euler–Lagrange equation, **16**:81, **16**:87,
　　16:98

Euler–MacLaurin formula, **12**:51
Europium neutron scattering, **5A**:137,
　　5A:138, **5A**:141, **5A**:142, **5A**:143
Europium oxide surfaces, polarized
　photoemission, **8**:56
Europium oxide, **5A**:135, **5A**:136,
　　5A:137, **5A**:138, **5A**:139, **5A**:142,
　　5A:143, **5A**:145, **5A**:315, **5A**:316,
　　6:44
Europium sulphide, **5A**:135, **5A**:136,
　　5A:137, **5A**:138, **5A**:139, **5A**:142,
　　5A:143, **5A**:145
Europium sulphide, model, **7**:206
EuS, **2**:194
Evaporating edge [of interface], **17**:86
Evaporation, **1**:228
Exact calculations, finite size scaling,
　　8:201–223
Exact exponent identities, **19**:272
Exact finite methods, **2**:363
Exact results, **8**:50–64
Exact simulation, **18**:69
Exact solution
　dynamical equations, **19**:5
　equilbrium systems, **19**:4
　exclusion processes, **19**:136, **19**:148
　many body systems, **19**:30–31, **19**:33,
　　19:34
　nonequilibrium systems, **19**:4
　random sequential absorption
　process, **19**:167
　reaction–diffusion systems, **19**:5
　three state systems, **19**:29
Exact solutions, **3**:183, **10**:78
Exactly soluble models, **7**:173–202
Exactly solved models, surfaces, critical
　exponents, **8**:54
Excess energy, **17**:84–85
　as function of shift angle, **17**:*88*
Excess n-point potentials, **5B**:216
Exchange anisotropy, **6**:526
Exchange constants, **8**:71
Exchange coupling, **1**:228, **14**:47,
　　15:55
$(1/n)$-expansion, **14**:52
Exchange energy, **3**:247
Exchange enhancement, **8**:32, **8**:44
　at surfaces, **8**:22
Exchange integral, **8**:15

Exchange interaction, **5A:**199
Exchange interaction, dilute magnets, **7:**155
Exchange interactions, **6:**358, **6:**361, **8:**20, **8:**64
  cubic, **6:**361
  dipolar, **6:**386
  Dyzaloshinski–Moriya, **6:**361
  isotropic, **6:**361
    dipolar, **6:**361
    long-range, **6:**361
      isotropic, reviewing the dipolar problems, **6:**382
  spin-anisotropic, **6:**361
ϵ-Expansion, **8:**48, **8:**49, **8:**168
Exchange models, two spin, **2:**461, **2:**465
Exchange terms, **6:**360
Exchanged-coupled spin system, **2:**449
Excitation, **3:**371
Excitons, **19:**13, **19:**49, **19:**176, **19:**196, **19:**222–223
Excluded volume, **3:**118, **12:**24, **12:**51, **12:**67
Exclusion process
  asymmetric, **19:**43, **19:**101, **19:**104, **19:**158
  discrete time, **19:**225–229
  elementary move, **19:**41, **19:***42*
  exact results, **19:**136, **19:**148
  generalized, **19:**144
  integrability, **19:**50–51
  interaction, **19:**86, **19:**114–115, **19:**116
  and interface dynamics, **19:**231
  k-step, **19:**125
  nonequilibrium, **19:**103
  partial, **19:**43, **19:**51
  partially asymmetric, **19:**113
  partially symmetric, **19:**96–97
  with particle injection and absorption, **19:**79
  quantum Hamiltonian formalism, **19:**41–45
  single species, **19:**45–47
  symmetric, **19:**43, **19:**79–102, **19:**89, **19:**101
  traffic flow, **19:**154–157
  two-type, **19:**51

universality, **19:**199
  see also asymmetric simple exclusion process (ASEP); symmetric simple exclusion process (SSEP)
Expanded cactus, **2:**211
$1/n$-Expansions, **6:**218, **6:**249–292, **6:**359, **6:**373, **6:**378, **6:**522
Expansion
  bare, **3:**163
  ε, **9:**21, **9:**54
  Flory approximation, **19:**354–355
  high-temperature, **3:**506, **3:**600, **3:**663
  $1/d$, **19:**449–450
  $1/n$, **9:**21
  low temperature, **3:**225, **3:**371, **3:**405, **3:**506, **3:**571, **3:**654, **3:**663
  of tricritical exponents, **9:**122
  parameters, **19:**348
  renormalized, **3:**140
    see also perturbative expansion
  unrenormalized, **3:**140, **3:**163
Expectation operators, **19:**4
Expectation values
  calculation, **19:**204
  connected and nonconnected, **19:**306
  decay, **19:**66
  density, **19:**168
  equal time, **19:**394
  experimental measurement, **19:**22–23
  observables, **19:**280, **19:**282, **19:**293, **19:**305–307, **19:**366–367, **19:**378, **19:**467
  quantitative behaviour, **19:**193
  spectral decomposition, **19:**62
  stationary, **19:**54, **19:**58
  transformed systems, **19:**72
Experimental data, **14:**19
Experimental error estimate, **5B:**19
Experimental error, **5B:**13
Experimental measurement, **14:**12
Experimental realizations, **19:**215–223, **19:**385
Experimental results, **14:**5, **14:**42, **14:**76–92, **14:**120
Experimental studies, **14:**12, **14:**14
Exponent inequalities, **1:**103
Exponent relations, **2:**440
  critical, **2:**440

Exponent renormatization, 3:325
Exponent z, 5A:170
Exponent α, 6:554
Exponent γ
evaluation, 6:280
Exponent η, 6:73–77, 6:182, 6:280
higher order calculations, 6:76
Exponential decay, 19:63, 19:65
Exponential decays in two-point
correlation functions, 17:32–33
Exponential relaxation, 19:67
Exponentially weak-mixing, 18:72,
18:77, 18:84–91, 18:116–23
Exponents, 6:128, 6:257, 6:276, 6:285,
6:288, 6:290, 6:293–354, 6:511,
6:512, 6:513, 6:537 (see also
Critical exponents)
calculation of, 6:276–292
cubic, 6:287
dipolar, 6:388
higher order relevant, 6:97
renormalized, critical, 6:414
Extended scaling
method, 12:224, 12:275–277
relations, 12:280, 12:291–292
Extensive operators, 5A:3
Extensive property, 3:74, 3:75, 3:76
Extraordinary transitions, 8:12, 8:20,
8:23, 8:29, 8:37, 8:41, 8:43, 8:44,
8:50
lower critical dimensionality, 8:53
to bulk exponents, 8:49
Extrapolation length, 8:6–19, 8:20, 8:30,
8:48, 8:66, 10:92, 10:94
demagnetizing fields and, 8:32
microscopic interaction parameters
and, 8:15–18
Extrapolation methods, finite size
scaling, 8:224–228
Extrapolation, 3:183, 3:189, 3:194,
3:197, 3:198, 3:199, 3:200, 3:207,
3:212, 3:213, 3:216, 3:230, 3:232,
3:234, 3:302, 3:304, 3:323, 3:324,
19:349–351, 19:406, 19:429,
19:430, 19:433, 19:447, 19:448
Extremal dynamics, 18:195–6
Extremal point see Extremum point
Extreme anisotropic rates, 17:148–154
Extremum point, 15:97, 15:98, 15:102

ε-expansion
divergences, 19:360
double, 19:364–368
extrapolation, 19:349, 19:350, 19:429,
19:446–447
numerical predictions, 19:264
renormalization, 19:393, 19:439
technical convenience, 19:256
and variational estimates, 19:446–447
Wilson–Fisher, 19:446
ε-expansion, 11:86, 14:45, 14:46, 14:52,
14:55, 14:59, 14:60, 14:63–9,
14:71–5, 14:81, 14:86, 14:87,
14:92, 14:95, 14:96, 14:101,
14:105–7, 14:114, 14:117,
14:364
φ-Expansions, 6:378
ε-expansion, 10:82, 10:340
ε′ (= d − 2) expansion, 10:209
critical surface exponents, 10:186
ordinary and special transition, 10:183
ε-Expansions, 6:293–354, 6:373, 6:379,
6:392, 6:420, 6:510, 6:522, 6:537,
6:544
in Feynman diagrams, 6:1

F

F model, 3:657, 3:661, 3:662, 3:664,
3:665, 11:30, 11:31, 11:35, 11:39
Kagome, 11:46
low temperature series, 3:665
F-model, 6:99, 6:103, 10:41, 10:44,
12:303–4
general, 1:344, 1:345
modified, 1:456, 1:466
on square lattice, 1:343, 1:385, 1:423,
1:427, 1:433, 1:449
on triangular lattice, 1:469
Facets, 14:139, 14:140
Fast rate limit [for standard model],
17:8, 17:149–154
FCC lattice, 14:60
FDT see Fluctuation-dissipation theorem
Fe₃(PO₄)₂. 4H₂O, 3:582
Fermi annihilation, 1:208
Fermi anticommutation relations, 1:209,
1:210
Fermi edge, 19:40

Fermi gas, entropy, **10**:33
Fermi numbers, **1**:250
Fermi operators, **1**:206, **1**:208, **1**:209,
    1:233, **1**:234, **1**:236, **1**:254, **1**:262,
    1:263, **1**:266
Fermi particles, **2**:468
Fermi statistics, **1**:128
Fermi surface, **12**:253, **12**:261–263,
    12:282, **15**:2–3
Fermion interaction quartics, **19**:194
Fermion operators, **2**:469, **3**:175
Fermion theory, **12**:221, **12**:247, **12**:249,
    12:253, **12**:258, **12**:286–288,
    12:294–296, **12**:329–333
    Hamiltonian, **12**:250
Fermion variable, **3**:175
    α-Fe$_2$O$_3$, **3**:582
Fermionic operators, **19**:175, **19**:177
Fermions *see* free fermion approach
Fermions, **1**:32, **1**:38, **1**:50, **1**:94, **1**:129
Ferrielectric model,
    related problems, **1**:333, **1**:445
Ferrimagnet, **1**:307, **1**:308, **3**:300, **3**:364,
    3:372, **3**:373
    Ising, **3**:363
Ferrimagnetic polynomial, **3**:417
Ferrimagnetism, **1**:271, **1**:289, **3**:294,
    3:363
Ferromagnet,
    dilute, **1**:312, **1**:314
Ferromagnetism,
    dilute, **1**:271, **1**:312
Ferro-electrics, order-disorder,
    2:491–2
Ferroelectric model, **1**:9, **1**:25, **3**:183
    general, **1**:346
Ferroelectric transition, **1**:426, **1**:436,
    1:437
Ferroelectric transitions, **5A**:297,
    14:145
Ferroelectrics, **1**:25, **1**:266, **3**:646,
    5B:5, **8**:6, **8**:29, **8**:30, **8**:31, **8**:33,
    15:23
    displacive, **3**:647, **3**:649
Ferromagnet, **3**:365, **3**:366, **3**:367,
    3:372, **3**:444, **3**:453, **5A**:36, **5A**:37,
    5A:138, **5A**:273, **5A**:275, **5A**:277,
    5A:287, **5A**:323, **5A**:325, **5B**:5
    amorphous, **5B**:339

classical, **3**:300
dilute, **5B**:260, **5B**:319, **5B**:335
insulating, **3**:572
isotropic, **5A**:203, **5A**:205, **5A**:257,
    5A:258, **5A**:282
planar, **5A**:280, **5A**:282, **5A**:284,
    5A:294
random, **5B**:43, **5B**:325
random dilute, **5B**:317
randomly dilute, **3**:293
spin $\frac{1}{2}$, **5B**:260
three-dimensional, **5A**:135–147
Ferromagnetic exchange, **15**:92
Ferromagnetic Heisenberg models,
    coherent potential approximation,
    7:217
Ferromagnetic interactions, **14**:47
Ferromagnetic interbranch interactions,
    15:37
Ferromagnetic model, **3**:307
Ferromagnetic ordering, **3**:309, **15**:94,
    15:97, **15**:99
Ferromagnetic polynomial, **3**:413, **3**:414,
    3:415, **3**:416, **3**:417
Ferromagnetic spin system, **5B**:260
Ferromagnetic structure, **5A**:93
Ferromagnetic system, **6**:296
Ferromagnetic transition, **5A**:7, **14**:59
Ferromagnetism, **3**:358, **3**:361, **19**:32,
    19:200–201, **19**:230
    dilute, **2**:199, **2**:249, **2**:253, **2**:255,
    2:259
    see also Ising model
Ferromagnets Ising, molecular field
    theory, **8**:25
    Ising, surfaces, local critical
        behaviour, Landau theories,
        8:6–10
    non-ferromagnetic sheet at surfaces of,
        8:56
Ferromagnets, **14**:85
Ferromagnets, anisotropic, **6**:390
    anisotropic Ising-like, **6**:392
    isotropic, **6**:387
    dipolar, **6**:420
Ferrous fluoride, **5A**:120, **5A**:121,
    5A:122, **5A**:129, **5A**:131, **5A**:134,
    5A:279, **5A**:282, **5A**:283, **5A**:315,
    5A:325

Feynman diagrammatics, **5B**:215
Feynman diagrams, **6**:1, **6**:4, **6**:169,
    6:173, **6**:174, **6**:203, **6**:217, **6**:241,
    6:525, **6**:526, **6**:537
Feynman
    diagrams, **19**:286, **19**:290, **19**:318
    integrals, **19**:256–257, **19**:318,
        19:319, **19**:408, **19**:436
Feynman graph expansion, **10**:124,
    10:129
Feynman graph, **6**:294, **6**:299, **6**:332
    expansion, **6**:298, **6**:301, **6**:307,
        6:328, **6**:359, **6**:367, **6**:373
Feynman integral, **1**:127
Feynman integrals, **6**:170
Feynman parameter methods, **6**:323
Feynman path integrals, **6**:128, **6**:132
Feynman rules, **6**:300, **6**:302, **6**:304,
    6:305, **6**:328, **6**:329
Feynman–Kac formula, **1**:123, **1**:124,
    1:125, **1**:127, **1**:128, **1**:130
Field derivative,
    second perpendicular, **3**:607
Field h, **5A**:8
Field points, **5B**:174
Field t, **5A**:8
Field theoretic expansions, **14**:57–8
Field theoretical methods
    convenience, **19**:256
    and fluctuating lines, **19**:408
    multilocal, **19**:257, **19**:258
    nonlocal, **19**:260
    O (*N*) model, **19**:413, **19**:414
    renormalization, **19**:333–334,
        19:392–393
    tethered membranes, **19**:279–305
Field theoretical renormalization group,
    6:509, **6**:528, **6**:540–544
Field theory of surfaces, **10**:256 *et ff*
Field theory, **6**:508, **6**:522, **6**:524,
    14:365
Field variables, **6**:527
Field-space diagram, **9**:173
Field-theoretic methods, **8**:118–128
    models, **8**:287–300
    nucleation theory, **8**:300–319
Field-theoretic renormalization group
    treatments, dilute magnets,
    7:242–247

Fields, **5A**:6, **5A**:7, **5A**:16
"Fields" and "densities", **9**:171–6, **9**:180
Figure eight, **3**:11, **3**:70
Figure generating function, **3**:28
Film, **10**:77
    geometry (FG), **10**:226, **10**:231,
        10:237
Films (*see also* Thin films) critical
    temperature, asymptotic shifts,
    8:219
    helium, specific heat, **8**:251–254
    Ising, **8**:4
    Ising, scaling picture, **8**:243
    2, 6–lutidine and water, coexistence
        curves, **8**:256
    nickel, resistivity, **8**:256
Finger formation, **17**:88, **17**:112–118
    factors affecting, **17**:91, **17**:92,
        17:117
Finite cluster effects, quenched models,
    7:182
Finite cluster method, **3**:73, **3**:74, **3**:253,
    3:268, **3**:271, **3**:272, **3**:273, **3**:289,
    3:291, **3**:292, **3**:297, **3**:360, **3**:389,
    3:474
Finite cluster singularities, **7**:180
Finite cluster technique, **3**:475
Finite cluster theory, **3**:76
Finite clusters
    bond diluted square lattices,
        7:156–157
    quenched models, **7**:180
Finite convergence radius, **1**:43
Finite size effect, **3**:361, **5B**:53, **5B**:61,
    5B:95
Finite size effects
    critical temperature and, **8**:32
    renormalization, **8**:247
Finite size scaling theory, **5B**:100,
    5B:101
Finite size scaling, **8**:2, **8**:45, **8**:63,
    8:195–266
    applications, **8**:223–250
    critical dynamics, **8**:199
    defect fields, **8**:233
    exact calculations, **8**:201–223
    experimental tests, **8**:250–257
    exponents and, **8**:35–50
    extensions, **8**:181–201

extrapolation method, **8:**224–228
hypothesis, **8:**159
Monte Carlo calculations, **8:**245–247
numerical test, **8:**223–250
specific heat of helium in pores and
    films, **8:**253
theory, **8:**39, **8:**40, **8:**42
theory, exponents and, **8:**38–42
theory, homogeneity and, **8:**34, **8:**41
Finite size, **2:**105, **2:**150, **5B:**95
Finite systems, **1:**11, **19:**62–63, **19:**65
    boundary conditions, **8:**148
    correlation length, **8:**157–158
    critical point, distortions, **8:**153–157
    geometry, **8:**148
    periodic boundary conditions, **8:**164
Finite volume correlation functions,
    1:113
Finite-interaction-radius model, **15:**192
Finite-size amplitudes, **14:**41, **14:**120,
    14:364
Finite-size effects in dimers, **13:**273–277
    and anisotropy, **13:**276–277
    K models, **13:**274–275
    scaling function form, **13:**275–276
Finite-size effects, **10:**5, **10:**14, **10:**62,
    10:67, **10:**76, **10:**78, **12:**229,
    12:232, **12:**282, **12:**289, **12:**316
    scaling, **10:**78, **10:**230–1, **10:**285
    slab, **10:**333
Finite-size scaling, **11:**57, **11:**68, **11:**69,
    11:72, **11:**79, **11:**88, **11:**115,
    11:121, **14:**107, **14:**117–18
    anisotropic, **17:**44, **17:**51–52, **17:**103,
    17:147
    corrections to, **11:**75
    in mean-field approaches, **17:**16
    isotropic, **17:**7, **17:**44, **17:**51, **17:**52,
    17:140, **17:**143
Finite-size systems, **14:**4–8, **14:**11–13,
    14:26, **14:**40, **14:**42, **14:**44,
    14:99–120
First moment frequency matrix, **5A:**195,
    5A:200, **5A:**367
First order phase transition, **5A:**5, **5A:**6,
    6:159, **6:**272, **6:**347, **6:**351, **6:**365,
    6:398, **6:**409, **6:**414, **6:**416, **6:**417,
    6:420
    equilibrium properties and, **6:**8

First-order phase transition, **5B:**110,
    5B:118, **5B:**133, **5B:**147,
    5B:149,153, **5B:**194, **5B:**346
First-order
    phase transition, **9:**11
    transitions, **9:**17, **9:**22, **9:**24
First-order phase transitions, **10:**14,
    10:102, **11:**137, **11:**139
First-order transition kinetics, **19:**145
First-order transitions bulk, surface
    effects at, **8:**33–34
    dead layer and, **8:**34
    dynamics, **8:**267–465
    essential singularity, **8:**316–319
    finite size scaling, **8:**195–198
    Monte Carlo studies, **8:**374–395
    64–state Potts model, **8:**238
First-order transitions, **14:**102
First-passage time, **19:**75–77, **19:**79,
    19:84, **19:**217–218
    distribution, **19:**83–84, **19:**89
Fish shape of three-phase body,
    16:7–8
Fisher exponent renormalization,
    6:540
Fisher relation
    for correlation exponents, **3:**439
Fisher renormalization, **9:**24, **12:**227
Fisher waves, **19:**172
Fisher–de Gennes critical adsorption,
    10:210
Fisher–Essam relation, **9:**46
Fisk–Widom theory, **10:**27, **10:**284,
    10:292, **10:**305
Five-component system, **9:**227
Fixed point
    cubic, **19:**432, **19:**433
    Gaussian, **19:**365, **19:**369, **19:**404,
    19:432
    Hamiltonian, **9:**305
    Heisenberg, **19:**365, **19:**369, **19:**404,
    19:432, **19:**433
    infrared (IR), **19:**305, **19:**354, **19:**357,
    19:358, **19:**368, **19:**369–370,
    19:426, **19:**446, **19:**457, **19:**464,
    19:466
    isotropic, **19:**399, **19:**405–407
    perturbative, **19:**389
    pure self-avoidance, **19:**451

renormalization group flow,
19:404–405
topology, 9:139, 9:143
Fixed point theory, 5A:24, 5A:25,
5A:26
Fixed point, 5A:23, 5A:24, 6:34, 6:39,
6:59, 6:62, 6:87, 6:99, 6:128,
6:129, 6:175, 6:193, 6:195, 6:220,
6:222, 6:228, 6:229, 6:232, 6:235,
6:258–267, 6:272, 6:276, 6:291,
6:359, 6:364, 6:373, 6:374, 6:380,
6:382, 6:383, 6:387, 6:402, 6:426,
6:427, 6:432, 6:435, 6:436, 6:441,
6:443, 6:447, 6:449, 6:450, 6:456,
6:458, 6:462, 6:470, 6:477, 6:481,
6:482, 6:486, 6:493, 6:516, 6:522,
6:534, 6:536, 6:537, 6:539, 6:545,
6:548, 6:550, 8:48
antiferromagnetic, 6:493, 6:495
asymptotic, 6:420
Baxter–Wu, 6:493
biconical, 6:406
bifurcation, 6:66
critical, 6:61, 6:89
cubic, 6:394, 6:395, 6:396, 6:398,
6:400, 6:401
dipolar, 6:401, 6:402
decoupled, 6:406
discontinuity, renormalization group,
8:196
equivalent, 6:40, 6:41
even, 6:436
ferromagnetic, 6:495
Gaussian dipolar, 6:387
Heisenberg, 6:348, 6:351, 6:394,
6:395, 6:396, 6:398, 6:400,
6:402, 6:403, 6:404, 6:409,
6:414, 6:416
Heisenberg-like, isotropic short range,
6:386
infinite Gaussian, 6:89
infrared, 6:223
infrared stable, 6:180, 6:231
interaction, 6:229
interaction parameters, 6:484
Ising, 6:395, 6:396, 6:398, 6:409
isotropic, 6:78, 6:377, 6:390
dipolar, 6:389, 6:390
Heisenberg, 6:397, 6:416

line of, 6:99, 6:101, 6:498
long range, 6:382, 6:383
m-component, 6:403, 6:404
mixed, 6:403, 6:404, 6:408, 6:409
non-critical, 6:10, 6:61–63, 6:89
non-trivial, 6:65–80, 6:375
branching off, 6:66
odd-dominated, 6:76
operators, 6:50
range of, 6:265
renormalization group and, 6:3
renormalized, 6:414
spherical, 6:414, 6:415
stable, 6:222, 6:314
symmetry conserving operators, with,
6:44
transformation properties of
Hamiltonians and, 6:8
tricritical, 6:409
trivial (Gaussian), 6:54–60, 6:67,
6:73, 6:98, 6:121, 6:231, 6:368,
6:369, 6:375, 6:395, 6:398,
6:401, 6:403, 6:406, 6:409,
6:414
$X Y$, 6:416
Fixed points
infrared stable, 10:152–3, 10:155,
10:171, 10:219, 10:245
m-special, 10:255
Fixed points, 9:92, 9:114, 9:127, 9:135,
9:137, 9:142, 9:150, 9:292, 11:11,
11:13, 11:15, 11:16, 11:18, 11:60,
11:81, 11:90, 11:160, 11:163–4,
14:32, 14:35, 14:37
Hamiltonian, 11:61–3, 11:65, 11:67
Fixed-line, Gaussian, 17:33–37
Fixed-point, see also Standard model;
Wilson–Fisher...
Hamiltonians, 17:101–102, 17:173
randomly driven and multi-
temperature models, 17:101
Fixman theory, 5A:168
Flat phase
fluid membranes, 19:258
persistence, 19:277
self-avoiding membranes, 19:277,
19:356
in simulations, 19:451
stability, 19:263, 19:272, 19:278

Flatness criterion, **5B**:86
Flip-flop symmetry, **1**:151, **1**:152
Floating phases, **10**:5
Floating-commensurate solid transitions, **7**:64
Floquet–Bloch form, **15**:162
Flory approximations
    crumpled phase, **19**:275
    disordered system, **19**:391
    expansion, **19**:348, **19**:354–355, **19**:466n
    fractal phase, **19**:388
    one loop order, **19**:407
    phase separation, **19**:371
    self-avoidance, **19**:266–267, **19**:276, **19**:278, **19**:376
Flory scaling, **14**:42
Flory θ-temperature, **9**:21
Flory–Huggins form of entropy of mixing, **16**:72, **16**:121
Flory–Huggins theory, **9**:218
Flow algorithms, **18**:158–74
Flow augmentation lemma, **18**:173–4
Flow diagram, **6**:397, **6**:408
Flow diagrams, **19**:*368*, **19**:369, **19**:403, **19**:*404*, **19**:*432*
Flow equation, **6**:127, **6**:174, **14**:175, **14**:177
Flow in parameter space, **7**:240
Flow network, **18**:160–2
Flow, **6**:364, **6**:365
Flowchart,
    for generation of configurations, **3**:102, **3**:103
Fluctuating lines, and field theories, **19**:408
Fluctuating membrane, **16**:134–41, **16**:157–61
Fluctuating quantitites, **14**:32
Fluctuation amplitude, **3**:640
Fluctuation matrix, **3**:144
Fluctuation operator D, **10**:286
Fluctuation quantities, **2**:5
Fluctuation relation, **1**:105, **2**:116, **2**:119, **2**:377, **2**:428, **2**:429
Fluctuation series, **3**:616, **3**:620, **3**:637
    fourth order, **3**:611
Fluctuation theorem, **5B**:161, **5B**:176

Fluctuation, **3**:599, **5B**:172
    fourth order, **3**:600, **3**:607, **3**:610, **3**:623, **3**:629, **3**:636, **3**:640, **3**:647
    higher order, **3**:600
    higher order perpendicular, **3**:599
    long range order, **3**:637
    perpendicular, **3**:599, **3**:603, **3**:606
    second order, **3**:601, **3**:607, **3**:610, **3**:623, **3**:647
Fluctuation-dissipation relation, **3**:524
Fluctuation-dissipation theorem (FDT), **2**:496, **5A**:94, **5A**:193, **5B**:22, **10**:248, **10**:345, **17**:21, **17**:101, **19**:62, **19**:70, **19**:159, **19**:380, **19**:383, **19**:389, **19**:393–394
    effects, **17**:24, **17**:38–39, **17**:104
    perturbative, **19**:396, **19**:399, **19**:401
    violation of, **17**:23, **17**:25, **17**:35, **17**:192–193
Fluctuation-induced interactions, **14**:189, **14**:190, **14**:192, **14**:217
Fluctuations, **5A**:11, **5A**:12, **5A**:16, **5A**:28, **5A**:52, **5A**:62, **5A**:70, **5A**:77, **5A**:86, **5A**:356, **5A**:357, **5A**:375, **5A**:376, **5A**:379, **6**:250, **6**:511, **6**:523, **14**:32, **19**:230–236, **19**:272, **19**:374
    anharmonic, **5A**:55
    longitudinal, **5A**:94
    of order parameter, **5A**:53, **5A**:302, **5A**:313
    phase transitions and, **7**:2
    relaxation, quenching and, **8**:436–439
    transverse, **5A**:94
Fluid mechanics applications, **13**:130–134
    collapsing spherical piston shock wave, **13**:131–133
    flow problems, **13**:133–134
    Janzen–Rayleigh expansion extension, **13**:130–131
    phase transitions, **13**:130
    regular perturbation series, **13**:130
4–8/1 dimer model, **13**:244–245
    conservation property, **13**:251
    thermodynamic properties, **13**:258
4–8/2 dimer models, **13**:245
    conservation property, **13**:251

thermodynamic properties,
13:266–269
4–8/2/1 commensurate-
incommensurate transitions,
13:292–293
domain walls, **13**:249–250
4–8/4 dimer models, **13**:246–247
thermodynamic properties,
13:269–270
4–8s/2/l dimer model, **13**:245–246
Fluid Membranes, **19**:256, **19**:257–258,
19:261–262, **19**:431
almost flat, **16**:134–7
bending elasticity of, **16**:131–34
free energy of, **16**:131–34
long wavelength behavior, **16**:136
Fluid phase, **1**:172, **1**:173
Fluid, **3**:444
Fluid-fluid displacement, **12**:343–344,
12:384, **12**:387, **12**:391,
12:393–397, **12**:469, **12**:472,
12:474
Fluids, **14**:22
capillary wave theory, **8**:72
mean-critical, nucleation, **8**:395–404
mixtures, phenomenological scaling
theory for, **8**:370
Fluids, binary
hydrodynamic effects, **8**:327–331
nucleation models, **8**:310–316
spinodal decomposition, experimental
studies, **8**:411–421
Fluids, non-equilibrium steady states,
17:187–191
Flux creep, **17**:196
Flux lattice, **18**:235–6, **18**:239–41
Flux, **5A**:231
Flux-line lattice *see* Abrikosov lattice
Fock space, **1**:144, **9**:249, **9**:250
Fokker–Planck equation, **7**:67, **17**:25,
19:4, **19**:65, **19**:394
Folded phase, molybdenum disulphide,
19:274
Folding, crystallization by, **7**:121–131
Folds, number per unit of length,
infinitely long macromolecules,
7:128
Force, elastic, **12**:190
solvation, **12**:162, **12**:163, **12**:166

Forest construction, **19**:264, **19**:318,
19:320, **19**:321, **19**:322,
19:334–335
Forest fire algorithm, **18**:188–9
Forest fire models, **17**:186
Forest formula, **10**:137
FORTRAN, **3**:108
Fortuin–Kasteleyn model *see* random-
cluster model
Fortuin–Kasteleyn–Ginibre (FKG)
inequality, **18**:25–6
Fortuin–Kastelyn–Rushbrooke
inequality, **2**:248
Four loop calculations, **19**:434
Four point correlator, **19**:82
Four vertex model, **19**:160, **19**:225
Four-component fluid mixtures, **9**:59
Four-field
region, **9**:31
space, **9**:83
Four-point function, **6**:201
Four-point graphs, **6**:326
Four-spin cell approximation, **6**:485
Fourier components, Ising models
Hamiltonian, **6**:15
Fourier space, **6**:542
Fourier transform field, **6**:300
Fourier transform methods
density distribution, **19**:116,
19:208
disorder model, **19**:391
dynamic matric ansatz, **19**:93, **19**:94,
19:95
dynamical structure function,
19:59–60
flat phase stability, **19**:268
free fermion systems, **19**:192
Gaussian variational approach,
19:442–443
longitudinal and transverse projectors,
19:454–456
master equation, **19**:63
normalization, **19**:280
self-duality, **19**:82, **19**:85
string expectation value, **19**:183
Fourier transform, **6**:370, **6**:384,
6:548
Fourier transformation, **6**:553
Fourier transformed space, **6**:526

FQS (Friedan, Qiu and Shenker), **11**:57,
    11:58, **11**:99–100, **11**:103, **11**:107,
    11:111, **11**:113–6
Fractal dimension
    aluminium foil crumpling,
        19:275–276
    calculation, **19**:264, **19**:278, **19**:356,
        19:446
    crumpled swollen phase, **19**:257,
        19:259
    crumpling transition, **19**:263,
        19:264
    graphite oxide, **19**:275
    and renormalization, **19**:385
    Sierpinsky gasket, **19**:264, **19**:278
Fractal exponent, **19**:273
Fractal phase, **19**:77, **19**:277, **19**:356,
    19:388
Fractal substrates, **14**:341, **14**:345–6
Fractals, **12**:167, **12**:362
    aggregate, **12**:336, **12**:387,
        12:405–418, **12**:442, **12**:471,
        12:476
    dimensionality, 338–341, **12**:342,
        12:348, **12**:350–355, **12**:362,
        12:366–367
    geometry, **12**:336–341, **12**:342,
        12:350, **12**:395, **12**:400, **12**:403,
        12:469, **12**:470
    growth, **12**:470
    measure, **12**:336, **12**:353, **12**:354–357,
        12:405–418, **12**:427,
        12:429–430, **12**:460–462,
        12:469, **12**:474, **12**:476
    scaling, **12**:339
    self affine, **12**:341
    self similar, **12**:365
    structure, **12**:336, **12**:342, **12**:398,
        12:430–432
    substrates, 350, **12**:469
Fracton, **12**:351
Frank constant, **7**:91, **7**:93
Fredholm integral equation, **1**:186
Free 'phantom' surface, **19**:280
Free boundary condition, **18**:52–3
Free boundary conditions, *see* Boundary
    conditions
Free boundary, **5B**:3, **5B**:64
Free energy bound, **5B**:121–127

Free energy
    diluted Ising model, impurity
        concentration and, **7**:185
    for scaling of normalization factor in
        Boltzmann distribution, **7**:256
    one-dimensional diluted systems,
        7:182
    quenched models, **7**:179, **7**:184
    reference Ising model, **7**:198
    renormalization group theory and,
        7:233
    scaling and, **7**:234
Free energy functional coarse grained,
    8:295–298
    renormalization group calculations,
        8:298–300
Free energy functional, **3**:149, **9**:65–7,
    9:79, **9**:80, **9**:83, **9**:85, **9**:93, **9**:95
    coarse grained, **10**:17
Free energy, **1**:59, **1**:138, **1**:178, **1**:180,
    1:198, **1**:199, **1**:200, **3**:138, **3**:141,
    3:143, **3**:144, **3**:146, **3**:149, **3**:151,
    3:163, **3**:166, **3**:167, **3**:170, **3**:173,
    3:250, **3**:252, **3**:255, **3**:256, **3**:264,
    3:290, **3**:314, **3**:362, **3**:447, **3**:459,
    3:647, **5A**:17, **5A**:18, **5A**:25, **6**:85,
    6:365, **6**:436, **6**:440, **14**:6–13,
    14:26, **14**:29, **14**:33, **14**:35–8,
    14:40, **14**:49, **14**:51, **14**:65,
    14:103–16, **15**:88–93, **15**:105,
    15:123, **15**:138, **15**:139, **15**:157,
    19:265, **19**:*266*, **19**:279, **19**:374
    as function of scaling fields, **6**:117,
        6:118
    at condensation point, singularity,
        8:283
    concave, **1**:33
    convex, **1**:33
    density, **6**:21, **19**:436, **19**:439, **19**:442
    F model on square lattice, **1**:409
    F model on triangular lattice, **1**:469
    fluctuations, **14**:282–3
    free fermion model, **1**:452
    homogeneous equation for, **6**:452
    ice rule model, $\lambda = 0$, **1**:348, **1**:350
    IKDP model, **1**:345
    KDP model, **1**:343, **1**:394, **1**:402,
        1:408, **1**:411
    Landau Hamiltonian and, **6**:16, **6**:17

large-n limit of non-translationally
  invariant n-vector model,
  15:108–13
model system, extensive, **1**:11
modified F model, **1**:456
modified KDP model, **1**:439, **1**:453
non-analytic dependence, **1**:42
of humps, **14**:160
scaling, **6**:41–45
self-averaging, **15**:92
shape-dependent, **1**:39
singular part, **3**:450
spherical model, **15**:103
transformation law, **6**:266
unrenormalized, **3**:167
vertex renormalized, **3**:148
Free fermion approach
  boundary conditions, **19**:211–212,
    19:213
  classification, **19**:175, **19**:178,
    19:181–187
  dynamical properties, **19**:191–193
  exact results, **19**:197–200
  formalism, **19**:24, **19**:175
  Hamiltonian, **19**:178, **19**:180, **19**:189,
    19:194
  interacting particle system,
    19:199–200
  as mathematical tool, **19**:5, **19**:51
  nearest neighbour interaction, **19**:191
  one dimensional, **19**:200
  physical meaning, **19**:193
  relaxation times, **19**:191–193
  stationary states, **19**:191
  translation invariant, **19**:175–176
Free fermion model, **1**:452
Free fermions, **11**:108
Free graph enumeration, **3**:375
Free multiplicity, **3**:127, **3**:176
Free propagator *see* response function
Free propagator, **6**:302, **6**:323
Free surface, **5B**:4
Free surfaces, **2**:104
  boundary conditions, **8**:149
β-Function, **8**:175–176
  Roomany-Wyld approximants, **8**:194
  two-dimensional Ising model, **8**:177
Free-boundary conditions, **14**:106,
    14:108, **14**:109, **14**:111

Free-embedding expansion, **3**:117
Free-energy amplitudes, **14**:44
Free-energy density, **14**:32, **14**:35
Free-energy function, **5A**:3, **5A**:6, **5A**:23
Freezing, **1**:228
Frenkel–Kontorova (FK) model, **15**:3–4,
    15:58
  continuum limit, **15**:7–14
  discrete case, **15**:14–19
  dynamics, **15**:12
  extensions of, **15**:29
  fundamental features, **15**:18
  generalized, **15**:20, **15**:22
  ground states, **15**:17–19
  momentum, **15**:14
  potential energy, **15**:14
  quantum version, **15**:27
  two-dimensional variants, **15**:27-9
Frequency spectrum, **14**:20, **14**:72
Friction coefficient, **19**:401
Frobenius theorem, **1**:161, **1**:162, **1**:198
"Frozen" system, **1**:96, **1**:97
"Frozen-in" disorder, **1**:96
Frobenius' method, **2**:399
Frozen impurity, **5B**:361
Frozen randomness, **14**:161,
    14:179–80
Frozen-in problem, **3**:473, **3**:474
Frustrated magnets, **18**:197
Fugacity expansion, **5B**:172
Fugacity, **3**:145, **5B**:144–147, **5B**:171,
    5B:174, **5B**:208, **5B**:289, **11**:4,
    11:6, **11**:8, **11**:9, **11**:11–19, **11**:25,
    11:26, **11**:31, **11**:38, **11**:45, **11**:49,
    19:408, **19**:412
  electric, **11**:28
Fully packed loops (FPLs), **18**:260–1
Function,
  concave, **1**:18, **1**:19, **1**:23, **1**:36, **1**:41,
    1:59, **1**:63, **1**:84, **1**:103
  convex, **1**:18, **1**:19, **1**:33, **1**:34, **1**:35,
    1:36, **1**:95, **1**:103
Function–tangent contact, **2**:13
Functional derivative, **3**:54
Functional differential equation, **3**:122,
    3:171
Functional differentiation, **3**:53, **3**:145,
    3:170, **6**:191, **6**:526
Functional equations, **6**:526, **6**:528

Functional integral, **1**:114, **5B**:182, **5B**:185, **6**:133, **6**:151, **6**:298, **6**:524
Functional renormalization, **14**:137, **14**:200–17, **14**:276–8
Functional RG equation, **14**:46
Fusion
  asymmetry, **19**:183
  branching process, **19**:167, **19**:169, **19**:191
  diffusion-limited, **19**:163, **19**:164, **19**:168–169, **19**:181
  –pair annihilation process, **19**:183–184
  reactions, **19**:72

G

G (Griffiths, 1972), **11**:131
G-M-L equations, **6**:509
G-phase, **11**:150
Galilean invariance, **14**:295
Galilean transformation, **17**:63, **17**:145
Galilei transformation, **19**:66, **19**:199
Gallavotti —Miracle equations, **1**:149
Gap exponent Δ, **3**:435, **3**:444, **3**:600, **3**:648
Gap exponent, **2**:252, **2**:335, **2**:412, **3**:436, **3**:444, **3**:465, **14**:8
Gap exponents, **8**:38
"Gap" index, **1**:99
Gap index, *see* Gap exponent
Garden of Eden, **19**:160
Garnet structure, **3**:300
Gas-liquid
  coexistence, **12**:9–14, **12**:17–24, **12**:95–101, **12**:162
  interface, **12**:27
Gauge field, **6**:291
Gauge glasses *see* vortex glasses
Gauge invariance, **1**:152
Gauge theories, **11**:140, **11**:172, **11**:197, **11**:200
Gauge theories, and random surfaces, **19**:256
Gauss Bonnet theorem, **16**:133
Gauss looping integral, **7**:134, **7**:135
Gauss' *theorema egregium*, **16**:133, **16**:134

Gauss's continued fraction, **9**:277
Gaussian approximation, **6**:524, **6**:525, **6**:528, **6**:554
Gaussian behaviour, **6**:372
Gaussian curvature, **16**:97, **16**:133, **16**:143, **16**:149, **16**:162
Gaussian
  crossover exponent, **9**:129
  density profile, **19**:67
  disorder force, **19**:392
  elastic energy, **19**:280
  fields, **19**:390, **19**:413
  fixed point, **9**:106, **9**:135, **9**:143, **19**:365, **19**:369, **19**:404, **19**:432
  model, **9**:98, **9**:152, **9**:241, **9**:246–7, **9**:284
  moments, **9**:265
  noise, **19**:377, **19**:390, **19**:392
  phase, **19**:*386*
  random walk, **19**:64–65
  tricritical exponents, **9**:127, **9**:132
  variational ansatz, **19**:277, **19**:352, **19**:355, **19**:371, **19**:442–444
Gaussian distribution function, **15**:210
Gaussian distribution, **5B**:17
Gaussian dynamic models, **17**:33–37
Gaussian fixed point, **14**:39, **14**:170
Gaussian integrals, **6**:379
Gaussian model, **2**:120, **2**:125, **2**:126, **2**:127, **2**:130, **2**:135, **2**:138, **2**:146, **2**:147, **2**:148, **2**:149, **2**:154, **2**:156, **2**:158, **3**:183, **6**:359, **6**:366, **6**:368, **6**:371, **6**:385, **8**:60, **8**:69, **8**:72, **8**:73, **8**:74, **11**:2, **11**:24, **11**:42, **11**:70, **11**:71, **11**:84, **11**:104, **11**:107, **11**:115, **11**:166, **12**:32, **12**:71, **12**:277, **12**:279–282, **12**:327, **12**:331, **12**:332
  discrete, **10**:33, **10**:35, **10**:59, **10**:64, **10**:67, **10**:68, **10**:94, **11**:27, **11**:28, **11**:29
Gaussian orthogonal ensemble (GOE), **15**:171, **15**:179, **15**:180, **15**:224
Gaussian probability, **6**:277
Gaussian process, **5A**:192
Gaussian random field, **14**:64, **16**:162
Gaussian random matrices, **15**:192
Gaussian random variables, **15**:201, **15**:207, **15**:209

Gaussian stochastic process, **5B**:140
Gaussian white-noise potential, **15**:217
Gd, **2**:67
$Gd_2(SO_4)_3.8H_2O$, **3**:580
Gel electrophoresis, **17**:9, **17**:127, **17**:179, **17**:182–183, **19**:8, **19**:16, **19**:159, **19**:215–216
Gel point, **2**:199
Gelation, **2**:199, **12**:439, **12**:450
Gell–Mann and Low approach, **6**:523, **6**:550
Gell–Mann and Low condition, **6**:550
Gell–Mann and Low normalization point, **6**:529
Gell–Mann and Low transformation, **6**:526
Gell–Mann–Low, *see* Wilson
Gels, **8**:452
Gels, two-dimensional, **19**:278
Generalized deformed Wigner ensemble *see* Generalized Wigner ensemble
Generalized homogeneous function, **3**:503, **10**:113
Generalized hydrodynamics, **5A**:232
Generalized inverse Padé approximants, **13**:80–83
Generalized scaling, **3**:477
Generalized susceptibility, **5A**:4
Generalized Wigner ensemble, **15**:188, **15**:189, **15**:192, **15**:196
Generating function, **2**:388, **3**:16, **3**:17, **3**:18, **3**:20, **3**:21, **3**:23, **3**:25, **3**:27, **3**:29, **3**:30, **3**:31, **3**:34, **3**:39, **3**:405
  partial, **3**:405, **3**:412
Generating functional, **5B**:206, **5B**:208, **5B**:214, **6**:134, **6**:135, **6**:154, **6**:155, **6**:178, **6**:189, **6**:241, **6**:298, **6**:299, **6**:304, **6**:326, **9**:237, **9**:281, **9**:284
Generating integral, **6**:151
Generic scale invariance, **17**:26–37, **17**:183–186
  compared with self-organized criticality, **17**:185
Geological systems, **8**:451
Geometric neighbours, **2**:275, **2**:288, **2**:289, **2**:297
Geometrical disorder, **14**:341–6

Geometry
  defect plane (DP), **10**:89
  edge, **10**:241
  film (FG), **10**:89
  finite systems, **8**:148
  semi-infinite (SI), **10**:89, **10**:241
  wedge-shaped, **10**:238
Gerschgorin inequality, **15**:187
Ghost coordinates, **19**:66, **19**:87
Gibbs absorption isotherm, **10**:30
Gibbs distributions, finite volume, **18**:12
Gibbs double tangent construction, **5B**:116, **5B**:131, **5B**:132
Gibbs factor, **7**:155
Gibbs free energy functional, **5A**:46–49, **5A**:81
Gibbs free energy, **5A**:38, **5A**:39, **5A**:40, **5A**:41, **5A**:44, **5A**:47, **5A**:49
  equilibrium, **5A**:47, **5A**:50, **5A**:59, **5A**:60, **5A**:81
  equilibrium per spin, **5A**:45
  generalized, **5A**:38–40, **5A**:45
  generalized per spin, **5A**:42
Gibbs isotherm, **16**:129
Gibbs measure, **19**:57
Gibbs measures, **18**:9–13
  correlation decay, **18**:72
  extremal, **18**:13–14
  infinite volume, **18**:11, **18**:12–13
  multiple, **18**:13–14
  as phases, **18**:14
  structure of set of, **18**:13–14
  uniqueness, **18**:72–8
Gibbs phase prism, **16**:6, **16**:8
Gibbs phase rule, **9**:169
Gibbs potential, **3**:503, **3**:507, **3**:512, **3**:514, **3**:536, **3**:540, **3**:548, **3**:551, **3**:552, **5A**:38, **5A**:57, **5A**:62, **5A**:67, **5A**:69
  equilibrium, **5A**:52, **5A**:62
Ginzburg criterion, **5A**:54, **5A**:55
Gibbs probability, **7**:156
Gibbs state, **1**:144, **1**:149, **1**:152, **1**:160, **1**:163, **1**:164, **1**:170, **1**:171
  euclidean—invariant, **1**:172
  strongly transitive, **1**:171, **1**:172
Gibbs states, **11**:184–5, **11**:187–8, **11**:193–5

boundary conditions, **11**:135–6, **11**:140–2

phase rule, **11**:138

Gibbs systems, computer simulation of, **18**:67–9

Gibbs–Thomson relation, **17**:90, **17**:119

Gibbs triangle, **16**:*11*

Gibbs–Duhem equation, **9**:172

Gibbs space, **2**:2, **2**:7, **2**:8, **2**:9, **2**:10, **2**:11, **2**:12, **2**:13, **2**:18

Ginzburg criterion, **5A**:54, **5A**:55, **6**:511, **6**:525, **9**:8, **9**:92, **9**:94, **9**:95, **9**:103, **9**:123, **9**:127, **9**:132, **12**:41, **12**:64

Ginzburg critical region, **5A**:55

Ginzburg Landau model (TDGL), time-dependent, **10**:245, **10**:343, **10**:355

Ginzburg–Landau ansatz, **15**:63

Ginzburg–Landau free energy, **15**:63, **15**:64

Ginzburg–Landau free-energy density, **15**:60

Ginzburg–Landau free-energy functional, **15**:57, **15**:58

Ginzburg–Landau model, **6**:252, **6**:260, **6**:273, **6**:274, **6**:277, **6**:288, **8**:303, **16**:78–87, **16**:98, **16**:165

one-order-parameter model, **16**:79–82, **16**:87–115

phase diagram of, **16**:105–09, **16**:*106*, **16**:*109*

three-order-parameter model, **16**:85–7

time-dependent, **8**:373

two-order-parameter model, **16**:83–5

Ginzburg-Landau theory (GL-theory), **18**:236–7

Ginzburg–Landau theory, **8**:12, **8**:23, **14**:87, **16**:20–1, **16**:55, **16**:76–129

Ginzburg–Landau–Wilson Hamiltonian, **15**:64

Ginzburg–Pitaevskii theory, **5A**:67, **5A**:68, **5A**:69, **5A**:76, **5A**:79

GKS inequalities (Griffiths–Sherman–Kelly), **11**:183, **11**:184

GKS inequality, **1**:72, **1**:75, **1**:76, **1**:78, **1**:79, **1**:80, **1**:81, **1**:93, **1**:104, **1**:105

GKSA *see under* Kirkwood

Glass transition, icosahedral symmetry and, **7**:88

Glasses, spinodal decomposition, experimental studies, **8**:421–422

Glassy dynamics, **19**:389

Glauber dynamics

boundary conditions, **19**:213

decoupling, **19**:185

and DLPA, **19**:74

diluted Ising systems, **7**:207

enantiodromic, **19**:164

equations of motion, **19**:187

equilibrium system, **19**:57, **19**:191

free fermion systems, **19**:176

Ising model, **19**:47–49

nonfactorized state, **19**:191

and pair annihilation–creation process, **19**:51

spin flip, **19**:13, **19**:49–50, **19**:76, **19**:213, **19**:214

stochastic rules, **19**:188

zero temperature, **19**:163, **19**:193, **19**:206–207, **19**:213, **19**:264

Glauber model, **2**:466, **2**:481, **2**:492

Glauber spin-flip dynamics, **17**:17, **17**:171

compared with Kawasaki dynamics, **17**:171–172

multi-temperature models with, **17**:173–175

Global rescaling, and equations of motion, **19**:305–307

Global symmetries, typical results, **19**:5–6

Gluck's theorem, **18**:268

GNS construction, **1**:142, **1**:143, **1**:146, **1**:147, **1**:150, **1**:169, **1**:172, **1**:173

Goldstone excitations, **7**:66

Goldstone mode, **8**:75

Goldstone models, **6**:214

Goldstone modes, **7**:4, **9**:129, **10**:208, **10**:209, **10**:336, **10**:351, **10**:355, **17**:104, **17**:133

Goldstone's Theorem, **6**:333

Grain boundaries, **10**:3, **10**:4, **10**:48, **10**:52, **10**:53

Grain size, **2**:199

Grand canonical distribution, **19**:62, **19**:80, **19**:105, **19**:108, **19**:123

Grand canonical ensemble, **5A**:178,
  5A:354, **5A**:376, **19**:457, **19**:458
Grand canonical formalism, **1**:112,
  1:114, **1**:129
Grand canonical pair distribution
  function, **5B**:158
Grand canonical pressure, **5B**:128
Grand partition function, **3**:43, **3**:50,
  3:52, **3**:71, **3**:364, **3**:366, **5B**:144,
  5B:186, **5B**:206, **5B**:208, **5B**:209,
  5B:222
  monomer-dimer, **3**:654, **3**:655
  osmotic, **5B**:222
  zeros, **3**:359
Grand pressure partition function,
  5B:145
Granular conductors, **14**:364
Graph collapse, **3**:176
Graph expansion method,
  weak, **3**:660
Graph expansion, **5B**:170, **5B**:172
  weak, **3**:661, **3**:665
Graph generating function,
  weak, **3**:653, **3**:654, **3**:655, **3**:659
Graph group, **3**:7
  Γ, **3**:41
Graph symmetry number, **3**:7
Graph symmetry, **3**:7
Graph theory, **3**:103, **3**:116, **3**:124
  terminology, **18**:6–8, **18**:148–9
Graph, **3**:99, **3**:128, **3**:130, **3**:132, **3**:134,
  3:135, **3**:141, **3**:143, **3**:158, **3**:161,
  3:264, **3**:269
  allowed, **3**:585
  articulated, **3**:5, **3**:67, **3**:85
  bare, **3**:584, **3**:585, **3**:588, **3**:590,
    3:593, **3**:601, **3**:602, **3**:603,
    3:605, **3**:608, **3**:609, **3**:610,
    3:613, **3**:614, **3**:615
  bare free energy, **3**:150
  basic, **3**:269, **3**:270, **3**:271, **3**:272,
    3:273, **3**:274, **3**:275, **3**:276,
    3:281, **3**:285, **3**:287
  bond, **3**:153, **3**:154, **3**:156, **3**:157,
    3:159
  bond renormalized, **3**:158
  bubble, **3**:604, **3**:606, **3**:632
  connected, **3**:4, **3**:10, **3**:11, **3**:16, **3**:17,
    3:18, **3**:19, **3**:23, **3**:25, **3**:29,
    3:31, **3**:32, **3**:36, **3**:37, **3**:38,
    3:40, **3**:46, **3**:47, **3**:53, **3**:54,
    3:55, **3**:60, **3**:63, **3**:67, **3**:68,
    3:73, **3**:79, **3**:83, **3**:84, **3**:85,
    3:90, **3**:124, **3**:125, **3**:136, **3**:139,
    3:154, **3**:157, **3**:158, **3**:257,
    3:263, **3**:268, **3**:276, **3**:282,
    3:283, **3**:284, **3**:289
  2-connected, **3**:32
  disconnected, **3**:2, **3**:4, **3**:10, **3**:17,
    3:61, **3**:90, **3**:134, **3**:281, **3**:282
  double-cross, **3**:283, **3**:287
  n-edged, **3**:128
  elementary, **3**:153, **3**:157
  free, **3**:7, **3**:8, **3**:27
  free connected, **3**:25
  homeomorphic, **3**:9, **3**:10, **3**:11, **3**:61
  homogeneous, **3**:67, **3**:84, **3**:399
  horizontal weight of, **3**:586
  hypermagnetic, **3**:377, **3**:378
  1-irreducible, **3**:136, **3**:137, **3**:138,
    3:142, **3**:153, **3**:157, **3**:158
  1-irreducible connected, **3**:165
  1-irreducible 2-rooted, **3**:169
  1-irreducible unrooted, **3**:148
  2-irreducible, **3**:153
  isomorphic, **3**:4, **3**:14, **3**:83
  isospectral, **3**:15
  labelled, **3**:7, **3**:16, **3**:32, **3**:38
  labelled connected, **3**:39
  ladder, **3**:40, **3**:89, **3**:153, **3**:154,
    3:156, **3**:157
  linear, **3**:1, **3**:2, **3**:3, **3**:16, **3**:23,
    3:124
  linked cluster, **3**:135
  magnetic, **3**:377, **3**:380
  m-line bonding, **3**:72
  multiply bonded, **3**:387, **3**:388
  multiply connected, **3**:2, **3**:5
  nodal, **3**:153, **3**:156, **3**:157
  non-ladder, **3**:40
  non-nodal, **3**:157
  non-separable, **3**:32
  non-simple, **3**:4, **3**:14
  ordered directed, **3**:585
  partial, **3**:78, **3**:79
  1-irreducible, **3**:136, **3**:137
  regular, **3**:68
  ring, **3**:151

rooted, **3**:7, **3**:20, **3**:51, **3**:129, **3**:136,
        3:137, **3**:139, **3**:153
n-rooted, **3**:124, **3**:158, **3**:177
0-rooted, **3**:142
1-rooted, **3**:129, **3**:143, **3**:168, **3**:178
2-rooted, **3**:140, **3**:152, **3**:154, **3**:155,
        3:156, **3**:158, **3**:159, **3**:160,
        3:168, **3**:174
rooted connected, **3**:22
1-rooted connected, **3**:56
2-rooted connected, **3**:56, **3**:130,
        3:174
2-rooted simple, **3**:160
3-rooted, **3**:159
3-rooted connected, **3**:130
self-field, **3**:160
simple, **3**:4, **3**:154, **3**:156, **3**:157,
        3:160
simple labelled, **3**:14
skeleton, **3**:136
l-skeleton, **3**:136, **3**:137, **3**:138, **3**:139
2-skeleton, **3**:153, **3**:157, **3**:158, **3**:159
star, **3**:60, **3**:67, **3**:87, **3**:89, **3**:289,
        3:382
undirected, **3**:584
unlabelled, **3**:23, **3**:28, **3**:29, **3**:34
unrooted, **3**:133, **3**:138, **3**:143, **3**:146,
        3:148, **3**:153, **3**:155, **3**:162,
        3:164, **3**:173, **3**:176
unrooted connected, **3**:147, **3**:167,
        3:173
vertex labelled, **3**:127, **3**:267
vertex-labelled connected, **3**:265,
        3:266
vertical weight of, **3**:586
weak, **3**:135
weight, **3**:116
zero field, **3**:377, **3**:380
Graph, locally finite, **18**:6
Graphical distribution, **18**:79–82
Graphite, **19**:256, **19**:274
    argon on, **12**:140
    Br$_2$, intercalated on, **12**:285
    bromide, intercalated on, **12**:226,
        12:247, **12**:251
    CF$_4$ on, **12**:225
    helium monolayer on, **12**:221,
        12:224–226, **12**:229, **12**:232,
        12:237, **12**:244, **12**:309

hydrogen monolayer on, **12**:221,
        12:224–226, **12**:309
    krypton monolayer on, **12**:221,
        12:224–225, **12**:228–230,
        12:238, **12**:245, **12**:309
    methaheon, **12**:15
    N$_2$ and CO on, **12**:224, **12**:225–226,
        12:232, **12**:235, **12**:251,
        12:285
    Sb CI$_5$ intercalated on, **12**:228
    Xenon on (herringbone ordered),
        12:226
Graphite oxide, **19**:275
Graphs, **6**:277, **6**:279, **6**:287
    with up to four loops, **6**:317
Gravitational field, **5B**:163, **10**:281,
        10:291, **10**:308, **10**:318, **14**:164–5,
        19:104
Gravity field, **2**:62
Gravity waves, third sound and, **7**:32
Gravity, **12**:68, **12**:75, **12**:101, **12**:150,
        12:155
Greedy algorithms, **18**:150–1, **18**:155,
        18:195–6
Greek cross, **1**:265
Green function, **6**:132, **6**:299, **6**:319,
        6:508, **7**:105, **7**:106, **7**:215,
        15:169–70
    coherent potential approximations,
        7:219
    derivation, **19**:459–461
Green's function approximation,
        5B:260
Green's function equation of motion,
        5B:302
Green's function matrix, **5B**:325
Green's function theory
    second-order, **3**:317
Green's function, **2**:385, **2**:387, **2**:390,
        2:397, **2**:409, **2**:437, **2**:438,
        5A:218, **5B**:260–267, **5B**:279,
        5B:285, **5B**:288–293, **5B**:297,
        5B:301, **5B**:303–306, **5B**:321–328
        passim, **5B**:336, **5B**:337
    connected, **5B**:215
    double time, **5B**:261, **5B**:321
    retarded, **5B**:261, **5B**:262, **5B**:321
    thermodynamic, **5B**:260, **5B**:261,
        5B:321

three-spin, **5B**:322
two-spin, **5B**:322
Green's functions for dimer correlation
   functions, **13**:271–272
Green's functions
   time-dependant, **1**:115
   connected, **17**:60, **17**:64
Green–Kubo formulae, **2**:444, **2**:452
Gregorshin theorem, **19**:54
Grey measure *see* graphical distribution
Griffiths–Kelly–Sherman inequalities,
   9:253, **9**:256, **9**:269, **9**:273, **9**:297
Griffiths analyticity, **6**:191
Griffiths inequalities, **7**:189, **15**:107
Griffiths
   inequality, **9**:252, **9**:253, **9**:255, **9**:266,
      9:268, **9**:269
   sum rules, **9**:177, **9**:179
Griffiths regime, **18**:116–17
Griffiths singularity, **7**:180, **7**:226
Griffiths' inequalities, **10**:16, **10**:61
Griffiths–Blume model, **3**:164
Griffiths–Kelly–Sherman (GKS)
   inequalities, **10**:29
Griffiths–Kelly–Sherman inequality, *see*
   GKS inequality
Gross variables, **5A**:171, **5A**:172,
      5A:173, **5A**:176, **5A**:181, **5A**:182,
      5A:186, **5A**:187, **5A**:189, **5A**:190,
      5A:192, **5A**:194, **5A**:199, **5A**:200,
      5A:206, **5A**:210, **5A**:213, **5A**:234,
      5A:236, **5A**:237, **5A**:238, **5A**:242,
      5A:243, **5A**:244, **5A**:251, **5A**:257,
      5A:258, **5A**:260, **5A**:267, **5A**:280,
      5A:281, **5A**:287, **5A**:294, **5A**:298,
      5A:299, **5A**:317, **5A**:335, **5A**:342,
      5A:345, **5A**:366, **5A**:372, **5A**:373,
      5A:388, **5A**:391
   complete set, **5A**:171, **5A**:172,
      5A:190, **5A**:208
   elimination, **5A**:234
   equilibrium probability distribution
      function, **5A**:174
   J-mode, **5A**:257, **5A**:258, **5A**:259,
      5A:260, **5A**:265, **5A**:266,
      5A:267, **5A**:268, **5A**:269
   kinetic equations, **5A**:189–216
   mutually orthogonal set, **5A**:186
   random force elimination, **5A**:217

reduced, **5A**:236, **5A**:237
   time correlation function, **5A**:216–236
   time derivatives, **5A**:176
Ground state energy, **19**:439
Ground state entropy, **11**:200
Ground state, *n*-vector models, **8**:56–57
Ground states [for half-filled lattices]
   17:*13*
Ground-state phase diagrams, **15**:17–19,
      15:20, **15**:21, **15**:22, **15**:25, **15**:28,
      15:51
Group equations, **6**:533
Growth algorithms, for percolation,
      18:189
Growth
   diffusion limited, **12**:337
   Eden, **12**:474
   mode, **12**:184
   non equilibrium, **12**:383, **12**:427,
      12:474
   probability, **12**:385, **12**:410,
      12:418–430, **12**:471, **12**:474–476
Growth of crystals, **14**:141
Growth, late stage, theories, **8**:333–339
Gudermannian function, **1**:323
Γ-function, **19**:402, **19**:444
Γ-ordering, **5B**:206, **5B**:234, **5B**:235,
      5B:236, **5B**:238, **5B**:242, **5B**:246
γ-ordering, **5B**:234, **5B**:235, **5B**:238,
      5B:246

H

Hadron, **1**:4
Hafnian, **1**:235
Hairpin diagram, **7**:117
Half-plane geometry, **14**:109
Hamaker coefficient, **12**:144,
      12:154–155
Hamiltonian
   anisotropic transverse *XY* model, **19**:6
   Canham–Helfrich, **19**:261–262
   counterterms, **19**:298, **19**:299
   diffusion-limited pair annihilation,
      19:73
   driven and undriven systems, **19**:197
   effective, **19**:269, **19**:270, **19**:279,
      19:436
   equivalent, **19**:72

exclusion process, **19**:41–45
free, integration by parts, **19**:306–307
free energy, **19**:279
free fermion approach, **19**:178,
  19:180, **19**:189, **19**:194
Heisenberg, **19**:34–35, **19**:165
integral counterterms, **19**:298
membrane, **19**:278
modifed, **19**:297
nonstochastic, **19**:178–180
quantum *see* quantum Hamiltonian
quantum spin model, **19**:5, **19**:33–34
renormalized, **19**:341
rescaled, **19**:436
static, **19**:377
stochastic, **19**:104, **19**:178–180
trial Gaussian, **19**:442–444
two-membrane model, **19**:358
Hamiltonian space
under transformation, **6**:364
Hamiltonian, **1**:23, **3**:246, **3**:247, **3**:248,
  3:252, **3**:269, **3**:271, **3**:284, **3**:291,
  3:301, **3**:326, **3**:358, **3**:363, **3**:418,
  3:464, **3**:571, **3**:572, **3**:581, **5A**:17,
  5A:36, **5A**:39, **5A**:40, **5A**:41,
  5A:46, **5A**:48, **5A**:79, **5A**:80,
  5A:81, **5A**:89, **5A**:107, **5A**:153,
  5A:199, **5A**:203, **5A**:220, **5A**:221,
  5A:223, **5A**:234, **5A**:235, **5A**:237,
  5A:238, **5A**:240, **5A**:243, **5A**:247,
  5A:248, **5A**:249, **5A**:251, **5A**:252,
  5A:254, **5A**:255, **5A**:256, **5A**:257,
  5A:260, **5A**:266, **5A**:275, **5A**:286,
  5A:287, **5A**:288, **5A**:290, **5A**:294,
  5A:311, **5A**:330, **5A**:335, **5A**:383,
  5A:387, **5A**:388, **6**:510, **18**:9
anisotropic, **3**:311
anisotropic spin, **3**:294, **3**:298
cell spin, **6**:427, **6**:430
critical, **6**:31, **6**:517
effective, **6**:405
effective model, **6**:523
equivalent, **6**:36
fixed point, **6**:29, **6**:30, **6**:34, **6**:36,
  6:39, **6**:45, **6**:49, **6**:86, **6**:88,
  6:91, **6**:93
Gaussian fixed point, **6**:10
homogeneous, **6**:428
Landau, **6**:14–17

reduced, **6**:359, **6**:360, **6**:371
relative, **18**:10
spin- $\frac{1}{2}$ Ising, **6**:524
symmetry of, **6**:358
transformation and, **6**:8
XY-, **18**:238
Heisenberg, **3**:251
Heisenberg-Ising classical, **3**:253
mixed Heisenberg-Ising, **3**:298
planar, **3**:636
spin, **3**:252, **3**:283, **3**:577, **3**:578
Hard circles, **1**:183
Hard core (lattice gas) model, **18**:18–20,
  18:77, **18**:108
agreement percolation, **18**:103
stochastic domination, **18**:30–1
Hard core condition, **1**:164
Hard core
constraint, **19**:84
interaction, **19**:79, **19**:96, **19**:103–104
repulsion (site exclusion),
  19:149–150, **19**:155, **19**:194,
  19:363
Hard core gas, **1**:153
Hard core model, **2**:323
Hard core potentials, **1**:124
Hard core, **1**:12, **1**:20, **1**:24, **1**:25, **1**:27,
  1:28, **1**:29, **1**:36, **1**:39, **1**:47, **1**:66,
  1:69, **1**:89, **1**:90, **1**:94, **1**:116, **1**:125
continuous one-dimensional, **1**:163
extended, **1**:24
Hard cores, **5B**:109, **5B**:189, **5B**:234,
  5B:239
Hard discs, **5B**:2
Hard disk fluid, **2**:313, **2**:314
Hard Hexagon problem, **11**:51
Hard hexagon model, critical activity,
  8:231
Hard molecule transition, **2**:325
Hard rods, **1**:184, **1**:186
Hard rods, **5B**:110, **5B**:159, **5B**:196
"Hard-rods" gas,
one-dimensional, **1**:164, **1**:182
Hard sphere aggregates, **2**:286, **2**:287
Hard sphere models, **2**:314, **2**:315, **2**:324
Hard spheres, **1**:183, **5B**:137, **5B**:240
charged, **5B**:240
dipoles, **5B**:240
Hard Square model, **11**:51

Hard square model, **1**:467
Hard squares, critical behaviour, **8**:232
Hard-core condition, **5B**:130, **5B**:235
Hard-core gas quantum, **5B**:196
Hard-core molecule, **5B**:206
Hard-core potential, **5B**:139, **5B**:149, **5B**:161, **5B**:177, **5B**:231
Hard-core system, **5B**:191
Hard-hexagon model, **12**:290, **12**:293
square model, **12**:290, **12**:293, **12**:297
Hard-sphere gas, **5B**:189, **5B**:191, **5B**:192
Hard-sphere ion, **5B**:180
Hard-sphere mixture, **9**:25
^{3}He–^{4}He mixtures, **9**:5, **9**:15, **9**:25, **9**:26, **9**:31, **9**:54, **9**:63, **9**:76, **9**:108, **9**:110, **9**:112, **9**:170
^{4}He + ^{3}He system, **9**:164, **9**:215, **9**:218, **9**:223
Hard-sphere transition, **5B**:192
Harmless staircase, **15**:6
Harmonic interactions, **15**:24
Harper's equation, **12**:262
Harris argument, **7**:169, **7**:171
striped randomness model, **7**:181
Harris criteria, **7**:170, **7**:246
Harris criterion, **12**:170, **12**:172–173, **14**:327–9, **17**:144, **19**:433, **19**:434
Hartree approximation, **3**:150, **6**:255
Hartree–Fock approximation, **5A**:53, **19**:442, **19**:443
Hausdorff dimension, **15**:49
He^3, **2**:68
He^4, **2**:57, **2**:58, **2**:59, **2**:62, **2**:67, **2**:68, **2**:70, **2**:71, **2**:76
Heat capacity singularity, **2**:84
Heat capacity, **5B**:349, **5B**:354, **5B**:356, **5B**:358, **5B**:360, **5B**:363, **5B**:364, **5B**:365, **5B**:371, **5B**:376, **5B**:382–389 *passim*
of air, **5B**:361
of argon, **5B**:343, **5B**:348, **5B**:366
of carbon dioxide, **5B**:352
of ethane, **5B**:356, **5B**:357, **5B**:358, **5B**:366, **5B**:372, **5B**:373, **5B**:377
of ethane/carbon dioxide mixture, **5B**:358, **5B**:361, **5B**:377

of ethane/carbon dioxide azeotropic mixture, **5B**:358, **5B**:361, **5B**:377
of ethane/heptane mixture, **5B**:372, **5B**:373, **5B**:377
gravity effect, **5B**:353
isobaric, **5B**:345
temperature gradient effect, **5B**:353
of xenon, **5B**:352, **5B**:353, **5B**:364
Heat capacity, C_h, **5A**:5
Heat capacity, *see* Specific heat
Heat conduction mode, **5B**:29
Heat flux, **5A**:335
Hecke algebra, **19**:50, **19**:63, **19**:68, **19**:188, **19**:211, **19**:213
Hedvall effect, **10**:81
Heisenberg antiferromagnet, **1**:86, **1**:88, **5A**:123, **5A**:151
isotropic, **5A**:123, **5A**:205–208, **5A**:243–247, **5A**:262–264, **5A**:275–279, **5A**:392–394
Heisenberg antiferromagnets, mixed two-dimensional, Monte Carlo methods, **7**:204
Heisenberg chain, **1**:214, **1**:224
Heisenberg chains, pure one-dimensional properties, **7**:178
Heisenberg crossover exponent, **7**:259
Heisenberg ferromagnet, **1**:52, **1**:84, **1**:85, **1**:86, **1**:87, **5A**:37, **5A**:123, **5A**:129, **5A**:135, **5A**:136–143, **5A**:145, **5B**:20, **5B**:301, **5B**:317, **10**:77
classical, **5A**:180
dilute, **5B**:320, **5B**:336
isotropic, **5A**:136, **5A**:199–205, **5A**:239–243, **5A**:261, **5A**:262, **5A**:269–275, **5A**:361–366, **5A**:388–392, **10**:289
s.c. classical, **5B**:45, **5B**:47
spin $\frac{1}{2}$, **5B**:262
system, **10**:255
Heisenberg fixed point, **19**:365, **19**:369, **19**:404, **19**:432, **19**:433
Heisenberg Hamiltonian, **1**:20, **1**:116, **3**:251
Heisenberg interaction, **1**:80
Heisenberg magnet, **2**:470, **5A**:243, **5A**:286, **5A**:334, **5A**:344, **5B**:19

anisotropic, **5A**:279, **5A**:285
classical, **5B**:21, **5B**:36
three-dimensional, **5A**:147
Heisenberg magnets
    See also under Antiferromagnetic
        Heisenberg models; Bond diluted
        Heisenberg ferromagnets;
        Classical Heisenberg
        ferromagnet; Dilute anisotropic
        Heisenberg model; Dilute
        Heisenberg and antiferromagnets;
        Dilute Heisenberg chains; Dilute
        Heisenberg ferromagnets; Dilute
        Heisenberg layer magnets; Dilute
        Heisenberg magnet; Dilute
        Heisenberg quadratic layer
        magnet; Dilute isotropic
        Heisenberg model; Dilute
        magnets; Dilute spin half
        Heisenberg model; Diluted
        anisotropic Heisenberg
        antiferromagnets; Dilute
        anisotropic Heisenberg
        ferromagnets; Diluted anisotropic
        Heisenberg model; Diluted
        classical Heisenberg model;
        Diluted Heisenberg
        antiferromagnets; Diluted
        Heisenberg chain magnet;
        Diluted Heisenberg
        ferromagnets; Diluted
        Heisenberg layer magnet; Diluted
        Heisenberg magnets; Diluted
        isotropic Heisenberg model;
        Diluted spin half Heisenberg
        magnet; Diluted uniaxially
        anisotropic Heisenberg model;
        Diluted zero temperature
        Heisenberg models; Disordered
        Heisenberg magnets;
        Ferromagnetic Heisenberg
        models; Heisenberg
        antiferromagnets; Heisenberg
        chains; Isotopic Heisenberg layer
        magnets; Low temperature
        diluted Heisenberg magnets;
        Mixed Heisenberg
        antiferromagnets; Mixed
        Heisenberg ferromagnets;

    Quenched diluted Heisenberg
        models; Random bond
        Heisenberg model. Random
        diluted Heisenberg
        antiferromagnets; Site diluted
        Heisenberg antiferromagnets;
        Site diluted Heisenberg
        ferromagnets; Site mixed
        Heisenberg antiferromagnets;
        Site diluted Heisenberg
        ferromagnets; Site diluted
        Heisenberg magnets; Spin half
        Heisenberg model; Uniaxially
        anisotropic Heisenberg magnets
    model, diluted, **7**:191
    exact limiting slope methods, **7**:194
    one-dimensional, percolation fixed
        point, scaling, **7**:261
    striped randomness models, **7**:181
    three-dimensions, transition
        temperatures, **7**:164
    two dimensional, critical exponents
        and parameters, **7**:176–177
    quasi-one-dimensional, correlation,
        length, **7**:265
    transition curves, experimental,
        7:263
Heisenberg model, **1**:19, **1**:96, **1**:104,
    1:115, **1**:116, **1**:178, **1**:181, **1**:205,
    2:249, **2**:253–5, **2**:261–2, **2**:340,
    2:341, **2**:353, **3**:2, **3**:57, **3**:58, **3**:69,
    3:72, **3**:74, **3**:76, **3**:118, **3**:119,
    3:173, **3**:174, **3**:184, **3**:186, **3**:192,
    3:208, **3**:246, **3**:248, **3**:251, **3**:252,
    3:253, **3**:271, **3**:275, **3**:288, **3**:291,
    3:294, **3**:298, **3**:301, **3**:302, **3**:305,
    3:310, **3**:314, **3**:319, **3**:321, **3**:323,
    3:325, **3**:326, **3**:328, **3**:358, **3**:382,
    3:487, **3**:500, **3**:501, **3**:506, **3**:540,
    3:543, **3**:546, **3**:556, **3**:557, **3**:571,
    3:621, **3**:622, **3**:630, **3**:647, **5A**:89,
    5A:93, **5A**:96, **5B**:4, **5B**:26, **5B**:52,
    5B:56, **5B**:57, **5B**:260, **5B**:318,
    6:11, **6**:210, **6**:339, **6**:343, **6**:526,
    8:56, **8**:57, **8**:103–107, **11**:2, **14**:85,
    15:76
anisotropic, **1**:80, **1**:205, **3**:170, **3**:572,
    3:576, **3**:596, **3**:611, **3**:630
anisotropic spin ½, **3**:574

anisotropic classical, **3**:498
antiferromagnetic, **3**:231, **3**:571
classical, **1**:179, **1**:200, **3**:118, **3**:165,
 3:167, **3**:168, **3**:224, **3**:247,
 3:250, **3**:272, **3**:288, **3**:295,
 3:299, **3**:318, **3**:488, **3**:489,
 3:496, **3**:499, **3**:502, **3**:543,
 5B:14, **5B**:25, **5B**:34, **5B**:64,
 5B:94, **6**:296
dilute, **2**:263
generalized classical, **5A**:55, **5A**:56,
 5A:82
interfaces, **8**:75
isotropic, **1**:123, **1**:152, **2**:387, **3**:573,
 3:577, **3**:635, **6**:347, **6**:387,
 6:513
isotropic ferromagnet, **3**:582
Monte Carlo calculation, **8**:109–114
nest-nearest neighbour interaction,
 1:154
of spin, **1**:71, **1**:99, **1**:112
one-dimensional classical, **1**:181
quantum, **3**:169
quantum mechanical, **3**:119, **3**:503
s.c., **5B**:64, **5B**:67
spin ∞, **3**:624
spin ½, **3**:186, **3**:506, **3**:525, **3**:646
three-dimensional, **5A**:89, **5A**:129,
 5B:44, **5B**:53
two-dimensional, **3**:252, **5B**:44
Heisenberg power law critical behaviour,
 crossover from, **7**:262
Heisenberg quantum chain
 anisotropic, **19**:11, **19**:34–35, **19**:43,
  19:114–117, **19**:165, **19**:175
 Hamiltonian, **19**:34–35, **19**:43, **19**:83,
  19:163, **19**:165, **19**:216
 integrability, **19**:35, **19**:101, **19**:220
 isotropic, **19**:111, **19**:163, **19**:216
 properties, **19**:104
 representation, **19**:23, **19**:33–35
 stationary states, **19**:80
 SU (2) symmetry, **19**:35
 wave function, **19**:97
 zero-field, **19**:43
Heisenberg quantum ferromagnet, **19**:6,
 19:10, **19**:34–35, **19**:41–42, **19**:89
Heisenberg series, **3**:302, **3**:303
Heisenberg symmetry, **14**:69

Heisenberg system, classical, **5B**:6,
 5B:10
 b.c.c., **5B**:30, **5B**:58
 magnetization, **5B**:35
 three-dimensional, **5B**:36
Heisenberg systems, **6**:229
Heisenberg thermal exponent, at
 percolation fixed point, **7**:269
Heisenberg thermal variable, **7**:259
Heisenberg, Paul, **19**:33
Heisenberg-Ising classical Hamiltonian,
 3:253
Heisenberg-Ising crossover, **7**:167,
 7:168
Heisenberg-Ising mixed model, **3**:281
Heisenberg–Ising model, **1**:23
Hele Shaw cells, **12**:343–345,
 12:392–393, **12**:400, **12**:472
Helfrich Hamiltonian, **16**:101, **16**:134,
 16:143
Helfrich interaction, **16**:139–41, **16**:146,
 16:164
Helical ground state, **15**:51
Helical structure, macromolecules, **7**:103
Helicity modulus, **8**:152, **8**:213
 finite size scaling, **8**:191–192
Helicity modulus, **10**:39, **10**:40, **14**:16
Helicity, **7**:114, **7**:121
Helium
 confined, superfluidity onset in,
  8:254–255
 on graphite, finite size scaling, **8**:256
 specific heat, in pores and films,
  8:251–254
Helium films
 diverging, transport coefficients, **7**:39
 dynamic scaling, **7**:31–39
 hydrodynamics, **7**:31–33
 melting, **7**:45
 superfluid, **7**:13
  Kosterlitz–Thouless theory, **7**:83
  phase transitions, **7**:7
  specific heat, **7**:22
 third sound in, **7**:4, **7**:31–39
 dynamic scaling and, **7**:35
Helium
 liquid, **6**:526
 superfluid, **6**:11, **6**:44
 He³–He⁴ mixtures, **6**:170

Helium mixtures, **9**:18, **9**:21, **9**:151, **9**:153
Helium superfluid, **14**:73, **14**:90–1
    superfluid transition in, **14**:71–3, **14**:82–4, **14**:366
Helium
    λ-line, **5B**:380
    λ-point, **5B**:365
    λ-transition, **5A**:317–320
    liquid, **5A**:293–296, **5A**:316
    superfluid velocity, **5A**:198
Helium, **12**:152
    wetting experiment, **12**:102–104, **12**:193
Helium, liquid, **5B**:378
    λ-point, **5B**:381
    λ. transition, **3**:572, **3**:643, **3**:646, **3**:647, **3**:648, **3**:649
    superfluid transition, **3**:502
Helium-3/helium-4 mixtures, **8**:429–432
Helium-4 film
    superfluid flow, **5A**:71
Helium-4, liquid critical point, **5A**:306
    λ-transition, **5A**:67
Helium-4, superfluid, **5A**:57, **5A**:62, **5A**:67–71, **5A**:72, **5A**:75, **5A**:78, **5A**:79, **5A**:81, **5A**:88
Helium³, **5B**:370, **5B**:392, **5B**:393
Helium⁴, **5B**:392, **5B**:393
Helix-coil transitions, **7**:109–121
    in branched synthetic polynucleotides, **7**:121
    in macromolecules, surface adsorption and, **7**:107
    order, **7**:115, **7**:133
    synthetic polynucleotides, **7**:116
Helmholtz fluctuation theory, **19**:230
Helmholtz free energy infinitely long macromolecules, **7**:128
    of infinitely long chains, **7**:130
Helmholtz free energy, **5A**:38, **5A**:39, **5A**:41, **14**:106
Hemmer, Kac and Uhlenbeck, **5B**:153, **5B**:154
Hendrickson's matching algorithm, **18**:270
    modified, **18**:276–9
Hendrickson's theorem, **18**:273

Hepp sectors, **19**:318, **19**:323, **19**:325–326
Heptane/ethane system, **5B**:370, **5B**:371, **5B**:372, **5B**:374, **5B**:376, **5B**:377
Herglotz functions, **15**:174, **15**:181
Hermite polynomial, **6**:57
Hermitian model, **2**:462
Hermitian, symmetric Hamiltonian, **19**:58
Herringbone
    orientational order, **12**:225
    structure, **12**:223, **12**:225
Heterogeneous catalysts, **12**:337
Heterophase fluctuations, **8**:69
Hexagonal phases, **16**:4, **16**:73, **16**:106, **16**:*107*, **16**:125, **16**:*126*
Hexatic free energy, **7**:51
Hexatic liquid crystals, melting, **7**:52
Hexatic membranes, **19**:264–265
Hexatic phase, **7**:54
Hexatic-solid transitions, **7**:44, **7**:45, **7**:54
Hexatics, **7**:43
    disclinations, **7**:72, **7**:78
    hydrodynamics, **7**:66
HIC phase (honeycomb incommensurate), **12**:228, **12**:231, **12**:288, **12**:307–311, **12**:313–315
    floating solid, **12**:307–309
Hierarchical model, **12**:441–443, **12**:453, **12**:463, **12**:468, **12**:476
Hierarchical models, **14**:44
High field, **1**:48
High temperature expansion parameter, **3**:248
High temperature expansion, **3**:71, **3**:231, **3**:246, **3**:248, **3**:250, **3**:253
    cumulant, **3**:368
    moment, **3**:368
High temperature expansions, **7**:224
    quenched site-diluted systems, **7**:227–228
High temperature gap, **3**:321
High temperature probability, **2**:222
High temperature series expansion, **3**:529, **6**:319, **7**:12, **9**:16, **9**:300–4
    general-D, **3**:512, **3**:513
    in Feynman diagrams, **6**:1

High temperature series, **2:**155, **2:**158, **2:**403, **2:**405, **2:**424, **2:**426, **2:**486, **2:**488, **3:**358

High-density incommensurate phase, **12:**227, **12:**229, **12:**232, **12:**238, **12:**240, **12:**247, **12:**309

High-density phase, **19:**132, **19:**133, **19:**138, **19:**139, **19:**140, **19:**142, **19:**145, **19:**146, **19:**172

High-T_c superconductor, **14:**87

High-temperature expansion, **5B:**76, **5B:**79, **5B:**167, **11:**48–49

  Ising model, **19:**257, **19:**408, **19:**431

  O (N) model, **19:**260, **19:**409–412, **19:**421

High-temperature expansions, **8:**103–109

High-temperature series, **6:**215, **6:**319, **6:**358

Higher order critical points, **9:**225

Higher-field derivatives, **2:**420, **2:**421, **2:**422, **2:**424

Higher-order diagrams, **6:**323

Hilbert space, **1:**115, **1:**117, **1:**129, **1:**139, **1:**141, **1:**142, **1:**143, **1:**144, **1:**165

Hildebrand solubility parameter, **9:**167, **9:**184

HKU *see* Hemmer, Kac and Uhlenbeck

Hohenberg–Mermin–Wagner theorem, **6:**289

Holders inequality, **19:**362

Holley's inequality, **18:**24–5

Holmium, **5A:**315, **15:**56

Homcomorph, **3:**11

  irreducible, **3:**11

Homeomorphic classification, **3:**41, **3:**59, **3:**68

Homeomorphic type, **3:**34, **3:**39, **3:**42

Homogeneity conjecture, **2:**80, **2:**130, **2:**139

Homogeneity for dilute magnets, **7:**232–238

Homogeneity hypothesis, **5B:**50, **5B:**62

Homogeneity law, **6:**10, **6:**42, **6:**49, **6:**82

Homogeneity postulate, **3:**599

  generalized, **3:**465

Homogeneity properties, **6:**512, **6:**533

Homogeneity theorem, *see* Homogeneity conjecture

Homogeneity, **10:**270

Homogeneity, finite size scaling and **8:**34, **8:**39

Homogeneous function, **2:**30, **2:**31, **2:**36, **5B:**254, **6:**512

Homogeneous nucleation rate, **5B:**134

Homogeneous state condition, **5B:**7

Homogeneous systems

  nonlinear theory, **6:**80–105

Homogenous factorized transformations, **19:**179

Homogenous function, generalized, **9:**32, **9:**35, **9:**36, **9:**38, **9:**41

Honeycomb-incommensurate phase, *see* HIC phase

Hopf–Cole transformation, **19:**158

Hopping

  asymmetry, **19:**104, **19:**183, **19:**197, **19:**203, **19:**212

  biased, **19:**66

  matrices, **19:**42, **19:**43, **19:**50, **19:**91, **19:**110, **19:**158, **19:**220

  nearest neighbour, **19:**84, **19:**85

  rate, **19:**9, **19:**19, **19:**27, **19:**57, **19:**103, **19:**145

  time, **19:**217

Hoshen–Kopelman algorithm, **18:**189

Hottest-bond algorithm, **18:**195

Hunter and Guerrieri method, **13:**22–23

Husimi function, **5B:**206, **5B:**209

Husimi tree, **3:**6, **3:**22, **3:**33

  mixed, **3:**6, **3:**21, **3:**34, **3:**36, **3:**37

  pure, **3:**6

Hydrocarbon mixtures with ethane, **9:**188–91

Hydrodynamic approach, **17:**109

Hydrodynamic divergenceless flow, **19:**388

Hydrodynamic effects, in binary fluids, **8:**327–331

Hydrodynamic equation

  linearized, **5A:**265

Hydrodynamic interaction, **19:**387

Hydrodynamic limit, **19:**62, **19:**124–125

Hydrodynamic mode coupling

  as equal time correlation of fluctuations, **5A:**179–185

in one-component fluid, **5A:**176, **5A:**182, **5A:**183
with two other modes, **5A:**184
see also Mode coupling
Hydrodynamic mode, **5A:**175, **5A:**176, **5A:**236
coupling, **5A:**175–185
coupling theory, **5A:**188, **5A:**189
Hydrodynamic radius, **12:**452, **12:**454, **12:**459–460, **12:**476, **14:**95
Hydrodynamic regime, **5A:**143, **5A:**216, **5A:**260, **5A:**265, **5A:**272, **5A:**289
Hydrodynamic turbulence, **5A:**227, **5A:**330
Hydrodynamic variables, **5A:**337
Hydrodynamical mode, low-frequency, **5B:**29
Hydrodynamics
helium films, **7:**31–33
melting, **7:**66–69
linearized, **5A:**340, **5A:**341
linearized equations, **17:**187–189
Zimm model, **19:**259, **19:**385–388
Hydrogen bonded model, **3:**661
Hydrogen bonded problem, **3:**656, **3:**658, **3:**665
Hydrogen bridges, conformational phase transitions in macromolecules and, **7:**102
Hydrogen, on Fe, **12:**226, **12:**241, **12:**247, **12:**251, **12:**286, **12:**294, **12:**333
on palladium, **12:**226
Hydrogen-metal systems, **8:**443–444
Hydrostatic effect, **5B:**352–360 *passim*, **5B:**364
Hydrostatic equilibrium condition, **5B:**166
Hyperbolic model, **6:**99, **6:**100, **6:**105
Hyperchain equation, **2:**272
Hypercritical point, **2:**9
Hypercubic-shaped Ising models, **14:**100
Hypercubical lattice
in *d* dimensions, **3:**468
Hyperfine interaction experiments, **14:**92
Hypergeometric function, **3:**232, **19:**238

Hyperlattice, cubic, **6:**384
Hypernetted chain approximation, **3:**118
Hypernetted chain equation, **3:**157, **5B:**219, **5B:**221, **5B:**230
Hypernetted chain expansion, **5B:**219, **5B:**228
Hyperscaling relation, **9:**286, **9:**297, **9:**301, **12:**30, **12:**31, **12:**35, **12:**38, **12:**64, **12:**66, **12:**258, **12:**298
Hyperscaling, **8:**39, **8:**46, **8:**67, **10:**113, **10:**163, **10:**171, **10:**224, **10:**233, **14:**4, **14:**7, **14:**8, **14:**10, **14:**17, **14:**24, **14:**26, **14:**27, **14:**34, **14:**39–40, **14:**42, **14:**44
interfacial, **10:**273
Hyperuniversal amplitude combination, **14:**28, **14:**42
Hyperuniversal combination, **14:**54, **14:**364
Hyperuniversal relations, **14:**104
Hyperuniversality, **14:**4, **14:**10, **14:**26, **14:**40, **14:**96–104
Hypervertex function, **5B:**227
Hypervertex, **5B:**173
Hypervertices, **5B:**171, **5B:**173, **5B:**174, **5B:**181, **5B:**182, **5B:**187, **5B:**188, **5B:**228, **5B:**233, **5B:**234, **5B:**237

I

Ice condition, **1:**25, **1:**266
Ice
dielectric constant, **3:**664
residual entropy, **3:**663
Ice model, **3:**183, **3:**657, **10:**2
Ice problem, **1:**363
on general lattice, **1:**335
on square lattice, **1:**333
on triangular lattice, **1:**337, **1:**475
Ice rule, **1:**343, **3:**656, **11:**31
model on square lattice, **1:**348, **1:**350
transfer matrix, **1:**364, **1:**390, **1:**393, **1:**408
Ice-like model, **1:**266
Icosahedral symmetry, bond orientation and, **7:**86–87

Ideal Bose gas, **6:**94
  finite size scaling, **8:**217–222
Ideal fluid, **5B:**191
Identification of vertices method,
  3:590
Identity group, **3:**26
1($\frac{1}{2}$) lattice, b.c.c., **3:**227
IF model, **1:**392
IKDP model, **1:**345, **1:**390, **1:**402
Images, method of, **10:**238
Imbalance, **18:**171
Immediate reversals, **1:**263
Immune response, configuration of
  adsorpted macromolecules and,
  7:109
Implicit function theorem, **3:**33
Importance sampling, **5B:**6, **5B:**7
Impurities, **1:**237
Impurity bonds, **2:**163
Impurity effects, **1:**232
Impurity-like interactions, **19:**463–464
Imry-Ma hypothesis, **15:**82, **15:**119
Incidence matrix, **3:**14, **3:**15
Incommensurability, **12:**225, **12:**245,
  12:254, **12:**268, **12:**269, **12:**308,
  12:310, **12:**332
Incommensurate configurations, **15:**18
Incommensurate structures, **15:**2, **15:**11,
  15:15, **15:**48, **15:**51
Incommensurate wavenumber, **15:**29
Incomplete unbinding, **14:**183
Incomplete wetting, **14:**141, **14:**142,
  14:183
Independent percolation *see* Bernoulli
  percolation
Indicator function, **18:**9
Indices (see exponents)
  classical, **6:**528
Indirect neighbours, **2:**275, **2:**278
Inelastic neutron scattering function, site
  mixed layer antiferromagnets,
  7:209
Infinite cluster, **18:**32–5
Infinite clusters, **7:**237
  bond diluted square lattices, **7:**157
  number of, **18:**42–7
  percolating, **7:**237
  percolation correlation lengths and,
  7:165

Infinite membranes, **19:**417, **19:**418,
  19:456
Infinite space dimension, **15:**206–10
Infinite spin dimensionality, **3:**491
1-Insertions, **3:**137, **3:**139, **3:**140, **3:**147,
  3:160, **3:**168
2-Insertions, **3:**153, **3:**154, **3:**158
Infinite spin, **1:**23, **1:**54
Infinite systems
  Bethe ansatz, **19:**114–117
  density relaxation, **19:**98–99
  and dynamical scaling, **19:**63–65
  exponential decay, **19:**65
  hard-core interaction, **19:**103–104
  late time behaviour, **19:**159
Infinite time limit, **19:**53–54
Infinite volume correlation functions,
  1:113
Infinite volume equations, **1:**120
Infinite volume limit, **1:**113, **1:**121,
  1:125, **1:**133, **9:**251, **9:**263, **9:**267,
  9:268, **9:**270, **19:**63, **19:**64
Infinitesimal dilatation, transformation
  for, **6:**23
Infinitesimal rigidity, **18:**266–8, **18:**267
Information content, **2:**293, **2:**295,
  2:296, **2:**299
Information theory, **2:**291
Infrared (IR)
  convergence, **19:**285, **19:**299
  cutoff, **19:**272, **19:**321, **19:**419
  divergences, **19:**280, **19:**282, **19:**284
  finite observable, **19:**281, **19:**366–367
  fixed point, **19:**305, **19:**354, **19:**357,
    19:358, **19:**368, **19:**369–370,
    19:426, **19:**446, **19:**457, **19:**464,
    19:466
Infrared absorption, moment
  calculations, **7:**222
Infrared divergence, **6:**156, **6:**167,
  6:168, **6:**294, **6:**523, **6:**550
Infrared problems, **6:**198, **6:**218,
  6:306
Infrared singularities, **6:**238, **6:**343,
  6:348, **10:**208, **10:**232
Initial conditions, random, **19:**202,
  19:203
Injection rate, overfeeding, **19:**135
Inner opening angle, **14:**116

Inside/outside transitions, **16**:115–21
Instanton methods, **9**:154, **19**:260,
  19:434, **19**:435–439, **19**:441–442,
  19:443
Insulating ferromagnet
  $CrBr_3$, **3**:506
Insulating ferromagnetism, **2**:66
Integer linear programming (ILP),
  18:182
Integrability
  checking, **19**:52
  concept, **19**:4–6
  consequences and practical
    applications, **19**:31
  and matrix representation, **19**:50,
    19:101
  multi-species processes, **19**:51
  scattering amplitude, **19**:101
Integrable systems
  algebraic properties, **19**:50–51
  nearest neighbour processes, **19**:47
  quantum spin models, **19**:51
  relaxation times, **19**:63
  stochastic processes, **19**:6,
    19:30–52
Integral approximant method, **13**:4
Integral counterterms, **19**:298, **19**:299,
  19:341
Integral equation method, **5B**:138–142
Integral equation, **5B**:143, **5B**:145,
  5B:146, **5B**:149, **5B**:150, **5B**:151,
  5B:153, **5B**:158, **5B**:161, **5B**:162,
  5B:166, **5B**:167, **5B**:169, **5B**:188,
  5B:237, **5B**:238, **5B**:240
  HNC, **5B**:237
  matrix, **5B**:162
  PY, **5B**:237
Integral methods, **2**:371
Integral operator, slowly varying,
  5B:163
Integral representation, energy
  expression, **19**:86
Integrated density of states (IDS),
  15:76–8, **15**:90, **15**:103, **15**:129–30,
  15:136, **15**:137, **15**:139, **15**:170,
  15:178, **15**:179, **15**:182, **15**:183,
  15:185, **15**:188, **15**:189, **15**:192,
  15:195, **15**:197, **15**:198, **15**:201–10,
  15:216

Integration measure
  analytical continuation, **19**:309–310
  normalization, **19**:286, **19**:378,
    19:379, **19**:451–452
Interacting dislocation loops in
    superftuid helium, **7**:85
Interacting particle systems
  free fermion nature, **19**:199–200
  quantum Hamiltonian formalism,
    19:41–50
  stochastic dynamics, **19**:3–4
Interacting spin cluster, **3**:264
Interacting vortex lines in superfluid
    helium, **7**:85
Interaction graph, **3**:254, **3**:257, **3**:258,
    3:259, **3**:260, **3**:265, **3**:267, **3**:281,
    3:284, **3**:285, **3**:288, **3**:291, **3**:293,
    3:328
nnn Interactions, **3**:498
Interaction matrix, **15**:96
Interaction picture, **6**:329
Interaction radius, **15**:74–5
Interactions
  anisotropic, **6**:337
  antiferromagnetic, **1**:229, **1**:231
  attractive, **19**:199, **19**:441–442
  contraction, **19**:383–384
  dipolar, **6**:290, **6**:383, **6**:384
  effective, **6**:18
  exclusion, **19**:86, **19**:114–115, **19**:116
  finite-range, **1**:162, **1**:181, **1**:186,
    1:197
  infinite-range, **1**:91, **1**:92, **1**:161,
    1:162
  irrelevant, **6**:525
  local, **19**:68–69
  long-range, **1**:17, **1**:18, **1**:24, **1**:153,
    6:289, **6**:382–394, **8**:75, **12**:16
  many-body, **1**:17, **1**:113, **1**:114
  nearest-neighbour, **1**:179
  on site, **19**:6
  parameters, microscopic, extrapolation
    length and, **8**:15–18
  $r^{-d-\sigma}$, renormalization group and,
    6:14
  random, **6**:428
  relevant, **6**:525
  renormalization group and, **6**:14
  repulsive, **19**:84, **19**:368, **19**:435

see also long-range interactions; short-range interations
short-range, **6:**523, **12:**16
  renormalization group and, **6:**14
time-ordered disorder, **19:**392
translationally invariant, **1:**17
two-body, **1:**113, **1:**123, **1:**124, **1:**161, **1:**162
Intercalation compounds, **8:**446–447
Intercalation, **17:**112
Interconnected structures, droplet-like structures and, **8:**273
Interface
  dynamics, **19:**76, **19:**231
  fluctuations, **19:**79
  growth, **19:**104, **19:**158
Interface free energy, **5B:**66, **8:**5, **8:**64, **8:**66, **8:**67, **8:**69, **8:**75
  essential singularity, **8:**73
Interface growth kinetics, **5B:**94
Interface model, random field Ising model, **7:**247
Interface orientation
  bulk properties affected by, **17:**83–87, **17:**92
  finger formation in combined drive systems affected by, **17:**117
Interface potentials, **14:**346–53
Interface profile, **14:**240–4, **14:**307
Interface roughening, **5B:**103
Interface specific heat, **8:**73
Interface stability, effect of transverse chemical potential gradient, **17:**119
Interface tension, **8:**5, **8:**65, **8:**66, **8:**70
  anisotropy, **8:**71, **8:**72
  critical exponent, **8:**67
  effective, **8:**71
Interface, **1:**90, **2:**81, **2:**85, **2:**86, **2:**87, **2:**93, **2:**94, **2:**95, **5B:**4, **5B:**65, **5B:**66, **5B:**67, **5B:**94, **5B:**102, **5B:**104, **10:**272–8, **12:**138, **12:**143
  dynamics, **10:**342, **10:**355–6
  potential, **12:**22, **12:**43, **12:**113, **12:**126, **12:**139, **12:**142–143, **12:**145, **12:**151, **12:**154–155, **12:**170, **12:**174, **12:**180, **12:**183
  profile, **12:**127
  rough, **12:**172

roughness, **10:**292
s.c. Ising, **5B:**66
stability of, **10:**275
stiffness, **12:**34, **12:**172
structure, **2:**86, **2:**98
structure (2-dimensional Ising model), **10:**294
thickness, **2:**81, **2:**84, **2:**93
wandering, **10:**292–3, **10:**295
Interfaces, **9:**153, **14:**136, **14:**137
  between bulk ordered phases, **8:**34
  bulk second-order transitions, **8:**34
  critical behaviour, **8:**64–76
  delocalization, **8:**65
  dynamics, for models with nonconserved order parameter, **8:**335–339
  field-theoretic methods, **8:**126–128
  in Ising systems, Monte Carlo methods, **8:**116–118
  in *n*-vector models, **8:**75–76
  localization-delocalization transition, **8:**73
  phase transition, **8:**76, **8:**89–91
  pinning, **8:**73
  profile, **8:**67, **8:**68, **8:**70, **8:**72, **8:**76
  roughening transitions, capillary waves and, **8:**69–74
  roughness, **8:**72
  scaling properties of, **14:**150–220
  shape fluctuations of, **14:**151–4
  thickness, **8:**67
  unpinning transition, **8:**73
  width, **8:**68, **8:**70, **8:**71, **8:**72
Interfacial
  dynamics, **10:**354
    (angle-dependent), **10:**12
  finite-size effects, **10:**20, **10:**62
  floating, **10:**62
  free energy, **10:**3, **10:**4, **10:**13, **10:**17, **10:**26, **10:**30, **10:**40, **10:**50, **10:**56, **10:**280
  pinned, **10:**63
  phemomena, **10:**271
  profile, **10:**272, **10:**275, **10:**278, **10:**288
  reflectivity, **10:**314–15
  Weeks model, **10:**65
Interfacial energy, **17:**83

Interfacial fluctuations, **14**:119–20
anomalous correlations, **17**:103–105
Interfacial free energy, **2**:80, **14**:26,
14:138, **14**:139, **14**:153
Interfacial phenomena, **14**:18, **14**:136
Interfacial profiles, **16**:61, **16**:*62*, **16**:*54*,
16:*55*, **16**:61, **16**:*62*, **16**:77, **16**:79,
16:87–105, **16**:*89*, **16**:*100*, **16**:*125*,
16:127–28
Interfacial properties,
randomly driven and two-temperature
models, **17**:103–105
standard model, **17**:80–93
Interfacial roughening transition, **7**:10
Interfacial roughness, **14**:151, **14**:165
suppression of, **17**:7, **17**:81–83
Interfacial tension, **2**:79, **14**:138, **14**:139,
14:142, **16**:13–15, **16**:*14*, **16**:48–53,
16:*51*, **16**:*52*, **16**:57, **16**:59, **16**:61,
16:75, **16**:87–115, **16**:129,
16:141–43, **16**:149, **16**:164–65
Intermediate fluctuation regime, **14**:173,
14:192, **14**:195, **14**:215–17, **14**:246
Internal energy density, **5A**:183
Internal energy, **1**:180, **1**:199, **1**:212,
1:273, **1**:277, **2**:423, **3**:362, **3**:427,
3:532, **3**:584, **14**:265–7
fluctuations in, **17**:49–50
local, **8**:36
Monte Carlo methods, **7**:204
of a fluid, **1**:11, **17**:47, **17**:58
Internal interfaces, **16**:130
Internal stress (IS) percolation, **18**:284
Interparticle distribution function,
19:184
Interparticle interactions
attraction, **17**:20
mixture of competing interactions,
17:195–196
repulsion, **17**:18–19, **17**:138–144
Intrinsic space symmetry, **1**:172
Intrinsically antiferroelectric model,
1:432
Intrinsically ferroelectric model, **1**:430
Invariance properties, **6**:37, **6**:85–88
derivation, **6**:36–41
fixed point Hamiltonians, **6**:8
Invariant, **3**:89, **3**:90
of topology, **3**:89

Invariants, **2**:409, **2**:413
Invasion algorithms, **18**:189–90
Invasion percolation, **18**:69
Inverse correlation length, **5B**:40,
5B:52
of s.c. lattice, **5B**:50
Inverse cut-off, **6**:544
Inverse hexagonal phase, **16**:125,
16:*126*
Inverse range of correlation, **2**:432,
2:433
Inverse range parameter, **5B**:234
Inverse-range expansion, **3**:151
Inversion centre, **3**:581
Involutive Banach algebra, **1**:140
Ionic amphiphiles, **16**:5, **16**:120 *see also*
AOT, SDS
Ionic composition, cells, phase
transition, adsorption and, **7**:109
Ionic conductors, charge carriers in,
17:127
coarse-grained dynamics, **17**:20
modelling, **19**:159
Ionic crystal, **3**:252
Ionic force, **3**:45
Ionic solution theory, **5B**:222, **5B**:223
Ionic solution, **5B**:226, **5B**:238
IR *see* infrared
Iron, **5A**:135, **5A**:143, **5A**:144, **5A**:272,
5A:274
critical neutron scattering, **5A**:143,
5A:144
inelastic neutron scattering, **5A**:272
Irreducible diagram series, **6**:320
Irreducible diagram, **5A**:229, **5A**:230
Irreducible diagrams, **6**:324
Irreducible four-point graphs, **6**:325
Irreducible representation, **3**:292
Irrelevant
bulk operators, **10**:218
eigenvalues, **9**:140, **9**:151
surface operators, **10**:218
variables, **9**:41, **9**:42, **9**:134
Irrelevant field, **5A**:24, **5A**:25
Irrelevant fields, **6**:435, **6**:528, **14**:37
Irrelevant parameters, **6**:379, **6**:383
Irrelevant scaling fields, **14**:38
Irrelevant variables, **6**:379, **6**:520, **6**:533,
6:536

Irrelevant-variable correction to scaling,
    14:55
Irrelevant-variable corrections, **14**:37
Irrelevant-variable, **14**:40, **14**:50
Irreversible thermodynamics, **5A**:167,
    5A:185
Ising antiferromagnet, **1**:224, **3**:251,
    5A:108, **5B**:43
Ising behaviour,
    dipolar, **6**:392
Ising chain, **1**:191, **1**:192, **1**:194, **1**:201
    closed, **1**:203
    kinetic, **5B**:74
    linear, **5B**:77
Ising chains,
    diluted weakly coupled, virtual crystal
        approximations, **7**:213
    dynamics, **7**:196
    pure one-dimensional properties,
        7:178
Ising critical dynamics, Monte Carlo
    methods, **7**:208
Ising cube, rectangular, **5B**:54, **5B**:57
Ising cubes, **14**:106
Ising cylinders, **14**:106
Ising disease, **1**:3
Ising energy, **19**:36
    spin configuration, **19**:32
Ising excluded volume, **2**:158
Ising exponential behaviour, crossover
    from Heisenberg power law critical
    behaviour, **7**:262
Ising ferromagnet, **1**:9, **1**:52, **1**:56, **1**:57,
    1:58, **1**:65, **1**:66, **1**:72, **1**:78, **1**:84,
    1:92, **1**:97, **1**:98, **1**:99, **1**:104,
    1:197, **3**:251, **5A**:83, **5A**:106,
    5A:120
    GKS inequality, **1**:72
    spin greater than $\frac{1}{2}$, **1**:84
Ising ferromagnetic with impurity,
    5B:345
Ising film
    s.c., **5B**:59
    thin, **5B**:53, **5B**:54, **5B**:59
Ising Hamiltonian, **5B**:2
Ising lattice
    finite square, **5B**:55
    s.c., **5B**:37
    16 x 16 x 16 simple cubic, **5B**:41

simple cubic, **5B**:66
s.q., **5B**:37, **5B**:39, **5B**:40, **5B**:83,
    5B:90, **5B**:100
Ising fixed point, **19**:432, **19**:433
Ising free energy, **3**:126
Ising Hamiltonian, **1**:20, **5A**:106,
    5A:107
Ising lattice, **1**:270, **1**:273, **1**:325, **2**:113,
    2:135–6, **2**:163, **2**:252, **2**:371
    b.c.c., beta-brass uniformly
        compressible, **5A**:118
    b.c.c., rigid, **5A**:118
    body centred cubic, **3**:215, **3**:216,
        3:217, **3**:218, **3**:226, **3**:228
    decorated, **1**:271, **1**:291
    decorated honeycomb, **1**:291
    decorated square, **1**:308
    ferromagnetic, **2**:111, **2**:142–3, **2**:250
    finite, **2**:150, **2**:153
    half decorated square, **1**:300
    infinite, **2**:158
    isotropic, **2**:137
    non-crossing diagonal interaction
        square, **1**:302
    planar, **2**:105, **2**:111, **2**:114–6, **2**:139,
        2:145, **2**:149
    s.q., **3**:201, **3**:214, **3**:224, **3**:233, **3**:238
    simple cubic, **3**:211, **3**:212, **3**:213,
        3:214, **3**:215, **3**:238
    square, **1**:310, **2**:114, **2**:140, **2**:150
    three-dimensional, **2**:138
    two-dimensional, **1**:270, **5A**:64
Ising lattice gas, **1**:48
Ising limit, **15**:25
Ising magnet, three-dimensional, **5A**:147
    magnetization, s.c., **5B**:31
Ising magnets
    See *also under* Annealed bond diluted
        Ising magnets; Bond diluted Ising
        model; Bond disordered Ising
        magnets; Bond random Ising
        model; Bond random quantum
        transverse Ising chain; Classical
        Ising magnets; Decorated Ising
        models; Dilute chain Ising
        magnets; Diluted frustrated Ising
        systems; Dilute Ising chain;
        Dilute Ising ferromagnets; Dilute
        Ising magnets; Dilute layer Ising

magnets; Dilute magnets; Dilute
spin half Ising system; Diluted
Ising chains; Diluted Ising
ferromagnets; Diluted Ising layer
magnet; Diluted Ising magnets;
Diluted Ising quadratic layer
magnet; Diluted transverse Ising
model; McCoy–Wu Ising model;
Mixed bond Ising magnets;
Mixed Ising magnets; Pure Ising
magnets; Quenched bond diluted
Ising model; Quenched diluted
Ising models; Quenched site
diluted Ising ferromagnets;
Quenched site diluted Ising
model; Quenched site diluted
transverse Ising model; Random
bond Ising chains; Random field
Ising model; Random Ising
model; Site diluted simple cube
Ising model; Site diluted Ising
ferromagnet; Site diluted Ising
model; Site diluted triangular
lattice Ising model; Site-
disordered Ising model; Spin half
Ising model. Striped random
Ising model; Transverse Ising
models
model, bond diluted, two-dimensional
zero temperature, in transverse
field, phase boundary, **7:**195
bond mixed, **7:**191
self duality, **7:**191
coherent potential approximations,
7:219
exactly soluble, with striped dilution,
phase boundary for, **7:**191
exponential low temperature
dependence, **7:**167
in transverse field, **7:**179
one-dimensional, in transverse field,
zero temperature transitions,
7:178
percolation fixed point, scaling,
7:261
percolation-thermal crossover
exponents, **7:**246
solution, **7:**199
striped randomness models, **7:**181

three-dimensional, exponential
variables, **7:**164
simple cubic lattice, **7:**188
transition temperature, bounds, **7:**189
two-dimensional, critical exponents,
7:178
parameters, **7:**176–177
phase diagrams, **7:**229
specific heat singularity, **7:**188
with arbitrary quenched randomness,
high temperature series
expansion, **7:**229
Ising magnets
transition curves, experimental,
7:263
two-dimensional, intrinsic critical
exponents, **7:**265
Ising model
antiferromagnetic, **18:**17–18, **18:**30–1,
18:47–55, **18:**107–8
agreement percolation, **18:**102–3
application of random cluster
measures to percolation, **18:**65
computer simulation, **18:**67–9
dependent percolation, **18:**40–1
ferromagnetic, **18:**4, **18:**15–17,
18:55–9, **18:**75–7, **18:**87–8,
18:106–7
agreement percolation,
18:94–100
diluted, **18:**115, **18:**116
stochastic domination, **18:**26–30
random, **18:**117–23
see also random-bond magnets;
random-field Ising magnets
(RFIM); random Ising magnets;
triangular Ising solid-on-solid
model (TISOS)
Ising model
b.c.c. low-temperature spin-half series.
Padé analysis, **13:**60–61
spin-*s*, multiparameter fitting method
for, **13:**48–50
square-lattice asymptotic form from
Darboux's theorem, **13:**12
high-temperature susceptibility,
13:9–10, **13:**17
three-dimensional differential
approximants for, **13:**87, **13:**97

triangular-lattice, function-changing
transformation, **13**:125
two-dimensional coefficient
recurrence relations, **13**:83–84
correlation functions, **13**:271
differential approximants for,
13:96–987
temperature susceptibility, **13**:136
Ising model scaling function, **3**:506
Ising model series, **3**:224, **3**:225
high-temperature, **3**:224
low-temperature, **3**:224, **3**:225
Ising model, **1**:12–14, **1**:18, **1**:55, **1**:59,
1:70, **1**:77, **1**:79, **1**:82, **1**:96, **1**:99,
1:104, **1**:151, **1**:152, **1**:153, **1**:155,
1:156, **1**:158, **1**:179, **1**:190, **1**:225,
1:270, **1**:276, **2**:43, **2**:48, **2**:54–5,
2:63, **2**:74, **2**:96, **2**:98, **2**:101–2,
2:104, **2**:112, **2**:119, **2**:120, **2**:123,
2:125, **2**:130–1, **2**:135, **2**:138–9,
2:148–9, **2**:155–8, **2**:162, **2**:221,
2:224, **2**:227, **2**:229, **2**:249, **2**:251,
2:254–7, **2**:261–2, **2**:264, **2**:266,
2:307, **2**:330, **2**:332, **2**:336, **2**:340,
2:342, **2**:357, **2**:370, **2**:372, **2**:376,
2:378, **2**:387, **2**:410, **2**:473, **2**:477,
2:481, **3**:2, **3**:4, **3**:57, **3**:58, **3**:69,
3:72, **3**:73, **3**:74, **3**:76, **3**:84, **3**:85,
3:87, **3**:89, **3**:99, **3**:118, **3**:119,
3:120, **3**:121, **3**:122, **3**:128, **3**:129,
3:131, **3**:133, **3**:135, **3**:149, **3**:162,
3:167, **3**:168, **3**:170, **3**:183, **3**:185,
3:187, **3**:191, **3**:192, **3**:195, **3**:201,
3:209, **3**:224, **3**:228, **3**:229, **3**:232,
3:233, **3**:234, **3**:241, **3**:251, **3**:252,
3:253, **3**:257, **3**:288, **3**:293, **3**:298,
3:299, **3**:301, **3**:304, **3**:307, **3**:313,
3:487, **3**:488, **3**:491, **3**:499, **3**:501,
3:506, **3**:507, **3**:540, **3**:545, **3**:555,
3:556, **3**:557, **3**:571, **3**:573, **3**:611,
3:628, **3**:646, **3**:647, **3**:661, **3**:662,
3:663, **5A**:2, **5A**:3–6, **5A**:7, **5A**:18,
5A:19, **5A**:20, **5A**:22, **5A**:64,
5A:69, **5A**:89, **5A**:93, **5A**:96,
5A:105, **5A**:118, **5A**:119, **5B**:5,
5B:6, **5B**:11, **5B**:13, **5B**:21, **5B**:26,
5B:37, **5B**:51, **5B**:170, **5B**:318,
5B:382, **5B**:383, **5B**:387, **5B**:392,
5B:393, **6**:11, **6**:158, **6**:210, **6**:229,
6:289, **6**:296, **6**:339, **6**:341, **6**:344,
6:382, **6**:394, **6**:429, **6**:440, **6**:462,
6:476, **6**:493, **6**:513, **6**:525, **8**:5,
8:71, **8**:72, **8**:103–107, **9**:16, **9**:140,
9:234, **9**:252, **10**:2, **10**:3, **10**:4,
10:38, **10**:48, **10**:109, **10**:211,
11:26, **11**:51, **11**:71, **11**:73,
11:76–77, **11**:88, **11**:109, **11**:116,
11:119, **11**:132, **11**:143, **11**:186,
11:191, **12**:32, **12**:39, **12**:41,
12:118, **12**:120, **12**:124, **12**:224,
12:236–237, **12**:248, **12**:271, **14**:6,
14:7, **14**:19, **14**:44, **14**:46,
14:47–50, **14**:58–60, **14**:64,
14:86–7, **14**:100, **14**:103, **14**:107,
14:109, **14**:110, **14**:112, **14**:113,
14:115, **14**:118, **14**:119, **14**:151–3,
14:267–8, **14**:364, **14**:365, **15**:42,
15:44, **15**:54, **15**:63, **15**:64, **15**:78,
15:84, **15**:95, **16**:25–6, **16**:148–49,
19:32–35, **19**:47
anisotropic, **10**:19
anti-ferromagnetic, **12**:137, **12**:178
antiferromagnetic (FCC) lattice,
11:134, **11**:139, **11**:145, **11**:168
antiferromagnetic, **8**:230
square lattice, **8**:230
surface exchange, **8**:56
triangular lattice, **8**:230
see also Axial-next-nearest-neighbor
Ising model
b.c.c, **5A**:115, **5A**:117, **10**:41
bond disorder, **19**:433
classical, **1**:22, **1**:202
continuous spin, **9**:281–6, **9**:297
dead layers, **8**:58
decorated lattice, **15**:161
dilute, **2**:244, **2**:261–3, **3**:368, **9**:23
energy function, **19**:48
exact results, **8**:48
ferrimagnetic, **3**:400
ferromagnetic, **3**:205, **3**:209, **11**:139,
11:144
ferromagnets, **8**:280, **10**:5, **10**:27,
10:28, **10**:54
finite size scaling, **8**:229–233
for beta-brass, **5A**:118
frustrated, **11**:3, **11**:50
gauge invariant, **6**:13

geometrical description,
  19:430–431
generalized, **1:**323
Hamiltonian, **6:**14, **11:**137
high-temperature, **3:**117
high-temperature expansion, **19:**257,
  19:408, **19:**431
in zero magnetic field, **1:**9
isotropic, **2:**377
Kawasaki dynamics, **19:**68
kinetic, Ch, 11, **2:**444, **2:**457–9,
  2:460, **2:**464–5, **2:**468, **2:**470,
  2:477, **2:**479, **2:**480, **2:**485–6,
  2:489, **2:**491–2, **5A:**77, **5A:**78,
  5A:344, **5B:**3, **5B:**4, **5B:**13,
  5B:14, **5B:**16, **5B:**19, **5B:**21,
  5B:22, **5B:**25, **5B:**26, **5B:**28,
  5B:29, **5B:**73, **5B:**74, **5B:**77,
  5B:88, **5B:**90, **5B:**95, **10:**250,
  12:270, **12:**325, **19:**76, **19:**185,
  19:186, **19:**187
low-temperature expansion, **19:**256,
  19:408, **19:**431
magnetization profile, **8:**45
Monte Carlo calculations, **8:**109–114
nearest-neighbour, **1:**166
nearest neighbour, molecular theory,
  8:22
of spin s, **1:**23, **1:**99
on a triangular lattice, **11:**144, **11:**172
on the sub-lattice, **11:**199
one-dimensional, **1:**153, **1:**181, **1:**187,
  2:378, **2:**481, **2:**498, **5A:**26,
  9:213, **11:**142, **11:**193–4, **19:**13,
  19:154, **19:**156, **19:**162, **19:**191
partition function, **19:**431
phase diagram, **10:**86, **10:**90, **11:**148,
  11:180
phase diagrams, **8:**57
planar, **10:**48, **10:**49, **10:**62, **10:**67,
  19:230
random bond, **19:**260, **19:**430, **19:**433
random magnetic field, **9:**25
rectangular s.c., **5B:**58
s.c., **5B:**56, **5B:**63, **5B:**95
s.q., **5B:**95
semi-infinite, **10:**92, **10:**95, **10:**110,
  10:160, **10:**187, **10:**219, **10:**251
simple, **3:**361

single spin-flip, **5B:**74
singularities, **19:***430*, **19:**431
smoothly inhomogeneous, **10:**58
specific heat, **8:**153
spin-$\frac{1}{2}$, **3:**182, **3:**223, **3:**232, **3:**489,
  3:578, **3:**621, **3:**622, **3:**646,
  3:654, **9:**18, **9:**273, **9:**287, **9:**296,
  9:298, **11:**145, **11:**196
spin-1, **9:**141, **11:**128, **11:**130
spin configuration, **19:***33*
spin s, **3:**162, **3:**283
spontaneous magnetization, **11:**50
surfaces, **8:**5
  critical exponents, **8:**54
susceptibility, **1:**65
three-dimensional, **1:**75, **2:**432, **3:**200,
  3:209, **3:**629, **5A:**10, **5A:**33,
  5A:78, **5A:**110, **5A:**118, **5A:**119,
  5A:120, **5A:**147, **5B:**24, **5B:**37,
  5B:56, **5B:**61, **8:**73, **9:**288,
  10:113, **11:**142, **12:**42, **15:**45
3-dimensional, renormalization group
  equations, **6:**28
toroidal, **10:**56
transverse, **8:**222–223
triangular, **10:**46
tricritical, **11:**59, **11:**111–21, **11:**118
two-dimensional, **1:**3, **1:**9, **1:**206,
  2:378, **2:**465, **3:**2, **3:**114, **3:**182,
  3:188, **3:**198, **3:**209, **3:**210,
  3:302, **3:**440, **3:**629, **3:**630,
  3:635, **5A:**33, **5A:**37, **5A:**45,
  5A:57, **5A:**61, **5A:**147, **5B:**2,
  5B:33, **5B:**37, **5B:**41, **5B:**57,
  5B:72, **5B:**85, **5B:**104, **6:**95,
  8:34, **8:**48, **8:**57, **8:**59, **9:**241,
  9:291, **10:**87, **10:**242, **10:**294,
  11:82, **11:**187, **11:**195
  bulk exponents, **8:**53
  exact calculations, **8:**49,
    8:201–208
  linear defects, **8:**233
  phenomenological
    renormalization, **8:**176–178
  renormalization group equation,
    6:28
  specific heat, **6:**94
  with free surface, exact results,
    8:50–55

(2 + 1)-dimensional transfers, **8**:249
universality class, **8**:42
two-phase, **19**:*231*
with a free surface, **10**:83
with competing interactions, **9**:139
with general spin, **1**:78
with infinite spin, **1**:78
universality class, **11**:35
Ising model, three-dimensional
high-temperature specific heat, **3**:200
Ising model, two-dimensional
susceptibility, **3**:183
Ising problem, **1**:193, **1**:256, **1**:263
two-dimensional, **1**:194
Ising problems,
short range, **6**:393
Ising random magnet, **6**:420
Ising renormalized coupling constant, **14**:58
Ising result, **1**:205
Ising series, **2**:245
Ising specific heat series
spin ½, **3**:655
Ising spin glasses, **18**:197, **18**:221–34
Ising spin system, **1**:20, **1**:54, **1**:277, **5B**:128, **5B**:182
Ising spin, **1**:316
higher, **1**:271
Ising spin-½ series
low temperature, **3**:656
Ising spins, anisotropic magnets, **8**:18
Ising strips, two-dimensional, exact
calculations, **8**:47
Ising susceptibility configuration, **3**:70
Ising susceptibility series, **3**:199
Ising susceptibility, **3**:235
high-temperature, **3**:232
two-dimensional, **3**:189
Ising system, **6**:327
beta-brass, **5A**:111
three-dimensional, **5A**:89, **5A**:105–120
Ising systems, **8**:69, **8**:74
antiferromagnetic, **8**:231
interfaces, Monte Carlo methods, **8**:116–118
position renormalization group
calculations, **8**:128–134

surface free energy, **8**:64
two-dimensional, **8**:56, **8**:57, **8**:71
long-range modification of surface
interactions, **8**:59–61
Ising variable, **7**:259
Ising walk, **3**:473, **3**:475
Ising–Heisenberg–*XY* critical point,
partial differential approximants
for, **13**:117
Ising-like system,
dipolar, **6**:421
Ising-susceptibility series high
temperature generalized inverse
Padé approximants for, **13**:80–83
Roskies approach, **13**:72
Roskies' quadratic transformation for, **13**:72
Zinn–Justin method for, **13**:23–25
Ising-universality critical point, **14**:42
Isingantiferroroagnet, **1**:224
Isobaric heat capacity, **5B**:345
Isochore, **5B**:190
Isomorphism, **5B**:365, **5B**:384, **5B**:389
Isomorphy, **5B**:382
of critical phenomena, **5B**:345
of phase transitions, **5B**:347
of second-order phase transitions, **5B**:344
Isooctane/nitroethane mixture, **5A**:327
Isothermal compressibility, **1**:99, **1**:190, **5B**:250, **5B**:345
Isothermal susceptibility, **1**:190, **5B**:44, **5B**:45
Isotopic Heisenberg layer magnets,
transition temperatures,
experimental, **7**:264
Isotopic XY layer magnets, transition
temperatures, experimental, **7**:264
Isotropic case, **14**:48
Isotropic index, **6**:513
Isotropic magnet, **5A**:281
Isotropic *n*-vector. *see* *O*(*n*) model
Isotropic systems, **6**:293–354
Isotropic three-dimensional systems, **14**:84
Isotropy, **2**:116
Iteration, **1**:295
extended, **1**:271, **1**:312

Itinerant electron ferromagnet, **5A**:286, **5A**:287
Itinerant electron model, **5A**:286
Ito (prepoint) discretization, **19**:377, **19**:387, **19**:392
Ice models, **10**:2

J

J model, **1**:345
Jacobi imaginary transformation, **1**:387
Jacobi matrices, **15**:163, **15**:164
Jacobian, **3**:144
Janzen-Rayleigh expansion, computer extension, **13**:130–131
Jastrow assumption, **5B**:217
Joint probability distributions, dilute magnetism, **7**:156
Jordan–Wigner transformation, **1**:250, **12**:252, **12**:264, **12**:272, **12**:277, **19**:175, **19**:177–178
Josephson inequality, **5A**:53, **5A**:56, **5A**:61–63, **5A**:74, **5A**:75
Josephson relation, **7**:23, **8**:192, **8**:222
Josephson-junction arrays, **12**:329

K

K dimer models, **13**:240–241
  3–d, **13**:278–280
  area per chain, **13**:287
  for biomembranes, **13**:282–283
  for commensurate-incommensurate transitions, **13**:290–291
  correlation functions, **13**:271–273
    and anisotropy, **13**:272–273
    correlation lengths, **13**:272
    Green's functions in, **13**:271–272
  entropy, **13**:287
  finite-size scaling, **13**:274–275
  phase diagram, **13**:287–289
K models, **17**:52
K-type transitions in dimer models, **13**:239, **13**:247–252
  3–12/1 model, **13**:244
  4–8 models, **13**:245–247
  commensurate/incommensurate, **13**:293
  conservation property, **13**:249, **13**:250–251
    4–8 models, **13**:250–251
    VH models, **13**:251–252
  domain wall perturbations, **13**:248
    4–8/2/1 model, **13**:249–250
    K models, **13**:261
    lipid bilayers, **13**:285
    and scaling theory, **13**:274
    spatial anisotropy, **13**:252
    SQK model, **13**:244
    VH models, **13**:241, **13**:261–263
K-weights, **2**:239, **2**:260
k-weights, **2**:234–7, **2**:239, **2**:241
Kac integral equation, **5B**:142, **5B**:153, **5B**:157
Kac inverse range parameter, **5B**:207
Kac limit, **12**:50, **12**:51, **12**:74
Kac potential, **5B**:112, **5B**:113, **5B**:118, **5B**:122, **5B**:127, **5B**:131, **5B**:132, **5B**:136, **5B**:138, **5B**:169, **5B**:170, **5B**:178, **5B**:183, **5B**:186, **5B**:187, **9**:97, **9**:103
  long-range, **5B**:128
  oscillatory, **5B**:136
Kac, Uhlenbeck and Hemmer, **5B**:148, **5B**:149, **5B**:151
Kac-determinant, **11**:56, **11**:57
  formula, **11**:96, **11**:100, **11**:103, **11**:106, **11**:107, **11**:112, **11**:116
Kac–Szego theorem, **2**:108, **2**:112
Kac–Ward determinant, **1**:235, **1**:236, **1**:263, **1**:265
Kac–Ward method, **2**:141
Kadanoff's cell model, **6**:42
Kadanoff–Wilson Groups, **6**:540–544
Kadanoff–Wilson transformation, **6**:542
Kadanoll–Wilson approach, **6**:514, **6**:523, **6**:552
Kagomé lattice, **2**:223
  see Lattice, Kagomé expanded, **1**:297
Kagome SOS (KSOS), **11**:43
  F-model, **11**:46
  lattice, **11**:44–45
Kardar–Parisi–Zhang (KPZ) equation, **17**:80, **17**:170, **17**:175, **17**:176, **18**:187, **18**:192, **18**:194, **19**:52, **19**:158

and Burgers equation, **17**:177
conserved version, **17**:179
and driven interfaces, **17**:9, **17**:175,
17:176, **17**:177
and Navier–Stokes equation, **17**:177
Kasteleyn, *see* K dimer models: K-type
transitions
Kaufman–Onsager spinor treatment,
1:236
Kawasaki dynamics, **17**:11, **17**:95,
17:141, **17**:191
compared with Glauber spin-flip
dynamics, **17**:171–172
with infinite range, **17**:172
Kawasaki spin-flip dynamics, **19**:43,
19:68, **19**:108
Kawasaki-type calculations, **14**:89
KDP model, **1**:343, **1**:394, **1**:402, **1**:408,
1:411, **3**:657, **3**:664, **12**:300–303,
see Phase transition, KDP type
general, **1**:413
modified, **1**:439, **1**:440, **1**:441,
1:453
KDP, **3**:656
Kelly–Sherman expansion, **9**:296
Kelly–Sherman theorem, **1**:72–74
Kelvin equation, **12**:159, **12**:163
Kikuchi's approximation, **2**:342, **2**:345,
2:348, **2**:351, **2**:354, **2**:355, **2**:357,
2:360, **2**:361, **2**:362, **2**:365, **2**:366,
2:368, **2**:371
Kinematic interaction, **3**:250
Kinetic coefficient, **2**:480, **14**:20
Kinetic equation, **5A**:200, **5A**:372
for gross variables, **5A**:189
Kinetic gelation, **14**:66
Kinetic matrix, **2**:452, **2**:454, **2**:455,
2:479, **2**:480
Kinetic phenomena, **5B**:389
Kinetic slowing down of fluctuations,
5B:76
Kinetic theory of gases, **5A**:190
Kinetics of liquid–gas transitions,
2:444
Kinetics of order–disorder, **2**:444
Kink point, **2**:62
Kink solution, order parameter profile,
8:65
Kinks, **9**:112

Kirkwood superposition approximation,
5B:219, **5B**:221
generalized (GKSA), **5B**:221
Kirkwood transition, **1**:183
Kirkwood-Riseman theory, **12**:459,
12:461, **12**:476
Kirkwood–Salsburg equations, **11**:157
see K.S equations
Kirkwood–Salsburg method, **10**:24
Kjaer–Hilhorst model, **14**:224–5
Klauder model, partial differential
approximants for, **13**:118–119
KMS boundary conditions, **1**:123, **1**:139,
1:144, **1**:145, **1**:146, **1**:147, **1**:148,
1:150, **1**:151, **1**:166, **1**:173
dynamical, **1**:149
Knot
algebraic invariant, **7**:146
integral invariant for, **7**:145
numerical enumerations, **7**:147
Knot formation, double-stranded DNA,
7:133
Knot theory, **7**:132, **7**:146
Kolmogorov–Arnold–Moser (KAM)
theorem, **15**:15
Kondo effect, **6**:8
Kondo problem, **6**:5
transformation equations for, **6**:27
Kosterlitz and Thouless transition (KT),
11:20, **11**:22, **11**:25–29
Kosterlitz recursion relations, **7**:21
universal jump and, **7**:18–25
Kosterlitz Thouless transition, **14**:140,
14:174
Kosterlitz–Thouless-type phase
transition, **13**:126
singularities, **13**:26–29, **13**:70
Kosterlitz–Thouless (Berezinskii)
transition, **10**:159, **10**:187, **10**:253
Kosterlitz–Thouless (KT) phase,
15:39
Kosterlitz–Thouless theory, superfluid
helium films, **7**:83
Kosterlitz–Thouless transition, **7**:160,
17:143, **17**:186
at finite temperatures, **7**:79
helium films, third sound, **7**:35
in superfluids, **7**:69
vortex dynamics near, **7**:31

Kosterlitz–Thouless transitions, **8**:56, **8**:57
finite size scaling, **8**:192–195
Kosterlitz–Thouless, *see* KT transition
melting, **12**:237, **12**:253, **12**:284
type, **12**:279
Kramer doublet, **3**:578
Kramers–Wannier transformation, **12**:324
Kruskal's algorithm, **18**:158
KS equations, **1**:43, **1**:45, **1**:48, **1**:56, **1**:57, **1**:65, **1**:111, **1**:113, **1**:115, **1**:117, **1**:119, **1**:122, **1**:132, **1**:133, **1**:149
KSA *see* Kirkwood superposition approximation
KT transition (Kosterlitz–Thouless), **12**:255, **12**:281–283, **12**:287, **12**:288–290, **12**:295, **12**:329–332
Kubo canonical correlation, **5A**:198
Kubo method, indirect, **2**:453
Kubo–Martin–Schwinger boundary conditions, *see* KMS boundary conditions
Kubo–Martin–Schwinger state, **1**:145, **1**:147, **1**:149
extremal, **1**:147, **1**:148, **1**:149, **1**:151, **1**:167, **1**:169, **1**:170
extremal time-invariant, **1**:148
KUH *see* Kac, Uhlenbeck and Hemmer

L

L_3 phase, **16**:5, **16**:13, **16**:115–21, **16**:164
light-scattering data, **16**:*118*
$La_2Ni_3(NO_3)_{12}.24H_2O$, **3**:580
$LaAlO_3$, **3**:583, **3**:647
Label correcting algorithms, **18**:153
minimal path, **18**:156–7
Label setting algorithms, **18**:153
Labelled configuration, **3**:101
Ladder graph, **2**:232
Ladder operators, **19**:20, **19**:35–36, **19**:107
Ladder, **1**:244, **1**:245
Lagrange method, **3**:49
Lagrange multiplier, **15**:80
Lagrange theorem, **3**:21, **3**:22

Lagrange's inversion formula, **2**:412, **2**:415, **2**:419
λ-line, **2**:10
λ-transition state of liquid helium, **2**:12, **2**:19
Lagrangian field theory, **9**:251
Laman's theorem, **18**:270, **18**:289–90, **18**:293–5
body Laman theorem, **18**:271
Lambda line, **9**:3, **9**:6, **9**:9, **9**:36, **9**:37, **9**:53, **9**:54, **9**:57, **9**:68, **9**:69, **9**:72, **9**:73, **9**:75, **9**:76, **9**:78, **9**:85, **9**:91, **9**:92, **9**:100–3, **9**:106, **9**:107, **9**:110, **9**:111, **9**:125–9, **9**:131, **9**:132, **9**:152, **14**:90
Lame coefficients, **7**:5
Lamé coefficients, **19**:268
Lamé equation, **15**:13
Lamellar phases, **16**:*4*, **16**:*5*, **16**:*41*, **16**:53, **16**:57, **16**:68, **16**:74, **16**:105, **16**:107, **16**:110, **16**:112–13, **16**:*115*, **16**:*125*, **16**:151–5
Laminar flow through coiled pipe, **13**:133–134
Landau argument, **1**:172, **1**:174
Landau expansion, **8**:13, **8**:18, **8**:29, **8**:33, **8**:66, **16**:36–37, **16**:44, **16**:82–3
Landau free energy, **5A**:38
Landau functional, **5A**:56, **5A**:82
classical, **5A**:49–55, **5A**:56, **5A**:76, **5A**:83
generalized, **5A**:48, **5A**:57, **5A**:61, **5A**:62, **5A**:81, **5A**:83
generalizing, **5A**:56
non-local term, **5A**:56
Landau–Ginzburg-Wilson functional, **6**:170
Landau levels, **15**:216–17
Landau model, **6**:55
Landau–Peierls Hamiltonian, **16**:151
Landau theory, **5A**:35, **5A**:36, **5A**:37, **5A**:38, **5B**:345, **6**:168, **6**:170, **6**:330, **7**:7, **8**:14, **8**:15, **8**:18, **8**:19, **8**:22, **8**:45, **8**:49, **10**:93, **10**:98, **10**:99, **10**:102, **10**:104, **10**:106, **10**:127, **10**:156, **10**:157, **10**:161, **10**:232, **15**:57–9, **15**:62
amplitude fluctuations and, **7**:16–18

bulk smectics, **7**:81
classical, **5A**:37, **5A**:38, **5A**:44–46,
    5A:55–71
critical phenomena, **6**:9
ε-expansion and, **6**:1
equilibrium, **5A**:37
for local critical behaviour, Ising
    ferromagnets, **8**:6–10
generalized, **5A**:36, **5A**:37, **5A**:38,
    5A:44, **5A**:55–71, **8**:46, 48
mean field (MF) theory, **10**:109
Onsager rejection, **5A**:45
predictions, **5A**:36
time-dependent, **5A**:37, **5A**:73–75
two-dimensional melting, **7**:40–45
Wilson modification, **5A**:55
Landau, **9**:2, **9**:3, **9**:207
theory, **9**:15, **9**:16, **9**:18, **9**:22, **9**:53,
    9:58, **9**:59, **9**:60, **9**:96, **9**:104,
    9:171
Landau–Ginsburg–Wilson model, **9**:153,
    9:154
Landau–Ginzburg expansion, **10**:90
Landau–Ginzburg Hamiltonian,
    11:98
theory, **11**:114
Landau–Ginzburg–Wilson free energy,
    12:113, **12**:123–124
Hamiltonians, **12**:176, **12**:224
model, **12**:66
theory, **12**:16, **12**:39, **12**:123–127,
    12:131–135, **12**:154–155,
    12:165, **12**:189, **12**:194
Landau–Ginzburg–Wilson Hamiltonian,
    10:276, **10**:280, **10**:298, **15**:60,
    15:65
Landau–Ginzburg–Wilson interaction,
    6:128
Landau–Khalatnikov theory, **5A**:72,
    5A:73, **5A**:76
Landau–Ginzburg–Wilson theory,
    19:440, **19**:442, **19**:445, **19**:446
Lanes, **14**:326
Langer–Bar-on–Miller approximation,
    spinodal decomposition, statistical
    theories, **8**:322–327
Langevin approach, **19**:4, **19**:234,
    19:235, **19**:236, **19**:377–380,
    19:385, **19**:390–391, **19**:394

Langevin dynamics, **12**:438
Langevin equation, **5A**:193, **10**:343,
    17:5–6, **17**:19–25
and dynamic functional, **17**:35, **17**:60,
    17:61
for driven interfaces, **17**:175–178
generalized, **5A**:361
multi-species model, **17**:131, **17**:177,
    17:181
noiseless version, **17**:78
randomly driven and multi-
    temperature models, **17**:97
standard model, **17**:22, **17**:27, **17**:34,
    17:78,
systems driven by chemical
    potential gradient, **17**:109,
    17:115
systems with generic scale invariance,
    17:184
systems with quenched random
    impurities, **17**:145–146
systems with repulsive interactions,
    17:139
two-layer model, **17**:125
Langevin force, **17**:20, **17**:109
Langevin function, **3**:225, **5B**:27
Laplace equation for pressure difference,
    16:100, **16**:101
Laplace equation, **12**:384,
    12:387–388, **12**:395, **12**:400,
    12:427, **12**:473, **12**:475, **19**:412,
    19:422, **19**:452
transform, **19**:315
Laplace transform, **1**:185, **7**:123, **7**:124,
    7:126, **15**:91
inversion, **7**:126–127
Laplace–Beltrami operator, **16**:133
Large canonical ensemble, **19**:80
Large-interaction-radius model,
    15:233–5
Large-*n* limit conductivity in Wegner
    model, **15**:210–15
in continuous models, **15**:215–17
in statistical mechanics, **15**:73–165
of disordered *n*-vector model,
    15:116–37
general one-site anisotropy,
    15:128–33
random external field, **15**:116–21

random uniaxial model, **15:**121–8
of non-translationally invariant
  n-vector model, **15:**108–16
  correlation functions, **15:**113–16
  free energy, **15:**108–13
Large-*n* amplitudes, **14:**51
Large-*n* limit, **14:**51, **14:**52, **14:**55–7,
  14:105
Larson model, **16:**68–70
Laser optics, **1:**4
Late time behaviour *see* asymptotic
  behaviour
Latent heat, **2:**36, **8:**51
  finite size scaling, **8:**196
Lattice animals, **12:**445, **12:**451, **14:**43,
  14:67–8
  multiparameter fitting, **13:**50
Lattice
  anisotropic *d*-dimensional, **3:**466,
    3:467
  anisotropic f.c.c., **3:**466
  anisotropic rectangular, **3:**464
  anisotropic s.c., **3:**466, **3:**467
  b.c.c. (body centred cubic), **3:**90,
    3:92, **3:**104, **3:**200, **3:**216,
    3:217, **3:**218, **3:**223, **3:**228,
    3:246, **3:**249, **3:**250, **3:**251,
    3:261, **3:**273, **3:**274, **3:**275,
    3:285, **3:**286, **3:**287, **3:**294,
    3:295, **3:**296, **3:**297, **3:**298,
    3:306, **3:**307, **3:**308, **3:**309,
    3:313, **3:**314, **3:**317, **3:**319,
    3:321, **3:**327, **3:**342, **3:**344,
    3:345, **3:**346, **3:**347, **3:**349,
    3:350, **3:**363, **3:**373, **3:**384,
    3:385, **3:**401, **3:**405, **3:**407,
    3:408, **3:**412, **3:**415, **3:**416,
    3:417, **3:**419, **3:**420, **3:**421,
    3:422, **3:**425, **3:**426, **3:**427,
    3:429, **3:**431, **3:**432, **3:**433,
    3:434, **3:**435, **3:**436, **3:**437,
    3:438, **3:**440, **3:**442, **3:**448,
    3:449, **3:**452, **3:**454, **3:**457,
    3:458, **3:**459, **3:**461, **3:**463,
    3:464, **3:**497, **3:**498, **3:**506,
    3:525, **3:**530, **3:**531, **3:**581,
    3:594, **3:**595, **3:**601, **3:**604,
    3:607, **3:**617, **3:**618, **3:**619,
    3:621, **3:**622, **3:**625, **3:**628,

    3:629, **3:**641, **3:**644, **3:**645,
    3:646, **3:**647, **3:**648
  b.c.c. (12), **3:**286, **3:**296, **3:**297,
    3:298, **3:**306, **3:**307, **3:**313,
    3:314, **3:**345, **3:**349
  b.c.c. (123), **3:**286, **3:**298
  Bethe, **3:**400, **3:**528
  computer, **3:**105
  cristobalite, **3:**462, **3:**581
  decorated honeycomb, **3:**461
  diamond (d.), **3:**90, **3:**92, **3:**104,
    3:200, **3:**201, **3:**218, **3:**373,
    3:381, **3:**384, **3:**405, **3:**408,
    3:411, **3:**417, **3:**419, **3:**420,
    3:421, **3:**422, **3:**425, **3:**426,
    3:427, **3:**432, **3:**433, **3:**434,
    3:435, **3:**437, **3:**438, **3:**441,
    3:442, **3:**452, **3:**581, **3:**664
  f.c.c. (face centred cubic), **3:**69, **3:**90,
    3:91, **3:**92, **3:**104, **3:**112, **3:**128,
    3:189, **3:**191, **3:**195, **3:**200,
    3:213, **3:**217, **3:**218, **3:**246,
    3:249, **3:**250, **3:**273, **3:**274,
    3:275, **3:**287, **3:**291, **3:**294,
    3:295, **3:**297, **3:**298, **3:**299,
    3:301, **3:**305, **3:**306, **3:**307,
    3:308, **3:**309, **3:**312, **3:**313,
    3:314, **3:**316, **3:**317, **3:**319,
    3:320, **3:**321, **3:**323, **3:**324,
    3:325, **3:**327, **3:**341, **3:**344,
    3:345, **3:**346, **3:**349, **3:**350,
    3:373, **3:**381, **3:**384, **3:**385,
    3:389, **3:**403, **3:**405, **3:**411,
    3:415, **3:**419, **3:**420, **3:**421,
    3:425, **3:**426, **3:**427, **3:**429,
    3:431, **3:**432, **3:**433, **3:**434,
    3:435, **3:**436, **3:**437, **3:**438,
    3:440, **3:**441, **3:**442, **3:**452,
    3:458, **3:**462, **3:**463, **3:**464,
    3:494, **3:**497, **3:**498, **3:**506,
    3:507, **3:**529, **3:**531, **3:**535,
    3:536, **3:**548, **3:**555, **3:**581,
    3:589, **3:**594, **3:**595, **3:**601,
    3:604, **3:**606, **3:**607, **3:**611,
    3:615, **3:**616, **3:**617, **3:**618,
    3:619, **3:**621, **3:**622, **3:**623,
    3:624, **3:**625, **3:**628, **3:**629,
    3:630, **3:**632, **3:**634, **3:**641,
    3:644, **3:**645, **3:**646, **3:**647

f.c.c. (12), **3:**286, **3:**296, **3:**297, **3:**298,
   3:306, **3:**307, **3:**313, **3:**314,
   3:320, **3:**345, **3:**349
f.c.c. (123), **3:**286, **3:**298
hexagonal close-packed, **3:**297,
   3:462
honeycomb (h.c.), **3:**90, **3:**92, **3:**217,
   3:231, **3:**380, **3:**381, **3:**386,
   3:405, **3:**408, **3:**409, **3:**410,
   3:411, **3:**417, **3:**419, **3:**420,
   3:421, **3:**422, **3:**425, **3:**426,
   3:427, **3:**430, **3:**431, **3:**434,
   3:435, **3:**448, **3:**450, **3:**454,
   3:456, **3:**457
hydrogen peroxide, **3:**92, **3:**461, **3:**581
hypercubical, **3:**522
hyperkagomé (h.k.), **3:**462
hypertriangular (h.t.), **3:**462
kagomé, **3:**104, **3:**202, **3:**461
linear chain, **3:**510, **3:**523, **3:**524,
   3:553, **3:**554
p.t. (plane triangular), **3:**90, **3:**91,
   3:92, **3:**104, **3:**106, **3:**128, **3:**182,
   3:185, **3:**189, **3:**191, **3:**193,
   3:195, **3:**202, **3:**213, **3:**217,
   3:229, **3:**231, **3:**234, **3:**246,
   3:273, **3:**274, **3:**275, **3:**294,
   3:296, **3:**297, **3:**298, **3:**299,
   3:301, **3:**310, **3:**317, **3:**345,
   3:347, **3:**348, **3:**349, **3:**359,
   3:373, **3:**374, **3:**380, **3:**381,
   3:386, **3:**409, **3:**411, **3:**413,
   3:417, **3:**419, **3:**420, **3:**421,
   3:424, **3:**425, **3:**426, **3:**427,
   3:429, **3:**430, **3:**431, **3:**434,
   3:435, **3:**437, **3:**448, **3:**450,
   3:457, **3:**463, **3:**464, **3:**497,
   3:544, **3:**545, **3:**636, **3:**637,
   3:638, **3:**639, **3:**641
regular, **3:**104, **3:**105, **3:**462
regular non-Bravais, **3:**462
s.c. (simple cubic), **3:**90, **3:**92, **3:**104,
   3:186, **3:**195, **3:**196, **3:**197,
   3:199, **3:**200, **3:**210, **3:**211,
   3:212, **3:**213, **3:**217, **3:**218,
   3:235, **3:**236, **3:**237, **3:**240,
   3:241, **3:**246, **3:**249, **3:**250,
   3:261, **3:**273, **3:**274, **3:**275,
   3:285, **3:**286, **3:**294, **3:**295,

   3:296, **3:**297, **3:**298, **3:**306,
   3:307, **3:**309, **3:**310, **3:**313,
   3:314, **3:**317, **3:**320, **3:**327,
   3:343, **3:**344, **3:**345, **3:**347,
   3:349, **3:**350, **3:**359, **3:**363,
   3:373, **3:**380, **3:**381, **3:**384,
   3:385, **3:**402, **3:**405, **3:**408,
   3:412, **3:**416, **3:**417, **3:**419,
   3:420, **3:**421, **3:**422, **3:**425,
   3:426, **3:**427, **3:**429, **3:**431,
   3:432, **3:**433, **3:**434, **3:**435,
   3:436, **3:**437, **3:**438, **3:**440,
   3:442, **3:**452, **3:**454, **3:**457,
   3:458, **3:**459, **3:**460, **3:**461,
   3:463, **3:**464, **3:**494, **3:**497,
   3:498, **3:**506, **3:**510, **3:**581,
   3:601, **3:**604, **3:**607, **3:**617,
   3:618, **3:**619, **3:**622, **3:**625,
   3:628, **3:**641, **3:**647, **3:**648
s.c. (12), **3:**286, **3:**296, **3:**297, **3:**298,
   3:306, **3:**307, **3:**313, **3:**314,
   3:345, **3:**349
s.c. (123), **3:**286, **3:**298
shadow, **3:**408, **3:**409, **3:**410, **3:**411,
   3:422
spinel, **3:**462
s.q. (simple quadratic), **3:**90, **3:**92,
   3:101, **3:**104, **3:**108, **3:**185,
   3:195, **3:**196, **3:**197, **3:**198,
   3:210, **3:**211, **3:**213, **3:**217,
   3:235, **3:**236, **3:**246, **3:**273,
   3:275, **3:**294, **3:**296, **3:**297,
   3:298, **3:**310, **3:**345, **3:**348,
   3:349, **3:**358, **3:**363, **3:**373,
   3:381, **3:**386, **3:**402, **3:**405,
   3:406, **3:**408, **3:**411, **3:**414,
   3:415, **3:**417, **3:**419, **3:**420,
   3:421, **3:**422, **3:**424, **3:**425,
   3:426, **3:**427, **3:**430, **3:**431,
   3:433, **3:**434, **3:**435, **3:**437,
   3:440, **3:**448, **3:**453, **3:**454,
   3:457, **3:**459, **3:**460, **3:**461,
   3:463, **3:**464, **3:**467, **3:**497,
   3:510, **3:**548, **3:**549, **3:**636,
   3:637, **3:**638, **3:**639, **3:**655,
   3:656, **3:**663
two-layer quadratic, **3:**462
Lattice anisotropy, **3:**489, **3:**494, **3:**506,
   3:573, **3:**579

Lattice anisotropy, **14**:48
Lattice
  b.c.c., **5A**:105, **5A**:107, **5A**:110
  Brownian motion, **19**:9
  Burgers equation, **19**:104
  derivative, density profile,
    19:130–131
  diffusion, with absorbing
    boundary, **19**:170
  equation, solution, **19**:173
  f.c.c., **5A**:136, **5A**:138
  gas
    collective velocity, **19**:147
    diffusive, **19**:157–158
    driven, **19**:3, **19**:103–161, **19**:171
    hard core, **19**:41–45
    as model system, **19**:8–9, **19**:13
    multi-species, **19**:16, **19**:97
    one-dimensional, **19**:8–10
    particle number conservation,
      19:55
    shock, **19**:124–125
  gauge theory, **19**:256, **19**:408
  Ising rigid, **5A**:110
  s.q., **5A**:20, **5A**:64, **5A**:65
  p.t., **5A**:65
  random walk, **19**:23, **19**:82, **19**:412
  sawtooth configuration, **19**:231,
    19:232, **19**:235
  sites, finite number of particles, **19**:6
  spacing, vanishing, **19**:62
  three-dimensional reciprocal, **5A**:149,
    5A:150
  transformation, **5A**:21, **5A**:22
  triangular, **5A**:64, **5A**:65
  two-dimensional, **5A**:21
Lattice colouring, of hexagonal, **1**:342,
  1:476
  of square, **1**:461
Lattice constant expansion connected,
  3:84, **3**:382
  star, **3**:84, **3**:382, **3**:398, **3**:405
  weak, **3**:396
Lattice constant, **3**:2, **3**:3, **3**:13, **3**:57,
  3:58, **3**:59, **3**:60, **3**:61, **3**:62, **3**:65,
  3:66, **3**:70, **3**:71, **3**:75, **3**:77, **3**:78,
  3:90, **3**:92, **3**:100, **3**:108, **3**:269,
  3:271, **3**:272, **3**:360, **3**:375, **3**:378,
  3:379, **3**:387, **3**:388, **3**:393, **3**:395,

  3:462, **3**:463, **3**:522, **3**:558, **3**:600,
  3:601
  articulated, **3**:65, **3**:84, **3**:399
  articulated graph, **3**:68
  closed graph, **3**:70
  connected, **3**:58, **3**:59, **3**:60, **3**:65,
    3:66, **3**:67, **3**:71, **3**:73, **3**:74,
    3:75, **3**:76, **3**:77, **3**:90, **3**:390,
    3:398
  disconnected, **3**:58, **3**:59, **3**:65, **3**:71,
    3:87, **3**:89
  disjoint, **3**:381, **3**:382
  full perimeter, **3**:77, **3**:382
  high temperature, **3**:58, **3**:59
  irreducible, **3**:274
  low temperature, **3**:58, **3**:59
  magnetic, **3**:379
  separated, **3**:58
  simple chain, **3**:69
  star, **3**:58, **3**:59, **3**:60, **3**:65, **3**:67,
    3:68, **3**:69, **3**:71, **3**:86, **3**:90,
    3:92, **3**:387, **3**:398, **3**:400, **3**:401,
    3:475
  strong, **3**:62, **3**:63, **3**:67, **3**:69, **3**:70,
    3:73, **3**:76, **3**:89, **3**:90, **3**:92,
    3:127, **3**:176, **3**:178, **3**:390,
    3:392
  strong full perimeter, **3**:77
  tabulation, **3**:90
  weak, **3**:13, **3**:62, **3**:63, **3**:67, **3**:69,
    3:89, **3**:90, **3**:92, **3**:127, **3**:128,
    3:135, **3**:176, **3**:178, **3**:395,
    3:587
  weak f.c.c., **3**:588, **3**:602, **3**:603,
    3:605, **3**:606, **3**:608, **3**:609,
    3:610, **3**:613, **3**:614
  weak full perimeter, **3**:77
  zero field, **3**:379
Lattice constants,
  strong, **2**:241, **2**:260
  weak, **2**:241
Lattice count, **3**:254, **3**:273, **3**:274,
  3:275, **3**:276, **3**:285, **3**:286
Lattice defect, **5B**:349
Lattice fluid kinetic energy operator,
  3:575
Lattice gas model, **1**:162, **1**:232, **1**:241,
  2:8, **2**:18, **2**:41, **2**:54, **2**:55, **2**:85,
  2:96, **2**:104, **3**:502, **8**:68

Lattice gas problem, **2**:366, **2**:370
Lattice gas, **1**:3, **1**:12, **1**:13, **1**:14, **1**:17,
    1:18, **1**:23, **1**:24, **1**:48, **1**:49, **1**:53,
    1:56, **1**:59, **1**:60, **1**:61, **1**:63, **1**:64,
    1:65, **1**:66, **1**:69, **1**:84, **1**:148,
    1:153, **1**:163, **1**:164, **1**:187, **1**:241,
    1:242, **1**:243, **2**:199, **2**:305, **2**:306,
    2:307, **2**:308, **2**:314, **2**:315, **2**:316,
    2:321–3, **2**:347–9, **2**:358–9, **2**:448,
    3:2, **3**:394, **3**:398, **3**:400, **5B**:128,
    5B:143, **5B**:145, **5B**:148, **5B**:185,
    5B:207, **5B**:208, **5B**:248, **5B**:251,
    5B:252, **5B**:253, **5B**:255, **5B**:257,
    5B:375, **5B**:387
  Bose, **1**:116
  hard cores **1**:69
  hard core, **2**:347, **2**:349, **2**:363–4,
      2:368, **2**:371
  hard sphere, **2**:307, **2**:308, **2**:310–12,
      2:314, **2**:325
  hard-square, **1**:69, **1**:71, **2**:323, **2**:457,
      2:462
  imperfect, **1**:232
  mixtures, **1**:69
  relation to spin system, **1**:14
  triangular, **2**:213, **2**:325
  van der Waals-like, **1**:243
Lattice
  gas, **9**:204
  Green's function, **9**:245, **9**:263
Lattice gases, **8**:5
  finite size scaling, **8**:229–233
  Potts, finite size scaling, **8**:235
Lattice gauge theories, **12**:248
Lattice gauge theory four-dimensional
      non-Abelian SU(2), **8**:250
  four-dimensional $U(1)$, **8**:250
  two-dimensional SU(2), **8**:250
Lattice insensitive, **1**:266
Lattice model, **1**:23, **1**:228, **1**:232
  decorated, **5B**:345
Lattice models, **14**:119, **15**:29, **16**:22–74
  results of, **16**:33–74
Lattice site, **1**:23, **1**:24
Lattice spacing, **14**:47, **14**:99
Lattice system, **1**:10, **1**:59
  thermodynamic limit, **1**:12
Lattice, **1**:3–12, **1**:4–8, **1**:286, **1**:296,
    1:297, **1**:298, **1**:286, **1**:289

antiferromagnetic triangular, **1**:280,
    1:328
asymmetric square, **1**:285
body-centred cubic (b.c.c.), **1**:231,
    1:300, **1**:314
"brick-wall", **1**:248
chequer, **1**:286
close-packed, **1**:231, **1**:249
cyclic change, **1**:280, **1**:281, **1**:284,
    1:294, **1**:295, **1**:298
decorated, **1**:291, **1**:312, **1**:313, **1**:314,
    1:316
decorated honeycomb, **1**:291, **1**:292,
    1:304, **1**:305
decorated square, **1**:307, **1**:308, **1**:313,
    1:315
diamond, **1**:314
diced, **1**:275, **1**:293, **1**:295, **1**:304,
    1:314
double bond square, **1**:318, **1**:319
doubly decorated honeycomb, **1**:296,
    1:297
dual, **1**:229, **1**:240, **1**:241, **1**:273,
    1:274, **1**:276, **1**:277, **1**:282,
    1:283, **1**:286, **1**:298
expanded, **1**:260, **1**:263
face-centred (f.c.c.), **1**:249, **1**:314
ferrimagnetic square, **1**:290
generalized square, **1**:285, **1**:286,
    1:288, **1**:322, **1**:323
hemp-leaf, **1**:297, **1**:298
hexagonal, **1**:261
honeycomb, **1**:271, **1**:274, **1**:278,
    1:279, **1**:280, **1**:281, **1**:282,
    1:283, **1**:285, **1**:286, **1**:287,
    1:288, **1**:293, **1**:304, **1**:305,
    1:306, **1**:312, **1**:314, **1**:322,
    1:326, **1**:327, **1**:328
Kagomé, **1**:271, **1**:275, **1**:286, **1**:292,
    1:293, **1**:294, **1**:295, **1**:303,
    1:304, **1**:306, **1**:314, **1**:323,
    1:328
linear chain, **1**:322
loose packed, **1**:231, **1**:249
non-crossing diagonal interaction
      square, **1**:288, **1**:289
non-planar, **1**:231, **1**:232, **1**:237,
    1:250
planar, **1**:232, **1**:249

plane hexagonal, **1:**241, **1:**248, 264
plane honeycomb, **1:**231, **1:**240
plane square, **1:**240, **1:**241, **1:**242,
    1:246, **1:**247, **1:**248, **1:**250,
    1:260
plane triangular, **1:**231, **1:**240, **1:**241,
    1:248, **1:**249, **1:**264
rectangular, **1:**278, **1:**285, **1:**286,
    1:287, **1:**322
regular, **1:**237, **1:**256
self-dual, **1:**241, **1:**275
semiferromagnetic, **1:**326
semiferromagnetic honeycomb, **1:**287,
    1:288
simple cubic (s.c.), **1:**314
square, **1:**59, **1:**66, **1:**270, **1:**272,
    1:274, **1:**277, **1:**288, **1:**289,
    1:293, **1:**294, **1:**302, **1:**308,
    1:310, **1:**312, **1:**314, **1:**317,
    1:319
triangular, **1:**261, **1:**274, **1:**278, **1:**279,
    1:280, **1:**281, **1:**282, **1:**283,
    1:285, **1:**286, **1:**287, **1:**288,
    1:293, **1:**295, **1:**303, **1:**312,
    1:314, **1:**322, **1:**326, **1:**327
"union jack", **1:**231, **1:**238, **1:**250,
    1:258, **1:**264, **1:**265
Lattice, body-centred cubic, **2:**224
    diamond, **2:**224
    face-centred cubic, **2:**223, **2:**224
    honeycomb, **2:**224
    simple cubic, **2:**223, **2:**224
    triangular, **2:**224
Lattice-gas, **11:**5
    animals, **11:**116
Lattice-lattice scaling, **3:**361, **3:**450
Lattice-translation invariant, **1:**149,
    1:166
Lattices, **6:**524, **18:**6–8
    anisotropies, **6:**359, **6:**417
    approximation, **6:**522
    distortion, interaction due to,
        renormalization group and, **6:**14
    face-centred cubic, polar angles, **8:**56
    (hyper-)cubic, **8:**15
    Ising, simple cubic, Monte Carlo
        calculations, **8:**246
    Ising square, two-dimensional, **8:**55,
        8:67

quadratic, **6:**474, **6:**484
scale invariants and renormalization
    group, **6:**17
spacing, **6:**127, **6:**524, **6:**525
square, antiferromagnetic ordering,
    8:25
systems, **6:**510
triangular, **6:**431, **6:**473
    transformation, **6:**448
    with free surfaces, percolation on,
        8:108–109
Laurent expansion, **19:**299, **19:**342,
    19:343–344
Law of corresponding states, quantum
    deviations, **5B:**196
Law of large numbers, **18:**14
Layer susceptibility, **8:**216
Layer systems
    phase transitions, **8:**186–189
    three-dimensional, finite size scaling,
        8:241–245
Layered compounds, staging in, **17:**112,
    17:122, **17:**196
Layered materials, melting, **7:**76–79
Layering transitions, **14:**326
Layers (*see also* Monolayers)
    finite systems, thickness, finite size
        scaling, **8:**245
    Heisenberg, three-dimensional,
        8:243
    Ising, three-dimensional, critical
        temperature, **8:**242
    local susceptibility, finite size scaling,
        8:206
    multilayer adsorption, **8:**83–94
    at surfaces, **8:**5
Lebesgue bounded convergence
    theorem, **1:**127
Least integer dimensionality for long-
    range order, **7:**175
Leath algorithm, **18:**189
Lebowitz and Penrose, **5B:**111,
    5B:115
Lebowitz inequalities, **9:**271, **9:**274,
    9:279
Ledges, **14:**151
Lee–Yang circle theorem, **1:**9, **1:**98
LEED, **12:**96, **12:**127, **12:**140, **12:**225,
    12:269

LEED, low-energy electron diffraction, **10**:78

Legendre transform, **1**:64, **2**:9, **2**:11, **2**:13, **2**:14, **2**:15, **2**:19, **2**:24, **2**:25, **2**:32, **2**:35, **5B**:214, **9**:66, **9**:124, **10**:44, **15**:92

Legendre transformation, **3**:118, **3**:144, **14**:182

Legendre transformations, **1**:33, **1**:34, **1**:36, **6**:27, **6**:135, **6**:138, **6**:151, **6**:154, **6**:158, **6**:166, **6**:269, **6**:304, **6**:527
  functional, **6**:303
  generalized, **1**:35

LEIS, **12**:128

Length scales, **5A**:12, **5A**:20, **5A**:22, **5A**:23
  separate, **19**:131, **19**:149, **19**:171

Length transformation, **5A**:20–23

Length, scaling, **3**:444, **3**:477

Lennard–Jones fluid, spinodal decomposition, **8**:454

Lennard–Jones interaction, **12**:66, **12**:74
  potentials, **12**:50–52, **12**:57

Lennard–Jones potential, hexatic, **7**:57

Lennard–Jones potentials, **1**:88

Lenz, W., **19**:32

Lenz–Ising model, **1**:228

Leonard–Jones potential, **2**:296

Level surfaces, **16**:161–63

Levin transforms in sequence extrapolation, **13**:38–39
  series analysis application **13**:42–48

Lie algebra, **1**:229, **1**:247, **19**:34, **19**:158

Lie equations, **6**:546

Lieb-type operator, **1**:266

Lifshitz critical endpoint, **16**:95

Lifshitz invariants, **15**:64

Lifshitz line, **16**:42, **16**:48, **16**:81, **16**:82, **16**:92, **16**:92, **16**:*106*, **16**:111

Lifshitz multicritical behaviour, **15**:63

Lifshitz multicritical point, **15**:43

Lifshitz point, **11**:60, **12**:287, **12**:292, **12**:297, **12**:305, **14**:69, **15**:37, **15**:47, **15**:48, **15**:50, **15**:54–6, **15**:59–65, **16**:58, **17**:52

Lifshitz tricritical point (LTP), **15**:63, **16**:*56*, **16**:58, **16**:95, **16**:96

Lifshitz–Slyozov theory, **8**:333–335, **8**:355–356

Light
  cone, **19**:141–142
  scattering methods, **19**:385

Light scattering, **5B**:388, **5B**:389

Light-scattering experiment, **10**:312

Light-scattering techniques, **14**:91

Light-scattering, **9**:197
  studies, **9**:199–203, **9**:223

Light-scattering, **12**:452, **12**:455, **12**:464, **12**:476

Lily pond model, **18**:124

Limit distributions, **6**:552

Limit-cycle orbits, **15**:15

Limiting cycles, **6**:228

Limiting eigenvalue distribution, **15**:195

Limits of infinite radius of interaction, **15**:206–10

Lindeberg condition, **15**:178

Lindeman theory, **2**:271

Line defects, **11**:88
  effects, **17**:118–119

Line of
  critical end-points, **9**:84, **9**:142
  first order transitions, **9**:154
  triple points, **9**:68, **9**:83

Line of critical points, **9**:67, **9**:68, **9**:79, **9**:100, **9**:150, **9**:183

Line of fixed points, **14**:203

Line of renormalization group fixed points, **14**:203–7

Line of triple points, **14**:143

Line singularities in three dimensions, **7**:83–93

Linear chain, **3**:250, **3**:251, **3**:275, **3**:297, **3**:491, **3**:510, **3**:532

Linear chains, with long-range forces, **1**:78

Linear functionals, **1**:139, **1**:143

Linear graph theory, **2**:200

Linear graph, **3**:1, **3**:2, **3**:3, **3**:16, **3**:60, **3**:124
  ordered directed, **3**:584

Linear intercept, **3**:190

Linear model, **2**:76

Linear parametric equation of state, **5B**:86, **5B**:88

Linear parametric model, **6**:341, **6**:342
Linear programming, **18**:181–3
Linear renormalization of interface
    potentials, **14**:349–50
Linear response theory, **2**:452, **2**:471,
    3:630, **5B**:22
Linear response, function, **3**:631
Linear weight functions, **6**:495
Linear weight-factors, **6**:451, **6**:452,
    6:463
Linear σ-model, **6**:344
Linearized group transformation, **6**:518
Linearized theory, **6**:29–66
Linewidth broadening, **5B**:100
Link, **3**:395
Linked cluster, **5B**:207
Linked-cluster expansion, **3**:3, **3**:74,
    3:117, **3**:118, **3**:119, **3**:120, **3**:121,
    3:128, **3**:131, **3**:133, **3**:134, **3**:135,
    3:144, **3**:162, **3**:163, **3**:166, **3**:176,
    3:264
Linked-cluster method, **3**:165
Linked-cluster property, **3**:123
Lipid bilayers, **19**:261, **19**:*262*
    see also fluid membranes
Lipid membranes, exactly solvable
    models, **7**:104
Lipid monolayers, melting, **7**:9–10, **7**:45
Lipschitz condition, **1**:95
"Liquid" system, **1**:96
Liquid crystal films
    melting, **7**:45
    smectic, melting, **7**:8
Liquid crystal nematic, **12**:393
Liquid crystal, **14**:82
Liquid crystalline systems, **2**:326
Liquid crystals, **2**:327, **5B**:5
    bulk, melting, **7**:81–82
    bulk smectic, dislocations, **7**:7
        phase transitions, **7**:4
    cholesteric, **7**:74–75
    melting, **7**:11
    nematic-smectic-A transition, **7**:44
    smectic, melting, **7**:10
    smectic-A, melting, **7**:88–93
    smectic-C, melting, **7**:82
        melting, vortices and, **7**:78
    smectic-F, melting, **7**:82
    tilted films, **7**:79

Liquid mixtures, **5B**:362
Liquid sulfur, **9**:218
Liquid-gas critical point, **5B**:345
Liquid-gas critical points, **14**:5, **14**:19,
    14:76–82, **14**:89–90
Liquid-gas transition, **5A**:2, **5A**:7,
    5A:188, **5B**:132, **14**:5, **14**:70–1
    nucleation models, **8**:310–316
Liquid-liquid coexistence curve, **9**:184
Liquid-liquid critical point, **5B**:378
Liquid-liquid mixture, **5B**:380
Liquid-vapour transition line, **2**:8
Liquid-vapour transition, **6**:91
    symmetry, **6**:12
Liquids
    binary mixtures, **8**:47
    supercooled, crystal growth, **8**:454
    supercooled, nucleation, **8**:454
Liquids in non-equilibrium steady states,
    17:187–192
    and Brillouin lines, **17**:188, **17**:189
    and Rayleigh line, **17**:188
    and temperature gradients, **17**:189
    under shear, **17**:190–192
Lithium terbium fluoride, **5A**:120
Little–Hopfield model, **15**:83, **15**:136
Local anisotropy field, **3**:163
Local concentration, **5A**:181, **5A**:213
    C_q, **5A**:214
Local current, time evolution, **19**:158
Local divergences, **19**:282–284,
    19:380–381, **19**:395–396
Local entropy, **5A**:213
    S, **5A**:214
Local equilibrium approximations, **2**:478
Local equilibrium state, **5A**:182
Local equilibrium, **5A**:183
Local exponents, **8**:3, **8**:75
Local field theory, **19**:317
Local field, **3**:121
Local fields, **8**:39
Local longitudinal velocity, **5A**:213
Local observables algebra, **1**:141
Local operators (definition), **10**:191
Local operators, **5A**:3
Local order parameter, **5A**:189, **5B**:36
    gauging variant Ising models and,
        6:13
Local pressure, **5A**:176, **5A**:181, **5A**:213

Local stress tensor, **5A**:176
Local temperature, **5A**:176
Local transverse velocity, **5A**:213
Local variables
  fluctuations, **6**:523
  $S(r)$, **6**:11
Local velocity, **5A**:181
Localization lengths, **19**:145, **19**:149,
  19:173, **19**:174
Localization, position space methods,
  7:250
Localization-delocalization transition,
  8:74
Locked incommensurate structures,
  15:16
Logarithmic anomalies, **6**:94–98
Logarithmic corrections in four
  dimensions, **10**:219, **10**:221
Logarithmic corrections, **6**:195, **9**:42,
  9:121, **9**:123, **9**:124, **9**:135, **9**:137,
  9:154, **9**:203, **14**:11, **14**:40, **14**:101
  factors, **9**:45
Logarithmic divergences, **6**:199, **6**:307
Logarithmic factors, **14**:64
Logarithmic singularities, **14**:11
Logarithmic singularity, **3**:302, **5A**:8,
  5A:45, **5A**:68
Logarithmic term, **6**:276, **6**:281, **6**:282
  anomalous, **6**:285
Long contour, **10**:49, **10**:50, **10**:59,
  10:65
Long range exchange interaction, **2**:477
Long range magnetic order effective
  dimensionality and, **7**:270
  fluctuations and, **7**:7
  in crystals, broken continuous
    translational symmetry, **7**:3
  in two-dimensional magnetic models,
    7:159
  quenched bond diluted magnets,
    7:158
  suppression by phase fluctuations, **7**:6
Long time tail, **5A**:169, **5A**:340
Long wavelength fluctuations, **6**:427
  at critical point, **6**:1
  characteristic length, **6**:2
Long-period superstructures, **15**:38
Long-range correlation function, **5B**:181,
  5B:188

Long-range correlations, **17**:25–40,
  17:93
  see also Power law decays
Long-range forces, **1**:38, **1**:78
Long-range
  forces, **9**:101
  interactions, **9**:93, **9**:97, **9**:102
Long-range interaction, **10**:76
Long-range interactions, **5B**:125,
  5B:195, **5B**:196
  competition, **19**:363
  correlated disorder, **19**:404,
    19:407–408
  and fractal phase, **19**:277
  hydrodynamic, **19**:387
  in membranes, **19**:272
  nonrenormalization, **19**:303–305
  one-dimensional systems, **19**:54
  and phase transitions, **19**:125
  physical importance, **19**:305
  tethered membranes, **19**:304–305
Long-range inverse power law
  interactions, **2**:396, **2**:401, **2**:407,
    2:423, **2**:427, **2**:430, **2**:434
Long-range order, **1**:150, **1**:194, **1**:197,
  1:199, **1**:200, **1**:202, **1**:214, **1**:251,
  1:310, **1**:326, **3**:299, **3**:300, **3**:366,
  3:373, **3**:374, **3**:458, **3**:543, **3**:635,
  5B:44, **5B**:168, **5B**:315, **5B**:318,
  5B:319, **6**:289
Long-range ordering, **2**:272, **2**:279,
  2:290, **2**:294, **2**:295, **2**:297, **2**:300,
  2:301, **2**:309, **2**:334, **2**:344, **2**:346
Long-range potential, **5B**:111, **5B**:139,
  14:169
Long-range spherical model, **14**:50
Longitudinal
  bulk susceptibility, **10**:209
  spin-spin correlation function,
    10:224
Longitudinal correlation length, **14**:165
Longitudinal projectors, Fourier
  representation, **19**:454–456
Longitudinal sound, **7**:71
Longitudinal susceptibility, **5A**:129,
  5A:130
Loops see contour loops (CLs); fully
  packed loops (FPLs)
Loops, **18**:260–1

Lorentzian form, **5A**:93, **5A**:113,
  5A:114
Lorentzian line shape, **5A**:114, **5A**:115,
  5A:126, **5A**:135, **5A**:139
Lorentzian, **5A**:112, **5A**:115, **5A**:125,
  5A:138, **5A**:140, **5A**:152, **5A**:158,
  5A:160
Low density expansions, **1**:41
Low lying excitations in quenched
  diluted magnetic models, **7**:159
Low temperature diluted Heisenberg
  magnets, static critical properties,
  scaling methods, **7**:259
Low temperature expansion, amplitude
  fluctuations in, **7**:17
Low temperature series expansion, *see*
  series expansion
Low-density phase, **19**:134, **19**:135,
  19:139, **19**:140, **19**:142, **19**:145,
  19:146, **19**:171
Low-dimensional systems, **19**:4
Low-energy electron diffraction (LEED)
  experiments, **14**:120
Low-frequency mode, **5B**:73
Low-temperature amplitude, **3**:441,
  3:444
Low-temperature approach, **10**:336
  to dynamics, **10**:355
Low-temperature configuration, **3**:392
Low-temperature expansion, **3**:225,
  3:371, **3**:405, **3**:506, **3**:571, **3**:654,
  3:663, **5B**:103, **5B**:167
  Ising model, **19**:256, **19**:408, **19**:431
Low-temperature expansions,
  8:103–109
2, 6–Lutidine, films of water and,
  coexistence curves, **8**:256
Low-temperature series, **3**:187, **3**:214,
  3:216, **3**:219, **3**:358, **3**:360
Lower critical dimension, **7**:7
  smectic liquid crystals, **7**:10
LP *see* Lebowitz and Penrose
LRO *see* Long-range order
Lubkin's three-term transformation in
  sequence extrapolation, **13**:40
  series analysis application **13**:42–48
Luttinger model, **1**:181
Lymphocytes, configuration of adsorpt
  macromolecules and, **7**:109

Lyotropic phases, **16**:72, **16**:121–26 *see
  also* Hexagonal phases. Inverse
  hexagonal phase. Cubic phase,
  Lamellar phases

M

m-special, *see* Transition
Macromolecules
  adsorption to a surface, **7**:104
  conformational phase transitions in,
    exactly solvable models,
    7:101–149
  crystallization, **7**:103
  entanglements, **7**:131–147
    with continuous curve, **7**:134–138
  folded, configuration, **7**:122
    crystallization, **7**:121
  infinitely long, **7**:127
    folds per unit of length, **7**:128
Macroscopic mechanisms, **19**:6, **19**:7
Magnet
  dilute, **3**:473
  one-dimensional, **5A**:149, **5A**:150
  two-dimensional, **5A**:154–158
Magnetic concentration, quenched site
  diluted Ising ferromagnet, **7**:159
Magnetic equation of state, **3**:316
Magnetic exponent, **6**:521
Magnetic field variable, **5A**:6
Magnetic insulator, **3**:579, **3**:580, **3**:647,
  3:649, **5A**:315
Magnetic long-range order, **5A**:148
Magnetic materials, **14**:84
Magnetic moment, **14**:47, **15**:86, **15**:102,
  15:149, **15**:158
Magnetic phase boundary, **3**:252, **3**:314,
  3:315, **3**:316, **3**:317, **3**:318
Magnetic relaxation, **2**:489, **2**:490
Magnetic resonance, **2**:489, **2**:490
Magnetic screening length, **7**:8
Magnetic susceptibility
  calculation, **7**:209
  concentration dependence, **7**:204
  concentration expansion method,
    7:224
  dilute magnets, experimental, **7**:264
  exponent, annealed bond diluted Ising
    magnets, **7**:229

in annealed site-diluted Ising magnets, **7**:229
dilute Heisenberg model, series expansion methods, **7**:230
dilute XY models, series expansion methods, **7**:231
in quenched bond diluted Ising magnets, **7**:229
in quenched site-diluted Ising magnets, **7**:229
    quenched site diluted Ising model in transverse field, series expansion methods, **7**:231
in magnetic systems, mean cluster size in bond diluted square lattices and, **7**:157
Monte Carlo methods, **7**:204, **7**:205
reference Ising model, **7**:198
site diluted Ising ferromagnet, **7**:158
two-dimensional bond diluted Ising model, position space method, **7**:248
virtual crystal approximation, **7**:213
layered, continuous symmetry, **7**:10
with two-dimensional continuous symmetry, **7**:10
Magnetic susceptibility, **3**:454, **5A**:10, **19**:32
local, **8**:3, **8**:19
see 'magnetic' under susceptibility
Magnetic symmetry, **3**:369
Magnetic system
one-dimensional, **5A**:147
two-dimensional, **5A**:147
Magnetic systems, **6**:361
Magnetic transitions, **5A**:311–316, **14**:73–5, **14**:84–9, **14**:91–2
Magnetization profile, **10**:17, **10**:31, **10**:51
local, **10**:78
near a boundary, **10**:56
Magnetism
critical behaviour, **6**:14
n-vector model, **8**:18–19
Magnetization
bond diluted two-dimensional Ising model, **7**:256
concentration dependence, **7**:204
decay, **7**:198

dilute magnets, experimental, **7**:264
low temperature, coherent potential approximation, **7**:217
Monte Carlo methods, **7**:204
two-dimensional bond diluted Ising model, position space method, **7**:248
virtual crystal approximation, **7**:213
Magnetization critical exponent β, **5A**:43
Magnetization density, **14**:14
Magnetization fluctuation dynamics, **5A**:240
Magnetization
local, **8**:74, **8**:75
staggered, **8**:26
surface, **8**:3, **8**:11, **8**:12, **8**:13, **8**:32, **8**:38, **8**:45, **8**:53, **8**:62, **8**:63
surface, finite size scaling, **8**:184
surface, scaling, **8**:188
Magnetization M, **5A**:39
Magnetization M(T), **5A**:115
Magnetization operator, **3**:596
Magnetization pattern, **15**:36
Magnetization per spin, **14**:100
Magnetization profiles, **8**:14, **8**:16, **8**:17, **8**:18, **8**:29, **8**:30, **8**:38, **8**:44, **8**:45, **8**:48, **8**:55, **8**:76, **14**:240–4
near free surfaces, **8**:12
Magnetization, **1**:77, **1**:101, **1**:109, **1**:193, **1**:200, **1**:213, **1**:227, **2**:334, **2**:384, **3**:362, **3**:371, **3**:543, **5A**:37, **5B**:14, **5B**:22, **5B**:28, **5B**:35, **5B**:46, **5B**:48, **5B**:49, **5B**:70, **5B**:338, **6**:273–276, **14**:49, **14**:60, **19**:5, **19**:230, **19**:233
concavity, **1**:84
critical behaviour, **5B**:38
density, **6**:295
2-dimensional systems with rotational symmetry, temperature and, **6**:13
Landau Hamiltonian and, **6**:15
non-analytical part, **6**:43
operator, **6**:42
spontaneous, **6**:130, **6**:160, **6**:197, **6**:216, **6**:296, **6**:436, **6**:447, **6**:449, **6**:473, **6**:478, **6**:479, **6**:480, **6**:494, **6**:495
easy plane, **3**:502

fluctuations, **3**:596, **5A**:11
layer, **5B**:62, **5B**:64
mean square, **5B**:30
metastable, **5B**:33
of metastable state, **5B**:87, **5B**:88
of s.c. classical Heisenberg
    ferromagnet, **5B**:45, **5B**:46
of s.c. Ising film, **5B**:59
of simple s.c. Heisenberg ferromagnet,
    5B:54
parallel, **3**:572, **3**:597, **3**:630
perpendicular, **3**:571, **3**:572, **3**:597,
    3:604, **3**:607, **3**:630
See also Spontaneous magnetization
scaled, **5B**:49
sub-lattice, **3**:363
surface, **5B**:62, **5B**:64
uniform, **5A**:38–46
zero field, **3**:540, **3**:543
Magnetization-magnetization correlation
    function, **1**:99
Magneto-optic Kerr effect (MOKE),
    10:189
Magnets
    anisotropic, **8**:5
    anisotropic, Ising spins, **8**:18
    dipolar, **8**:6
    Ising, simple cube lattice, **8**:26
    isotropic, **8**:45
    itinerant, molecular field treatments,
        8:18
    m-component, **6**:406
    random, **6**:408
Magnons, **19**:36–37
Main leaves, **3**:20
Manganese fluoride, **5A**:120, **5A**:121,
    5A:122, **5A**:123, **5A**:129, **5A**:131,
    5A:133, **5A**:140, **5A**:161, **5A**:279,
    5A:282, **5A**:283, **5A**:315, **5A**:316,
    5A:325
Manifold
    closed compact, **19**:421
    compact, **19**:422
    free Gaussian, **19**:435
    generalized model, **19**:430
    integrals, **19**:459–460
    isotropic, **19**:404
    single noninteracting, **19**:428
    size, **19**:427

theory, **19**:408–409
Many body systems
    conservation laws, **19**:32
    exact solutions, **19**:30–31, **19**:33,
        19:34
    master equation, **19**:5
    modelling, **19**:3–4, **19**:23–27
    tensor basis, **19**:23–26
Many-body forces, **1**:76
Many-component fluid, **3**:418
Many-particle transition, **5B**:21, **5B**:27
Many-spin correlation functions, **10**:21
Mapping, discrete, mean-field phase
    diagrams and, **8**:96–99
Marginal dimensionality, **8**:34, **8**:39,
    8:76
Marginal excitations, **12**:259–261,
    12:263, **12**:271–276, **12**:281,
    12:283, **12**:328
Marginal fields, **6**:435, **6**:520
Marginal operator, **8**:75
Marginal parameter, **6**:393
Marginal variables, **9**:42, **9**:44, **9**:45
Marginally rough interface, **14**:156
Markov chain Monte Carlo method,
    18:68
Markov chain, **2**:444, **5B**:8, **5B**:9,
    5B:17, **5B**:18
Markov process, **5B**:7, **5B**:9
    generator, **19**:18
Markov property, **9**:238, **9**:241, **9**:247,
    19:5, **19**:17
Markov random field, **18**:11
    see also quasilocality
Markovian master equation, **5B**:3,
    5B:25, **5B**:94
Martin–Siggia–Rose response field,
    17:35, **17**:56
Mass density, **14**:70
Mass gap, **8**:181
Mass operator approximation, **5B**:294,
    5B:296
Mass operator decoupling, **5B**:280
Mass operator, **5B**:288, **5B**:292, **5B**:293,
    5B:298, **5B**:300, **5B**:301
Mass renormalization graphs, **6**:373
Mass renormalization, **6**:301, **6**:378,
    9:274, **9**:279, **9**:310
Mass, **6**:529

Massive *see* bulk
Massless modes, **6:**192
Massless phases, finite size scaling, **8:**192–195
Master equation, **2:**445, **2:**451–3, **2:**460, **2:**464, **2:**465, **2:**466, **2:**473–4, **2:**478, **2:**491, **2:**493, **2:**495, **2:**496, **5B:**6, **5B:**13, **5B:**14, **5B:**15, **5B:**24, **5B:**73, **5B:**74, **5B:**89, **5B:**104
  and conditional probability, **19:**84–85
  ASEP, **19:**114
  biased single-particle diffusion, **19:**63
  boundary terms, **19:**91
  determinant representation, **19:**158
  formulation, **19:**4, **19:**102
  Markovian, **5B:**3, **5B:**25, **5B:**94
  Markov property, **19:**5
  quantum Hamiltonian formulation, **19:**17–29
  single particle, **5B:**25
  stationary form, **19:**59
  symmetric simple exclusion process (SSEP), **19:**10
  three particle, **19:**117
  two-particle, **19:**85, **19:**117
  vector form, **19:**21
Matching algorithms, **18:**175–81, **18:**272–6
Matching graphs, **2:**218
Matching lattices, **2:**218
Matching problem, **1:**233, **1:**259
Matching problems, history of, **18:**175
Matchings, terms, **18:**175
Matrix algebra, **19:**96, **19:**101, **19:**159, **19:**160
Matrix method, **1:**243, **2:**112, **2:**113, **2:**308, **2:**313, **2:**316, **2:**317, **2:**322, **2:**323, **2:**325, **2:**327, **2:**370
Matrix product ansatz, **19:**52, **19:**90, **19:**137, **19:**159, **19:**161
Matrix representation, **19:**50, **19:**53, **19:**97
Matrix, time-dependent, **19:**91
Matsen–Sullivan model, **16:**30, **16:**59–62, **16:***60*, **16:***61*, **16:***62*, **16:**71, **16:**72
Matsubara technique, **6:**526

Maximal current, **19:**133–134, **19:**143, **19:**144, **19:**146, **19:**155, **19:**157
Maximal transport capacity, **19:**135, **19:**147
Maximum matching on general graphs, **18:**179–81
Maximum-cardinality bipartite-matching algorithm, **18:**179
Maximum-cut problem, **18:**225–7
Maximum-flow problem, **18:**160–7, **18:**199–200, **18:**208–11, **18:**255–6
Maximum-weight algorithm, **18:**175
Maximum-weight forest (MWF), **18:**155
Maximum-weight-matching problem, **18:**179, **18:**184
Maxwell construction, **2:**361, **5B:**110, **5B:**111, **5B:**112, **5B:**114, **5B:**117, **5B:**132, **5B:**148, **5B:**149, **5B:**156, **5B:**189, **5B:**192, **5B:**193, **5B:**196, **5B:**256
Maxwell's equations, third sound, **7:**36–39, **7:**69
Maxwell's rule, **5B:**111
Maxwell–Boltzmann–Gibbs theory, **1:**4
Mayer cluster coefficients, **8:**282
Mayer expansion, **3:**84
Mayer *f*-function, **3:**148, **5B:**224
Mayer theory, **3:**3, **3:**74, **3:**394, **3:**398
  multicomponent, **3:**400
Mayer–Montroll equations, **1:**149
MC *see* Maxwell construction
McCoy–Wu Ising model critical behaviour, **7:**181
  striped randomness, **7:**181
  variant, transition temperature, **7:**182
McCoy–Wu model, vertical random interaction version, **7:**190
MCD *see* Moment conserving decoupling
ME *see* Mid-point envelope
Mean cluster size
  bond diluted square lattices, divergence, **7:**157
  percolation and, in site diluted f.c.c lattices, **7:**157
Mean Field theory, **11:**80, **11:**86
Mean field analysis
  continuum limit, **19:**172

diffusion-limited pair annihilation,
19:195–197
domain wall dynamics, 19:135
limitations, 19:4
membranes, 19:265–267
pertubative expansion, 19:348–349
phase diagram, 19:126, 19:*127*
tubular phase, 19:375
and variational approximation,
19:354
Mean field approximation, 2:333, 2:335,
2:336, 2:337, 2:338, 2:340, 2:363,
2:346, 2:351–3, 2:365, 2:368,
3:450, 3:570, 5B:23, 5B:24, 5B:26,
5B:27, 5B:30, 5B:54, 5B:184,
5B:251, 5B:339, 6:137, 6:210,
6:217, 7:210–213
Mean field critical temperature,
quenched models, 7:179
Mean field model, 2:43, 2:48, 2:73,
2:473–4, 2:470, 2:477
Mean field representation, 5B:263
Mean field solution, 3:463
Mean field theory, 2:415, 2:416,
2:418–19, 2:444, 3:251, 3:252,
3:301, 3:306, 3:309, 3:316, 3:453,
3:468, 3:491, 3:543, 5A:2,
5A:12–16, 5A:242, 5A:296, 5B:67,
5B:189, 5B:320, 6:129, 6:157,
6:165, 6:171, 6:294, 6:295, 6:301,
6:306, 6:307, 6:319, 6:363, 6:365,
6:380, 6:416
failure, 5A:15, 5A:16
Mean field values, 3:468
Mean field, 3:114, 3:287, 3:447, 3:449,
3:492, 3:549, 5A:13, 6:398
Mean number expansion, 2:237
Mean number of clusters, 2:212, 2:216,
2:226, 2:229, 2:234, 2:239, 2:241,
2:244, 2:264
Mean reduced trace, 3:258, 3:259,
3:260, 3:261, 3:263, 3:277, 3:281,
3:282, 3:284, 3:328
Mean size expansion, low density,
2:221
Mean size exponent, 2:245
Mean size of clusters, 2:239, 2:243–4,
2:255, 2:264–5, 2:268
Mean size weights, 2:238

Mean size, 2:224, 2:226–7, 2:229
Mean spherical approximation, 5B:238,
5B:239, 5B:241, 5B:242, 5B:251,
5B:252, 5B:253
Mean spherical equation, 5B:207
Mean spherical model, 5B:207, 5B:234,
5B:240, 5B:246, 5B:256, 5B:257
Mean trace, 3:257, 3:272, 3:277, 3:285,
3:288
Mean-field (MF) theory, 10:53, 10:82,
10:85, 10:88, 10:92–3, 10:98,
10:104, 10:109–13, 10:157, 10:174,
10:222, 10:224–5, 10:240, 10:274,
10:335
renormalized, 10:274, 10:283, 10:303,
10:315, 10:327
Mean-field approximation, 8:19, 8:29,
8:34, 14:47, 14:196, 15:207
interfaces, 8:65
Mean-field
approximation, 9:17, 9:19, 9:20,
9:142, 9:217, 9:221, 9:227
like behaviour, 9:67, 9:180
theory, 9:12, 9:16, 9:22, 9:58, 9:59,
9:141, 9:174, 9:178, 9:180,
9:199, 9:217
Mean-field exponents, 14:40, 14:47,
14:65
Mean-field phase diagrams, 15:34,
15:47
Mean-field regime, 14:191
Mean-field relation, 14:82
Mean-field results, 14:52
Mean-field theory, 8:41, 8:44, 8:48,
8:62, 8:64, 8:75, 8:76, 14:11,
14:26, 14:39–40, 14:43–8, 14:330,
16:34, 16:*35*, 16:55, 16:58–60,
16:*60*, 16:73, 16:99, 16:110,
16:146, 17:5, 17:16–19, 17:141,
17:160, 17:192
analysis, 12:406
correlation length and, 8:36
microscopic, 8:19
result, 12:383
see MFT
surface critical behaviour, 8:6–34
two-dimensional Ising model, 8:49
Mean-field values, 14:27, 14:48, 14:55,
14:101

Medium, **2:**202, **2:**204, **2:**205, **2:**210, **2:**211
  branching, **2:**208
  covering, **2:**205
  random, **2:**202, **2:**203
Meeron, $\mathcal{M}(v)$-bond function, **5B:**225
Mellin transform, **6:**324
Melting
  anisotropic, **7:**74–75
  anisotropic lattices, **7:**79–81
  computer simulations, **7:**53–57
  dislocation lines and, **7:**85
  dynamics, **7:**66–74
  grain boundary-mediated, **7:**55
  incommensurate, **7:**10
    on periodic substrates, **7:**57–62
  layered materials, **7:**76–79
  lipid monolayers, **7:**9–10
  liquid crystal phases, **7:**11
  smooth substrate, **7:**45–53
  smectic, dislocation model, **7:**90
  smectic-A liquid crystals, **7:**88–93
  smectic liquid crystal films, **7:**8
  two-dimensional, **7:**8
    Landau theories, **7:**18
    statistical mechanics, **7:**40–66
Melting line, **5B:**192
Melting point, **5B:**385
Melting transition, **5B:**191
Melting, **3:**367, **11:**2, **12:**19, **12:**93, **12:**137–146, **14:**145
  curve, **12:**17, **12:**102, **12:**120–121, **12:**137, **12:**142, **12:**162, **12:**191–192
  grain boundary, **12:**142–146
  surface, **12:**139–142
Membrane depolarization,
  effect on activation of contraction, **2:**46–54
Membrane systems, **16:**21–2, **16:**129–64
  elastic modulii, **16:**155–56
  phase diagram, **16:***141*, **16:**141–45, **16:***142*
    of ternary system, **16:**145–51, **16:***148*, **16:***150*
  scaling considerations, **16:**137–39
Membranes, **14:**116, **14:**136
  of arbitrary dimension, **19:**258
  characteristic function, **19:**361

N-coloured, **19:**408–434
  density, **19:**422, **19:**423, **19:**425, **19:**427
  ϵ-expansion, **19:**256, **19:**349
  fluctuations, **19:**267
  Hamiltonian, **19:**278
    with intrinsic disorder, **19:**278–279
  local field theory, **19:**317
  mean field description, **19:**265–267
  O (N) model generalization, **19:**421–426
  partition function, **19:**359–361
  properties, **19:**261–279
  self-avoiding, **19:**319
  self-energy, **19:**361
  tethered (polymerized), **19:**262–265
  tricritical point, **19:**363
  tubular phase, **19:**374–377
  two-loop calculations, **19:**350
  see also fluid membranes
Memory function, **5A:**232
3-Methylpentane/nitroethane mixture, **5A:**327
Memory, **1:**4
Mermin–Wagner theorem, **8:**244, **19:**272
Mesoscopic, **12:**152
Messenger RNA *see* biopolymerization
Metal insulator transition, **12:**252–258, **12:**300
Metal–hydrogen alloys, **10:**76
Metal–hydrogen systems, **8:**443–444
Metal–insulator transitions, **14:**364
Metamagnet, **3:**496
Metamagnetic transitions, **6:**170
Metamagnetic tricritical behaviour, **6:**413
Metamagnetic-antiferromagnetic transition, **9:**171
Metamagnets, **9:**7, **9:**10, **9:**11, **9:**12, **9:**13, **9:**15, **9:**16, **9:**17, **9:**25, **9:**26, **9:**31, **9:**45, **9:**47, **9:**52, **9:**53, **9:**54, **9:**63, **9:**65, **9:**76, **9:**84, **9:**88, **9:**90, **9:**108, **9:**110, **9:**115, **9:**117, **9:**153, **9:**208
  $FeCl_2$, **9:**44
  spin-$\frac{1}{2}$, **9:**142, **9:**143
  two-dimensional model, **8:**427
Metastability limit, **5B:**86, **5B:**88, **5B:**89

Metastability, **5B**:37, **5B**:132, **8**:68,
    8:432–436, **9**:153, **12**:160, **12**:193
Metastable approximation, **3**:360
Metastable drops, **10**:55
Metastable equilibrium, **5B**:82
Metastable state, **3**:471, **5B**:4, **5B**:21,
    5B:72, **5B**:82, **5B**:85, **5B**:88,
    5B:90, **5B**:96, **5B**:112, **5B**:118,
    5B:133, **5B**:134, **5B**:163
Metastable states, **2**:4, **2**:476, **2**:481,
    9:68
Methane
    + 2,2-dimethylbutane, **9**:168, **9**:186,
        9:187
    + 3,3-dimethylpentane, **9**:184
    + *n*-hexane, **9**:173, **9**:184
    + (2-methylpentane + 2-ethyl-l-
        butane), **9**:185
    + *n*-pentane, **9**:186, **9**:187
Methane/cyclohexane system, **5B**:388
Methanol
    + carbon dioxide + ethane, **9**:181
    + ethane, **9**:181
Methanol/cyclohexane system, **5B**:360,
    5B:378, **5B**:379, **5B**:380, **5B**:392,
    5B:393
Method of plaquettes, **15**:46
Metric factors, **14**:7, **14**:8, **14**:11–13,
    14:18, **14**:24
Metric tensor, **16**:131
Metropolis rates, **17**:12, **17**:128, **17**:135,
    17:141, **17**:152, **17**:*153*
MF *see* Mean field approximation
MFA *see* Molecular field approximation
MFT (Mean field theory), **12**:16, **12**:17,
    12:19, **12**:21, **12**:27, **12**:29–32,
    12:36, **12**:40, **12**:44–50, **12**:52–58,
    12:62, **12**:64, **12**:73, **12**:84,
    12:86–88, **12**:117, **12**:123, **12**:126,
    12:131–135, **12**:145–148, **12**:152,
    12:155, **12**:169, **12**:185, **12**:194,
    12:468, **12**:474
MHT scaling function, **3**:504, **3**:505,
    3:507
Micelle 3 *see also* Critical micelle
    concentration
Microcanonical ensemble, **14**:103
Microcanonical partition function, **15**:91
Microcanonical subspace, **5A**:173

Microcrystals, **2**:103
Microemulsion model, **15**:47
Microemulsion, **16**:4
    structure, **16**:16–18, **16**:40–8, **16**:*110*,
        16:*112*
Microemulsions, **12**:5, **12**:192–193,
    17:127
    model for, **17**:128, **17**:135–138
Microscopic models, **16**:19–20,
    16:22–76, **16**:98, **16**:164
Mid-point envelope, **5B**:137
Mimic function, **3**:199, **3**:200, **3**:201,
    3:429
Mimic partition function, **3**:470
Minimal current phase, **19**:144, **19**:152,
    19:*153*
Minimal path, **18**:153–7
Minimal sensitivity, **19**:350,
    19:354–355
Minimal subtraction (MS), **19**:299,
    19:340–342
Minimal-energy-interface problem,
    18:196
Minimal-path algorithm, **18**:192–5
Minimal-path problem, **18**:194–5
Minimal-path tree, **18**:153–4
Minimal-spanning trees, **18**:155,
    18:157–8
Minimum path dimensionality, **12**:391
Minimum-cost path, **18**:153
Minimum-cost-flow problem, **18**:167–9,
    18:175, **18**:183, **18**:248–52,
    18:254–5
Minimum-cut problem, **18**:226
Minimum-cut/maximum-flow theorem,
    18:161–2
Minimum-energy interface problem,
    18:196, **18**:199–200
Minkowski space field theory, **9**:248,
    9:298
Minlos–Sinaï
    equations, **10**:9
    boundary condition, *see* Boundary
        conditions
    theory, **10**:17
Minlos–Sinai method, **11**:157–8,
    11:161
Miscibility gap, **6**:91
    critical point and, **6**:12

Misfit, **12**:232, **12**:235–236, **12**:240, **12**:258, **12**:268, **12**:288–293, **12**:297–299, **12**:302, **12**:305–306, **12**:329, **12**:331
Missing spin, **5B**:67
MIT bag, **10**:81
Mixed bond Ising magnets, critical curves, **7**:257
Mixed ferromagnets. coherent potential approximation, **7**:216
Mixed Heisenberg antiferromagnets, coherent potential approximation, **7**:217
Mixed integer linear programming (MILP), **18**:185–6
Mixed Ising magnets
  position space methods, **7**:248, **7**:257
  three-dimensional, smeared transitions, **7**:265
  two-dimensional, smeared transitions, **7**:265
Mixed magnets, **7**:154
  competing anisotropics, **7**:270
Mixtures, **14**:42, **14**:61
ML *see* Mubayi–Lange decoupling
$MnCO_3$, **3**:582
MnP magnet, experimental phase diagram, **15**:55
Möbius function, **2**:237, **2**:268
Mobius transformation, **11**:66, **11**:97
Mode coupling theory, **5A**:168, **5A**:169, **5A**:170, **5A**:188, **5A**:189, **5A**:232, **5A**:262, **5A**:266, **5A**:274, **5A**:275, **5A**:298, **5A**:304, **5A**:307, **5A**:309, **5A**:336, **5A**:340, **5A**:341, **5A**:343, **5A**:344, **5A**:380
  extended, **5A**:190, **5A**:236
Mode coupling, **5A**:220, **5A**:223, **5A**:224, **5A**:225, **5A**:226, **5A**:227, **5A**:236, **5A**:253, **5A**:258, **5A**:259, **5A**:266, **5A**:270, **5A**:280, **5A**:294, **5A**:295, **5A**:300, **5A**:304, **5A**:310, **5A**:331, **5A**:334, **5A**:342, **5A**:360, **5A**:387
  see also Hydrodynamic mode coupling
Mode mixing, **5A**:179
Mode-coupling, **14**:46, **14**:71, **14**:73, **14**:75

Model A, **17**:52, **17**:80, **17**:126, **17**:139, **19**:259, **19**:377
Model B, **17**:20, **17**:52, **17**:63, **17**:80, **17**:101
Model C, **17**:80, **17**:126, **17**:139
Model
  one-dimensional, **3**:114
  two-dimensional, **3**:114
Modelling, **19**:3–4, **19**:6–13, **19**:43, **19**:47, **19**:104, **19**:215–223, **19**:258–261
Models (*see also* Baxter model, Baxter–Wu model, Droplet model. Eight-vertex model, Exactly solved models, Gaussian model, Ginzburg–Landau model, Hard hexagon model, Heisenberg model, Ising model, Lattice gas model, *n*-vector models, nn/nnn model, $0(3)$ model, Potts model, Schwinger model, Solid-on-solid models, Spherical models, XY model)
  A, in critical dynamics, **8**:290
  B, free-energy functional, **8**:295
  B, in critical dynamics, **8**:290
  C, in critical dynamics, **8**:291
  C, late stage growth law, **8**:425
  C, nucleation rate, **8**:425
  C, nucleation rate, calculation, **8**:426
  H, in critical dynamics, **8**:292
  nucleation, in binary fluids and liquid-gas transitions, **8**:310–316
  with nonconserved parameter, interface dynamics, **8**:335–339
Models, exactly solvable. conformational phase transition in macromolecules, **7**:101–149
Models, *see* Ginzburg (TDGL); Ice; Ising; Planar; Random surface; Rotor; Solid-on-solid; String; Terrace–ledge–kink
Modified array, **2**:111, **2**:126, **2**:131, **2**:140
Modified lattice, **2**:102, **2**:104–5, **2**:108, **2**:139
  honeycomb, **2**:108, **2**:109, **2**:114
  square, **2**:107, **2**:109, **2**:113–14
  triangular, **2**:108, **2**:109, **2**:114
Moebius function, **3**:81, **3**:82

Moebius inversion, **3:**77, **3:**78, **3:**81
Molar volume, **14:**14
Molecular distribution function
canonical, **3:**53
grand canonical, **3:**53
Molecular dynamics algorithm, **19:**377
Molecular dynamics method, **5B:**3,
  5B:18
Molecular dynamics simulation, **16:**32
Molecular dynamics, **2:**272, **2:**274,
  2:289, **5B:**192, **7:**202, **8:**454–455,
  12:39, **12:**142–143, **12:**162
simulation, **7:**55
Molecular field approximation
Landau Hamiltonian, **6:**16
Molecular field approximation, **3:**175,
  5A:40–44, **5B:**272, **5B:**276,
  5B:277, **5B:**282, **8:**15, **8:**73
see Mean field approximation
Molecular field method, **1:**152, **1:**166
Molecular field model, **1:**170, **5A:**36,
  5A:37
Molecular field phase diagram, **8:**26
Molecular field theory, **1:**169, **5B:**329,
  8:17, **8:**74
  (*see also* Mean-field theory)
    Ising ferromagnet, **8:**25
  nearest neighbour Ising model, **8:**22
Molecular field treatments, itinerant
  magnets, **8:**18
Molecular field, **5A:**45
Molecular-field approximation, **1:**82
Molybdenum disulphide, folded phase,
  19:274
Moment calculations for dynamic
  response, **7:**222–223
Moment conserving decoupling,
  5B:303–306
self-consistent, **5B:**306
Moment equations, **15:**176, **15:**190,
  15:211, **15:**227–9
Moment expansion, **3:**71, **3:**368, **3:**631
Moment function, **3:**265
Moment generating function, **3:**368
Moment method, **3:**253, **3:**254, **3:**258,
  3:261, **3:**276, **3:**281, **3:**289, **3:**291,
  3:293, **3:**297
Moment, **3:**45, **3:**54, **3:**254, **3:**262,
  3:265

Moment-cumulant transformation,
  3:261, **3:**263, **3:**264
Moment-of-inertia tensor, **14:**43
Moments, **9:**244, **9:**264
Momentum space formulation, **19:**95,
  19:459
Momentum space, **6:**142, **6:**300
correlation functions in, **6:**45–49
variables, **6:**361
Momentum-shell integration, **10:**117,
  10:118
Momomers, **14:**116
Monge representation, **16:**134
Monochromator span, **5A:**99
Monohedron three phase, **9:**14, **9:**59–63,
  9:88, **9:**111, **9:**112, **9:**143, **9:**169,
  9:178
Monolayers (*see also* Layers),
  adsorbed, on crystal surfaces,
  antiferromagnetic Ising systems
  and, **8:**231
Monolayers, dimer models for,
  13:286–287
Monomer–dimer model, **13:**237
Monomer–dimer problem, **1:**55, **3:**665
Monomials, **11:**190
Monotonicity intervals, **15:**182
Monte Carlo (MC) methods, **14:**42,
  14:44–46, **14:**58–61, **14:**65, **14:**66,
  14:82, **14:**101, **14:**364
Monte Carlo
approach, **9:**304
simulations, **9:**17, **9:**20, **9:**141,
  9:142
Monte Carlo averaging, **5B:**9, **5B:**17,
  5B:72
Monte Carlo calculations, **5B:**29,
  5B:68, **5B:**70, **5B:**71, **5B:**78,
  5B:192, **8:**109–118
finite size scaling, **8:**245–247
first-order phase transitions,
  8:374–395
tricritical systems, **8:**427
Monte Carlo cluster statistics, **5B:**339
Monte Carlo computations
for b.c.c. lattice, **5B:**44
for f.c.c. lattice, **5B:**44
for s.c. lattice, **5B:**44
for s.q. lattice, **5B:**38, **5B:**44

for three-dimensional lattice, **5B**:41, **5B**:44

Monte Carlo estimate
in critical region, **5B**:18

Monte Carlo estimates, **2**:224, **2**:227, **2**:242–4, **2**:272, **2**:274, **2**:280, **2**:283, **2**:289, **2**:301, **2**:349

Monte Carlo method, **5B**:2–17 *passim*, **5B**:24, **5B**:26, **5B**:29, **5B**:32, **5B**:63, **5B**:70, **5B**:73, **5B**:74, **5B**:90, **5B**:91, **5B**:94, **5B**:95, **11**:73, **18**:68
accuracy, **5B**:16
boundary conditions, **5B**:29
conservation law, **5B**:21
convergence, **5B**:16
dynamic interpretation, **5B**:13
for thin Ising film, **5B**:59
master equation approach, **5B**:6
self-consistent, **5B**:33, **5B**:34, **5B**:45
simulations, **11**:85, **11**:86

Monte Carlo methods, **7**:202–210
equilibrium systems, **19**:57
gel electrophoresis, **19**:216
in modelling, **19**:5
phase transitions, **19**:*151*, **19**:152, **19**:*153*, **19**:154
taking averages, **19**:28
TASEP, **19**:144
traffic models, **19**:157
two-loop diagrams, **19**:347

Monte Carlo
methods, **10**:3, **10**:62, **10**:78
calculations, **10**:207, **10**:250
estimates, **10**:188

Monte Carlo procedure, **5B**:319

Monte Carlo simulations, **16**:20–21, **16**:55, **16**:108–15, **16**:140, **16**:153–54, **16**:157–61

Monte Carlo study, **5B**:42, **5B**:43, **5B**:44, **5B**:53, **5B**:56, **5B**:66, **5B**:82, **5B**:103
of correlations, **5B**:42
of specific heat, **5B**:42
susceptibility, **5B**:42

Monte Carlo work, **3**:461

Monte-Carlo simulations, **12**:21, **12**:39, **12**:41, **12**:111–112, **12**:116, **12**:120, **12**:122, **12**:127, **12**:137, **12**:145, **12**:162, **12**:169, **12**:170, **12**:180–181, **12**:243, **12**:294, **12**:298, **12**:438, **12**:466–467

MOPE *see* multilocal operator product expansion (MOPE)

Morphology, **12**:345, **12**:389–390, **12**:397, **12**:454

Mössbauer effect, **2**:62, **10**:78
local quantities from, **8**:3

Motion, semi-phenomenological equations, **8**:287–295

MSA *see* Mean spherical approximation

Mubayi–Lange decoupling, **5B**:316

Müller–Hartmann Zittartz method, **16**:34

Multi-spin interactions, **11**:183

Mullins–Sekerka instability, **17**:73, **17**:89, **17**:91, **17**:120

Multi-component systems, **5B**:161, **5B**:178

Multi-point correlation function, **11**:56, **11**:58, **11**:62

Multi-species models, **17**:127–138

Multi-temperature models, **17**:95, **17**:96, **17**:98
with Glauber dynamics, **17**:173–175

Multi-time correlation functions, **19**:74

Multicomponent expansion, **3**:84

Multicomponent fluid
mixtures, **9**:4, **9**:13, **9**:63, **9**:65, **9**:153
systems, **9**:7, **9**:9, **9**:10, **9**:85, **9**:112

Multicomponent gas, **3**:372

Multicomponent system, **3**:48, **3**:50, **3**:71

Multicomponent systems, **2**:9

Multicritical behaviour, **8**:6
(*see also* Critical behaviour) at surfaces, **8**:23–27

Multicritical exponents, ordinary transition, **8**:34

Multicritical
fixed point, **9**:150
points, **9**:121, **9**:130, **9**:163 *et ff.*

Multicritical loci, **14**:69

Multicritical phenomena, **14**:10

Multicritical point, **8**:20, **8**:23, **8**:26, **8**:32, **8**:36, **8**:44, **8**:53, **8**:57, **11**:81, **11**:113, **11**:114, **12**:34, **12**:287, **12**:301, **12**:303, **12**:305
first-order transition and, **8**:33, **8**:34

Multicritical points, **10:**86, **10:**94,
 10:105, **10:**113, **10:**157, **10:**159–60,
 10:164, **10:**166, **10:**190, **10:**242,
 10:271, **14:**28, **14:**29, **14:**35,
 14:68–9, **14:**75, **14:**364, **15:**43,
 15:64, **17:**73
 behaviour of the surface, **10:**190
 isotropic, **10:**254
 phenomena, **10:**358
Multifractal, **12:**412–413, **12:**416,
 12:474
Multilayer adsorption, **10:**82
Multilayer models, **17:**8, **17:**121–126,
 17:196
Multilocal operator product expansion
 (MOPE)
 coefficients
  evaluation, **19:**292–297, **19:**372,
   19:461–463, **19:**464
  factorization, **19:**334, **19:**345–346,
   19:372–373
  integral, **19:**341
  Laurent series, **19:**343–344
  in renormalization, **19:**298–299
  residue extraction, **19:**310–313
 definition, **19:**291–292
 dipole contraction, **19:**360
 dipole divergence, **19:**418
 disordered system, **19:**395–396
 dynamic case, **19:**381–385
 important technique, **19:**259
 notation, **19:**454
 one-loop order, **19:**298
 in renormalization, **19:**419
 residue, **19:**425
 in Taylor expansion, **19:**321–322
 Zimm model, **19:**387
Multiparameter fitting, **13:**48–50
Multiple commutators, **1:**121
Multiple correlation function, **3:**444,
 11:50
Multiple critical points, **9:**169
Multiple decoration, **1:**295, **1:**301
Multiple occupancy, **19:**41
Multiple transitions, **1:**300
Multiplicative factors, **6:**529
Multiplicative transformation, **6:**549
Multiplicity factors, **6:**526
Multiplicity functions, **11:**136, **11:**173

Multiplicity, **3:**178
Multivariables, **13:**105–120
 behaviour, two-variable, **13:**106
 Canterbury approximants, **13:**107–110
  test series performance,
   13:109–110
 partial-differential approximants,
  13:110–113
  applications, **13:**116–120
  matching set, **13:**112
  multicritical behaviour
   determination, **13:**113–116
  multisingular point, **13:**111
  scaling axes, **13:**112–113
Multiwall expansions, **15:**34
Monotonicity, **1:**77, **1:**104

N

$n \to \infty$ ∞ limit, **8:**63–64
 finite size scaling and, **8:**217
 n-component spin model, **8:**157
 n-component spin system, spherical
  models and, **8:**208–217
n-butane + acetic acid + water, **9:**181
n-component classical field, **6:**523
n-component d-dimensional spin,
 6:250
n-component field model, **6:**295
 isotropic, **6:**77–80
n-component Heisenberg system,
 6:327
n-component order parameter, **5A:**56
n-component spin, **5A:**55
N-point fit, **3:**219, **3:**222, **3:**223, **3:**224,
 3:228, **3:**229, **3:**442
N-point function, **6:**145
n-point cumulant, **6:**48, **6:**109
N-step walks, **14:**92, **14:**98
n-vector model, **6:**375, **9:**98, **9:**217,
 10:39, **10:**82, **10:**92, **15:**78, **15:**81,
 15:83, **15:**84, **15:**87, **15:**89, **15:**95,
 15:167
 infinite-range limit, **15:**217–24
 large- n limit of disordered,
  15:116–37
 large- n limit of non-translationally
  invariant, **15:**108–16
 phase diagram, **10:**93

semi-infinite, **10**:83, **10**:90, **10**:108, **10**:116–18, **10**:138, **10**:143, **10**:155, **10**:158–9, **10**:185, **10**:202, **10**:209, **10**:213, **10**:220, **10**:250
three-dimensional, **10**:184, **10**:243
with magnetic fields, **10**:101, **10**:104
n-vector models, **8**:5, **8**:19, **8**:34, **8**:45, **8**:49, **8**:61, **14**:5, **14**:45, **14**:51–63, **14**:93, **14**:109
defects, **8**:75
ground state, **8**:56–57
interfaces, **8**:75–76
magnetic transitions, **8**:5
magnetism, **8**:18–19
n→∞ limit, **8**:63–64
phase diagram, **8**:57
three-dimensional, **8**:56
n-vector spherical model, **15**:122
N_2 on graphite, **12**:226
N_2O, **2**:63
Nagel–Schreckenberg model, **19**:155, **19**:157
Naive dimensional analysis, **6**:511
Natural phenomena
modelling, **19**:3–4, **19**:6–13, **19**:43, **19**:47, **19**:104, **19**:215–223, **19**:258–260
universality, **19**:256
see also biological systems; complex processes
Navier–Stokes equation, **5A**:210, **17**:177, **17**:178
NbO₂, **15**:64
Nearest neighbour
annihilation rate, **19**:195
distances, ordering, **19**:318
hopping, **19**:84, **19**:85
interaction, **19**:191, **19**:194
processes, one dimensional, **19**:47
spin–spin correlation, **19**:206
Nearest neighbour model, **1**:193, **1**:229
Nearest neighbour, two-dimensional, **1**:227
Nearest-neighbour Heisenberg model, **5A**:150
Nearest-neighbour interaction, **15**:207

Nearest-neighbour number, **5A**:13
Néel point
antiferromagnetic, **3**:231
Néel temperature, **3**:251, **3**:307, **3**:453, **3**:455, **3**:458, **9**:2, **9**:26, **9**:117, **17**:139
Néel temperatures, coherent potential approximations, **7**:217
Negative cycle cancelling algorithm, **18**:169–70
Negative cycle cancelling theorem, **18**:171
Nelson–Fisher transformation, **6**:410
Nematic lamellar phase, **16**:*142*
Nematic phase, **12**:191
Nematic-order parameter, **7**:76
Nematic-smectic *A* transition, **6**:417
Nematogens, two-dimensional order, **7**:74
Neon, **5B**:386
Nernst–Einstein relation, **19**:215
Nest formulation, **19**:318, **19**:323, **19**:324, **19**:327, **19**:328
Net
homogeneous, **3**:396
Network embedding, counting, **3**:97, **3**:98
Network, **3**:97, **3**:98, **3**:103, **3**:109
computer representation, **3**:103, **3**:104, **3**:105
embedding, **3**:97, **3**:98
Neumann boundary condition, **10**:200, **10**:226
Neumann series, **1**:112
Neutron scattering
critical, **5A**:89–97, **5A**:143
cross-section, **5A**:89–92
spectrometry, **5A**:97–105
Neutron scattering methods, **19**:217, **19**:385
Neutron scattering spectroscopy, **5A**:97
inelastic, **5A**:97
Neutron scattering, **3**:252, **16**:16, **16**:43, **16**:46, **16**:*47*, **16**:92, **16**:117, **16**:*118*, **16**:154
correlation lengths and, **7**:165
low-angle, **10**:78, **10**:172
Neutron, magnetic moment, **5A**:90
Neutron-scattering experiment, **12**:452

Neutron-scattering, **14:**85, **14:**91–2
NEVBARB, **13:**150, **13:**154–156
  listing, **13:**224–228
Neveu–Schwartz algebra, **11:**118
Neville–Aitken extrapolation, **13:**21–22
Neville table extrapolation, **3:**321
Neville tables, **3:**191, **3:**192, **3:**302,
  3:304, **3:**313, **3:**320, **3:**624, **3:**641
NEWGRQD/TABUL, **13:**96, **13:**97,
  13:139–159
  NEWGRQD listing, **13:**158–171
  TABUL listing, **13:**172–197
Newtons equations of motion, **19:**17,
  19:19
Next nearest neighbour interactions,
  19:156
Next-nearest neighbour interaction,
  3:496, **3:**506
NH_4Cl, **9:**208, **9:**224
Ni, **2:**67, **2:**194
Nickel, **5A:**274, **5A:**316
$NiCO_3$, **3:**582
NiF_2, **3:**582
Nitrobenzene/n-hexane mixture, **5A:**292,
  5A:309, **5A:**310
Nitroethane/iso-octane system, **5B:**380,
  5B:381, **5B:**389, **5B:**392, **5B:**393
Nitromethane + ethylene
  glycol + ethanol + n-dodecanol,
  9:199
nn/nnn model, **8:**229
Nodal graph, **2:**231–2
Nodal order, **5B:**238, **5B:**239
Nodal ordering, **5B:**206, **5B:**234
Nodal point, **3:**153, **3:**155
Node, **3:**11
Noise
  correlation matrix, **17:**21–24,
    17:27–30
  correlation, **19:**386
  function, **19:**4
  Gaussian, **19:**377, **19:**390, **19:**392
  1/f, **17:**182, **17:**183
Non-Abelian symmetry, **19:**80, **19:**82
Non-analytic behaviour, **1:**50, **1:**51,
  1:52, **1:**59, **1:**91
Non-classical corrections to tricritical
  points, **9:**179, **9:**180
Non-commutativity of operators, **1:**114

Non-commuting operator, **3:**253, **3:**258
Non-deterministic polynomial (NP)
  algorithms, **18:**150
Non-deterministic polynomial-complete
  (NP-complete) algorithms, **18:**150
Non-equilibrium statistical mechanics,
  5A:166
Non-equivalent transformation, **6:**540
Non-ergodic system, **2:**473
Non-Gaussian case, **6:**367
Non-Gaussian fluctuations, **14:**198
Non-Hermitian model, **2:**462
Non-ionic amphiphiles **16:**8 *see also n-*
  Alkyl polyglycol ethers, C_iE_j
Non-linear groups, **6:**545, **6:**548
Non-linear hydrodynamic interactions,
  5A:168
Non-linear terms, **6:**520, **6:**539
Non-linear theory, **6:**66
  correlation, **6:**105–121
  homogeneous systems, **6:**80–105
Non-linearity, **6:**547
Non-local term generalization, **5A:**56
Non-locality, **5A:**290
Non-physical singularities, **2:**404–6,
  2:409, **2:**424
Non-propagating modes, **5A:**248
Non-renormalizable theories, **10:**132
Non-self-avoiding membrane *see*
  phantom membrane
Non-singular part, **14:**114
Non-universal behaviour, **8:**75
Non-universal
  parameter, **9:**90, **9:**110
  term, **9:**111
Non-universal property, **10:**200
Non-universality, **9:**55, **9:**107, **9:**135,
  9:136, **9:**153
Nonequilibrium systems
  asymptotic behaviour, **19:**53–71
  behaviour, **19:**80–83
  boundary conditions, **19:**103
  exact solution, **19:**4
  exclusion process, **19:**103
  maintaining, **19:**89
  modelling, **19:**3, **19:**104
  phase transitions, **19:**6
  randomness, **19:**4
  statistical mechanics, **19:**3

Nonergodic systems, **19:**66
Noninteracting particles, **19:**116–117
Nonlinear growth, **19:**373
Nonlinear magnetization, **14:**102
Nonlinear recursion relations, **14:**90
Nonlinear relaxation, **14:**69
Nonlinear renormalization of interface
    potentials, **14:**350–3
Nonlinear scaling fields, **14:**38
Nonlinear susceptibility, **14:**42, **14:**55
Nonlocal interactions, polymer, **19:**259
Nonmagnetic impurities, **1:**96
Nonrandom Toeplitz matrix, **15:**201
Nonrenormalization, long-range
    interaction, **19:**303–305
Nonstochastic generators, **19:**28
Norm–asymptotic–abelian manner,
    1:150
Normal distribution, **5B:**8
Normal ordered products, **9:**249–51
Normal ordering, **19:**286–287, **19:**293,
    19:395, **19:**396
Normal-normal correlation function,
    16:136
Normalization condition, **5B:**7
Normalization factor, **15:**189
Normalization point, **6:**544
Normalization, **19:**84, **19:**294,
    19:451–452
    see also renormalization
Normalized distribution function (NDF),
    15:170, **15:**172, **15:**176, **15:**177,
    15:187, **15:**188, **15:**189, **15:**192,
    15:193–5, **15:**198–200, **15:**205,
    15:206
Normalized relaxation function, **5A:**92
Normed algebra, **1:**140
Normed *-algebra, **1:**140
    of local observables, **1:**142
North-east–centre (NEC) model, **17:**169,
    17:174
    see also Toom model
Notation, **19:**239–241, **19:**453–454
Novaco–McTague rotations, **12:**232,
    12:244–245
Nuclear magnetic resonance (NMR),
    5A:324–326, **10:**77
    experiments, **19:**26
    quantities from, **8:**3

Nucleation
    barrier, **8:**68
    classical theory, **8:**68, **8:**279–286
    coagulation equation, **8:**352
    completion time, **8:**399–404
    field-theoretic, **8:**300–319
    in binary fluids, **8:**274
    in near-critical fluids, **8:**395–404
    in polymer systems, **8:**447–449
    in supercooled liquids, **8:**454
    models, in binary fluids and liquid-gas
        transitions, **8:**310–316
    rates, calculation, **8:**307–310
    spinodal decomposition as generalized
        theory of, **8:**360–366
    theory, **8:**352–355
Nucleation rate, **5B:**70
Nucleation theory, **3:**471, **5B:**88, **5B:**89
Nucleation time, **5B:**89
Nucleation, **5B:**5, **5B:**85, **5B:**86,
    5B:134, **12:**7–8
    heterogeneous, **12:**9
    homogeneous, **12:**9
Number operators, **19:**20
Numerical estimates, experimental
    results and, **8:**123–125
Numerical methods, **19:**5, **19:**15, **19:**28,
    19:113, **19:**276–278, **19:**363–364
    critical behaviour at surfaces,
        8:103–118
    see also Monte Carlo methods
Numerical results, **14:**46, **14:**255–6
Numerical test, finite size scaling,
    8:223–250

O

$0(3)$ model, $(1 + 1)$-dimensional, finite
    lattice calculations, **8:**248
$0\{n\}$ model, **12:**279, **12:**281
$O(N)$ model
    applications, **19:**429–434
    behaviour for large N, **19:**427–429
    field theoretical description, **19:**256,
        19:413, **19:**414
    generalization to membranes,
        19:421–426
    high-temperature expansion, **19:**260,
        19:409–412

O(n) models, **11**:3, **11**:42, **11**:45–46, **11**:48–50, **11**:82, **11**:112, **11**:121
O(n) symmetry, **9**:62
Observable, **1**:139
Observables, **18**:8–9
  quasilocal, **18**:8
Occupancy, unrestricted, **19**:29
Occupation number representation, **1**:210
Octahedron, **1**:320, **2**:216
Odd/even oscillation, **3**:190, **3**:197
Off-lattice model, **12**:367, **12**:377–378, **12**:390, **12**:392, **12**:426, **12**:436–448, **12**:453, **12**:461, **12**:463
OH networks, **12**:312–315, **12**:320
Oil-water-amphiphile mixtures
  interfacial properties, **16**:13–16
  phase behavior, **16**:5–13
  structure, **16**:16–18
Oil/microemulsion interface, at three-phase coexistence, **16**:87–92, **16**:*89*, **16**:*91*, **16**:*92*
  elastic property of, **16**:*104*
Oil/microemulsion interfacial tension, **16**:*14*, **16**:15, **16**:59, **16**:*61*
Oil/water interface
  at three-phase coexistence, **16**:87–92, **16**:*89*, **16**:*91*, **16**:*92*
  elastic properties of amphiphile monolayer at, **16**:97–105
  stress profile through monolayer at, **16**:*100*
  wetting transitions at, **16**:15, **16**:53–5, **16**:61, **16**:90–6
Oil/water interfacial tension, **16**:*14*, **16**:15, **16**:*51*, **16**:*52*, **16**:53, **16**:57, **16**:61, **16**:91, **16**:110, **16**:164
One-order-parameter model, **16**:79–82, **16**:87–115
Ordered bicontinuous minimal surfaces, **16**:113
On-site annihilation or interaction, **19**:6
One dimensional systems critical exponents, **7**:178
  and parameters, **7**:176–177
  pure, properties, **7**:178
  solution, **7**:182

One particle
  irreducible (IPI) graphs, **10**:126
  reducible graph, **10**:130
One-body approximation, **6**:158
One-component fluid, **5A**:176, **5A**:182, **5A**:183, **5A**:256, **5A**:257, **5A**:258, **5A**:289, **5A**:304, **5A**:305, **5A**:371, **5A**:374
  see also Single-component fluid
One-component fluids, **10**:211
One-density theory, **12**:88
One-dimensional gas, **1**:181
  One-dimensional systems, **1**:89
One-dimensional interfaces, fluctuation, **19**:43
One-dimensional models, **17**:9, **17**:154–155
  open boundary conditions, **17**:158, **17**:159–162
  shocks in, **17**:162–164
  systems with translational invariance, **17**:155–158
  Toom model, **17**:169–170
  two-species models, **17**:164–169
One-loop diagram, **17**:*67*
One-loop graph, **6**:306, **6**:312, **6**:350
One-loop order, **19**:292, **19**:296, **19**:298–303, **19**:367, **19**:381–385, **19**:407
One-particle irreducible function, **6**:178
Onsager
  function, **10**:12
  interfacial model, **10**:16
  sheet, **10**:33
  Temperley string, **10**:3
Onsager Kinetic coefficients, **2**:452, **2**:455, **2**:456, **2**:480, **2**:489, **2**:493
Onsager kinetic coefficient, **5A**:167, **5A**:185, **5A**:195, **5A**:196, **5A**:201, **5A**:211, **5A**:261, **5A**:262, **5A**:263, **5A**:295
  renormalized, **5A**:260
Onsager lattice, **1**:236
Onsager relation, **2**:454, **5A**:201
Onsager solution, **2**:465, **3**:464, **9**:273
  exact, **3**:555
Onsager temperature, **17**:10, **17**:40
Onsager–Ising model, **1**:232, **1**:234, **1**:235, **1**:236

Onsager-type phase transitions, **13**:239
    3–12/1 dimer model, **13**:244
    4–8 dimer models, **13**:245–247,
        13:270
OP (ordered phase), **12**:114–115,
    12:131, **12**:152, **12**:154
Opalescence critical, **9**:170, **9**:177 *(see
    also* light scattering)
Open boundary conditions
    and chemical potential gradients,
        17:108–118
    in ID models, **17**:158, **17**:159–162
Open chain, **1**:193
Open cluster, **18**:32, **18**:36
    infinite, **18**:32, **18**:42–7
Open isotropic chain, **1**:201
Open path, **18**:32, **18**:36
Operator product coefficients expansion,
    11:63
    universal, **11**:75
Operator product expansion (OPE), **6**:10,
    6:107, **10**:191–3, **10**:206–7, **19**:259,
    19:286–290, **19**:462
Operators
    algebra, **6**:65
    composite, **6**:148–154, **6**:198, **6**:200,
        6:238
    irrelevant, **6**:32, **6**:34, **6**:44, **6**:72,
        6:85, **6**:88, **6**:114, **6**:128
    linear, **6**:519
    local, **6**:49
    marginal, **6**:32, **6**:34, **6**:70, **6**:87, **6**:94,
        6:99, **6**:100, **6**:418
    n-point cumulant, **6**:48, **6**:109
    projection, **6**:67, **6**:391
    redundant, **6**:34–41, **6**:58, **6**:61, **6**:62,
        6:64, **6**:65, **6**:77, **6**:85, **6**:87,
        6:88, **6**:116, **6**:118, **6**:119
        RG equation and, **6**:9
        scaling fields *g* and, **6**:10
    relevant, **6**:32, **6**:33, **6**:44, **6**:58, **6**:72,
        6:91, **6**:97, **6**:98, **6**:114, **6**:118
        scaling fields of, **6**:114
    scaling, **6**:34, **6**:38, **6**:58, **6**:61, **6**:64,
        6:65, **6**:85
        bifurcation point and, **6**:10
        RG equation and, **6**:9
    special, **6**:33, **6**:61
    symmetry conserving, **6**:44

Operators, **5A**:7, **5A**:16, **5A**:17
    absorption, **1**:262, **1**:263
    emission, **1**:262, **1**:263
Optical instability, **8**:453
Optimal paths, **14**:275
Order
    of code, **3**:409
Order parameter correlation function,
    5A:38, **5A**:51, **5A**:74, **5A**:81
    dynamical, **5A**:38
    for phase transitions, **5A**:15
Order parameter correlation, **5B**:77
Order parameter fluctuation, **3**:600,
    3:601, **3**:636, **5B**:19
Order parameter operator, **3**:571,
    3:573
Order parameter profile (interfacial),
    10:4, **10**:32, **10**:88–9, **10**:93–4,
    10:99–100, **10**:105, **10**:109,
    10:204–10, **10**:231, **10**:240, **10**:271,
    10:282, **10**:284–5, **10**:293, **10**:308,
    10:311, **10**:350
    $d = 4 - \varepsilon$, **10**:301, **10**:306
    density, spatially varying, **10**:205
    mean-field, **10**:103
    non-linear relaxation, **10**:250
Order parameter profiles, **8**:14, **8**:23,
    8:31, **8**:45, **8**:65, **8**:67, **8**:68, **8**:75,
    14:115
    near surfaces, **8**:10–14
    interfaces, **8**:65
    scaling, **8**:44–47
Order parameter relaxation function,
    5B:74, **5B**:90
Order parameter relaxation time, **5B**:19,
    5B:78, **5B**:86, **5B**:88, **5B**:89
Order parameter, **1**:84, **2**:7, **2**:8, **2**:9,
    2:10, **2**:13–15, **2**:18, **2**:19, **2**:20,
    2:26, **2**:29, **2**:34, **2**:36, **2**:185,
    3:502, **3**:571, **3**:572, **3**:579, **3**:580,
    3:583, **3**:596, **3**:611, **3**:630, **3**:631,
    3:646, **3**:647, **3**:648, **3**:649, **5A**:18,
    5A:36, **5A**:37, **5A**:45, **5A**:47,
    5A:57, **5A**:88, **5A**:96, **5A**:167,
    5A:193, **5A**:205, **5A**:250, **5A**:260,
    5A:267, **5A**:279, **5A**:287, **5A**:298,
    5A:299, **5A**:310, **5A**:316, **5A**:317,
    5B:19, **5B**:20, **5B**:21, **5B**:26,
    5B:32, **5B**:33, **5B**:34, **5B**:38,

5B:43, **5B:**53, **5B:**70, **5B:**75, **5B:**80, **5B:**100, **5B:**345–349 *passim*, **5B:**366, **5B:**382–387, *passim*, **6:**11–14, **6:**50, **6:**91, **6:**93, **6:**128, **6:**132, **6:**159, **6:**160, **6:**163, **6:**171, **6:**188, **6:**189, **6:**217, **6:**221, **6:**222, **6:**416, **6:**512, **6:**526, **6:**528, **9:**6, **9:**66, **9:**67, **9:**69, **9:**70, **9:**73, **9:**83, **9:**89, **9:**153, **9:**174, **9:**178, **9:**215, **9:**224, **12:**123, **12:**126, **12:**130, **12:**133, **12:**136, **12:**140, **12:**151, **12:**176–179, **12:**188–189, **15:**12
  correlation, **6:**105–107
  correlation function, **6:**48, **6:**542
  detection of phase transition, **18:**13
  dimensionality, **6:**9
  dynamics, **5A:**250, **5A:**267–298
  fluctuations, **5A:**53, **5A:**302, **5A:**303, **5A:**313
  number of components, **6:**358, **6:**520
  of s.c. infinite spin Ising system, **5B:**43
  16 x 16 x 16 simple cubic Ising lattice, **5B:**41
  symmetry, **6:**526
  two-point correlation functions, **6:**511
Order parameters, **7:**158
  conserved, scaling, **8:**368–372
  correlation functions, **7:**2
  correlations, **7:**22
  many-component, **8:**18
  nonconserved, scaling, **8:**372–373
  one-component, **8:**18
  percolation and, in site diluted f.c.c. lattices, **7:**157
Order, optimal, **19:**446, **19:***448*
Order-disorder effect, **1:**228
Order-disorder transition, **3:**364, **3:**366, **3:**453, **3:**455, **5A:**78, **5A:**88
  in beta-brass, **5A:**105
Order-disorder transitions, **14:**145, **14:**147
Ordered phase, **5A:**274
Ordering field, **5B:**345, **9:**6, **9:**116
Ordering temperature, site diluted simple cubic Ising model, **7:**205

Ordinary transitions (surface), **8:**12, **8:**20, **8:**34, **8:**37, **8:**43, **8:**44, **8:**47, **8:**53, **8:**54, **8:**63
  scaling relations, **8:**41
  surface exponents, **8:**49
Orientation order, **12:**223, **12:**225, **12:**229, **12:**247
Orientational interactions, **16:**31
Orientational order, **7:**50, **7:**51
  parameter, **7:**44
    measurement, **7:**54
  two-dimensional melting, **7:**40–45
Orientational ordering, **2:**326
Ornstein–Uhlenbeck process, **5B:**162, **5B:**167
Ornstein–Zernicke formula, **10:**52, **10:**106
Ornstein–Zernike approximation, **5B:**238, **5B:**246, **5B:**258, **16:**41, **16:**44, **16:**86, **16:**110, **16:**116, **16:**148
  for hard spheres, **5B:**241
  three-particle, **5B:**242
Ornstein–Zernike behaviour, **5A:**118, **5A:**160, **6:**12, **6:**511
Ornstein–Zernike correlation, **12:**66
Ornstein–Zernike direct correlation function, **5B:**210
Ornstein–Zernike equation, **5B:**206, **5B:**213, **5B:**231, **5B:**232, **5B:**247, **6:**455
  Dyson form, **5B:**231
Ornstein–Zernike exponential decay, **5A:**56, **5A:**60
Ornstein–Zernike form [of structure factor), **17:**29, **17:**33, **17:**189
Ornstein–Zernike form, **6:**524, **8:**28
Ornstein–Zernike formula, **9:**199, **9:**200
Ornstein–Zernike pair correlation function, **5A:**94
Ornstein–Zernike relation, **6:**454
Ornstein–Zernike system, **2:**378, **2:**427, **2:**429, **2:**432
Ornstein–Zernike theory, **5A:**63, **5A:**65, **5A:**66, **5A:**67, **5B:**157, **5B:**160, **6:**427
Orthonormal set
  of gross variables, **5A:**345
  of polynomial functions, **5A:**174

Orthogonal matrix, **6**:52
Oscillatory correlation function, **16**:80, **16**:90
Osmotic compressibility, **16**:64
Osmotic pressure, **16**:138
Ostwald ripening, **8**:333, **8**:452
Overfeeding, **19**:135, **19**:147, **19**:153
Overhangs, **14**:152, **14**:153
Overlap partition, **3**:65, **3**:66, **3**:87, **3**:89, **3**:90, **3**:92
Overlap, **18**:217
Oxygen, **5B**:386, **5B**:392, **5B**:393
OZ *see* Ornstein Zernike equation
O–shaped honeycomb domain wall network, *see* OH network

P

P.A. analysis, **3**:466
Padé approximant method, **3**:240, **3**:319, **3**:320, **3**:436, **3**:442
basic **3**:303
Padé approximant, **2**:228–9, **2**:261, **2**:314, **3**:200, **3**:202, **3**:203, **3**:204, **3**:205, **3**:206, **3**:207, **3**:208, **3**:209, **3**:210, **3**:211, **3**:212, **3**:213, **3**:214, **3**:215, **3**:216, **3**:217, **3**:218, **3**:219, **3**:223, **3**:224, **3**:225, **3**:228, **3**:229, **3**:302, **3**:303, **3**:310, **3**:313, **3**:316, **3**:317, **3**:318, **3**:320, **3**:324, **3**:327, **3**:360, **3**:433, **3**:438, **3**:440, **3**:455, **3**:459, **3**:617, **3**:618, **3**:619, **3**:620, **3**:621, **3**:622, **3**:623, **3**:624, **3**:633, **3**:637, **3**:638, **3**:639, **3**:640, **3**:641, **3**:642, **3**:644, **3**:655, **6**:207, **6**:320, **6**:396, **6**:403
Padé approximants, **1**:58, **5B**:31, **5B**:38, **5B**:57, **5B**:58, **5B**:59, **5B**:63, **5B**:79, **5B**:189, **5B**:297, **5B**:333, **9**:259, **9**:261, **9**:278, **9**:301, **13**:51–75, *see also* Canterbury approximants, Rational-approximant method additive-singularity case, **13**:69
AMP method, **13**:73–75
applications, **13**:59–66
confluent singularities, **13**:61–63
confluent-singularity method, **13**:66–69

exponent-renormalization method, **13**:66
generalizations
differential approximants as, **13**:84–86
multidimensional, **13**:106
generalized inverse, **13**:80–83
invariance, **13**:95
Kosterlitz–Thouless-type singularities, **13**:26–29, **13**:70
and quadratic differential approximants, **13**:94
Roskies' quadratic transformation, **13**:72–73
theory, **13**:52–59
convergence properties, **13**:53–54
defective approximants, **13**:57
development, **13**:5
error analysis, **13**:57–59
polynomial coefficients, **13**:52–53
pseudoconvergence, **13**:55–56
two-point, **13**:70–72
Padé table **3**:204, **3**:211, **3**:222, **3**:223, **3**:303, **3**:310, **3**:320, **3**:321, **3**:326
and Shanks transformation, **13**:37
Pair annihilation process
and correlation, **19**:195
diffusion-limited, **19**:73, **19**:163, **19**:181, **19**:193–211
integrability, **19**:50–51
rate, **19**:222
on a ring, **19**:194–195
see also annihilation process
Pair annihilation–creation process, **19**:51, **19**:55–56, **19**:176, **19**:185, **19**:188, **19**:191
Pair annihilation–fusion process, **19**:193
Pair connectedness, **2**:201–2, **2**:229–30, **2**:239, **2**:244, **3**:76
Strong, **2**:231, **2**:234
weak, **2**:231
Pair correlation function, **1**:83, **1**:105, **1**:197, **1**:201, **3**:439, **3**:512, **5B**:77, **5B**:78, **5B**:92, **5B**:100, **5B**:131, **5B**:132, **5B**:159, **5B**:160, **5B**:163
Pair correlation, **2**:92, **2**:98, **2**:116, **2**:140, **2**:142, **2**:144, **2**:146, **2**:153, **2**:157

Pair correlations, **1**:41, **1**:83, **3**:76,
    3:129, **3**:130, **3**:139, **3**:140, **3**:150,
    3:161, **3**:167, **3**:168, **3**:174, **3**:235
Pair creation process, **19**:213–214
Pair density, **5B**:120
Pair distribution function, **2**:323,
    5B:176, **5B**:177
    of hard rods, **5B**:159
Pair exchange process, **19**:80
Pair excitations, **19**:201
Pair interaction, **15**:34
Pair interactions, **1**:32, **1**:42, **1**:48, **1**:55,
    1:80, **1**:82, **1**:84, **1**:90, **1**:91, **1**:92,
    1:98
Pair potential, **5B**:114, **5B**:139
Pair potentials, **1**:27, **1**:28, **1**:43, **1**:88,
    1:95, **1**:124, **1**:178
    negative, **1**:53
Pair transition matrix, **19**:46
Pair-correlation function, **5A**:88, **5A**:107
    for magnetic moments, **5A**:89
Pairwise additivity, **5B**:216
Papangelou intensities, **18**:127–8
Parabolic model, **6**:99, **6**:103-105
Parabolic renormalization group flow,
    14:211
Paraelectric transitions, **14**:145
Parafermion, *see* Spinor
Parallel correlation length, **14**:232,
    14:313–15
Parallel updating, **19**:28, **19**:137, **19**:156,
    19:158, **19**:160
Parallelogram geometry, **14**:113
Paramagnetic phases, diluted anisotropic
    Heisenberg antiferromagnets,
    coherent potential approximation,
    7:217
Paramagnetic transitions, **14**:145
Paramagnetism, **5A**:43
Paramagnons, **6**:8
Parametric model, **6**:340
Parametric representation, **2**:40, **2**:69
Parity, **3**:410
    alternate, **3**:409
    significant, **3**:410, **3**:411
Park method, **3**:495, **3**:499
Parquet approximation, **6**:196
Partial graph, **2**:201, **2**:233, **3**:61, **3**:78,
    3:79, **3**:82, **3**:83

Partial-differential approximants,
    13:105–106, **13**:110–113
    applications, **13**:116–120
        confluent singularities, **13**:117,
            13:120
        Ising–Heisenberg–*XY* critical
            point, **13**:117
        Klauder model, **13**:118–119
        slice method, **13**:119–120
    matching set, **13**:112
    muitricritical behaviour determination
        fidelity, **13**:115–116
        invariance, **13**:115
        method of characters, **13**:114
    multisingular point, **13**:111
    scaling axes, **13**:112–113
Partially ordered set, **3**:79, **3**:81, **6**:472
Particle annihilation, **11**:9
    fusion, **11**:8
n-Particle distribution function, **3**:145
Particle
    absorption, **19**:88
    –antiparticle excitations, **19**:40
    current, **19**:61–62
        inward and outward, **19**:122
        nonvanishing, **19**:110
        stationary, **19**:89, **19**:110, **19**:156
    density, **19**:5, **19**:183
    distributions, **19**:80, **19**:82
    energies, **19**:111
    –hole symmetry, **19**:9, **19**:82, **19**:126,
        19:134, **19**:139, **19**:147, **19**:155,
        19:227–228
    injection, **19**:88, **19**:226
    interaction, **19**:150
    number, **19**:197
        calculation, **19**:203, **19**:204
        change, **19**:197
        conservation, **19**:55, **19**:61–62,
            19:99, **19**:105, **19**:109, **19**:125,
            19:165
        decrease, **19**:211
        distribution, **19**:205
        dynamical, **19**:218
        even and odd, **19**:197, **19**:198
        fluctuations, **19**:206
        independent of bias, **19**:203
    parity operators, **19**:177
    reservoirs, **19**:89, **19**:98, **19**:99

systems
 late time behaviour, **19**:59–69
 and spin models, **19**:24, **19**:27,
  19:30
 two-type, **19**:27, **19**:118,
  19:121–122
 see also interacting particle
  systems
 transport, boundary conditions, **19**:44
Partile, current, stationary, **19**:96
Partition function, **3**:594, **3**:595, **3**:603,
  6:512, **6**:526, **15**:79, **15**:88, **15**:138,
  15:141
 canonical, **1**:11, **1**:13, **1**:20, **1**:189,
  1:242
 canonical configurational, **1**:25
 definition, **6**:18–22
 derivatives, **6**:18–22
 equilibrium distribution, **19**:106
 for two-dimensional lattices, **1**:322
 free, **1**:355, **19**:427
 free Gaussian manifold, **19**:435
 functional integral, **6**:18–22
 grand, **1**:13, **1**:20, **1**:50, **1**:130, **1**:189,
  1:232, **1**:242, **1**:312, **1**:314,
  1:316
 grand canonical, **1**:130, **1**:189
 high-temperature expansion, **19**:409
 Ising model, **19**:32, **19**:431
 membrane, **19**:359–361
 periodic, **1**:356
 polymer, **19**:314–315, **19**:408
 self-avoiding membrane, **19**:436–437
 singularities, **19**:431
 stationary distribution, **19**:62
 zero field, **3**:369, **3**:378, **3**:389, **3**:390,
  3:417
Partition functions, **14**:13, **14**:32,
  14:113
 crystal rarefied, **11**:154
Partition function zeros, **1**:50
Partition
 overlap, **3**:65, **3**:66, **3**:87, **3**:89, **3**:92
 of *r* labelled points, **3**:81
Path integral method, **6**:294
Path integrals *see* Feynman integral
Path integrals, **7**:135, **7**:137
Path integration, condensation
 phenomena and, **7**:104

Path probability method, **17**:16
Pattern formation, in chemical reactions,
  8:452
Pauli exclusion principle, **1**:38
Pauli matrices, **1**:206, **1**:208, **1**:210,
  1:211, **1**:245, **1**:251
 boundary conditions, **19**:178
 commutation relations, **19**:177
 equations of motion, **19**:182
 and fermionic operators, **19**:200,
  19:202
 in Heisenberg quantum formalism,
  19:33, **19**:41, **19**:48, **19**:106–107
 notation, **19**:20, **19**:239
 properties, **19**:26
 two-dimensional, **19**:203
Pauli operator, **5B**:261
Pauli spin matrices, **1**:115, **1**:153,
  1:178
Pauli-spin operators, **12**:249, **12**:252,
  12:272, **12**:278, **12**:322
Pauling model, **3**:656
Pecherski's model, **11**:149–150,
  11:172
Peierls argument, **1**:59, **1**:61, **1**:63, **1**:64,
  1:65, **1**:67, **1**:69, **1**:70, **1**:75, **1**:76,
  1:77, **1**:97, **10**:34, **10**:42, **10**:44,
  10:60, **10**:68
 contours, **10**:7
Peierls–Nabarro (PN) barrier, **15**:17
Peierls, argument, **11**:130, **11**:167,
  11:168, **11**:193
 bound, **11**:130–1, **11**:155
 condition, **11**:129, **11**:141–5,
  11:147–9
Peirls contour, **19**:231
Pentacritical point, **9**:164, **9**:225
Percolation behaviour, coherent potential
 approximations, **7**:221
Percolation cluster problems, position
 space methds, **7**:250
Percolation concentration
 Bethe lattice, **7**:184
 diluted layer magnets, **7**:258
 in dilute magnets, **7**:160
 McCoy–Wu Ising model variant,
  7:182
 quenched site diluted Ising
  ferromagnet, **7**:159

Percolation conductivity
dilute resistor networks, **7**:196, **7**:208
position space methods, **7**:247, **7**:248,
7:250, **7**:251
Percolation correlation length, **7**:237
infinite clusters and, **7**:165
Percolation critical behaviour, dilute
magnets, series expansion methods,
7:224–227
Percolation critical exponents, **7**:158,
7:161
Percolation
directed, **8**:241
essential singularity in, **8**:449–451
field-theoretic methods, **8**:126–128
finite size scaling, **8**:233–241
on lattices with free surfaces,
8:108–109
surface effects, **8**:99–103
Percolation effect, **5B**:103
Percolation effects
calculations, **7**:203
in quenched dilute magnets,
7:163–169
renormalization group theory and,
7:233
virtual crystal approximation, **7**:211
Percolation fixed point, **7**:245, **7**:253,
7:254
Heisenberg thermal exponent, **7**:269
in dilute magnets, **7**:241
Percolation function, **2**:226, **2**:247
Percolation model, **14**:64–7
Percolation order parameter,
concentration expansion methods,
7:225
Percolation point, dilute Ising model,
7:190
Percolation probability, **2**:198, **2**:201,
2:203, **2**:206, **2**:208, **2**:226–8,
2:242, **2**:243–4, **2**:246, **2**:254,
2:258, **7**:196
Percolation problem, **3**:89, **3**:655
bond, **3**:89
site, **3**:89
Percolation process, **3**:58
bond, **3**:86
site, **3**:85, **3**:474
Percolation process, Ch, **2**:6, **2**:200

Percolation theory, **3**:73, **3**:74, **3**:76,
5B:318, **5B**:333, **18**:4–5
see also Bernoullis percolation
Percolation thermal crossover, **7**:237,
7:261
exponent, Ising model, **7**:246
position space methods, **7**:247
Percolation threshold, **7**:196, **7**:253
cluster methods, **7**:213
correlation length, **7**:266
dilute Heisenberg layer magnet,
7:267, **7**:268
diluted Ising layer magnet, **7**:267
effective medium theory, **7**:221
position space methods, **7**:250
quasi-one-dimensional Heisenberg
system, **7**:265
Percolation transition, **7**:158
length invariants at, **7**:249
Percolation, **1**:266, **3**:71, **3**:87, **7**:205,
7:242, **11**:98, **11**:110, **12**:166,
12:351, **12**:353, **12**:396, **12**:429,
12:472–474, **14**:30, **14**:43, **14**:67–8,
14:365, **16**:65–8, **16**:141–42
dilute magnet, **7**:153, **7**:156–162
field-theoretic renormalization group
treatments, **7**:246
mean cluster size and, in site diluted
f.c.c. lattice, **7**:157
order parameter and, in site diluted
f.c.c. lattice, **7**:157
position space methods, **7**:247–262
scaling and, **7**:235
scaling laws, **7**:226
Percus–Yevick approximation, **5B**:220,
5B:240
for hard spheres, **5B**:241
Percus–Yevick equation, **2**:272, **5B**:189,
5B:207, **5B**:221
for hard spheres, **5B**:238
Perfect simulation, **18**:69
Perimeter method, **2**:243, **2**:266
Perimeter polynomial, **2**:227–8
Period-doubling commensurate phases,
15:51
Periodic boundary condition, **5B**:3,
5B:4, **5B**:11, **5B**:30, **5B**:34–37,
5B:44, **5B**:55, **5B**:58, **5B**:64,
5B:77, **5B**:83, **5B**:87, **5B**:100,

5B:127, **5B**:129, **5B**:130, **5B**:134,
   5B:169, **6**:466, **6**:467, **6**:474, **6**:485
Periodic boundary conditions, **3**:254,
   3:363, **5A**:46, **11**:68, **14**:6, **15**:150,
   15:162
Periodic elastic media, **18**:234–5
Periodic field, **15**:150–9
Periodic potential, **14**:157–8
Periodic substrates in commensurate
   melting on, **7**:57–62
Periodic systems, **14**:101
Periodic-strip relations, **14**:109
Periodically (AC) driven systems, **17**:94,
   17:197
Periodically diluted models, solutions,
   7:175
Permanent, **1**:235
Permutation group, **3**:26
Permutations, **3**:132
Perovskite-type crystals, **3**:583
Perpendicular field
   staggered, **3**:580
Perpendicular magnetization
   staggered, **3**:580
Perpendicular susceptibility amplitude,
   3:640
Perpendicular susceptibility, **3**:572,
   3:648
   frequency-dependent, **3**:572, **3**:630,
      3:633
Perron's theorem, **2**:320, **2**:321
Perron–Frobenius theorem, **15**:153
Persistence
   distributions, **19**:83–84
   probabilities, **19**:75–77
Persistence length, **16**:21, **16**:136,
   16:147, **16**:156–57, **16**:160,
   16:164
Pertubation
   and correlations, **19**:99
   anomalously small response, **19**:389
   diffusion, **19**:*61*, **19**:124
   expansion, **9**:282
   expansion
      critical exponents, **19**:351–352
      near critical point, **19**:366
      extrapolation, **19**:347–348
      $O(N)$ model, **19**:409–410,
        19:412

ϕ^4 theory, **19**:257
   polymer Hamiltonian, **19**:414
   R-operation, **19**:298
   second-order terms, **19**:288
   self-avoiding membrane, **19**:435
   simplification, **19**:313–314
   variational method, **19**:352–354
   large order behaviour,
      19:437–450
local, **19**:68, **19**:123–124, **19**:209
series, **9**:258–67
spread and decay, **19**:168, **19**:209
stationary state, **19**:59–60
theory, **9**:234
theory renormalized, **9**:293
theory, **19**:*281*, **19**:284–285, **19**:379,
   19:380–381
   analysis, **19**:117
   corrections, **19**:270–273
   divergent, **19**:438
   first-order, **19**:439
   fixed point, **19**:389
   large order results, **19**:434–450
   polymers, **19**:372–374
   renormalizability, **19**:318–340,
      19:371, **19**:446
Perturbation expansion, **3**:1, **3**:2, **3**:3,
   3:16, **3**:18, **3**:23, **3**:37, **3**:40, **3**:42,
   14:57, **14**:333–8
Perturbation method, **3**:375
Perturbation series, **1**:8, **1**:42
Perturbation theory, **3**:148, **3**:165, **6**:170,
   6:277
   unrenormalized, **3**:164, **3**:173,
      3:175
Perturbations, anisotropic, **6**:297
   cubic, **6**:266
   local, partition function and, **6**:22
Perturbative calculation, **6**:526
Perturbative expansion, **6**:533
Perturbative loop expansion, **14**:196–200
Pfaffian expansion, **1**:234
Pfaffian form, **2**:105
Pfaffian method, **1**:258, **1**:266, **2**:141,
   3:661, **3**:662
Pfaffian, **1**:233, **1**:234, **1**:236, **1**:237,
   1:255, **1**:256, **1**:257, **1**:259, **1**:260,
   1:261, **1**:262, **1**:263
   cyclic, 237

Pfafian method for transition behaviour, **13**:253–254

Phantom membranes, **19**:263, **19**:264, **19**:276, **19**:319, **19**:356, **19**:371, **19**:434, **19**:436, **19**:437

Phase
 angle, **19**:43
 diagram, **19**:138–139
  and boundary densities, **19**:*151*
  construction, **19**:153
  and current–density relation, **19**:144, **19**:153
  mean field approximation, **19**:126, **19**:*127*
  and particle interactions, **19**:150–151
 self-avoiding membrane, **19**:*386*
 separator, **19**:105, **19**:132–133, **19**:151–152, **19**:*364*, **19**:388
 transition
 boundary-induced, **19**:44, **19**:52, **19**:103, **19**:104, **19**:126, **19**:143–154, **19**:157
 and domain wall diffusion, **19**:171
 ferromagnetic systems, **19**:32
 field-induced, **19**:169, **19**:172
 first-order, **19**:147, **19**:172
 and long-range order, **19**:125
 nonequilibrium systems, **19**:6
 prediction, **19**:131
 second-order, **19**:34, **19**:135, **19**:147
 and shock dynamics, **19**:127
 surface, **19**:230
 symmetry breaking, **19**:256

Phase boundaries
 antiferromagnets, dilution and, **7**:270
 binary mixed bond disordered magnets, **7**:211
 bond annealed systems on Bethe lattice, **7**:201
 correlation lengths and, **7**:165
 critical singularity, **7**:188
 dilute bond disordered magnets, **7**:211
 dilute Ising case, exactly soluble, **7**:190
 diluted *q*-state Potts model on Bethe lattice, **7**:192
 dilute XY model, series expansion methods, **7**:231

exact, **7**:201
 for exactly soluble Ising model with striped dilution, **7**:191
 free energy, quenched models, **7**:184
 Monte Carlo methods, **7**:203
 quenched dilute Ising magnets, series expansion methods, **7**:229
 quenched magnets, **7**:191
 quenched site diluted transverse Ising model, **7**:232

Phase boundaries, methods of locating, **17**:17–18

Phase boundary equation, **2**:45

Phase boundary, **2**:42, **2**:44, **2**:47, **2**:50, **2**:73, **5A**:6, **14**:16, **14**:17, **14**:102

Phase diagram for the system methane + *n*-hexane, **9**:165, **9**:166, **9**:167

Phase diagram, **5A**:6

Phase diagrams
 dilute magnets, real space calculations, **7**:248
 dynamics affecting, **17**:18, **17**:99
 mean-field, discrete mapping, **8**:96–99
 Monte Carlo method, **7**:203
 n-vector model, **8**:57
 polarized lattice gas, **17**:*137*
 position space methods, **7**:247
 repulsive-interaction model, **17**:*140*
 site diluted Heisenberg antiferromagnets, virtual crystal approximation, **7**:212
 standard model, **17**:*13*
 two-species models, **17**:168

Phase separation, **3**:366, **14**:42
 dynamics, **17**:7, **17**:76–80
 liquid-liquid, **5B**:387

Phase transition displacive, **3**:583
 first order, **3**:470, **3**:662
 liquid vapour, **3**:366

Phase transition states, **2**:3

Phase transition, **5A**:15, **5A**:36
 definition, **1**:139
 first order, **1**:11, **1**:34, **1**:41, **1**:52, **5A**:6, **5B**:110, **5B**:133, **5B**:147, **5B**:153, **5B**:194
 fluid–crystal, **1**:174
 isomorphy, **5B**:344, **5B**:347
 KDP type, **10**:44, **10**:48
 problems, **5A**:7, **5A**:8

second order, **5A**:15, **5A**:35, **5A**:48,
　　5A:57, **5A**:71, **5A**:78, **5B**:344
solid–liquid, **1**:152
Phase transitions, **6**:358, **13**:130, **18**:13,
　　18:13–14, **18**:28–9, **18**:55, **18**:92–4,
　　18:105–11, **18**:113–16, **18**:125–9
　　boundary-induced, **17**:159–160
　　continuous, **6**:8, **17**:72–73, **17**:107
　　defect-mediated, **7**:1–93
　　　experiments, **7**:7–11
　　　theoretical background, **7**:2–7
　　effects of shear flow, **17**:189–191
　　in layered systems, **8**:186–189
　　Kosterlitz–Thouless type, **13**:126
　　of infinite order, **6**:10, **6**:98–105
　　phenomenological theory of,
　　　15:57–65
　　second-order, **6**:160
　　see also Transitions behaviour in
　　　dimer models
　　signals of, **17**:41
　　simple diluted magnets, **7**:165
　　splitting and merging, **17**:87–90
　　structural, **6**:295, **6**:394, **6**:416
Phenomenological renormalization,
　　7:203, **8**:171–181, **8**:229
Phenomenological theory of phase
　　transitions, **15**:57–65
Phenomenological theory of superfluid
　　helium-4, **5A**:56, **5A**:57
Phonon fluctuations, translational order
　　and, **7**:76
Phonon spectrum, **15**:13–14
Phonons, **1**:86
Photoemission, polarized, europium
　　oxide surfaces, **8**:56
Physical cluster, **3**:135
Physical neighbours, **2**:293
Physical phenomena *see* natural
　　phenomena
Physisorption commensurate-
　　incommensurate transitions,
　　13:289–294
　　K models, **13**:291–294
　　physical model, **13**:290–291
Physisorption, **8**:445–446
Piecewise parabolic model, **16**:89,
　　16:93, **16**:104
Pin, **3**:395

Pinned interfaces, **14**:118–19
Pinned-end interface, **14**:120
Pinning field, **10**:274
Pinning line, **14**:320
Pinning potentials, **8**:74
Pinning, **19**:389
Pions
　　renormalization group and, **6**:4
Pipes, coiled, laminar flow through
　　13:133–134
Pirogov–Sinai (PS) theory, **11**:128–131,
　　11:133–4, **11**:138, **11**:140–2,
　　11:152, **11**:161, **11**:164, **11**:166,
　　11:167–9, **11**:178, **11**:180, **11**:181,
　　11:193
Pirogov–Sinai analysis, **12**:118
Pirogov–Sinaï theory, **10**:30, **10**:59,
　　18:5, **18**:88, **18**:92–3
Pitch, inverse domain wall, periodicity,
　　see Quasi-particle pitch
Placzek correction, **5A**:101
Plait points, **9**:182
Planar magnetic insulator, **3**:577
Planar model, **3**:487, **3**:500, **3**:534
　　classical, **3**:636, **3**:637, **3**:642
　　two dimensional, **3**:635
Planar models, **10**:2, **10**:17
Planar rotor, **10**:2, **10**:7, **10**:9, **10**:39,
　　10:61
Plane rotator model, **1**:79, **1**:80, **3**:489,
　　3:636, **3**:637, **3**:641, **3**:642, **3**:648
　　classical, **3**:572
n-Point correlation, **3**:121
Plane wave ansatz, **19**:36, **19**:66–67,
　　19:183
Plane-rotator, two-dimensional,
　　divergent susceptibility, **13**:8
Plaquette models, **19**:256, **19**:258,
　　19:277
Plaquettes, **18**:109–11
　　frustrated, **18**:222–5
Plasma, **6**:279
2-Point functions, **6**:136, **6**:144, **6**:145,
　　6:152
3-Point functions, **6**:136
4-Point functions, **6**:144
4-Point proper vertex function, **6**:224
Plasticene models, **2**:283, **2**:293
Plumber's nightmare, **16**:143

Point defect system, **5B**:67
Point defect, Ising systems, **8**:34
Point defects, scaling hypothesis, **7**:187
Point pair group, **3**:28
Poisson blob model, **18**:124
Poisson bracket, **5A**:180, **5A**:247, **5A**:366, **5A**:367, **5A**:371
Poisson processes, **18**:123–5
Poisson random edge model, **18**:124–5
Poisson summation formula, **7**:142
Pokrovskii–Talapov (PT) transition, **15**:39
Pokrovsky–Talapov transition, *see* PT transition
Polar angle, **14**:98
Polarized lattice gas (PLG), **17**:135–138
Pole-zero pair, **3**:206
Poles *see* scattering amplitude
Poly amino acid, helical conformation, **7**:109
Polya relation, **3**:24
Polya theorem, **3**:16, **3**:25, **3**:26, **3**:27, **3**:29, **3**:30
Polydispersity, **12**:442–443, **12**:468
Polygon, **3**:69, **3**:92
Polygons, **14**:92–9, **14**:115
Polyhedra, **1**:320
  cyclic change, **1**:320, **1**:321
Polymer
  adsorption, **10**:188
  physics, **10**:217
  quantities, **10**:199
Polymer chain dynamics, **2**:492
Polymer chain shape, asymmetry of, **14**:95
Polymer chains, **14**:42, **14**:116
Polymer conformations, **14**:5, **14**:92–9
Polymer rings, interacting, **7**:84
Polymer sedimentation, **17**:9, **17**:179–183
Polymer solutions, **14**:42, **14**:61, **14**:82
Polymer systems, bending modulii in, **16**:98
Polymerization index, **14**:61
Polymerization, **12**:391, **12**:451, **12**:465
Polymerized membranes *see* tethered membranes
Polymers **11**:42, **11**:50

Polymers, **12**:193, **12**:339, **12**:353, **12**:386, **12**:388, **12**:392, **12**:427, **14**:364
  adsorption, **8**:5
  adsorption at surfaces, **8**:76–80
  branched configurations, **19**:431
  chains, **8**:5
  closed, self-entanglement and, **7**:145
  correlation function, **19**:315
  defects, **19**:8, **19**:9
  directed, **19**:158
  Edwards model, **19**:439–441
  entanglements, topology, **7**:147
  exact results, **19**:218, **19**:445
  exciton dynamics, **19**:13, **19**:176, **19**:222–223
  fully stretched, **19**:407
  globules, **19**:442
  in confined domains, finite size scaling, **8**:189–191
  linear, solutions, viscosity, **7**:134
  modelling, **19**:52
  nonlocal interactions, **19**:259
  nucleation in, **8**:447–449
  open and closed, **19**:412, **19**:413
  perturbation theory, **19**:372–374, **19**:413
  random flows, **19**:*390*
  renormalization, **19**:412–419
  reptation, **19**:8–10
  see also tethered membranes
  self-avoiding, **19**:256
  spinodal decomposition in, **8**:447–449
  stiff and flexible, **19**:375
  theory, **19**:305–317
  tricritical point, **19**:363
  two-dimensional network, **19**:274
  two-loop calculations, **19**:350
  variational estimates, **19**:445–449
Polynomial (P) algorithms, **18**:149–50
Polynucleotides
  double-stranded, conformations, **7**:110
  helical conformation, **7**:109
  helix-coil transitions, surface adsorption and, **7**:107
  synthetic, with branching structures, transitions in, **7**:116–121
  single-stranded, branching, **7**:117
Polyomino, **3**:99, **3**:112

Polypeptides, helix-coil transitions, surface adsorption and, **7**:107
Polytypism, **15**:38
Pores, helium in, specific heat, **8**:251–254
Porous solid, **2**:199
Porous, materials, **12**:400–401
    media, **12**:155, **12**:166, **12**:343–345, **12**:395, **12**:474
Position space methods
    dilute magnets, **7**:247–262
    for percolation, **7**:247–262
Position space renormalization methods, **7**:153
Positive correlation, **18**:25, **18**:28, **18**:47
Potassium manganese fluoride, **5A**:154, **5A**:323
Potassium nickel fluoride, **5A**:153, **5A**:154, **5A**:156, **5A**:158, **5A**:159, **5A**:161, **5A**:162
Potential (longitudinal) disorder, **19**:389, **19**:391, **19**:395, **19**:404–405
Potential lemma, **18**:173
Potential, **1**:18, **9**:172
    bounded, **1**:168
    finite range, **1**:154, **1**:168
    k-body, **1**:114
    strongly tempered, **1**:28
    two-body, **1**:114, **1**:164
    weakly tempered, **1**:31
Potts chains, pure one-dimensional properties, **7**:178
Potts
    lattice-gas, **9**:23, **9**:148, **9**:150
    model(s), **9**:21, **9**:22, **9**:143, **9**:227
    three-state, **9**:20, **9**:23, **9**:142, **9**:147, **9**:153, **9**:225
    -state, **9**:139, **9**:148, **9**:154
    symmetry, three-state, **9**:56
Potts model, **6**:351, **6**:417, **7**:27, **10**:342, **15**:42–3, **18**:18, **18**:55–9, **18**:108, **18**:109, **19**:77, **19**:214
    and parameters, **7**:176–177
    and random cluster model, **18**:47–59
    antiferromagnetic, **8**:240
    bond disordered q-state, **7**:193
    characteristic variables, **7**:192
    coherent potential approximations, **7**:219

computer simulation, **18**:67–9
constant spin clusters in, **18**:100–2
diluted, **7**:191, **7**:192
diluted q-state, on Bethe lattice, **7**:192
finite four-state specific heat, **8**:237
finite size scaling, **8**:233–241
one-dimensional, percolation fixed point, scaling, **7**:261
p-state clock, **8**:240
position space methods, **7**:248
q-state, **8**:58
quantum hamiltonian three-state, β-function, **8**:227
quenched bond diluted q-state, on square lattice limiting slopes, **7**:193
random, **18**:113–15
See also under Bond diluted Potts model; Diluted Potts models; Potts chains
solution, **7**:182
64–state, first-order transition, **8**:238
stochastic domination, **18**:30
three-state, **8**:230
    antiferromagnetic, **8**:240
    critical behaviour, **8**:244
two-dimensional, critical exponents, **7**:178
two-dimensional, transitions, **8**:238
Potts models, **11**:37–41, **11**:51, **11**:152, **11**:200, **14**:68, **14**:102, **14**:109, **14**:110, **14**:112, **14**:113, **14**:118, **14**:364, **17**:8, **17**:127, **17**:174, **17**:175
    antiferromagnets, **11**:3, **11**:50
    chiral 3 state, **12**:237, **12**:240–243, **12**:293–298
    chiral 4 state, **12**:292–298, **12**:314–315
    chiral (clock), **12**:109–110
    critical point, **11**:45, **11**:51
    four-state, **11**:77, **11**:84
    helical 3 state, **12**:233, **12**:237, **12**:244–246
    lattice gas, **12**:115, **12**:229
    model, **12**:109–116, **12**:133, **12**:181
    on the triangular lattice, **11**:45

q-state, **11**:3, **11**:36, **11**:59, **11**:70,
        11:78, **11**:108, **11**:111, **11**:121,
        11:167, **11**:201, **12**:116, **12**:145
RG flow lines, **11**:46
semi-infinite model, **12**:114, **12**:123
six-state, **12**:17
three-state, **11**:26, **11**:84–85, **11**:102,
        11:111, **11**:115
two dimensional 3 state, **12**:111,
        12:112, **12**:120
vector model (*see* Clock Models),
        11:201
Potts transition, **7**:30
Power counting, **12**:260, **12**:263,
        17:61–66, **17**:100, **17**:102, **17**:126,
        17:141, **17**:146, **17**:172
Power law approximations, **8**:331–332
Power law behaviour, asymptotic,
        6:518
Power law
        correction, **19**:133
        critical point, **6**:11
        decay, **19**:72, **19**:196
        divergence, **19**:124
        simple, **6**:512
Power law decays
        critical, **17**:45
        above criticality, **17**:26–32, **17**:97,
        17:98
Power law interactions, **14**:194
Power law singularities, **18**:116
Power laws, **5A**:8
Power series expansion, **3**:181, **3**:182,
        3:250
Power series expansions, asymptotic
        analysis, **13**:1–234, *see also*
        Differential approximants;
        Multivariables; Padé approximants;
        Ratio methods; Sequence
        extrapolation; Transformations
        basic problem, **13**:6–8
        Darboux's theorems, **13**:11–15
        in fluid mechanics, **13**:130–134
        renormalization group (RG) theory,
            early predictions, **13**:3–4
        integral approximant method, **13**:4
        programs, **13**:138–228
            ANALYSE, **13**:150–153,
            13:198–223

NEVBARB, **13**:150,
        13:154–156, **13**:224–228
NEWGRQD/TABUL, **13**:96,
        13:97, **13**:139–159,
        13:158–197
properties of power series and,
        13:8–11
singularity location and sign
        pattern, **13**:10–11
rational approximant method,
        13:75–80
singular perturbation expansions,
        13:135
Power series, **3**:2, **3**:33, **3**:184, **3**:186,
        3:187, **3**:205, **3**:271, **3**:423
Pre-wetting, **10**:104
critical point, **10**:106, **10**:163
Predecessor labels, **18**:153
Preflow, **18**:164
Preflow-push/relabel algorithm,
        18:165–6
Prepoint discretization *see* Ito (prepoint)
        discretization
Preprocess procedure, **18**:165
Pressure, **1**:33, **1**:38, **1**:42, **1**:46, **1**:47,
        1:56, **1**:57, **1**:59, **1**:90, **1**:91, **1**:94,
        1:134, **1**:138, **1**:185, **1**:186, **1**:189,
        5B:360
bulk, **1**:11
continuity, **1**:95
dependence on container shape, **1**:11
grand canonical, **1**:133
grand-canonical formula, **1**:11
in continuum systems, **1**:27
in one-component fluid, **1**:11, **1**:13
non-analytic dependence, **1**:42
Prewetting critical point, **14**:328
Prewetting line, **14**:326, **14**:328
Prewetting transition, **14**:145
Prim's algorithm, **18**:157–8, **18**:190
Primal linear programming problem,
        18:182–3
Primitive method, **3**:71, **3**:87, **3**:90
Primitive space, **2**:2, **2**:3, **2**:26, **2**:38
Principal point, **3**:11, **3**:39
of star, **3**:385, **3**:387
Principal radii of curvature, **16**:97
Principle of inclusion and exclusion,
        3:81, **3**:82

Pringsheim's theorem, **13:**10
Probabilistic approach, **19:**5, **19:**15, **19:**17
Probability distribution function, **6:**251
scaling, **7:**251
p-State clock models, **7:**10
Probability
distribution
master equation, **19:**17–18
time-dependent, **19:**90
vector, **19:**20
Probability distribution, **14:**98
Probability measures
finite energy, **18:**43
monotone, **18:**25
with positive correlations, **18:**25, **18:**28, **18:**47
weak topology of, **18:**9
Probability theory, **6:**510, **6:**515, **6:**552
Product measures, **19:**25, **19:**105, **19:**110, **19:**117, **19:**128
Product property, **3:**17, **3:**18, **3:**20, **3:**21, **3:**25, **5B:**216
Profiles, **2:**86, **2:**92
Programs, **13:**138–228
ANALYSE, **13:**150–153
listing, **13:**198–223
NEVBARB, **13:**150, **13:**154–156
listing, **13:**224–228
NEWGRQD/TABUL, **13:**96, **13:**97, **13:**139–159
NEWGRQD listing, **13:**158–171
TABUL listing, **13:**172–197
Projection operator, **5A:**173, **5A:**191, **5A:**242, **5A:**260, **5A:**345, **19:**56
Projection operators, **1:**207
Propagating modes, **5A:**78–81, **5A:**248, **5A:**251
Propagator bare, **3:**139
renormalized, **3:**139
Propagator, **5A:**228
Propagators, inverse, **6:**224
in momentum space, **6:**301
Propane, **5B:**386
Propp–Wilson algorithm, **18:**69
Protein synthesis *see* biopolymerization
Pseudo-binary model, **9:**213, **9:**214
Pseudo-Curie point, **3:**310, **3:**328
Pseudo-flow, **18:**171

Pseudo-polynomial algorithms, **18:**163
Pseudocritical temperature, **5B:**53
Pseudorandom numbers, **5B:**10, **5B:**11
PT transition, **12:**226, **12:**247, **12:**252, **12:**253–258, **12:**268, **12:**274–276, **12:**283–285, **12:**287, **12:**294, **12:**295, **12:**300, **12:**301, **12:**303, **12:**327, **12:**331–332
Pure annihilation process, **19:**206
Pure fixed point, **7:**245
Pure fusion process, **19:**213
Pure Ising critical parameter, **7:**253
Pure Ising fixed point, **7:**253
Pure Ising magnets, decimation procedure, **7:**251
Pure magnets
critical exponents, **7:**176–177
critical parameters, **7:**176–177
exact properties, **7:**174
one-dimensional, **7:**192
Pure self-avoidance, fixed point, **19:**451
Pure thermodynamic phase, **1:**150, **1:**151, **1:**152, **1:**167, **1:**170, **1:**171, **1:**172, **1:**173
Push-relabel algorithms, **18:**163–6
PY *see* Percus-Yevick equation
φ4-theory
correlation function, **19:**316
independent scaling exponent, **19:**360, **19:**363
Landau–Ginzburg–Wilson, **19:**440
limit behaviour, **19:**427
N-component, **19:**316, **19:**317
perturbation expansion, **19:**256
in renormalization, **19:**417
renormalized Hamiltonian, **19:**286
scalar, **19:**264
variational approximation, **19:**354

Q

q-state Potts models, **14:**41
Quadratic contact, **2:**10
pseudo, **2:**12
Quadruple point, **9:**19, **9:**22
Quadrupole field, **6:**258, **6:**272
Quantized Hall effect, **12:**262
Quantum algebra, **19:**51, **19:**106n, **19:**120, **19:**158

Quantum chain *see* Heisenberg
    quantum chain; quantum spin
    representation
Quantum classical crossover, **7:**261
Quantum continuum systems, **1:**30,
    1:114, **1:**115, **1:**123
Quantum effects and fluctuations,
    15:27
Quantum effects, **6:**526
Quantum electrodynamics, **6:**508,
    6:528
Quantum field theories (QFT), **11:**56,
    11:166
Quantum field theory, **3:**3, **3:**375, **6:**143,
    6:289, **6:**301, **6:**523, **8:**250, **10:**81,
    19:257, **19:**408
    estimates of physical quantities in,
        6:3
Quantum fluid, **3:**118, **3:**119, **3:**572
Quantum Hamiltonian
    construction, **19:**13–14, **19:**26–27
    DLPA, **19:**49
    first-passage time distribution, **19:**83
    formalism, **19:**21–22, **19:**80–81
    Heisenberg ferromagnet, **19:**10
    integrable, **19:**50
    interacting particle systems,
        19:41–50
    master equation, **19:**17–29
    mathematical properties, **19:**33–35
    in modelling, **19:**5
    nonstochastic, **19:**28
    particle and spin systems, **19:**30
Quantum hamiltonians finite size scaling,
    8:247–250
    limits, transfer matrices, **8:**178–181
    0(2)-symmetric, **8:**248
Quantum Ising chain, tricritical, **11:**71
Quantum lattice fluid model, **3:**570,
    3:578
Quantum lattice fluid, **3:**574, **3:**576
Quantum lattice gas, **1:**19, **1:**51
Quantum lattice systems, **1:**57, **1:**70,
    1:113, **1:**115
Quantum mechanical effect, **3:**500
Quantum mechanical self energy
    operator, **3:**138
Quantum mechanics
    phase transitions, **6:**14

Quantum models, solution, **7:**191
Quantum numbers, **19:**31, **19:**39, **19:**40,
    19:41, **19:**112–113
Quantum statistics, **1:**128, **1:**129, **1:**131,
    1:132, **1:**133, **1:**134, **1:**135, **3:**45
Quantum spin lattices, **1:**142
    one-dimensional, **1:**153
Quantum spin representation, **19:**6,
    19:14, **19:**30, **19:**45, **19:**51, **19:**72,
    19:90, **19:**97
Quantum spin system, **1:**54
Quantum states,
    macroscopic, **1:**4
Quantum-field theoretical method,
    5A:331–335
Quantun critical phenomena, **14:**364
Quartic interaction, **6:**523
Quartic spin interactions, **6:**394
Quartic symmetry, **6:**359
Quartic term, **6:**299
Quartz, **3:**647
Quasi-binary approximation, **9:**184
Quasi-chemical approximation, **2:**93,
    2:339
Quasi-elastic light scattering, **16:**155
Quasi-field treatment, **1:**234
Quasi-local algebra, **1:**146, **1:**165
Quasi-local observables, **1:**139
Quasi-long-range order, **7:**4
    melting and, **7:**80
Quasi-one-dimensional systems,
    19:125
Quasi-ordered phase, **3:**543
Quasi-particle energy spectrum,
    5B:280
Quasi-particle energy, **5B:**278, **5B:**281
Quasi-particle pitch, **12:**267–271
Quasi-stationarity, **19:**79, **19:**99–101
Quasi-two-dimensional system, **3:**502,
    3:510
Quasilocality, **18:**11
Quasiperiodic potential, **14:**158–9,
    14:177–9
Quaternary
    fluid mixtures – non symmetric, **9:**38
    liquid fluid mixtures, **9:**26, **9:**31, **9:**45,
        9:56
    mixture, **9:**13
    tricritical points, **9:**193, **9:**199

Quenched binary alloys, **5B**:5
Quenched bond diluted Ising models
  critical curves, **7**:228
  fixed points, position space methods,
    7:247
Quenched bond diluted magnets,
  percolation and, **7**:158
Quenched bond disorder systems, phase
  boundaries, **7**:202
Quenched dilute magnets aggregation in,
  7:156–162
  critical temperature, **7**:158
  cross over effects, **7**:163–169
  percolation in, **7**:156–162, **7**:163–169
  thermal effects, **7**:163–169
Quenched diluted Heisenberg models
  limiting concentrations, **7**:159
  transition temperatures, **7**:159
Quenched diluted Ising models, limiting
  concentrations, **7**:159
Quenched diluted XY models limiting
  concentrations, **7**:159
  transition temperatures, **7**:159
Quenched dilution, **7**:154–156
Quenched disorder, **7**:152, **14**:137
Quenched impurities, effects,
  17:144–148, **17**:175
Quenched magnetization, **18**:114–15
Quenched models
  exact results, **7**:179–198
  low impurity concentrations,
    solutions, **7**:175
  one-dimensional, solutions, **7**:175
Quenched problem, **3**:473
Quenched random system, **6**:406
Quenched random systems, **11**:98
Quenched random-bond spin models,
  coherent potential approximations,
  7:219
Quenched site diluted Ising
  ferromagnets, phase diagram,
  7:159
Quenched site diluted Ising model, in
  transverse field, high temperature
  series expansion methods, **7**:231
Quenched site diluted magnet,
  percolation and, **7**:158
Quenched site diluted transverse Ising
  model, phase boundaries, **7**:232

Quenched site disorder, **7**:154
Quenching, **5B**:92, **5B**:93
  relaxation of fluctuations and,
    8:436–439
Quintuple critical point, **9**:228

R

R-operation (subtraction operator),
  19:298, **19**:318, **19**:319, **19**:322,
  19:323, **19**:328, **19**:329, **19**:336,
  19:337
Radial distribution function, **5B**:119
Radioactive labelling, **19**:44–45
Radius of convergence, **3**:185, **3**:186,
  3:205
Radius of gyration exponent, **12**:381
Radius of gyration, **19**:391, **19**:457
Radius-of-gyration tensor, **14**:43
Radius-of-gyration, **14**:95, **14**:97
Raman absorption, moment calculations,
  7:222
Ramond algebra, **11**:118
Random anisotrophy, **7**:171, **7**:270
Random axis anisotropy, **7**:173
Random bond Heisenberg model,
  scaling, **7**:259
Random bond Ising chains,
  magnetization, Monte Carlo
  methods, **7**:203
Random bond system, cluster methods,
  7:213
Random bonds, **14**:257–9, **14**:261–2,
  14:267–75, **14**:277–91
Random close packings, **2**:273, **2**:286,
  2:288, **2**:289, **2**:300
Random coil configuration,
  macromolecules, **7**:103
Random diluted Heisenberg
  antiferromagnets, phase diagram,
  virtual crystal approximation, **7**:212
Random external field, **15**:93–5
  large-n limit of disordered n-vector
  model, **15**:116–21
Random ferromagnet, **5B**:43, **5B**:325
Random field Ising model,
  renormalization group treatments,
  7:247
Random field, **5B**:185, **5B**:187

Random fields, **7**:173, **7**:270, **14**:89,
  14:257, **14**:261–2, **14**:274–5, **18**:9
  critical properties and, **7**:247
  effects, **7**:171
      dilute antiferromagnets and,
      7:152
  perturbations, **7**:173
  renormalization group treatments,
      7:247
Random finite-difference operators,
  15:201–17
Random finite-range interaction,
  15:95–104
Random fixed points in dilute magnets,
  7:241
Random force field, correlation,
  19:390–391
Random force, **5A**:217, **5A**:220,
  5A:301, **5A**:322
  elimination, **5A**:217
Random function, **5B**:186
Random impurities, **2**:162
Random Ising magnets, **18**:113–16,
  18:196–234
  see also diluted anti-ferromagnets in a
      field (DAFF); Ising model
Random Ising model, critical behaviour,
  7:243
Random Ising system, Ch, **2**:5, **2**:161
Random lattice, **2**:163, **2**:164, **2**:168,
  2:171, **2**:175, **2**:194
Random loose packing, **2**:286
Random *m*-vector model, **6**:408
Random magnetic field, Ising model,
  9:25
Random matrices, **15**:168
Random media, **14**:366
Random mixed magnets, critical
  conditions, **7**:199
Random *n*-dimensional matrices, **15**:197
Random packings, **2**:273
Random phase approximation, **5B**:263,
  5B:266–292 *passim*, **5B**:299,
  5B:300, **5B**:301, **5B**:312, **5B**:317,
  5B:320, **5B**:323, **5B**:329, **5B**:330,
  5B:334
  decoupling, **5B**:277, **5B**:278, **5B**:286,
      5B:322, **5B**:324, **5B**:326
  Green's function equation, **5B**:279

theory, **5B**:283
Random potential, **14**:159
Random quantum *n*-vector models, exact
  results, **7**:194
Random rank-one projections,
  15:197–201
Random resistor network, **5B**:339
Random rods, **14**:259, **14**:260,
  14:302–3
Random sequential absorption,
  19:49–50, **19**:101, **19**:167
Random sequential updating, **19**:28
Random short-range interaction,
  15:105–7
Random standing wave, **16**:162
Random stress field, quenched, **19**:279
Random
  surface models, **10**:40
  walk, **10**:54, **10**:56
Random surfaces, and gauge theories,
  19:257
Random systems, **1**:96, **1**:97
  Anderson localization, **8**:250
Random uniaxial model, large-*n* limit of
  disordered *n*-vector model,
  15:121–8
Random variables, **6**:267, **6**:552
  in description of nonequilibrium
      systems, **19**:4
Random walk
  annihilating, **19**:175, **19**:199–200
  biased, **19**:113, **19**:122–123, **19**:146,
      19:148–149
  double-stranded DNA, **7**:112
  domain wall, **19**:122–123, **19**:135,
      19:143, **19**:148
  Edwards model, **19**:436
  free, **7**:116, **19**:436
  Gaussian distribution, **19**:64–65
  in disordered media, **19**:28
  lattice, **19**:23, **19**:82
  nearest neighbour moves, **19**:*18*
  polymers, **7**:109
  shock, **19**:173
  self-avoiding, **7**:116
  single loop, **19**:411
  two-class particles, **19**:122
  unbiased, **19**:153, **19**:172
Random walk enumeration, **3**:375

Random walk, **3**:3, **12**:343, **12**:350,
  12:363–364, **12**:368, **12**:374,
  12:375, **12**:378, **12**:385–386,
  12:406–408, **12**:419, **12**:423–429,
  12:436, **12**:439–440, **12**:460–461,
  12:463, **12**:475–476, **14**:43
Random walks, **2**:203, **2**:379, **2**:385–6,
  2:403, **2**:423, **2**:427–8
  self-avoiding, **2**:203, **2**:204, **2**:222,
    2:230–1, **2**:426, **2**:434
Random-bond Ising model, **14**:257
Random-bond magnets
  interfaces in, **18**:197–207
  see also random-surface model
Random-cluster model, **18**:47–55,
  18:59–65, **18**:70–2, **18**:78–84,
  18:100–2, **18**:104, **18**:113–14,
  18:119, **18**:126
Random-connection model, **18**:124–5
Random-exchange systems, **14**:88–9
Random-field Ising magnets (RFIM),
  18:196–7, **18**:207–21, **18**:207–27
  see also Ising model
Random-field Ising model, **14**:257
Random-field models, **14**:64, **14**:259
Random-phase sine-Gordon model,
  18:239–41, **18**:252–3
Random-rod model, **14**:159, **14**:179,
  14:258, **14**:262–7, **14**:302
Random-surface model, **18**:241,
  18:252–5, **18**:261–4
Random-surface problem, **18**:255–6
Randomly driven systems, **17**:94–107
Randomness
  ASEP, **19**:160
  critical behaviour and, **7**:169–173
  nonequilibrium systems, **19**:4
  traffic flow models, **19**:154
Range, interaction, **6**:357–421
Rank
  of code, **3**:409
Rare earth elements, **3**:503
Rate equation, **19**:4, **19**:5, **19**:172,
  19:196
Ratio analysis, **3**:218, **3**:466
Ratio estimate, **3**:211, **3**:213
Ratio method, **3**:187, **3**:197, **3**:202,
  3:206, **3**:213, **3**:214, **3**:230, **3**:232,
  3:240, **3**:302, **3**:304, **3**:305, **3**:308,

  3:319, **3**:359, **3**:526, **3**:616, **3**:617,
  3:618, **3**:623, **3**:624, **3**:655
Ratio methods, **13**:16–35, *see also*
  Darboux's theorems
  confluent logarithmic singularities,
    13:29–32
  confluent singularity case, **13**:20–21
  description, **13**:16–17
  error analysis, **13**:34
  Hunter and Guerrieri method,
    13:22–23
  Kosterlitz–Thouless-type singularities,
    13:26–29
  Neville–Aitken extrapolation,
    13:21–22
  ratio-type methods compared,
    13:32–34
  variants, **13**:17–20
  Zinn–Justin method, **13**:23–25
Ratio plot, **3**:436, **3**:557, **3**:559, **3**:620,
  3:623
Ratio tests, **3**:309, **3**:310
Rational-approximant method, **13**:75–80
Raw edges, **1**:253
Rayleigh–Bénard experiment, equivalent
  for lattice gas, **17**:108
Rayleigh–Benard problem, **7**:74–75
Rayleigh–Ritz calculation, **5B**:148
Rayleigh–Ritz technique, **2**:370
Rb_2ZnCl_4, incommensurate phase, **15**:29
$RbCaF_3$, **15**:64
$RbMnF_3$ **2**:195
RDM, **1**:91, **1**:124, **1**:128, **1**:129, **1**:130,
  1:131, **1**:132, **1**:133, **1**:134, **1**:135
Reaction kernel, **12**:437–443, **12**:458,
  12:464–467, **12**:470
Reaction rate, **19**:196
Reaction–diffusion rates, alternating *see*
  spin flip rates
Reaction–diffusion systems
  critical phenomena, **19**:70–71
  enantiodromy, **19**:162–164
  exact results, **19**:5
  experimental realizations, **19**:215–223
  Glauber dynamics, **19**:188
  integrability, **19**:50–51
  lattice gas modelling, **19**:13
  mean field approximation, **19**:4
  modelling, **19**:3

with nearest neighbour interaction,
19:162–174
quantum spin representation, 19:72
rate equations, 19:4, 19:172
single-species, 19:45–47, 19:162–174
statistical approach, 19:3
Real fluid, 5A:10
Real-space renormalization, 14:328
Real-space RG method, 14:46
Realisation, 3:99, 3:104, 3:108
Rectangular cube, 5B:56
Rectilinear diameter, 2:17, 2:18, 5B:383,
6:93
Recurrence relation method, 3:187
Recurrence relations, 3:420
Recurrence-relation method, 13:83–84
Recurrent events, 10:55
Recursion equation, 6:109
for correlation functions, 6:107
Recursion relation approach,
6:359–376
Recursion relations (Coulomb gas),
11:10
Recursion relations, 6:364, 6:368, 6:379,
6:385, 6:386, 6:387, 6:390, 14:35,
14:37, 15:49, 19:127, 19:128,
19:129, 19:137, 19:160
approximate, 6:522
bound vortices and, 7:25
exact, 6:358
for g, 6:370
for r, 6:370
for rescaling factor $b > 1$, 14:200–2
linearized, 6:388
in infinitesimal rescaling limit, 14:202
Red blood cells, 19:256, 19:273,
19:274
Reduced cost optimality theorem,
18:173
Reduced costs, 18:153, 18:172
Reduced density matrices see RDM
Reduced energy, 3:379, 3:453
Reduced enthalpy, 3:523
Reduced magnetization at critical field,
5B:69
Reduced mean trace, 3:328
Reduced models, 11:193
Reduced trace, 3:260, 3:279, 3:289
Redundant operator, 12:292–293

Redundant operators, 19:307–308,
19:464
Redundant variables, 6:272
Reference critical dimension, 12:276,
12:281, 12:317, 12:332
References listed, 17:198–213
Reflecting boundaries, 19:66, 19:67,
19:104, 19:*105*, 19:111
Reflecting principle, 19:66, 19:101
Reflectivity, 2:95
Reggeon field theory, 17:172, 17:173,
17:185
Regular close packing, 2:300
Regular lattice, 3:104, 3:105, 3:462
n-cluster counting, 3:105
Regular solution, 9:212
Regular trees, 18:6, 18:66–7
Related non-equilibrium steady-state
systems, 17:170–191
Relaxation behaviour, 5B:6
Relaxation
boundary effects, 19:98
DNA, 19:217–219
exponential, 19:99
late time, 19:110
order parameter, 19:99
rate, biased, 19:171
times, 19:142, 19:170–171, 19:218
finite systems, 19:62–63,
19:65–66
free fermion systems,
19:191–193
infinite systems, 19:65–66
polymers, 19:218
and system size, 19:63
Relaxation function, 5B:15, 5B:26,
5B:78
non-equilibrium, 5B:15, 5B:81,
5B:85, 5B:86, 5B:88
Relaxation kinetics, 2:492
Relaxation linear, finite size scaling,
8:200
non-linear, 8:200, 8:432–436
of fluctuations, quenching and,
8:436–439
Relaxation process, 5B:96
non-equilibrium, 5B:91
Relaxation processes, 2:478
Relaxation rate, 14:14, 14:19

Relaxation time, **2**:483–5, **2**:487, **5B**:4,
 5B:15, **5B**:16, **5B**:74, **5B**:80,
 5B:81, **5B**:359, **5B**:360, **5B**:364
 equilibrium, **5B**:84
 non-equilibrium, **5B**:16
 order parameter, **5B**:16
 scaled, **5B**:87
 thermal, **5B**:363
Relaxation, **5B**:5, **5B**:11, **5B**:27
 non-equilibrium, **5B**:82
Relaxational modes, **5B**:25
Relay station problem, **2**:200
Relevant direction, **6**:542
Relevant eigenvalues, **9**:140
Relevant field, **5A**:18, **5A**:24, **5A**:25,
 6:435, **6**:520, **14**:35
Relevant variables, **6**:533, **6**:535
Reliability function, **2**:202
Renormalizability
 theorem, **19**:322
 see also renormalization, criteria
Renormalizable theories, **10**:132, **10**:134
 multiplicatively, **10**:253
 super-renormalizable, **10**:132
Renormalizalion group (RG) theory,
 early predictions, **13**:3–4
Renormalization
 criteria, **19**:333–334, **19**:381, **19**:387
 disorder, **19**:397–399
 dynamic, **19**:381–385
 factors *see* Z factors
 generalization to *N* colours,
 19:420–421
 group
 analysis, **19**:377–378
 approach, **19**:13, **19**:70–71,
 19:72, **19**:104, **19**:256
 β function, **19**:446, **19**:464
 calculations, **19**:206
 critical phenomena, **19**:5
 equations, **19**:392–393,
 19:456–457
 factors, **19**:298
 flow, **19**:402, **19**:403, **19**:*404*,
 19:431–432, **19**:434
 functions, **19**:290, **19**:302,
 19:342–343, **19**:347, **19**:358,
 19:424, **19**:439
 polymers, **19**:412–419

O (*N*) model, **19**:414–418
 one-group order, **19**:298–303
 perturbative, **19**:318–340
 self-avoidance, **19**:356
 strategy, **19**:297–298
Renormalization factor, **3**:537
Renormalization group (Coulomb gas),
 11:6, **11**:56, **11**:57, **11**:60
 in real space, **11**:183
 trajectories, **11**:15
Renormalization group (RG), **14**:4, **14**:5,
 14:10, **14**:28, **14**:32, **14**:32–41,
 14:45–6, **14**:71
 additive, **10**:214–5
 approach, **10**:76, **10**:79, **10**:117–121,
 10:270
 amplitude, **10**:122
 dynamical, **10**:307, **10**:343
 equations, **10**:150, **10**:152, **10**:198,
 10:204, **10**:214, **10**:228
 field theories, **10**:81
 flow, **14**:35, **14**:36
 formalism, **14**:35
 formulation, **14**:73
 inhomogeneous, **10**:216
 iterations, **14**:33
 marginal perturbation, **14**:48
 multiplicative, **10**:129, **10**:202,
 10:207
 recursion relations, **14**:120
 semi-infinite *n*-vector model, **10**:150
 techniques, **14**:45–6
 theory, **14**:19, **14**:35, **14**:45, **14**:46,
 14:91
 trajectories, **10**:156
 trajectory, **14**:37
 transformations, **14**:33, **14**:34, **14**:39,
 14:161–2
 values, **14**:77
 with broken symmetry, **10**:203
Renormalization group analysis, **15**:62,
 15:63, **17**:6, **17**:21, **17**:52
 Gaussian dynamic models, **17**:33–37
 randomly driven and multi-
 temperature models, **17**:99–103
 standard model, **17**:59–73
 one-loop results, **17**:67–73
 systems with quenched random
 impurities, **17**:144–146

Renormalization group equation, **6:**173
    fixed point, linearized, **6:**29–34
    non-linear in *H*, **6:**27
    with smooth momentum cut-off, **6:**9,
        6:22–27
Renormalization group method, **8:**6,
        8:19, **8:**48, **8:**49, **8:**60, **8:**69, **8:**75,
        8:118–134
    differential, **8:**59
    finite size scaling, **8:**162–170
    first-order transitions, **8:**196
    free-energy functional, **8:**298–300
    position, **8:**128–134
    real space, **8:**163
Renormalization group methods, **7:**153,
        7:239–242
    ε-expansion, **7:**173
    for dilute magnets, **7:**232–262
Renormalization group recursion
        relations, **7:**48
Renormalization group technique,
        5B:76
Renormalization group theory, **5A:**344,
        6:3
    linear, **6:**66
    non-linear, **6:**66
Renormalization group transformation,
        6:18, **6:**426, **6:**430, **6:**514, **6:**516
    with sharp momentum cut-off, **6:**27
Renormalization group, **3:**2, **3:**468,
        3:473, **3:**477, **5B:**70, **5B:**257,
        6:250, **6:**258–267, **9:**4, **9:**10, **9:**17,
        9:25, **9:**41, **9:**43, **9:**64, **9:**92, **9:**95,
        9:105, **9:**180, **9:**234, **9:**267, **9:**285,
        9:291
    critical exponent, **6:**11–14
    critical phenomena, **9:**288–95
    discrete and continuous models and,
        6:14–17
    fixed points in, **6:**3
    group – position space, **9:**299
    homogeneous, **6:**510
    introduction, **6:**1–5
    order parameter, **6:**11–14
    other transformations, **6:**27–29
    real-space, **9:**20, **9:**23, **9:**55, **9:**154,
        9:304
    relinearized theory, **6:**29–65
    scale invariants and, **6:**17, **6:**18

    theory of
        tricritical points, **9:**113–52
Renormalization method, **5A:**27, **5A:**227
Renormalization
    of critical exponents, **5B:**345, **5B:**371,
        5B:372, **5B:**380
    of long-wavelength spin wave, **5B:**319
    of quasi-particle energies, **5B:**277,
        5B:278
    of spin-wave energy spectrum, **5B:**286
Renormalization of interface potentials,
        14:169–72
Renormalization, **3:**117, **3:**119, **3:**136,
        3:148, **3:**157, **3:**161, **3:**162, **3:**163,
        3:164, **3:**168, **3:**169, **3:**174, **3:**175,
        3:178, **5A:**168, **5A:**227, **5A:**228,
        5A:229, **5A:**258, **5A:**259, **5A:**260,
        5A:261, **5A:**262, **5A:**340, **6:**529
    bond, **3:**152, **3:**157
    critical exponenets, in annealed
        magnets, **7:**162–163
    exponent, **12:**136
    group, **12:**33, **12:**37, **12:**43, **12:**73,
        12:171
    interaction, **3:**157
    one-point, **3:**118
    two-point, **3:**152
    propagator, **5A:**228
    transform, **12:**362, **12:**474
    vertex, **5A:**229
Renormalized exponent, **5B:**372
Renormalized vertex function, **5B:**207
Renormalized coupling constant, **14:**42,
        14:44–5, **14:**55, **14:**60, **14:**100
Renormalized dimensionless coupling
        constant, **6:**531
Renormalized interaction parameters,
        6:432
Renormalized masses, **6:**331
Renormalized theory, boundary
        conditions, **10:**200
Renormalized vertex functions, **6:**317
Renormalized vertex, **5A:**229, **5A:**230
Renormalizing theory for Ising-like spin
        systems, **6:**425–505
Renormalizability of the semi-infinite
        theory, **10:**149
Reparametrization invariance, **19:**458
Replica approach, **14:**279–87, **14:**290–1

Reptation models, **17:**127, **17:**134, **17:**165–167, **17:**180–182
Reptation, **19:**8–10, **19:**43, **19:**217–219
Reptons, **19:**9, **19:**215, **19:**216, **19:**217, **19:**218
Repulsive interactions
mapping by gauge transformation, **17:**8, **17:**139
standard model with, **17:**18–19, **17:**138–144
Reservoir coupled systems, **19:**88–89, **19:**100, **19:**103, **19:**125–126, **19:**148, **19:**153–154
see also particle reservoir
Reshetikin relation, **19:**52
Residual correlation function, **3:**453
Residual costs, **18:**168
Residual polynomial, **3:**430
Residue extraction, **19:**310–313, **19:**399–402, **19:**425, **19:**449–450
Restricted geometries, **11:**68
Resistivity, nickel films, **8:**256
Resistor network, coherent potential approximation, **7:**220
Resolution ellipsoid, **5A:**104
Resonating valence bond (RVB) state, **15:**54
Response
fields, **19:**378–379, **19:**388
function, **19:**379–380, **19:**383, **19:**394
Response function, **3:**631, **5A:**92, **5A:**94, **10:**346–8, **10:**352, **10:**354, **14:**20, **14:**21
dynamic, **5A:**92
static, **5A:**92
Response functions, **17:**56
coherent potential approximation, **7:**217
Restricted equilibrium ensemble, **5B:**134
Restricted equilibrium state, **5B:**134
Restricted solid-on-solid model for combined effect of wetting and depinning, **14:**238–40
for depinning, **14:**237–8
for wetting, **14:**236–7
with $1/z$ interaction, **14:**245–6
Resummation procedures, **19:**256, **19:**349, **19:**446–447

Resummation, **3:**136
Retrograde condensation, **5B:**180
Reverse Coleman–Weinberg mechanism, **19:**260, **19:**430, **19:**431, **19:**432
Reversibility (time-reversal symmetry), **19:**58–59
RHEED, **12:**140
Rheology, **12:**337, **12:**391, **12:**393–394
Riemann curvature tensor, **16:**133
Riemann's zeta function, **7:**113
Rigidity percolation, **18:**279–89
Rigidity theory, **18:**264–95
Ring graph, **3:**151, **5B:**187, **5B:**228, **5B:**237
Ring topology, **3:**151
RKKY interaction, **12:**137
Romberg algorithm, extrapolation method using, **13:**33
Roomany–Wyld approximants, **8:**175–176
β-function, **8:**194
Root points, **5B:**174
Rooted union and subtraction, **19:**325
Roskies' quadratic transformation, **13:**72–73
Rotation group, **1:**229, **1:**252
Rotational symmetry, breaking, **19:**431
Rotor models, **10:**35, **10:**36, **10:**37, **10:**38
Rough interfaces, **14:**119, **14:**180–1
Roughening models, **11:**27
transition, **11:**28
Roughening
phase transition, **10:**5, **10:**31, **10:**32, **10:**40, **10:**46, **10:**53, **10:**59
temperature, **10:**295, **10:**336
Roughening transition, **5B:**102, **14:**139, **14:**174–7, **14:**221–8, **17:**81
effects of driving, **17:**179
Roughening transitions, **8:**65, **8:**70, **8:**72, **8:**73, **8:**74
Roughening with short-range forces, **14:**221–4
Roughening, temperature, **12:**14, **12:**112, **12:**126, **12:**135, **12:**141
transition, **12:**15, **12:**103, **12:**138, **12:**140, **12:**164, **12:**262, **12:**330
Roughness amplitude, **14:**271, **14:**289

Roughness exponent, **14:**154, **14:**155, **14:**165, **14:**187, **18:**200, **19:**271, **19:**272–273, **19:**403
Roughness, **14:**150
Rounding effect, **5B:**4, **5B:**41, **5B:**45, **5B:**50, **5B:**53, **5B:**55, **5B:**61
Rounding temperature, **8:**154, **8:**159
Rounding, **2:**157
Rouse model, **19:**259, **19:**377, **19:**385, **19:**386, **19:**387, **19:**388
RPA *see* Random phase approximation
RSM, **1:**9, **1:**18, **1:**28, **1:**33, **1:**41, **1:**50, **1:**78, **1:**85
Rubenstein–Duke model, **19:**215, **19:**216, **19:**220
Rubidium cobalt fluoride, **5A:**161, **5A:**162
Rubidium iron fluoride, **5A:**154
Rubidium manganese fluoride, **5A:**114, **5A:**120, **5A:**121, **5A:**122, **5A:**123, **5A:**124, **5A:**131, **5A:**132, **5A:**135, **5A:**154, **5A:**279, **5A:**314, **5A:**315, **5A:**316, **5A:**323
  critical scattering, **5A:**123–129
Rubinstein–Duke model *see* Reptation models
Ruelle Statistical Mechanics, *see* RSM

S

S (Sinai, 1982), **11:**131
Saddle point approximation, **14:**39
Saddle point equation, critical droplet solution, **8:**303–307
Saddle point methods, **19:**436, **19:**437, **19:**438
Saddle splay modulus, **16:**21, **16:**97–102, **16:**107, **16:***108*, **16:**134
Saddle-point equation, **2:**382, **2:**386, **2:**403, **2:**407
Saddle-point, **6:**166, **6:**364
Saffman–Taylor instability, **17:**89
Sandpile models, **17:**184–186
Sandwiching inequality, **18:**27–8, **18:**61
Saturated interface, **16:**130
Saturated matching, **1:**234
Saturated system, **16:**131

Saturation magnetization, **3:**247, **3:**315, **3:**316
SAW approximation, **3:**473, **3:**475
SAW polygonal closure, **3:**471
Scalar curvature, **16:**133
Scalar Laplacian (Laplace–Beltrami operator), **16:**133
Scalar spin system, **14:**44
Scale dimension, **6:**258
Scale factors, **14:**29
Scale invariance *see* Generic scale invariance
Scale invariance, **6:**228
  correlation functions, **6:**9
  renormalization group, **6:**17, **6:**18
Scale-invariant massless theory, **6:**220
Scaled field, **2:**414, **2:**417
Scaled particle model, **5B:**189
Scaling algorithm, **18:**166
Scaling ansatz, **14:**5, **14:**8
Scaling
  and self-similarity, **19:**3
  arguments, **19:**377–378
  autocorrelation function, **19:**385
  basic predictions and, **8:**158–162
  Baxter model, **11:**70
  behaviour, **19:**101, **19:**403, **19:**456
  corrections, **8:**170–171
  crossover, **8:**43–44, **8:**61
  densities, **11:**61
  dimensions, **11:**62, **11:**68, **11:**77–78, **11:**86, **11:**88, **11:**93–94, **11:**96–97, **11:**103–4, **11:**106–7, **11:**110, **11:**117, **11:**121
  exponents, **19:**65, **19:**357, **19:**360, **19:**439, **19:**446, **19:**457, **19:**464
    see also ε-expansion
  fields, **11:**19, **11:**57, **11:**60
  finite-size, **11:**115
  for systems with conserved order parameter, **8:**368–372
  for systems with nonconserved order parameter, **8:**372–373
  function, **19:**210, **19:**347–348, **19:**367, **19:**417
  functions, **11:**82, **11:**85
  invariance, **19:**72
  limit, **19:**446
  Monte Carlo studies, **8:**385–389

operators, **11**:73
radius of gyration, **19**:391
relation, **11**:115, **19**:428
structure function, **8**:419
theory, Widom, **19**:230
time dependent correlation function,
   19:142–143
universality and, **8**:66–69
variables, **19**:87
Scaling assumption, **14**:22, **14**:24, **14**:30
Scaling behavior, **16**:113, **16**:145,
   16:158, **16**:160, **16**:*161*
Scaling combination, **14**:34
Scaling corrections, **14**:7, **14**:37–8,
   14:44, **14**:50, **14**:52
Scaling equation of state, **3**:444, **3**:452
Scaling exponent, **3**:642
Scaling factor, **14**:24
Scaling fields, **8**:165, **14**:10, **14**:11,
   14:28, **14**:33, **14**:34, **14**:37
   irrelevant, in finite size scaling, **8**:170
Scaling for dilute magnets, **7**:232–262
Scaling form, **3**:441, **14**:8, **14**:10, **14**:21,
   14:27–9, **14**:31, **14**:38
   of equation of state, **3**:444
Scaling formulation, **14**:5, **14**:6, **14**:8,
   14:29
Scaling function, **3**:501, **3**:503, **3**:505,
   5B:5, **14**:4–7, **14**:12, **14**:13, **14**:24,
   14:25, **14**:27–31, **14**:35, **14**:37,
   14:44, **14**:45, **14**:73–5, **14**:81,
   14:82, **14**:85, **14**:89, **14**:102,
   14:104, **14**:105, **14**:120
   finite size, **5B**:61
   of f.c.c. lattice, **5B**:50
Scaling functions, **2**:434, **8**:38, **8**:44,
   8:45, **8**:60, **8**:242
   Monte Carlo methods, **7**:206
   universality, **8**:169
Scaling hypothesis, **2**:76, **2**:434, **3**:115,
   3:444, **3**:486, **3**:504, **3**:505, **3**:536,
   3:538, **3**:541, **5B**:62, **17**:52
   generalized, **3**:511
Scaling identity, **3**:626
Scaling law equation, **3**:322
Scaling law, **2**:40, **2**:46, **2**:130, **2**:139,
   2:218, **2**:415, **2**:433, **3**:323, **3**:326,
   3:444, **3**:451, **3**:470, **3**:542, **5B**:41,
   14:8, **14**:30, **14**:72

Scaling laws, **1**:166, **8**:49, **8**:63, **8**:67
   critical exponents and, **8**:34–76
   surface critical exponents and,
     8:118–123
   with strong anisotropy, **17**:53–59,
     17:192
Scaling method, **13**:33–34
Scaling properties of interfaces,
   14:150–220
Scaling relation, **2**:67, **2**:82, **2**:86, **2**:98,
   2:436, **3**:447, **3**:474, **3**:647, **5B**:47,
   5B:367
Scaling relations, **8**:34, **8**:38, **8**:39, **8**:43,
   8:44, **8**:50, **8**:53, **8**:62, **8**:63, **8**:64,
   8:74, **8**:75, **14**:9, **14**:14, **14**:17,
   14:25, **14**:51
   bulk and surface exponents, **8**:48
   correlation functions, **8**:63
   critical exponents at surfaces, **8**:47–50
   critical exponents in annealed magnets
     and, **7**:163
   crossover, **8**:23
   ordinary transition, **8**:41
   tricritical transitions, **8**:41
Scaling theories, **8**:60
   for structure functions, **8**:366–373
   phenomenological, **8**:342
     fluid mixtures, **8**:370
     binary alloys, **8**:370
Scaling theory, **3**:572, **3**:599, **3**:600,
   3:616, **3**:624, **3**:625, **3**:627, **3**:644,
   3:648, **5B**:60, **5B**:345, **5B**:369,
   5B:380, **5B**:382, **5B**:384, **5B**:387,
   5B:389, **14**:5, **14**:8, **14**:17,
   14:21–31
   dynamic, **3**:633
   finite size, **5B**:100, **13**:274
   lattice-lattice, **3**:625, **3**:627, **3**:649
   of finite size effects, **5B**:54
Scaling variable, **2**:410
Scaling variables, **14**:34
Scaling, **2**:24, **2**:26, **2**:30, **2**:31, **2**:33,
   2:35, **2**:38, **2**:54, **2**:56, **2**:60, **2**:76,
   3:472, **3**:626, **3**:642, **5A**:20–28,
   5A:168, **6**:511–514, **6**:516, **6**:518,
   6:528, **6**:533, **9**:4, **9**:8, **9**:31, **9**:69,
   14:4, **14**:6–9, **14**:45
   and homogeneity conjecture, **2**:80
   and parametrization, **2**:69

assumption, double power, **9**:36,
  9:37
asymptotic, **2**:17, **2**:30, **2**:34–7
behaviour, **6**:309, **6**:334
  vertex functions, **6**:311
corrections, **6**:366, **6**:376
correction to, **9**:73, **9**:78
crossover, **9**:125, **9**:141
density, **9**:130
deviations, **6**:198
dimensions, **6**:250, **6**:267–273
dynamic, **3**:571, **3**:648
equation of state, **6**:129
equations, **6**:508
exponents, **6**:38, **6**:57, **12**:355
fields, **6**:80–85, **6**:90, **6**:94, **6**:108,
  6:116-118, **6**:250, **6**:258–267,
  6:269, **6**:272, **6**:276, **6**:434,
  6:435, **6**:436, **6**:438, **6**:440,
  6:441, **6**:444, **6**:520, **9**:9, **9**:18,
  9:31, **9**:41, **9**:43, **9**:45, **9**:58,
  9:79, **9**:114, **9**:123, **9**:128, **9**:130,
  9:133
fields, even, **6**:439
  in homogeneous perturbations,
    6:115
  irrelevant, **6**:442
  odd, **6**:439
  relevant, **6**:452, **6**:461
  relevant operators, **6**:114
finite-size, **12**:316
form, **6**:161, **6**:327, **6**:336, **6**:340,
  6:346, **6**:517, **12**:358–359,
  12:455
free energy, **6**:41–45
functions, **6**:118, **6**:294, **6**:310, **6**:343,
  6:358, **9**:9, **9**:28, **9**:34, **9**:36,
  9:37, **9**:39, **9**:64, **9**:73, **9**:74–5,
  9:77–8, **9**:82, **9**:91, **9**:103, **9**:105,
  9:108, **9**:109, **9**:110, **9**:111,
  9:125, **9**:154, **12**:358, **12**:421,
  12:422, **12**:425, **12**:455, **12**:476
hypothesis, general, **9**:31, **9**:32,
  9:46
index, **12**:417, **12**:422
invariance, **5A**:2, **5A**:28, **6**:29
lattice-lattice, **3**:361, **3**:450, **3**:628,
  3:629, **3**:645, **3**:646
law, **12**:38, **12**:177

laws, **6**:128, **6**:129, **6**:131, **6**:177,
  6:184, **6**:188, **6**:202, **6**:242,
  6:319, **6**:337, **6**:350, **6**:520,
  6:533, **6**:534
laws, corrections, **6**:185, **6**:193, **6**:207,
  6:400
law, exact, **6**:84
length, **3**:444
linear, **9**:27, **9**:42, **9**:44, **9**:70, **9**:110,
  9:146
non-linear, **9**:25, **9**:30, **9**:41, **9**:71,
  9:91
non-symmetric, **2**:29, **2**:30
precise, **2**:31, **2**:34, **2**:36–7
product, **6**:270
properties, **12**:220, **12**:223, **12**:224,
  12:227, **12**:304, **12**:341, **12**:348,
  12:354, **12**:362, **12**:384, **12**:391,
  12:420, **12**:442, **12**:462, **12**:465,
  12:467, **12**:469
relation, **5A**:52, **5A**:68, **12**:256,
  12:280, **12**:289–290, **12**:342
relations, **6**:389, **9**:54
relevant and irrevelant, **9**:114
static, **5A**:170
strong, hypothesis, **6**:127, **6**:177
theory, **5A**:31, **6**:439
thermodynamic, **3**:444
transformation, **5A**:28
universality, **6**:115
variables, **6**:257, **6**:267–273, **6**:276,
  6:538, **6**:547, **9**:104, **9**:110,
  9:111
variable, irrelevant, **6**:348
variables, local, **6**:269
variables, product of, **6**:270
variables, relevant, **6**:348
Scattering amplitude, **19**:86, **19**:87,
  19:101, **19**:111, **19**:115, **19**:166
Scattering intensity, **16**:*16*, **16**:*47*,
  16:*71*, **16**:77, **16**:80, **16**:110,
  16:123, **16**:*124*, **16**:148,
  16:162
  at zero wavevector, **16**:*120*
  See also Structure function
Schauder–Tychonov theorem, **1**:163,
  1:165
Schrödinger equation, **15**:11, **15**:13,
  19:5, **19**:19, **19**:21, **19**:315

Schrödinger operator, **14**:177, **15**:165, **15**:167, **15**:216
Schwartz–Christoffel transformation, **11**:85
Schwarz inequality, **15**:118, **15**:131, **15**:135
Schwarz–Christoffel symbol, **16**:132
Schwinger formulation, **19**:318
Schwinger function, **5B**:215
Schwinger functions, **6**:132, **6**:147, **6**:525, **9**:238–9, **9**:243–8, **9**:253, **9**:255, **9**:258, **9**:266–7, **9**:274, **9**:276, **9**:279, **9**:281, **9**:297, **9**:298
Schwinger model, two-dimensional, **8**:250
Schwinger–Dyson equations, **11**:68
SCMCD *see* Self-consistent moment conserving decoupling
Screened Coulomb interaction, **6**:279
Screening, **12**:388, **12**:418
  growth model, **12**:418–423, **12**:426
Screw method, **1**:247
Screw, **1**:256, **1**:262
  construction, **1**:271
SDE, *see* short-distance expansion
SDS (sodium dodecyl sulfate), **16**:5, **16**:156, **16**:*16*
SDS–butanol–salt–toluene–water mixtures, **16**:*18*
SDS–pentanol–salt–water mixtures, **16**:120, **16**:142
SDS–toluene–salt–water mixtures, **16**:*16*, **16**:46, **16**:*47*, **16**:*50*
Sealing
  field, **10**:93, **10**:180
  form, **10**:221, **10**:249, (cross-over) **10**:242–3
  functions, **10**:201, **10**:205, **10**:217, **10**:271
  laws, **10**:76, **10**:83, **10**:113, **10**:154, **10**:163–70, **10**:183–4, **10**:213
  (Bray and Moore), **10**:223–5
  relation (Widom), **10**:11, **10**:29, **10**:79, **10**:109, **10**:216, **10**:270, **10**:273–4
Search algorithms, **18**:151–2
  for percolation, **18**:188–9
Second correlation moment, **3**:466
Second moment series, **3**:294, **3**:300, **3**:301

Second moment, **3**:496, **3**:546
Second neighbour interaction, **3**:246, **3**:261, **3**:272, **3**:287, **3**:295, **3**:296, **3**:297, **3**:307, **3**:309, **3**:314, **3**:320, **3**:341, **3**:489
Second order transition, **2**:324
Second quantization formalism, **5A**:221, **5A**:351
Second quantization, **9**:249
Second quantized operator, **1**:129, **5A**:351
Second sound, **7**:33, **7**:34, **7**:35
Second virial coefficient, **5B**:238, **19**:449
Second-moment correlation length, **14**:110–11
Second-moment, **14**:50, **14**:58, **14**:59
Second-order phase transition, **5B**:1, **5B**:344, **5B**:346
Section graph, **2**:200, **2**:215, **2**:234, **3**:61, **3**:83
  associated, **3**:61, **3**:63
  full perimeter, **3**:77
Segment, **3**:79, **3**:80, **3**:81, **3**:83, **3**:108, **3**:109, **3**:110, **3**:112
Segregation, alloys, **8**:94–96
Self avoiding walks
  percolative thermal behaviour, **7**:261
  position space methods, **7**:250
Self energy Σ, **6**:317
Self energy, **6**:313, **6**:325
  longitudinal, **6**:332
  transverse, **6**:332
Self matching lattice, **2**:212
Self-adjoint operator, **15**:168
Self-affine substrate, **14**:342–4
Self-affine, **14**:341, **14**:346
Self-assembling amphiphilic systems *see* Amphiphilic systems
Self-averaging property, **15**:183–7
Self-averaging, **14**:138
Self-avoidance, **16**:136
Self-avoiding branched polymer, **16**:158
Self-avoiding systems
  interaction, **19**:314
  membranes
    flat phase, **19**:356
    grand canonical ensemble, **19**:458

large orders and instantons,
19:435–439
modelling, 19:264
numerical simulations,
19:276–278
and phantom membrane, 19:434
phases, 19:*386*
two-loop extrapolation,
19:355–356
physical information, 19:347–356
polymers, 19:256, 19:263
renormalization, 19:356
restricted, 19:277
summing over, 19:411
tethered membranes, 19:258–259
Self-avoiding walk problem, 5B:56
additional singularity, 13:18–19
Self-avoiding walk triangular lattice
chain generating function, Padé
approximants, 13:55–57
series analysis, 13:28–29
Self-avoiding walk, 3:69, 3:70, 3:92,
3:103, 3:109, 3:110, 3:112, 3:188,
3:274, 3:344, 3:360, 3:471, 3:473,
3:475, 9:21
in computer memory, 3:112
Self-avoiding walks (SAWs), 14:92–6
Self-avoiding walks, 1:83, 11:83, 11:84,
11:112
Self-consistency equations, 1:169
Self-consistent approximation, 5B:113,
5B:188
Self-consistent boundary condition,
5B:36, 5B:67
Self-consistent field boundary condition,
5B:35, 5B:36, 5B:46, 5B:53
Self-consistent field theory, 5B:389
Self-consistent field, 6:255
Self-consistent moment conserving
decoupling, 5B:302, 5B:307,
5B:309, 5B:316, 5B:317
Self-consistent Γ-ordered scheme,
5B:239
Self-duality, 14:41, 19:81, 19:104–110
Self-enantiodromy, 19:74–75, 19:81n,
19:82, 19:108–110, 19:113,
19:211
Self-energy diagram, 5A:228
Self-energy function, 5B:231

Self-energy graphs, 6:302, 6:312, 6:334,
6:344
Self-energy, 19:361
Self-entanglement, closed polymers,
7:132, 7:145–146
Self-exclusion, 3:98, 3:109
Self-field, 3:138, 3:140, 3:141, 3:147,
3:160, 3:168, 3:174
Self-organized criticality (SOC), 17:9,
17:183–186
Self-organized criticality, 18:189–90
Self-similar function, 5B:254
Self-similarity, 19:3
Semi-infinite
continuum models, 10:211
Ising model, 10:82
model systems, 10:78, 10:123,
10:137, 10:212, 10:326–7,
10:329–332
theory, 10:192–3, 10:203
Semi-infinite geometry, 11:79
Semi-infinite systems, 11:58, 11:59,
11:119, 19:98, 19:100
Semi-invariants, 3:127, 3:128, 3:137,
3:140, 3:150, 3:152, 3:164, 3:165,
3:167, 3:168, 3:169, 3:172, 3:173
bare, 3:126, 3:129, 3:132, 3:134,
3:138, 3:141, 3:164, 3:166,
3:168
mixed, 3:164
renormalized, 3:129, 3:136, 3:139,
3:142, 3:143, 3:144, 3:168,
3:169
unrenormalized, 3:123, 3:146, 3:171
Semi-phenomenological equations of
motion, 8:287–295
Semicircle law, 15:171–83, 15:193,
15:194, 15:205
improvement of, 15:183–7
Semiconductors, electron-hole
condensation, 8:441–443
Semigroup property, 14:33
Sensitivity analysis, 18:166
Separation lines, 2:6, 2:7
Separation points, 2:3, 2:4
Sequence extrapolation, 13:35–51, *see
also* Multiparameter fitting
applications to series analysis,
13:40–48

Barber–Hamer algorithm, **13**:39–40
Brazinski's theta algorithm, **13**:37–38
BST algorithm, **13**:51
  error estimation, **13**:36
Levin transforms, **13**:38–39
Lubkin's three-term transformation,
      13:40
  methods compared, **13**:35
Wynn's epsilon algorithm, **13**:36–37
Series analyses, **10**:78, **14**:42, **14**:44,
      14:56, **14**:58–61, **14**:66, **14**:69,
      14:97
  see Power series expansions,
      asymptotic analysis
Series estimates, **14**:58–60, **14**:65,
      14:66
Series extrapolation, **2**:355, **2**:368
Series expansion high temperature, **3**:37,
      3:294, **3**:492, **3**:572, **3**:584, **3**:594,
      3:636
  low temperature, **3**:433
Series expansion methods, **7**:223–232
  dilute Heisenberg model, **7**:229–230
  dilute Ising model, **7**:227–229
  dilute XY model, **7**:230–231
Series expansion, **1**:3, **1**:228, **1**:231,
      1:232, **1**:266, **5B**:2, **5B**:39, **5B**:54,
      5B:70, **5B**:297
  high-temperature, **5B**:43
Series expansions, **2**:218, **2**:220, **2**:226,
      2:241, **2**:253, **2**:259, **2**:308, **2**:314,
      2:330, **2**:331, **2**:333, **2**:351, **2**:363,
      2:481, **2**:486, **2**:489, **2**:492, **9**:142,
      10:31
Series expansions, **12**:294, **14**:19, **14**:44
  low temperature, **12**:58, **12**:120–121
Series extrapolation, **5B**:42, **5B**:62
  high-temperature, **5B**:51, **5B**:52
Series methods, **14**:58
  for critical phenomena, **3**:115, **3**:116
Shadow graph, **3**:410, **3**:412, **3**:584,
      3:585, **3**:588, **3**:589, **3**:590, **3**:592,
      3:593, **3**:594, **3**:601, **3**:602, **3**:603,
      3:605, **3**:608, **3**:609, **3**:610, **3**:612,
      3:613, **3**:614, **3**:632
  connected, **3**:591
  decorated, **3**:612, **3**:614, **3**:615
  fourth order fluctuation, **3**:610
  ordered decorated, **3**:614

ordered directed, **3**:601, **3**:604, **3**:612
  perpendicular susceptibility, **3**:605
  susceptibility, **3**:604
Shadow system, **3**:409
Shadow, **3**:406, **3**:407, **3**:408
Shanks transform, **8**:225
Shanks transformation and epsilon
      algorithm, **13**:37
Shape dependence, finite size scaling,
      8:203
Shape effects, **14**:113–20
Shape fluctuations, **14**:137, **14**:151–4
Shape function, **14**:92
Sharp-kink, **12**:75, **12**:85, **12**:90
Shear
  and domain growth, **19**:389
  modulus, **19**:267, **19**:269, **19**:272
Shear modulus, **7**:8
  temperature dependent, determination,
      7:55
Shear viscosity in hexatic phase, **7**:73
Shear viscosity, **5A**:250, **5A**:289,
      5A:290, **5A**:291, **5A**:326, **5A**:340
  non-local, **5A**:291
Shear wall, **12**:238–239, **12**:241,
      12:245
Shear, phase transitions under,
      17:189–191
Sherrington–Kirkpatrick (SK) model,
      15:75, **15**:83, **15**:131, **15**:133–7
Sherrington–Kirkpatrick interaction,
      15:133–7
Shift exponent, **6**:370, **6**:379, **6**:381,
      8:36, **8**:41, **8**:153, **8**:161, **8**:242,
      8:244, **9**:9, **9**:27, **9**:30, **9**:54, **9**:70
Shifted periodic boundary conditions
      (SPBC), **17**:83–93
  and splitting/merging transitions,
      17:87–90
Shifting phenomena, **5B**:4
Shock
  ASEP, **19**:12
  in biopolymerization, **19**:12
  branching and coalescence,
      19:150–151, **19**:*152*
  diffusion and coalescence,
      19:117–123
  distribution, **19**:118, **19**:119, **19**:120,
      19:121, **19**:173

as domain wall, **19:**144–145
dynamics, **19:**6, **19:**127
evolution, **19:**195
formation, **19:**104
multiple, **19:**159–160
random walk, **19:**173
stability, **19:**124–125
structure, **19:**52
in traffic models, **19:**155
velocity, **19:***118*, **19:**123, **19:**143,
    19:172
Shocks
development in ID models, **17:**159,
    17:162–164
microscopic nature, **17:**162, **17:**167
Short-chain effects, **14:**95
Short-distance expansion, **6:**238
Short-distance expansions SDE, **10:**80,
    10:192–3, **10:**196–8, **10:**201,
    10:207, **10:**212
Short-range forces, **5B:**181,
    14:228–44
Short-range interaction, **10:**76
Short-range interactions, **5B:**125,
    5B:149, **5B:**161, **14:**47
correlations, **19:**391, **19:**404,
    19:407–408
disorder, **19:**388, **19:**406
and long-range order, **19:**54
N-component spins, **19:**255
repulsive, **19:**256, **19:**368
Short-range potential, **5B:**170, **5B:**180
Short-range renormalization group fixed
    points, **14:**202
Short-range spherical model, **14:**50–1
Short-range spin interaction, **15:**102
Shortest-path algorithms, **18:**153–7
SIC phase (stripped incommensurate),
    12:228, **12:**230, **12:**233, **12:**239,
    12:247, **12:**282, **12:**305, **12:**313
floating, **12:**252–254, **12:**256–259,
    12:261–263, **12:**268, **12:**271,
    12:273, **12:**276–281,
    12:282–286, **12:**290, **12:**295,
    12:300–301, **12:**303–304,
    12:311, **12:**315–316, **12:**330–333
fluid, **12:**263–271, **12:**282,
    12:287–290, **12:**295, **12:**300,
    12:302, **12:**327

SiC polytypes, **15:**38
SID (surface induced disorder),
    12:123–136
Sierpinski gasket, **12:**338
Sierpinsky gasket, **19:**264, **19:**278
Sign pattern of series and singularily
    location, **13:**10–11
Silhouette, **3:**388
Similarity transformation, stochastic,
    19:74
Similarity transformations, **19:**72–74,
    19:167–168, **19:**175, **19:**176,
    19:178
annihilation–fusion process, **19:**206
density profile, **19:**167–168
diagonal, **19:**105
equivalence and enantiodromy,
    19:72–74
factorized, **19:**101, **19:**189, **19:**191
in free fermion models, **19:**175,
    19:176, **19:**178
stochastic, **19:**74, **19:**185
typical results, **19:**5–6
Simple chain, **3:**69
Simple cubic bicontinuous phase,
    16:125
Simple cubic lattice, **14:**60
Simple cubic, **1:**300
Simple fluid, reduced critical
    temperature, **5B:**197
Simple graph, **2:**232, **5B:**212
Simple pole, **3:**303, **3:**316
Simple power law, **1:**98
Simplex, **5B:**217
Simplical graph, **2:**276, **2:**277, **2:**282,
    2:285, **2:**292, **2:**293, **2:**297
Simplicial complexes, **5B:**217
Simply connected graph, **5B:**212
Simulation techniques, **7:**202–210
Sine–Gordon equation, **15:**12
Sine–Gordon model, **12:**262,
    12:277–279, **12:**327–329
Sine–Gordon problem, **10:**324–5
Sine–Gordon, **17:**179
Single bond clusters, **7:**174
Single diamond phase, **16:***145*
Single ion terms, **6:**360
Single site clusters, **7:**174
Single spin-flip model, **5B:**95, **5B:**104

Single-component fluid, **5A**:208–213,
  5A:247–254, **5A**:265, **5A**:287,
  5A:289, **5A**:292, **5A**:336,
  5A:366–370, **5A**:394, **5A**:395
  classical, **5A**:302–310
  sound attenuation, **5A**:302
  see also One-component fluid
Single-ion anisotropy, **3**:579
Single-particle transition, **5B**:13, **5B**:21
Single-site basis vectors, **19**:239
Single-site heat-bath algorithm, **18**:68–9
Single-step surface growth model,
  17:154, **17**:162
Singular behaviour, **13**:7–8, *see also*
  Confluent singularities of
  differential approximants, **13**:89–90
Singular diffusion, **17**:186
Singular part, **14**:114
Singular perturbation expansions, **13**:135
Singular point, **3**:222, **5A**:268
Singular terms, **6**:267
Singularities, **12**:410, **19**:*430*, **19**:431,
  19:449
Singularity location and sign pattern,
  13:10–11
Singularity, **3**:184, **3**:186, **3**:187, **3**:188,
  3:194, **3**:200, **3**:202, **3**:206, **3**:210,
  3:232, **3**:234, **3**:239, **3**:367
  antiferromagnetic, **3**:186, **3**:195,
    3:214, **3**:234, **3**:235, **3**:237,
    3:238, **3**:319, **3**:321, **3**:327,
    3:430, **3**:431, **3**:495
  branch point, **3**:205, **3**:214
  coincident, **3**:209
  confluent, **3**:209
  dominant, **3**:184, **3**:185, **3**:187, **3**:202,
    3:209, **3**:228, **3**:309, **3**:423,
    3:424, **3**:434, **3**:616, **3**:637
  dominant ferromagnetic, **3**:201, **3**:454,
    3:457
  dominant non-physical, **3**:640
  essential, **3**:470
  ferromagnetic, **3**:186, **3**:214, **3**:235,
    3:238, **3**:240, **3**:241
  logarithmic, **3**:302
  non-Darboux, **3**:432
  non-physical, **3**:185, **3**:186, **3**:218,
    3:219, **3**:223, **3**:228, **3**:229,
    3:327, **3**:443, **3**:638

  physical, **3**:185, **3**:187, **3**:202,
    3:219, **3**:220, **3**:223, **3**:442,
    3:443
  residual, **3**:430
  spurious, **3**:360, **3**:442, **3**:443
  unphysical, **3**:442
  weak, **3**:188
Site dilute simple cubic Ising model,
  ordering temperature, **7**:205
Site diluted Baxter–Wu model, Monte
  Carlo methods, **7**:205
Site diluted Heisenberg
  antiferromagnets, phase diagram
  virtual crystal approximation,
  7:212
Site diluted Heisenberg ferromagnets
  spin wave stiffness, **7**:197
  two-dimensional, magnon modes,
    7:209
Site diluted Ising ferromagnet, transition
  temperature, **7**:158
Site diluted Ising models position space
  methods, **7**:248
  two-dimensional, Monte Carlo
    methods, **7**:204
Site diluted triangular lattice Ising
  model, Monte Carlo methods,
  7:205
Site dilution
  in disconnecting lattices, **7**:160
  position space method, **7**:256
Site disorder, **7**:155
Site exclusion, **19**:194
Site diluted Heisenberg antiferromagnets
  two-dimensional, density of states,
    7:209
  magnon modes, **7**:209
Site mixed layer antiferromagnets,
  inelastic neutron scattering
  function, **7**:209
Site mixed magnets, percolation concept,
  7:191
Site percolation
  concentrations, **7**:160
  field-theoretic renormalization group
    treatments, **7**:245
  position space methods, **7**:250
Site percolation problem, **5B**:339
Site percolation, **18**:32–6, **18**:42–7

Site problem, **2:**199, **2:**203, **2:**204,
    2:206, **2:**211, **2:**213, **2:**221, **2:**222,
    2:223, **2:**224, **2:**225, **2:**227, **2:**229,
    2:233, **2:**239, **2:**241, **2:**242, **2:**243,
    2:245, **2:**249, **2:**250, **2:**255, **2:**260,
    2:262, **2:**266
Site random-cluster measure, **18:**70–2
Site spins, **6:**432, **6:**464
Site substitutionally disordered
    ferromagnets, virtual crystal
    approximations, **7:**212
Site-diluted Heisenberg ferromagnets,
    coherent potential approximation,
    7:217
Site-diluted Heisenherg magnets,
    coherent potential approximations,
    7:221
Site-diluted magnets, coherent potential
    approximations, **7:**221
Site-disorder spin magnets, coherent
    potential approximations, **7:**218
Site-disordered Ising model, coherent
    potential approximations, **7:**218
Sites, **3:**98
Six vertex model, **17:**155–157
Six-vertex (6V) model, **11:**30, **11:**32,
    11:33, **11:**35, **11:**36, **11:**38–39,
    11:43, **11:**45
Six-vertex model, **10:**41, **10:**44, **10:**45,
    12:272–276, **12:**278, **12:**331, **19:**5,
    19:35, **19:**52, **19:**160
Sixteen vertex problem, **1:**350, **1:**436
    equivalence with Ising problem, **1:**350
Size effects, *see* Finite-size effects in
    dimers
Skeletal lines, **3:**136, **3:**158
Skeletal symmetry factor, **3:**139
Skeletal vertex, **3:**139
    n-valent, **3:**139
1-Skeleton, **3:**139
2-Skeleton, **3:**153, **3:**157, **3:**158, **3:**159
l-Skeleton, **3:**162
Skeleton expansion, **10:**132, **10:**133
    modified, **10:**144
SLAC approach, **19:**71
Slater KDP model, **3:**656, **3:**658, **3:**661,
    3:662, **3:**663
Sliding incommensurate structures,
    15:16

Small defect concentration, phase
    boundary, quenched models, **7:**184
Small particles, **5B:**4
Smeared transition, **6:**404
Smectic A-hexatic B transition, **14:**82
Smectic phase, **12:**191–192
Smectics, **7:**74–75
Smoluchowski equation, **12:**358, **12:**458,
    12:465–469
Smoluchowski theory, **19:**4, **19:**13,
    19:196–197, **19:**209–210, **19:**212
Smoothness postulate, **3:**361, **3:**455,
    3:456, **3:**459, **3:**461, **3:**465, **3:**477,
    3:572, **3:**582
Smoothness postulate, **6:**519
$Sn_2P_2(Se_xS_{1-x})_6$, **15:**64
Snowflakes, **12:**471–472
Sociological behaviour, **19:**3
Sodium dodecyl sulfate *see* SDS
Sodium-bis-ethylhexylsulfosuccinate *see*
    AOT
Soft disc pair potentials, **7:**54
Soft replusive core, **5B:**194
Sokal's inequality, **9:**297
Solid membranes *see* tethered
    membranes
Solid on solid model, **12:**31–32,
    12:41–44, **12:**64, **12:**69–70,
    12:73, **12:**117, **12:**170, **12:**172,
    12:179, **12:**181–182, **12:**329,
    12:330
Solid-liquid transition, **5B:**191
Solid-on-solid model (SOS), **18:**41,
    18:252–5
    continuum, **18:**198
    see also triangular Ising solid-on-solid
        model (TISOS)
Solid-on-solid model, **14:**137,
    14:220–56, **14:**268–74
    for wetting, **14:**230–6
    in continuum limit, **14:**226–8
    with $1/z^2$ interaction, **14:**247–9
Solid-on-solid models (SOS), **10:**2,
    10:3, **10:**33, **10:**34, **10:**36, **10:**40,
    10:41, **10:**46, **10:**53, **10:**54, **10:**55,
    10:59, **10:**65, **10:**67, **10:**68,
    10:342, **11:**28, **11:**29, **11:**43, **11:**59,
    11:113
    random surfaces, **10:**3

tube model, **10**:61
walk, **10**:19, **10**:20
Solid-on-solid models, **8**:72, **8**:74
    one-dimensional, **8**:73
Solids, dislocation lines in, bond
    orientational order and, **7**:85–88
Solids, one-dimensional, **19**:33
Soliton, **8**:65, **12**:227, **12**:262, **12**:277,
    12:327
Solitons, **19**:104
Solubility parameter, **9**:168
Solution, **3**:364, **3**:365, **3**:366
    regular, **3**:364
SOS-type approximation, **15**:47
Sound
    absorption, **5B**:380, **5B**:389
    critical frequency, **5B**:359
    velocity, **5B**:359
Sound attenuation, **5A**:72, **5A**:75,
    5A:299–320
    in aniline/cyclohexane, **5A**:309,
        5A:311
    coefficient, **5A**:305
    in helium, **5A**:306
    in nitrobenzene/n-hexane, **5A**:309,
        5A:310
    in xenon, **5A**:307
Sound dispersion, **5A**:76, **5A**:299–320
Sound propagation, **5A**:301
    adiabatic, **5A**:251
Sound velocity, **5A**:72, **5A**:301, **5A**:304,
    5A:305
    adiabatic, **5A**:210, **5A**:213, **5A**:252
Sound wave frequency, adiabatic,
    5A:258
Space dimensionality, **6**:523
Space of configurations, **15**:79
Space type, **2**:132, **2**:133
Space-time anisotropy, **19**:68
Spanning clusters, **18**:284
Spanning tree, construction, **19**:329–330
Spanning trees, **18**:153
Spatial correlation length, **19**:142
Spatial dimensionality, **15**:94, **15**:97,
    15:106
Spatial distribution function, normalized,
    19:60
Spatial homogeneity, **15**:88–9
Spatial inhumogeneity, **5B**:61

Spatial ordering, **5B**:138
Spatial rotation, **5A**:268
Spatially modulated structures
    basic definitions, **15**:4–5
    in systems with competing
        interactions, **15**:1–71
Special transitions (surface), **8**:12,
    8:20–21, **8**:37, **8**:38, **8**:41, **8**:43,
    8:44, **8**:50, **8**:54, **8**:64, **8**:125–126
    lower critical dimensionality, **8**:53
Species
    different, **3**:8
Specific heat amplitude, **3**:628, **3**:629
Specific heat
    annealed diluted magnets, **7**:163
    bond diluted two-dimensional Ising
        model, **7**:256, **7**:257
    coherent potential approximation,
        7:217
    dilute magnets, experimental, **7**:264
    of infinitely long chains, **7**:130
    Monte Carlo methods, **7**:204, **7**:205
    reference Ising model, **7**:198
    scaling and, **7**:234
    three-dimensional Heisenberg system,
        7:170
    three-dimensional Ising system, **7**:170
    three-dimensional XY magnets, **7**:264
    two-dimensional bond diluted Ising
        model, position space method,
        7:248
    two-dimensional Ising model, **7**:188
Specific heat anomaly, **3**:313, **3**:321,
    3:323, **3**:427
Specific heat coefficient, **3**:256, **3**:284,
    3:536, **3**:545
Specific heat curve, **3**:428, **3**:622
    effect of spin, **3**:428
Specific heat exponent
    α, **3**:235, **3**:321, **3**:323, **3**:426
Specific heat exponent, **6**:366
Specific heat exponent, **19**:354, **19**:431
Specific heat
    helium, in pores and films, **8**:251–254
    ideal Bose gas, **8**:221
    Ising model, **8**:153
    local, **8**:36
    Potts model, **8**:239
    surface, **8**:51, **8**:53

Specific heat jump, **1:**270
Specific heat per spin, **5A:**201
Specific heat series, **3:**271, **3:**297, **3:**321,
    3:323, **3:**528, **3:**531, **3:**532
Specific heat singularity, **3:**201, **3:**620
Specific heat, **1:**180, **1:**190, **1:**249,
    1:266, **1:**273, **1:**301, **1:**302, **1:**310,
    1:314, **1:**315, **1:**317, **1:**318, **2:**21,
    2:25, **2:**26, **2:**29, **2:**33, **2:**34, **2:**36,
    2:56, **2:**59, **2:**105, **2:**111, **2:**123,
    2:125, **2:**128, **2:**149, **2:**150–52,
    2:154, **2:**158, **2:**159, **2:**162, **2:**164,
    2:171, **2:**175, **2:**180, **2:**185, **2:**191,
    2:194, **2:**248, **2:**251–3, **2:**255–7,
    2:321, **2:**351, **2:**353, **2:**384, **2:**426,
    2:489, **3:**58, **3:**87, **3:**201, **3:**219,
    3:249, **3:**252, **3:**256, **3:**281, **3:**290,
    3:294, **3:**311, **3:**313, **3:**324, **3:**362,
    3:413, **3:**436, **3:**438, **3:**439, **3:**442,
    3:454, **3:**459, **3:**466, **3:**496, **3:**507,
    3:534, **3:**535, **3:**540, **3:**551, **3:**552,
    3:554, **3:**584, **3:**594, **3:**595, **3:**637,
    3:643, **3:**645, **3:**649, **5A:**14, **5B:**2,
    5B:254, **5B:**275, **5B:**294, **5B:**338,
    6:130, **6:**197, **6:**213, **6:**254, **6:**267,
    6:486, **6:**512, **6:**535, **10:**44, **10:**46,
    14:7, **14:**8, **14:**11–15, **14:**18, **14:**26,
    14:29, **14:**40–1, **14:**48, **14:**65,
    14:76, **14:**82, **14:**83, **14:**85, **14:**87,
    14:115, **14:**120, **17:**47, **17:**58
  critical point and, **6:**12
      continuous phase transition, **6:**8
  high-temperature, **3:**200
  high-temperature α, **3:**436
  Ising, **3:**92
  low-temperature, **3:**219
  magnetic, **5B:**295, **5B:**296, **5B:**297
  of rectangular s.c. Ising system, **5B:**58
  of 2-dimensional Ising model, **6:**94
  See also Surface specific heat
  zero-field, **3:**250
Spectator phase, **14:**143
Spectral density, **16:**163
Spectral dimensionality, **12:**391
Spectral functions, coherent potential
    approximation, **7:**217
Spectral properties, **19:**62, **19:**68, **19:**72
Spectral shape function, **5A:**92, **5A:**101
Spectral theory, **15:**165–235

Spectrin, in red blood cells, **19:**257,
    19:*273*, **19:**274
Spectrum of singularity, **12:**429–430
Spherical constraints, **15:**80, **15:**95,
    15:142–9
Spherical ferromagnet, **15:**93, **15:**161
Spherical model exponent
    renormalized, **3:**536
Spherical model series, **3:**558
Spherical model, **1:**24, **1:**81, **1:**200,
    3:183, **3:**190, **3:**224, **3:**232, **3:**326,
    3:450, **3:**451, **3:**468, **3:**487, **3:**488,
    3:489, **3:**491, **3:**498, **3:**499, **3:**506,
    3:512, **3:**534, **3:**537, **3:**538, **3:**540,
    3:546, **3:**552, **3:**555, **3:**557, **3:**571,
    3:628, **5A:**271, **5B:**56, **5B:**207,
    5B:240, **5B:**246, **5B:**256–257,
    5B:274, **5B:**329, **6:**94, **6:**217,
    6:220, **6:**255, **6:**344, **6:**526, **9:**4,
    9:96, **9:**97, **9:**101, **9:**102, **9:**106,
    9:112, **9:**152, **10:**39, **10:**40, **11:**79,
    14:44, **14:**45, **14:**50–2, **14:**56,
    14:64, **14:**104–5, **15:**78–80, **15:**83,
    15:84, **15:**87
  antiferromagnet, **15:**148–9
  approximation, **5B:**264
  disordered, **15:**89
  free energy, **15:**88–93, **15:**103,
      15:105, **15:**123
  in arbitrary periodic field, **15:**150–9
  on decorated lattice, **15:**159–65
  partition function, **15:**91
  phase diagrams, **15:**100, **15:**104
  planar, **15:**141, **15:**149, **15:**157
  random external field, **15:**93–5
  scalar, **15:**141
  translationally invariant, **15:**93, **15:**103
  with nonuniform spherical field,
      15:137–65
  with two spherical constraints,
      15:142–9
  with uniform spherical field, **15:**88–107
Spherical model, Ch, **2:**10, **2:**120, **2:**125,
    2:127, **2:**128, **2:**135, **2:**146, **2:**147,
    2:148, **2:**149, **2:**150, **2:**155, **2:**375,
    2:376, **2:**377, **2:**379, **2:**386, **2:**400,
    2:401, **2:**402, **2:**404, **2:**407, **2:**408,
    2:409, **2:**411–441, **2:**417, **2:**420,
    2:426–7, **2:**440

d-dimensional, **2**:415, **2**:416,
    2:418
mean, **2**:377
one-dimensional, **2**:387, **2**:395
two-dimensional, **2**:394
Spherical models, **8**:34, **8**:75
    exact results, **8**:48, **8**:49
    finite size scaling theory, **8**:40
    layered, **8**:224
    scaling law, **8**:63
    surfaces, critical exponents, **8**:54
    with free surfaces, **8**:61–63
    n-component spin systems, $n \to \infty$
        limit, **8**:208–217
Spherical moment series, **3**:320
Spherical particles, magnetization
    profiles, **8**:14
Spherical symmetry, **3**:248
Spheroidal wave functions, **1**:203,
    1:204
Spin
    antiparallel, **19**:36, **19**:188
    configuration, Ising model, **19**:32,
        19:*33*
    decoupling, **19**:427
    flip
        events, **19**:189
        in free fermion systems, **19**:186
        Glauber dynamics, **19**:48,
            19:49–50, **19**:76, **19**:77,
            19:213, **19**:214
        Kawasaki dynamics, **19**:43,
            19:68, **19**:108
        and pair creation–annihilation,
            19:188
        rates, **19**:212
        symmetry, **19**:76
        term, ladder operators, **19**:35–36
        times, **19**:49–50, **19**:69
        transformation, **19**:179
    interaction, **19**:36
    matrices, **19**:42
    operators, **19**:107
    orientation, **19**:32
    parallel, **19**:188
    relaxation, **19**:3, **19**:108, **19**:162–164,
        19:212
    –spin correlation, nearest neighbours,
        19:206

systems
    classical and quantum, **19**:30,
        19:53
    and particle systems, **19**:24,
        19:27, **19**:30
    two-state, **19**:20, **19**:*21*, **19**:23
    wave, **19**:37–38, **19**:81–82
Spin correlation, **1**:277, **5A**:92, **5A**:94
    nearest neighbour, **1**:280, **1**:313,
        1:314
    self dual, **1**:277
Spin correlations, **2**:471, **2**:476, **2**:483–4
Spin deviation, **5B**:68
Spin diffusion mode, **5B**:29
Spin diffusion, **2**:479, **2**:480, **5B**:25
Spin dimensionality
    systems with larger, **6**:416
Spin exchange model, **5B**:28, **5B**:29,
        5B:90, **5B**:91
Spin flop, **6**:380
Spin flop bicritical points, **14**:29
Spin flop field, **7**:270
Spin flop line, **14**:29
Spin flop phases, diluted anisotropic
        Heisenberg antiferromagnets,
        coherent potential approximation,
        7:217
Spin glass, **7**:152, **7**:270
    computer studies, **7**:207
    model, coherent potential
        approximations, **7**:218
    series expansion methods, **7**:232
    order, Monte Carlo methods, **7**:207
    system, **7**:190
Spin glasses, **15**:75, **15**:95, **18**:197,
        18:221–34
Spin half diluted XY magnet, transition
    curves, experimental, **7**:263
Spin half Heisenberg model, scaling,
        7:259
Spin half Ising model
    binary bond disorder, **7**:186
    solution, **7**:182
    three-dimensional, solution, **7**:186,
        7:187
    two-dimensional, solution, **7**:186
Spin half XY model, solution, **7**:182
Spin half-curve model, position space
    methods, **7**:248

Spin half-quadratic layer magnet, experimental results, **7**:264
Spin interaction, **15**:139
Spin model, continuous, **6**:360
Spin models, **14**:41, **14**:50, **15**:3, **15**:29–57
  n-vector, **15**:54
  thermodynamics, **15**:96
Spin pair correlation function, **5A**:92, **5B**:40, **5B**:67, **5B**:101 (*see also* Pair correlation function)
Spin pair correlation, **5B**:346
  for s.c. Ising model, **5B**:42
Spin relaxation, **2**:467, **2**:477, **2**:480, **2**:486, **2**:489
Spin reversal invariance, **1**:123
Spin reversal symmetry, **1**:52
Spin reversal, **1**:49
Spin rotations, **6**:265
Spin space anisotropy, **3**:573, **3**:577
Spin system, *n*-component, $n \to \infty$ limit, spherical models and, **8**:208–217
Spin variable, **14**:47
Spin vector, **6**:265
Spin wave dynamics
  diluted Heisenberg ferromagnets, coherent potential approximations, **7**:219
  diluted Heisenberg models, **7**:196
  Monte Carlo methods, **7**:208
Spin–wave expansion, **3**:249, **3**:250, **3**:571
Spin wave properties
  diluted Heisenberg antiferromagnets, **7**:207
  dilute Heisenberg ferromagnets, **7**:207
Spin wave spectrum, coherent potential approximation, **7**:217
Spin wave stiffness
  coherent potential approximation, **7**:217, **7**:219, **7**:221
  diluted Heisenberg ferromagnet, **7**:196, **7**:197, **7**:208
  diluted Heisenberg magnets, **7**:208
  dilute magnets, position space method, **7**:251
  site diluted Heisenberg ferromagnets, **7**:197
Spin wave theory, **1**:85

Spin wave, **3**:250, **3**:546
Spin waves, **2**:254, **2**:341, **5B**:25, **5B**:48, **5B**:68, **5B**:283, **5B**:284, **5B**:294, **5B**:317, **5B**:319, **5B**:339
  interacting, **5B**:272
  long wavelength, **5B**:319
  theory of, **2**:377
Spin weight function, **6**:360
Spin, **6**:359
Spin-(1/2) operators, **19**:108, **19**:175
Spin-flip dynamics, **17**:17, **17**:171
  see also Glauber spin-flip dynamics
Spin-flop phase, **9**:11
Spin-flop structure, **8**:56
Spin-glass model, **15**:82
Spin-polarized electrons, local quantities from, **8**:3
Spin-polarized
  low-energy electron diffraction (SPLEED), **10**:78, **10**:188, **10**:189
  wave energy, **10**:289
Spin-slip model, **15**:56
Spin-spin correlation function perpendicular, **3**:637
Spin-spin correlation function, **5A**:63
Spin-spin correlation, **3**:375, **3**:635, **5A**:14, **6**:130, **6**:215
  perpendicular, **3**:648
Spin-spin interaction
  anisotropic, **3**:489
Spin-wave approximation, **5B**:320
Spin-wave dispersion law, **5B**:291
Spin-wave energy, **5B**:319
Spin-wave interaction, **5B**:285
Spin–wave mode, **3**:633
Spin-wave stiffness, **5B**:336, **5B**:339
Spin-wave theories, **6**:344
Spin-wave theory, **3**:248, **3**:252, **3**:314, **5B**:282, **5B**:289, **5B**:293, **8**:45
  renormalized, **5B**:287, **5B**:288
Spinel structure, **3**:294, **3**:300
Spinodal curve, **5B**:87, **5B**:88
Spinodal decomposition as generalized nucleation theory, **8**:360–366
  experimental studies, **8**:404–422
  in coherent metal-hydrogen systems, **8**:444
  in Lennard-Jones fluid, **8**:454
  in polymer systems, **8**:447–449

in tricritical systems, theory, **8**:423
one-component fluids, **8**:330
statistical theories, **8**:322–327
theories, **8**:319–332
Spinodal decomposition, **5B**:92, **9**:153, **12**:7
Spinodal lines, **5B**:153, **5B**:178
Spinodal, **2**:64, **2**:76, **2**:97
Spinor analysis, **1**:250
Spinor group, **1**:229, **1**:252
Spinor method, **1**:248, **1**:249, **1**:257, **1**:258, **1**:266
Spinor operator *or* parafermion operator, **11**:42
Spinors, **1**:215
Spinor theory, **1**:257
Spiral structure, **5A**:93
SPLEED, **12**:128
Sponge phase *see* L_3 phase
Spontaneous curvature modulus, **16**:100–01, **16**:106, **16**:*108*, **16**:128, **16**:137, **16**:141, **16**:143, **16**:146–8
Spontaneous fluctuation, **5B**:133
Spontaneous magnetization, **1**:60, **1**:64, **1**:75, **1**:76, **1**:79, **1**:82, **1**:83, **1**:84, **1**:85, **1**:87, **1**:88, **1**:93, **1**:97, **1**:99, **1**:171, **1**:205, **1**:213, **1**:228, **1**:230, **1**:232, **1**:243, **1**:250, **1**:251, **1**:266, **1**:271, **1**:286, **1**:287, **1**:288, **1**:289, **1**:290, **1**:304, **1**:306, **1**:307, **1**:308, **1**:326
in XY model, 88
Spontaneous magnetisation, **7**:159, **7**:179
bond diluted two-dimensional Ising model, **7**:257
Spontaneous magnetization coefficient, **3**:420, **3**:464
Spontaneous magnetization exponent β, **3**:446
Spontaneous magnetization series, **3**:209, **3**:223
Spontaneous magnetization, **2**:120, **2**:130, **2**:141, **2**:142, **2**:162, **2**:163, **2**:171, **2**:184, **2**:185, **2**:190, **2**:199, **2**:250, **2**:251, **2**:253, **2**:254, **2**:335, **2**:336, **2**:351, **2**:359, **2**:366, **2**:384, **2**:407, **2**:420, **3**:185, **3**:210, **3**:215, **3**:218, **3**:219, **3**:224, **3**:226, **3**:227,

3:232, **3**:233, **3**:248, **3**:252, **3**:271, **3**:299, **3**:300, **3**:310, **3**:314, **3**:315, **3**:358, **3**:367, **3**:371, **3**:393, **3**:417, **3**:424, **3**:433, **3**:434, **3**:440, **3**:442, **3**:447, **3**:448, **3**:475, **3**:543, **3**:642, **5A**:96, **5A**:141, **5A**:142, **5B**:38, **5B**:44, **5B**:184, **5B**:282, **5B**:286, **5B**:311, **5B**:316, **14**:48, **15**:141
boundary, **2**:185, **2**:186, **2**:194
definition of, **10**:6
staggered, **5A**:129
Spontaneous moment, **5A**:44
Spontaneous order parameter, **5A**:58
Spontaneous symmetry breaking, **1**:138, **1**:151, **1**:152
Spread of disease, **2**:199
Spreading coefficient, **12**:175
Spreading pressure, **16**:143
Spring and bead model, **19**:263, **19**:279
Spurious pole, **3**:206, **3**:210, **3**:212, **3**:216, **3**:217
SQK dimer model, **13**:243–244
for biomembranes, **13**:283–285
K-type transition conservation property, **13**:249
thermodynamic properties, **13**:270
Square gradient approximation, **12**:44, **12**:74
Square gradient theory, **5A**:184
Square Ising lattice, **6**:489
Square lattice 2d Ising model, **14**:60
Square lattice, **14**:41, **14**:96, **14**:97, **14**:98, **14**:113
bond diluted, finite clusters, **7**:157
infinite clusters, **7**:157
diluted, percolation and, **7**:156
Square Model, **11**:186–8, **11**:193
Square-root power law, **15**:29
$SrTiO_3$, **3**:583, **3**:647, **3**:649
Stability conditions, **1**:26, **1**:27, **1**:30, **1**:33, **1**:103
Stability conditions, **2**:4, **2**:6, **2**:46
Stability, **1**:28, **1**:30, **1**:32, **1**:41
limit, first-order transition, **8**:33
linear, analysis, **8**:319–322
Stable distributions, **6**:553
Staggered field, **1**:444, **5B**:70
Staggered
field, **9**:116

magnetic field, **9:**4, **9:**12, **9:**16, **9:**66, **9:**115
magnetization, **9:**48, **9:**52, **9:**71, **9:**93, **9:**126
spin density, **9:**93
Staggered magnetization, **15:**146–7
Staggered susceptibility coefficients, **3:**261
Staging phenomena [in layered materials], **17:**112, **17:**122, **17:**196
Standard [non-equilibrium] model, **17:**4
    boundary conditions specified, **17:**12
    with chemical potential gradient, **17:**108–112
    in combination with electric field, **17:**112–118
    interface stability in transverse CPG, **17:**119–121
    co-existence curve for, **17:**76
    collective behaviour, **17:**95–98, **17:**192
    with combination of direct and random drives, **17:**105–107
    criticisms/limitations, **17:**5, **17:**187
    driving field introduced, **17:**11
    and dynamic mean-field theories, **17:**5, **17:**16–19
    fast rate limit, **17:**148–153
    finite-size effects, **17:**51–52
    fixed point, **17:**68
    interface fluctuations suppression, **17:**81–83, **17:**103–105
    lack of droplets in ordered states, **17:**75
    master equation, **17:**11
    mesoscopic approach, **17:**5–6, **17:**19–25, **17:**115
    microscopic dynamics, **17:**11–13
    and multi-layer models, **17:**121–126
    and multi-species models, **17:**127–138
    and multi-temperature model, **17:**95, **17:**96, **17:**98
    one-dimensional models, **17:**9, **17:**154–170
    phase separation, **17:**76–80
    with quenched impurities, **17:**144–148
    and randomly driven systems, **17:**95–98, **17:**193
    rates, microscopic, **17:**11–12

    with repulsive interactions, **17:**18–19, **17:**138–144
    scaling behaviour, **17:**67–73
Standard map, **15:**14, **15:**17
Standard ordering, **3:**177
Star algebra, **1:**140
    asymmetric, **1:**282
    extended, **1:**304
Star function, **5B:**209
Star generating function, **3:**33
Star graph contribution, **3:**472, **3:**473
Star graph, **3:**60, **3:**67, **3:**87, **3:**89, **3:**289
Star tree, **3:**6, **3:**22, **3:**33, **3:**37
    free, **3:**31
    mixed, **3:**31
    rooted, **3:**22, **3:**29
    unlabelled, **3:**29, **3:**31
    unrooted, **3:**31
Star, **3:**5, **3:**11, **3:**13, **3:**17, **3:**19, **3:**20, **3:**34, **3:**37, **3:**38, **3:**39, **3:**42, **3:**47, **3:**49, **3:**51, **3:**56, **3:**63, **3:**84
    homeomorphically irreducible, **3:**11
    labelled, **3:**22, **3:**39
    rooted, **3:**30
    unlabelled, **3:**31, **3:**37, **3:**40
Star, *HI*, **3:**11, **3:**13, **3:**14, **3:**15, **3:**41, **3:**42, **3:**68
Star-tetrahedron substitution, **3:**411
Star–triangle relation, **3:**411
Star-triangle transformations, **11:**88
Star-triangle transformation, **2:**213, **3:**450, **3:**461, **3:**462, **10:**16
Starting configuration, **5B:**11
Static correlations, **14:**77
Static critical phenomena, **5B:**37
Static crossover exponent, dilute Heisenberg model, **7:**259
Static properties, calculation, **7:**209
Static scaling hypothesis, **6:**438
Static scaling relation, **5B:**70
Static scaling, **5B:**57
Statics, **14:**76–89
Stationary algebra, **19:**92
Stationary distribution, **14:**288
    ASEP, **19:**117
    exponential, **19:**66
    grand canonical, **19:**62
    limiting, **19:**54

Stationary states
    classification, **19**:79–80
    construction, **19**:137–138
    exclusion process, **19**:95–97
    free fermion systems, **19**:191
    Heisenberg chain, **19**:80
    infinite time limit, **19**:53–54
    nonequilibrium systems, **19**:53
    obtaining, **19**:5–6
    perturbation, **19**:59–60
    and *SU* (2) symmetry, **19**:79–80
Stationary vector, **19**:53–54
Statistical ensemble, **6**:510
Statistical error, **5B**:3, **5B**:4, **5B**:6,
    5B:12
Statistical geometry, **2**:273, **2**:274,
    2:280, **2**:282, **2**:290, **2**:297
Statistical inaccuracy, **5B**:16
Statistical mechanical models, **6**:524
Statistical mechanics, **6**:508
    characteristic length and, **6**:2
Statistical mechanics, **19**:3, **19**:5
Statistical mechanics, large-*n* limit in,
    15:73–165
Statistical mechanics, two-dimensional
    melting, **7**:40–66
Statistical rotationally invariant force
    field, **19**:390
Statistical theories, spinodal
    decomposition, **8**:322–327
Steady state selection, **19**:125,
    19:144–148
Steam, **2**:59, **2**:60
Steepest descents, **1**:185, **3**:33
Steepest-descent method, **6**:165, **6**:170,
    6:218
Step free energy, **10**:31, **10**:35, **10**:36,
    14:140
Step function, **19**:107–108, **19**:117–118,
    19:135, **19**:158
Steps, **14**:151
Sticking probability, **12**:471
Stieltjes integral, **1**:58
Stieltjes series, **3**:204
Stieltjes transform, **15**:97, **15**:129,
    15:136, **15**:170–2, **15**:177, **15**:183,
    15:188, **15**:189, **15**:192, **15**:193,
    15:195, **15**:197, **15**:200, **15**:203–6,
    15:209, **15**:216

Stieltjes–Ostrovsky theorem, **15**:152
Stiffness constant, **14**:16, **14**:27, **14**:55,
    14:72
Stirling's formula, in Darboux's
    theorem, **13**:14
Stirred Burgers equation, **14**:291–7
Stochastic domination, **18**:21, **18**:23–31,
    18:78–84
Stochastic equation, **5A**:175
Stochastic processes, **19**:6, **19**:72–78
Stochastic variables, **6**:510
Stochastic vector model, **5B**:26, **5B**:27
Stochasticity conditions, **19**:178–180
Store, **3**:25
Strains, in alloys, **8**:322
Strassen's theorem, **18**:23–4
Stress tensor, **5A**:183, **5A**:335, **6**:10,
    6:63–65, **6**:87, **6**:119, **11**:90,
    11:105
    superstress, **11**:118
Stress, **6**:272
String expectation values, **19**:164,
    19:166–167, **19**:183
String models, **10**:81
String theory, **19**:256, **19**:257, **19**:260,
    19:262, **19**:408
Strip ordering, **17**:72, **17**:74, **17**:147
Striped dilution, exactly soluble Ising
    model, phase boundary for, **7**:191
Striped incommensurate phase, *see* SIC
    phase
Striped random Ising model, two-
    dimensional, bond random quantum
    transverse Ising chain, **7**:195
Striped randomness, **7**:173
    McCoy–Wu Ising model, **7**:181
    model, **7**:180
        Harris argument, **7**:181
Strips, **14**:110–11, **14**:114
Strong anisotropic scaling, **17**:53–59,
    17:192
Strong anisotropy, **17**:42
    implications, **17**:44
Strong coupling, **19**:404
Strong duality lemma, **18**:183
Strong scaling, **3**:361
Strong tempering, **1**:28, **1**:30, **1**:31
Strong-embedding expansion, **3**:117,
    3:118

Strong-fluctuation regime, **14**:173, **14**:192, **14**:193, **14**:214–15, **14**:343
Strontium titanate, **3**:502
Strontium titanium oxide, **5A**:298
Structural phase transition, **5B**:5, **5B**:21, **5B**:25
Structural phase transitions, **9**:7
Structural transitions, **5A**:297, **14**:14
Structure factor, **11**:86
    Monte Carlo studies, **8**:378–385
Structure factors, **17**:27–28
    above-criticality. *86*, **17**:*100*
    contour plots, **17**:*28*
    fluctuations in, **17**:49–50
    Ornstein–Zernike form, **17**:29, **17**:33, **17**:189
    see also Anisotropic structure factors
Structure function, **16**:43, **16**:45, **16**:47, **16**:110, **16**:116, **16**:117, **16**:*119*, **16**:123
Structure functions, scaling theories, **8**:366–373, **8**:419
    Superconductivity, **8**:6, **8**:440–441
    theory, **8**:7
STS model, **1**:346
SU(2) symmetry
    breaking, **19**:90
    Heisenberg quantum spin system, **19**:34, **19**:35, **19**:42
    and particle injections and absorption, **19**:88
    and scaling behaviour, **19**:101
    and stationary states, **19**:79–80
Sub-lattice magnetization, **5A**:244
Subdivergences, **19**:346–347
Subdominant operators, **19**:259
Subgraph, **3**:61
    connected, **3**:80, **3**:82, **3**:382
    edge disjoint, **3**:61
    full perimeter, **3**:77
    vertex disjoint, **3**:61
    weak, **3**:653, **3**:654, **3**:658
Subject Index 419
Sublattice magnetisation, **1**:67, **1**:88, **9**:3, **9**:48, **9**:116
Sublimating, **12**:19, **12**:93–97, **12**:99
    sublimation curve, **12**:138, **12**:192–193

Submanifold, **19**:162, **19**:164–165
Substitutional dilution, magnets, **7**:152
Substrate, **12**:3–7, **12**:9, **12**:14–18, **12**:22, **12**:68, **12**:139, **12**:150, **12**:164, **12**:167, **12**:189, **12**:191, **12**:385, **12**:474, **14**:346
    potential, **12**:16, **12**:20, **12**:23, **12**:37, **12**:42–45, **12**:49–52, **12**:58–61, **12**:96–103, **12**:107, **12**:109, **12**:113–115, **12**:140, **12**:147–150, **12**:158–159, **12**:162, **12**:169, **12**:173, **12**:189, **12**:193
    random, **12**:168–175
Subtraction scheme, **19**:409
Successive shortest-path algorithm, **18**:163, **18**:171–4, **18**:246
Sugihara–Hendrickson theorem, **18**:274
Sulfur + solvent, **9**:220, **9**:224
Sum graph, **3**:61, **3**:65
Sum rule, **14**:50
Sum rules, **9**:200
Superstable interactions, **1**:12
Super conductivity, **12**:194, **12**:341
Super stability condition, **1**:28
Super-exchange model, **3**:454, **3**:460
    antiferromagnet, **3**:454, **3**:460
Super-renormalizable theory, **6**:142
Super-rough phase, **18**:243–6, **18**:258–61
Super-symmetry, **11**:59, **11**:116
Superbond function, **5B**:229
Superconformal transformations, **11**:117
Superconducting films, phase transitions, **7**:8
Superconducting KY model, **7**:8
Superconducting transition, **5A**:296
Superconducting transitions, **6**:222
    ³He, **6**:416
Superconductivity
    BCS theory, **5A**:2
Superconductor, **5A**:193
    phase transition, **5A**:7
Superconductors, **1**:89, **6**:417, **18**:235–41
    flux creep in, **17**:196
    vortex rings in, **7**:83–84
Supercooled liquid, **5B**:133

Supercooled vapour, **5B:**133
Superdegenerate points, **15:**25
Superexchange, **5B:**67
Superfluid ^{4}He, **14:**14, **14:**90–1
Superfluid density areal, **8:**254
  confined helium, **8:**254
  finite size scaling, **8:**191–192
Superfluid density, **7:**8, **7:**13, **14:**55, **14:**120
  above $_c$, wave vector-dependent, **7:**25–27
  renormalized, **7:**19
  universal jump discontinuity in, **7:**18, **7:**23
  vortices and, **7:**25
Superfluid films, phase slippage, **7:**38
Superfluid flow, **5A:**71
Superfluid helium, **1:**89, **14:**28
Superfluid
  transition, **9:**5
  order parameter, **9:**171
Superfluid transition, **14:**71–3, **14:**82–4, **14:**365
Superfluid velocity, hexatic, **7:**72
Superfluid, **5A:**193
  phase transition, **5A:**7
Superfluidity, **5B:**363, **8:**440–441, **9:**6, **12:**193
  helium films, specific heat, **7:**22
  in confined helium, onset, **8:**254–255
  two-dimensions, **7:**11–31
Superfluids, **1:**84, **1:**89
  Kosterlitz–Thouless transition, **7:**69
  recursion relations, **7:**49
  two-dimensional, vortex pair excitations, **7:**17
  vortex-mediated process, **7:**70
  vortex mobility in, **7:**71
  vortex rings in, **7:**83–84
  vortices in, **7:**13–14, **7:**47
Superfluorescence, **8:**453
Superheated liquid, **5B:**134
Superionic conductors, **17:**4–5, **17:**8, **17:**187
Superlattice of domain walls, **14:**150
Superparamagmetism, **5B:**30
Superposition approximation, **5B:**206
Superposition-type approximation, **2:**279, **2:**299, **2:**300

Supersaturated solution, **5B:**133
Supersaturation, **12:**7
Superstable potential, **1:**51, **1:**59, **1:**95
Superstable reference potential, **5B:**117
Surface amplitude, **14:**364
Surface charge energy, **1:**39
Surface charges, **8:**30
Surface
  configurations, **19:**431
  growth, **19:**3
  phase transitions, **19:**230
Surface contribution, index, **2:**129
Surface corrections, to bulk quantities **8:**10–14
Surface couplings, **14:**10
Surface critical behaviour, **6:**419
Surface
  critical behaviour, **10:**58, **10:**83, **10:**220
  dynamic exponent, **10:**249
  effects (finite-size effects), **10:**76
  exponents, **10:**79, **10:**80, **10:**83, **10:**185–6
    numerical values, **10:**187
    series estimates, **10:**189
  magnetic field, **10:**83, **10:**109
  multicritical behaviour, **10:**190
  singularities, **10:**138, **10:**140, **10:**230, **10:**239, **10:**331
  specific heats, **10:**213
  spin anisotropies, **10:**188, **10:**207, **10:**218, **10:**250, **10:**254, **10:**256
  susceptibility, **10:**52
  transitions, **10:**91, **10:**160–3
    three-dimensional systems, **10:**58–61
Surface curvature, **16:**132
Surface disorder, **14:**326
Surface effect, **3:**361, **5B:**95
Surface effects, **1:**237, **14:**113–20
  percolation, **8:**99–103
Surface energy, **2:**149, **2:**150, **8:**8, **8:**59, **8:**61, **8:**68
  local, **8:**55
  Monte Carlo studies, **8:**389–391
Surface enrichment, **8:**5
  alloys, **8:**14, **8:**94–96
Surface entropy, **8:**51

Surface exchange, **8**:53
  antiferromagnetic, **8**:56–57
Surface exponent of Heisenberg model,
  5B:102
Surface exponents, **8**:2, **8**:3, **8**:49, **8**:62,
  8:63, **8**:64
  bulk and, scaling relations, **8**:48
  two-dimensional Ising model, **8**:53
Surface fields, **8**:9
  finite size scaling, **8**:184
Surface force apparatus, **16**:155
Surface free energy, **1**:25, **2**:121, **2**:122,
  2:124, **2**:125, **2**:127, **2**:129, **2**:131,
  5B:62, **8**:2, **8**:5, **8**:7, **8**:13, **8**:22,
  8:25, **8**:51, **8**:53, **8**:64, **14**:116–17
  definition, **8**:151
  free surface boundary conditions,
    8:150
Surface growth models, *see* Driven-
    interface models
Surface indices, **2**:130, **2**:131
Surface interaction, long-range
    modification, **8**:59–61
Surface lattice constant, **2**:132, **2**:133,
  2:134, **2**:135, **2**:158
Surface layer, **5B**:101
Surface layers
  magnetization, **8**:41
  susceptibility, finite size scaling,
    8:184
Surface melting, **14**:145–8
Surface of criticality, **6**:445
Surface order parameter, **14**:146,
  14:306
Surface ordering, **8**:32, **14**:107
  antiferromagnetic, **8**:57
Surface phenomena, **14**:18
Surface reconstruction, **8**:3, **8**:27,
  8:81–83
Surface scaling, **8**:52
Surface specific heat, **2**:128, **2**:135,
  2:136, **8**:2, **8**:14, **8**:219
  helium, in pores and films, **8**:253
Surface susceptibility, **8**:3, **8**:11, **8**:50,
  8:242, **8**:244
  local, finite size scaling, **8**:184
Surface tension of fluids, **5A**:63
Surface tension *see* Interfacial tension
Surface-to-volume ratio, **16**:163

Surface tension, **1**:229, **5B**:66, **10**:3,
  10:10, **10**:15, **10**:29, **10**:30, **10**:39,
  10:273, **10**:278, **10**:284–5, **10**:290,
  10:296, **10**:306–8, **10**:357, **14**:18,
  14:26, **14**:44, **14**:48, **14**:54, **14**:82,
  14:110, **14**:117–18
  angle-dependent, **10**:16, **10**:32
  boundary conditions, **8**:152
  Ch, **2**:3, **2**:79, **2**:104, **2**:113
  cylindrical definition, **10**:64
  Dobrushin, **10**:39
  experimental, **10**:308
  exponent, **10**:282
Surface transitions, **8**:12, **8**:19, **8**:20,
  8:21–23, **8**:26, **8**:36, **8**:37, **8**:41,
  8:43, **8**:44, **8**:53, **8**:62, **8**:64
  extraordinary, **8**:19–23
  lower critical dimensionality, **8**:53
  ordinary, **8**:19–23
  special, **8**:19–23
Surface–volume ratio, **1**:26
Surface wetting transition, **10**:48
Surface, critical behaviour, **11**:80, **11**:119
  critical exponents, **11**:82, **11**:120
  extraordinary transition, **11**:81, **11**:82,
    11:120
Surface, entropy, **12**:110
  exponents, **12**:113
  free enery, **12**:23–30, **12**:86, **12**:139,
    12:156, **12**:471
  mass exponents, **12**:422, **12**:425,
    12:430
  roughening, **12**:226, **12**:278
  spinodals, **12**:196
  stress, **12**:139, **12**:141
  tension, **12**:5, **12**:22–23, **12**:53, **12**:69,
    12:73, **12**:87, **12**:110, **12**:112,
    12:118–119, **12**:192, **12**:393
Surface, induced disorder, *see* SID
Surface, ordinary transition, **11**:120
  roughening, **11**:2
  scaling exponents, **11**:59
  special transition, **11**:81, **11**:82
Surface-bulk transition, **8**:21
Surface-induced disorder, **14**:145–8
Surface-tangent contact, **2**:13
Surfaces
  adsorption to, **7**:104–109
  roughening, **7**:11

Surfaces and interfaces, **12**:405–410
Surfaces free, percolation on lattices
with, **8**:108–109
long-range order, two-dimensional,
8:56
multicritical behaviour, **8**:23–27
polymer adsorption, **8**:76–80
properties, finite size scaling,
8:182–186
self-avoiding walks, Monte Carlo
methods, **8**:114–115
Surfaces, magnetic
dead layers at, **8**:57–59
ordering, phase diagram, **8**:4, **8**:6
reconstruction, **8**:27
Surfactant, **12**:5
Susceptibilities, **17**:46, **17**:56–57
Susceptibility amplitude
for s.q. lattice, **3**:476
Susceptibility amplitude, **2**:413
Susceptibility coefficient, **3**:281, **3**:282,
3:284, **3**:290, **3**:294, **3**:295, **3**:296,
3:301, **3**:311, **3**:318, **3**:341, **3**:378,
3:380, **3**:381, **3**:390, **3**:529, **3**:530,
3:544
for general spin s, **3**:390, **3**:391
generalized, **3**:295, **3**:341, **3**:344
higher order, **3**:296, **3**:318
low temperature antiferromagnetic,
3:422
low temperature ferromagnetic,
3:421
staggered, **3**:282, **3**:283, **3**:284
zero field, **3**:385
Susceptibility expansion coefficient,
3:285
Susceptibility expansion, **3**:195
high temperature, **3**:186, **3**:190, **3**:191,
3:249
Susceptibility exponent, **3**:305, **3**:319,
3:359, **3**:556, **6**:387
γ, **3**:361, **3**:496, **3**:500, **3**:503, **3**:531,
3:541, **3**:558
γ (d), **3**:468
high temperature, **3**:462
Susceptibility fluctuation theorem,
5A:94, **5A**:108
Susceptibility
generalized, **9**:177

non-ordering, **9**:53, **9**:76, **9**:100, **9**:141
ordering, **9**:72, **9**:73, **9**:94, **9**:99,
9:107, **9**:110, **9**:134, **9**:138,
9:199
staggered, **9**:48
uniform, **9**:77, **9**:108
Susceptibility graph, **3**:289
connected, **3**:386
Susceptibility matrix, **3**:167
Susceptibility series, **1**:327, **3**:271,
3:273, **3**:289, **3**:300, **3**:305, **3**:306,
3:308, **3**:309, **3**:310, **3**:311, **3**:319,
3:320, **3**:321, **3**:381, **3**:528, **3**:532,
3:536, **3**:557, **3**:655
high temperature, **3**:209, **3**:210, **3**:225,
3:232, **3**:241, **3**:252
higher order, **3**:290, **3**:297, **3**:315,
3:320
low temperature, **3**:229
perpendicular, **3**:624
staggered, **3**:286, **3**:287, **3**:288, **3**:295,
3:305, **3**:307, **3**:309
Susceptibility tensor, **6**:299
anisotropic, **6**:330
Susceptibility theorem, **2**:137
Susceptibility, **1**:83, **1**:99, **1**:104, **1**:105,
1:227, **1**:257, **1**:310, **1**:311, **1**:325,
1:326, **1**:328, **2**:22, **2**:33, **2**:40,
2:44, **2**:47, **2**:61, **2**:64, **2**:76, **2**:150,
2:153–7, **2**:159, **2**:191, **2**:221,
2:251, **2**:253–4, **2**:258–9, **2**:261,
2:351, **2**:353, **2**:404, **2**:487, **3**:69,
3:122, **3**:219, **3**:236, **3**:293, **3**:299,
3:300, **3**:315, **3**:316, **3**:327, **3**:362,
3:363, **3**:387, **3**:402, **3**:413, **3**:436,
3:438, **3**:442, **3**:448, **3**:466, **3**:467,
3:475, **3**:496, **3**:500, **3**:501, **3**:524,
3:526, **3**:540, **3**:543, **3**:546, **3**:547,
3:552, **3**:559, **5B**:2, **5B**:18, **5B**:39,
5B:47, **5B**:53, **5B**:70, **5B**:294,
5B:297, **5B**:364, **6**:197, **6**:513,
14:10, **14**:15, **14**:21, **14**:24, **14**:29,
14:48, **14**:49, **14**:51, **14**:102
adiabatic, **2**:472
antiferromagnetic, **3**:202, **3**:209,
3:231, **3**:235, **3**:325, **3**:364,
3:417, **3**:453, **3**:454, **3**:455,
3:458, **3**:461, **3**:552, **3**:554
boundary, **2**:116, **2**:118, **2**:125

bulk, **2:**118
critical point and, **6:**12
    continuous phase transition, **6:**8
dynamical, **2:**453, **2:**477, **2:**480,
    2:485–6, **2:**492, **2:**497–8
expansion, **5B:**296
ferromagnetic, **3:**417, **3:**459
for classical s.c. Heisenberg
    ferromagnet, **5B:**47
frequency-dependent, **3:**631
generalized, **3:**251
high temperature, **3:**215, **3:**232,
    3:424, **3:**425, **3:**429, **3:**431,
    3:432
high temperature derivative, **3:**444
higher order, **3:**292, **3:**299, **3:**314
initial, **2:**199, **2:**229, **3:**378, **3:**379
inverse, **2:**409, **2:**410, **6:**252, **6:**304,
    6:341
isothermal, **2:**384, **2:**472
Kubo, **2:**471
layer, **5B:**62
longitudinal, **5B:**48, **5B:**50, **5B:**52,
    6:237, **6:**273, **6:**344, **6:**400
low temperature, **3:**219
magnetic, **2:**480, **2:**484, **3:**252, **3:**359,
    3:465, **6:**44, **6:**130, **6:**161, **6:**166,
    6:186, **6:**192, **6:**214, **6:**216
of frozen-in dilute magnet, **3:**473
parallel, **3:**572, **3:**596, **3:**597, **3:**600,
    3:611, **3:**612, **3:**615, **3:**637
partial, **3:**404
perpendicular, **3:**572, **3:**596, **3:**598,
    3:599, **3:**600, **3:**604, **3:**606,
    3:607, **3:**611, **3:**623, **3:**625,
    3:630, **3:**632, **3:**633, **3:**637
reduced, **3:**379
singular part, **6:**43
staggered, **3:**186, **3:**251, **3:**260, **3:**285,
    3:294, **3:**308, **3:**364, **3:**455,
    3:458, **3:**460, **3:**547, **3:**665
static Kubo, **2:**472
surface, **2:**119, **2:**125, **2:**136, **5B:**62
temperature derivative, **3:**459
transverse, **5B:**48, **6:**237, **6:**273–274,
    6:337, **6:**398, **6:**399, **6:**400
zero field, **1:**232, **1:**328, **2:**244, **2:**352,
    2:345, **2:**384, **2:**400, **2:**401,
    2:403, **2:**411, **2:**420, **3:**250,

3:369, **3:**384, **3:**388, **3:**389,
    5B:264, **5B:**272, **5B:**273,
    5B:277, **5B:**295, **5B:**311–316
zero frequency, **2:**472
Swendsen–Wang algorithm, **18:**69
Sykes counting theorem, **3:**379
Sykes susceptibility theorem, **3:**453,
    3:467
symbols
    *-circuit, **18:**34–5
    *-clusters, **18:**44
    *-path, **18:**34
Symmetric 8-vertex model, **6:**429,
    6:437, **6:**497
Symmetric eight-vertex Baxter model,
    11:70
Symmetric exclusion process, **19:**43,
    19:79–102, **19:**217
    see also asymmetric simple exclusion
        process (ASEP); symmetric
        simple exclusion process
        (SSEP)
Symmetric group, **3:**26, **3:**27, **3:**28,
    3:291, **3:**292, **3:**293
Symmetric Hamiltonian, Hermitian,
    19:58
Symmetric simple exclusion process
    (SSEP), **19:**10
Symmetric vertex functions, **6:**347
Symmetrical tricritical point, **9:**164,
    9:168
Symmetry
    breaking
        phase transitions, **19:**255
        rotational, **19:**431
        spontaneous, **19:**16, **19:**32,
            19:68–69, **19:**375
    non-Abelian, **19:**80, **19:**82
    quantum algebra, **19:**51
    time reversal, **19:**58–59
Symmetry breaking, **1:**139, **2:**10
Symmetry
    charge conjugation (C), **17:**15
    Euclidean, **17:**84
    Galilean, *see* Galilean transformation
    Ising, **17:**26, **17:**38, **17:**39, **17:**44,
        17:84, **17:**95, **17:**96, **17:**123,
        17:139
    O(n), **17:**96

particle conservation, **17:**19
randomly driven and multi-
  temperature models, **17:**94–96
reflection (R), **17:**16
  reflection, in SPBC, **17:**85–86
standard model, **17:**15–16, **17:**24,
  17:38
supersymmetry, **17:**40
systems with repulsive interactions,
  17:139
time reversal, **17:**25
Symmetry
  conservation, **6:**33
  continuous, **6:**188
  critical point and, **6:**11, **6:**357–421
  cubic, **6:**390, **6:**394
  discrete, **6:**188
  spontaneously broken, **6:**188
Symmetry factor, **3:**125, **3:**126, **3:**128,
  3:129, **3:**130, **3:**133, **3:**138,
  3:139, **3:**140, **3:**143, **3:**146,
  3:147, **3:**154, **3:**156, **3:**158,
  3:159, **3:**160, **3:**162, **3:**167,
  3:168, **3:**169, **3:**173, **3:**174
Symmetry group, **5A:**18, **6:**349
Symmetry number, **3:**9, **3:**39, **3:**41, **3:**46,
  3:49, **3:**125, **3:**268, **3:**272, **3:**275,
  3:285, **3:**287
Symmetry number, **5B:**212
Symmetry plane, **9:**134
Symmetry point, **6:**181
Symmetry properties, **5A:**197
Symmetry, **2:**15, **2:**16, **2:**18, **2:**22, **2:**23,
  2:27–9, **2:**31, **2:**35, **2:**38
Symmetry, **3:**98
  of critical exponents, **3:**440, **3:**441
  spherical, **3:**248
Symmetry-breaking boundary
  conditions, *see* Boundary
  translational fields, **10:**21
"Symmetry breaking" field, **1:**89
Symmetry-breaking fields, clock models
  and, **7:**27–31
Symmetry-breaking, cubic and uniaxial,
  11:48, **11:**49, **11:**50
Symmmetry, quantum algebra, **19:**51
Synchrotron X-ray diffraction, **12:**225
Syozi model, **2:**224, **2:**251, **2:**253,
  2:255–6, **2:**258, **2:**262–4

Syozi model, **3:**474
Syozi–Heisenberg model, **2:**264

T

2d Ising model, **14:**153
3–12/1 dimer model, **13:**244
θ point, **19:**363, **19:**364, **19:**369–370
  see also Blume-Emery-Griffiths model:
  Potts model
T-matrix, **3:**74, **3:**77, **3:**90, **3:**269,
  3:271, **3:**272, **3:**275
Tableau formalism, **19:**318, **19:**324,
  19:325–326, **19:**327, **19:**335–336,
  19:337, **19:**338–340
TABUL, *see* NEWGRQD/TABUL
Tadpole graphs, **6:**328, **6:**332, **6:**336
Tadpole, **3:**11, **3:**69, **3:**70
Tagged particle process, **19:**44–45,
  19:50, **19:**52, **19:**214
Tail σ-algebra, **18:**8, **18:**13–14
Takagi model, **3:**656
Takahashi gas, **1:**184, **1:**186
Tangent vectors, **16:**131, **16:**135
Tauberian theorem, **15:**91, **15:**92
Tay's theorem, **18:**271
Taylor expansion, **13:**6, **19:**321, **19:**322,
  19:333, **19:**409
Taylor series, **15:**181
Taylor's theorem, as case of Darboux's
  theorem, **13:**11
Taylor–Green vortices, **13:**134
TDGL, *see* Ginzburg–Landau
Telephone switching networks, **2:**201
Temperature
  correlation length and, **7:**167
  dilute Heisenberg magnets, **7:**166
  diluted Ising model, **7:**168
Temperature expansions,
  high, **1:**204
  low, **1:**204
Temperature gradient, **5B:**353, **5B:**354
Temperature instability, **6:**378
Temperature scaling parameter, **3:**628
Temperature, increase, **19:**389
Tempering condition, **1:**38
Tempering, **1:**32
Temperley–Lieb algebra, **19:**50, **19:**159,
  19:188, **19:**211, **19:**213, **19:**220

Tense bicontinuous phase, **16**:142
Tensile strengths of liquid columns, **2**:97
Tensor product notation, **19**:239–240
Tensorial structure, **19**:23–26, **19**:294
Terbium, **3**:646, **3**:649, **5A**:135, **5A**:145,
    5A:146, **5A**:147
  critical fluctuations, **5A**:145–147
  magnetic structure, **5A**:145
Ternary
  diagrams, **9**:182, **9**:213, **9**:214
  mixtures, **9**:20, **9**:26, **9**:31, **9**:38, **9**:45,
    9:56
  system with threefold symmetry,
    9:225-7
Ternary fluid mixtures, **12**:154
Terrace–ledge–kink models (TLK), **10**:2,
    10:4, **10**:43, **10**:45, **10**:46, **10**:48
Tethered membranes
  anisotropy, **19**:375
  critical behaviour, **19**:259
  dynamics, **19**:377–388
  experimental realizations,
    19:262–265, **19**:273–276
  field theoretical treatment,
    19:279–305
  generalized $O(N)$ model, **19**:421–426
  grand canonical ensemble, **19**:457
  isotropically polymerized, **19**:374
  long-range interaction, **19**:304–305
  renormalization, **19**:318, **19**:417
  structure, **19**:258, **19**:*263*
Tethered polymerized surfaces, **19**:256
Tetracritical point, **6**:399, **6**:401, **6**:412,
    6:416, **9**:164, **9**:170, **9**:225, **9**:227,
    11:115
Tetracritical points, **14**:28
Tetragonal structure, **5A**:122
Tetrahedron graph, **6**:321
Tetrahedron, **1**:320, **1**:328
  composition, **9**:177
Tetramethylammonium manganese
    trichloride (TMMC), **19**:13, **19**:176,
    19:196, **19**:223
  see also polymers
Teubner–Strey form of structure
    function, **16**:80, **16**:92, **16**:110
Theoretical error estimate, **5B**:19
Thermal conductivity coefficient,
    5A:260

Thermal conductivity, **3**:649, **5A**:188,
    5A:264, **5A**:266, **5B**:90, **14**:90
Thermal diffusion coefficient, **5A**:260,
    5A:261
Thermal diffusion, **5A**:260, **5A**:262,
    5A:264, **5A**:266
Thermal diffusivity, **3**:649, **5A**:288
Thermal effects in quenched dilute
    magnets, **7**:163–169
Thermal expansion coefficient, **14**:83
Thermal expansion, helium, **8**:254
Thermal measurements, **14**:87
Thermal percolation behaviour, Monte
    Carlo methods, **7**:206
Thermal percolation crossover
  in diluted Heisenberg magnets,
    7:242
  in dilute isotropic n-vector models,
    7:194
Thermal properties, **14**:85
Thermal relaxation time, **5B**:363
  of xenon, **5B**:363, **5B**:364
Thermal roughness, **14**:264, **14**:273,
    14:310–12
Thermally excited fluctuations,
    14:155–7, **14**:160, **14**:167–79
Thermodynamic critical exponents,
    3:444
Thermodynamic function, **3**:119, **3**:131
  critical value, **3**:360
Thermodynamic functionals, **6**:527
Thermodynamic functions, **1**:49, **1**:58,
    1:77, **1**:77, **1**:90, **1**:125
  convexity, **1**:98
  microcanonical, **1**:33
Thermodynamic inequality, **2**:26, **2**:45
Thermodynamic isotropy, **2**:16, **2**:18
Thermodynamic limit, **1**:10, **1**:11, **1**:14,
    1:17, **1**:23, **1**:25, **1**:29, **1**:31, **1**:32,
    1:37, **1**:38, **1**:39, **1**:40, **1**:41, **1**:42,
    1:50, **1**:51, **1**:52, **1**:53, **1**:55, **1**:58,
    1:60, **1**:63, **1**:65, **1**:75, **1**:76, **1**:77,
    1:82, **1**:88, **1**:89, **1**:92, **1**:94, **1**:95,
    1:96, **1**:97, **1**:99, **1**:101, **1**:143,
    1:144, **1**:145, **1**:146, **1**:147, **1**:151,
    1:152, **1**:155, **1**:157, **1**:163, **1**:165,
    1:166, **1**:168, **1**:170, **1**:171, **1**:180,
    1:183, **1**:185, **1**:186, **1**:187, **1**:203,
    1:205, **1**:214, **1**:345, **1**:355, **3**:45,

3:47, 3:71, 3:84, 3:369, 3:371,
3:372, 3:378, 3:398, 5B:113–121,
6:430, 9:234, 9:246, 9:251, 9:252,
15:86, 15:89, 15:91, 15:139,
15:151, 15:158, 19:67, 19:110,
19:119, 19:120, 19:131–134,
19:138–139, 19:212
convexity properties, 1:18, 1:19
for general interactions, 1:17, 1:18,
1:22
for lattice system, 1:12
for nearest-neighbour interaction,
1:14–17, 1:21
passim, 5B:127, 5B:128, 5B:130,
5B:144, 5B:164, 5B:168
surface, 1:17
Thermodynamic perturbation theory for
single defects, 7:186
Thermodynamic potentials, 6:515,
6:516, 6:521, 6:531, 6:541
singular part, 6:512
Thermodynamic pressure, 1:43
Thermodynamic properties of dimer
models, 13:260–270
4–8 models, 13:265–270
entropy, 13:287
SQK model, 13:270
three-dimensional, 13:279–280
VH family, 13:260–265
Thermodynamic properties, Monte Carlo
method, 7:203
Thermodynamic quantities,
singularities, 6:522
Thermodynamic scaling, 3:444, 3:477
Thermodynamic singularity, 5A:2
Thermodynamic stability, 1:33, 1:36,
1:103, 2:4, 5B:110
Thermodynamic state
metastable, 5B:133
Thermodynamic surface quantities,
10:109, 10:110
Thermodynamic universality hypothesis,
14:22
Thermodynamics, Ch, 2:1
Thermodynamics, criticality and,
8:150–153
Thermogram, 5B:363, 5B:362
Theta algorithm in sequence
extrapolation, 13:37–38

Thin film calculation, 5B:4, 5B:31,
5B:63
Thin film, 12:337, 12:397–400
(see also Films)
finite size scaling, 8:39
homogeneity, 8:63
magnetic, 8:3
Thinning out process,
renormalization group transformation,
6:18
Third law of thermodynamics, 1:77
Third sound
in helium films, 7:4, 7:31–39
Maxwell's equations, 7:36–39, 7:69
superfluid helium films, 7:7
Third-order transition, 5B:346
Three component solution, 3:473
Three-component model, 16:22–4,
16:60, 16:82
phase behavior, 16:33–40
phase diagram, 16:34, 16:35, 16:38
results of, 16:33–55
Three-dimensional dimer models,
13:277–280
Three-field phase diagram, 9:82
Three-order-parameter model,
16:85–7
Three-particle distribution function,
5B:160
Three-phase
coexistence, 9:86, 9:173, 9:179
monohedron, 9:14, 9:59–63, 9:88,
9:111, 9:143, 9:169, 9:178,
9:192, 9:193, 9:195
Three-phase triangle, 16:6, 16:7, 16:11,
16:40, 16:41, 16:63, 16:148
Three-point correlation functions,
17:37–40, 17:48–49
Three-scale-factor universality, 14:24
Three-state systems, 19:363,
19:365–366, 19:370–371
exact solution, 19:29
Tight-binding model, 12:252, 12:253,
12:254, 12:258, 12:261,
12:264–267, 12:272, 12:273,
12:283, 12:297–303, 12:307–310,
12:315
Time correlation function, 5A:169,
5A:171, 5A:175, 5A:216, 5A:328

of gross variables, **5A**:176,
    5A:216–236
long time tail, **5A**:169
theory, **5A**:336
Time derivatives of gross variables,
    5A:172, **5A**:176
Time evolution, **2**:445
Time
    evolution, **19**:76
        density profile, **19**:99,
            19:117–118, **19**:122
        effect of driving, **19**:203
        operator, **19**:18, **19**:22, **19**:56,
            19:69–70, **19**:83, **19**:86,
            19:109
        spectral properties, **19**:6, **19**:72
        shock distribution, **19**:119,
            19:121
        TASEP, **19**:136
    reversibility, **19**:58–59
    scale separation, **19**:69–70, **19**:223
    translation operator, **19**:5
Time reversal, **2**:445
Time scale of fluctuations, **5A**:171
Time, continuum limit, **12**:323
    dependent model, **12**:445,
        12:455–456, **12**:459
Time-correlation function, **2**:449, **2**:450,
    2:451, **2**:489, **2**:490, **2**:491, **2**:497
Time-dependent correlation, **5B**:74
Time-dependent phenomena, **5A**:71–81
TMMC *see* tetramethylammonium
    manganese trichloride
TMMC, **5A**:148, **5A**:149, **5A**:150,
    5A:151, **5A**:152, **5A**:153
Tobolsky–Eisenberg theory, **9**:219
Toeplitz determinant, **2**:108, **2**:112,
    2:140, **2**:144
Toeplitz determinants, **1**:230, **1**:237,
    1:250
Tomonaga model, **12**:277, **12**:280,
    12:327–330
Tonks gas, **1**:182, **1**:183, **1**:191
Toom model, **17**:169–170, **17**:174
Töplitz determinants, **10**:4, **10**:16
Topological classes, entangled polymers,
    7:132
Topological constraints, statistical
    mechanics, **7**:103

Topological defects, statistical
    mechanics, **7**:11
Topological invariant, **2**:231, **2**:234,
    2:237–8
Topological repulsion, DNA, **7**:134
Topological type, **3**:268
Topology count, **3**:100
    computer approach, **3**:100
Topology, **3**:11, **3**:58, **3**:68, **3**:70, **3**:88,
    3:89, **3**:99, **3**:103, **3**:108, **3**:109,
    3:110, **3**:112, **3**:116, **3**:132, **3**:133,
    3:163, **3**:167, **3**:173, **3**:383
    bridge, **3**:99, **3**:104
    ladder, **3**:89, **3**:384
    non-ladder, **3**:89
    polymer entanglements, **7**:147
    realization, **3**:99, **3**:104, **3**:108
    ring, **3**:151
    star, **3**:383, **3**:386, **3**:387,
    θ, **3**:384, **3**:385, **3**:386
    tetrahedral, **3**:109
Toroidal boundary conditions, *see*
    Boundary conditions
Toroidal geometry, **11**:76
Toroidal lattice, **2**:105
Total energy, **3**:122
Total interaction, **14**:181
Totally asymmetric simple exclusion
    process (TASEP)
    as biopolymerization model,
        19:221
    collective velocity, **19**:147
    density profile, **19**:139
    exact results, **19**:148, **19**:*150*
    maximal current principle, **19**:144
    with open boundaries, **19**:125–126
    phase transitions, **19**:147
    physics, **19**:145, **19**:146
Toughening temperature, **14**:140
Toughness exponent, **14**:137
Trace
    basic, **3**:281
    calculation, **3**:520
    reduced, **3**:260, **3**:279, **3**:289
Trace problem, **3**:278, **3**:279, **3**:280
    single site, **3**:277
Tracer diffusion, **19**:44–45, **19**:89,
    19:101, **19**:220
Traffic flow model, **17**:134

Traffic models, **19**:3, **19**:12, **19**:118, **19**:122, **19**:123–124, **19**:148, **19**:154–157, **19**:160
Trajectories
  hyperbolic model, **6**:101
  renormalization group, **6**:31
Transfer matrices
  anisotropic two-dimensional Ising model, **8**:180
  conserved charges, **19**:35
  correlation length and, **8**:158
  energy gap, **19**:69
  equivalent, **19**:72
  formalism, **19**:30, **19**:31, **19**:32, **19**:225–226
  hard square lattice gases, thermodynamics, **8**:232
  in two-dimensional vertex model, **19**:225–226, **19**:227, **19**:229
  quantum hamiltonian limits, **8**:178–181
  statistical mechanics models, **19**:5
  vertex models, **19**:6
Transfer matrix algorithm, **18**:193–4, **18**:200
Transfer matrix approach, **7**:203
Transfer matrix eigenfunctions, **7**:184, **7**:192
Transfer matrix method, **14**:44–5, **14**:103, **14**:177, **14**:180, **14**:267–74
Transfer matrix techniques, **7**:178
Transfer matrix, **1**:90, **1**:153, **1**:155, **1**:156, **1**:157, **1**:158, **1**:159, **1**:161, **1**:192, **1**:193, **1**:194, **1**:195, **1**:196, **1**:197, **1**:198, **1**:201, **1**:203, **1**:206, **1**:461, **1**:469, **1**:477, **2**:105, **5B**:142, **9**:239, **10**:41, **10**:44, **10**:45, **10**:62, **11**:58, **11**:70, **11**:72, **11**:73, **11**:74, **11**:79, **11**:88, **11**:94, **11**:108, **11**:109, **11**:118, **12**:31, **12**:279, **12**:294–298, **12**:323–327
  corner, **11**:88
  diagonalization, **1**:361
Transfer operator, **1**:158
Transfer-matrix, **16**:34
Transformation
  dilatation, **6**:64
  homogeneous dilatation, **6**:52

non-linear, **6**:545
similarity, **6**:32
special conformal, **6**:51
Transformation law
  for correlation function, **6**:454, **6**:460
  for free energy, **6**:266
Transformation of parameters, dilatation and, **7**:239
Transformation of variables, **6**:24
Transformation, **3**:224, **3**:226, **3**:229, **3**:231, **5A**:20, **5A**:21, **5A**:22, **5A**:24, **5A**:29, **19**:73–74, **19**:179, **19**:182, **19**:189
  decoration, **1**:239
  decoration-iteration, **1**:270, **1**:271, **1**:291, **1**:294, **1**:298, **1**:302, **1**:321
  dual, **1**:237, **1**:247, **1**:248, **1**:270, **1**:271, **1**:279, **1**:281, **1**:284, **1**:294, **1**:298, **1**:321
  low → high temperature, **3**:455
  star-triangle, **1**:239, **1**:241, **1**:270, **1**:271, **1**:278, **1**:279, **1**:280, **1**:281, **1**:283, **1**:284, **1**:288, **1**:292, **1**:294, **1**:297, **1**:298, **1**:302, **1**:305, **1**:312, **1**:321, **3**:381
Transformations, **13**:120–129, **13**:138
  function-changing, **13**:120–121, **13**:124–126
  problems, **13**:121–122
  singularity-changing, **13**:121, **13**:126–129
  problems, **13**:122–124
  transformation function properties, **13**:127–128
Transition
  amplitudes, **19**:166
  matrices, **19**:45–46
  probabilities, **19**:17, **19**:199–200, **19**:226, **19**:255, **19**:408
Transition behaviour, dimer models, **13**:252–260, *see also* K-type transitions; Onsager-type transitions; Phase transitions
  critical point analytic behaviour, **13**:256–260
  energy, **13**:255
  matrix structure, **13**:254

Pfaffian method, **13**:253–254
pole movement, **13**:258–259
specific heat, **13**:256
Transition by breaking of analyticity,
  15:16
Transition curves, dilute Heisenberg
  model, series expansion methods,
  7:230
Transition
  displacive, **3**:488, **3**:646
  first order, **3**:163
  second order, **3**:163
Transition
  extraordinary, **10**:87, **10**:100, **10**:105,
    10:115–6, **10**:156–7, **10**:172,
    10:224–5, **10**:326
  ordinary, **10**:87, **10**:100, **10**:115,
    10:156–7, **10**:159, **10**:161,
    10:164, **10**:170–3, **10**:180–3,
    10:190, **10**:201, **10**:204, **10**:206,
    10:212, **10**:217, **10**:222, **10**:238,
    10:253, **10**:330
  special, **10**:88, **10**:100, **10**:115,
    10:156, **10**:159, **10**:164, **10**:167,
    10:169, **10**:171, **10**:180, **10**:183,
    10:185, **10**:193, **10**:204, **10**:212,
    10:222, **10**:248, **10**:331
  special anisotropic or m-special,
    10:190, **10**:253–5
  surface, **10**:87, **10**:100
Transition line, **2**:7, **2**:15, **2**:35, **2**:36,
  2:37
Transition metals,
  $3d$, **3**:503
  surfaces, dead layers, **8**:57
Transition points, **1**:301
Transition probability, **5B**:3, **5B**:7, **5B**:8,
  5B:9, **5B**:16, **5B**:21, **5B**:25, **5B**:28,
  5B:73, **5B**:74, **5B**:78, **5B**:94,
  5B:95, **5B**:104
  many-particle, **5B**:73
  single-particle, **5B**:73
Transition temperature,
  eight vertex problem, no field,
    1:454
  free fermion model, **1**:451
  general F model, **1**:427
  modified F model, **1**:427
  modified KDP model, **1**:439, **1**:441

ice rule model, no external field, **1**:391
  with external field, **1**:423
  with external field, $y = 0$, transition,
    1:416
  with external field, $y \pm 1$ transition,
    1:437
Transition temperatures
  coherent potential approximations,
    7:221
  cluster methods, **7**:214
  coherent potential approximation,
    7:217
  concentration and, cross over effects,
    7:165
  dilute Ising model, series expansion
    methods, **7**:227
  diluted Hieisenberg spin systems,
    coherent potential
    approximations, **7**:217
  dilute magnets, **7**:271
  dilute transverse Ising systems, **7**:270
  experimental results, **7**:263
  Hieisenberg models, **7**:164
  in Ising system, **7**:160
    bounds, **7**:189
  McCoy–Wu Ising model variant,
    7:182
  mean field approximations, **7**:211
  Monte Carlo methods, **7**:204
  quenched site diluted Ising
    ferromagnet, **7**:159
  scaling and, **7**:236
  site diluted Ising ferromagnet, **7**:158
  two-dimensional bond diluted Ising
    model, **7**:254
  XY models, **7**:164
Transition,
  conductor-insulator, **2**:199
  critical, **12**:17, **12**:24, **12**:26, **12**:31–35,
    12:38–39, **12**:40, **12**:47, **12**:171
  dewetting, **12**:15, **12**:18, **12**:88,
    12:95–97, **12**:100, **12**:155
  drying, **12**:17
  extraordinary, **12**:133, **12**:147
  first order wetting, **12**:26, **12**:27,
    12:32, **12**:45, **12**:49, **12**:52,
    12:59, **12**:71–74, **12**:81, **12**:84,
    12:96, **12**:100, **12**:102, **12**:105,
    12:149, **12**:165, **12**:193

fourth order wetting, **12**:56
gas-liquid, **2**:323, **2**:331, **2**:358,
 2:462
in binary liquid mixtures, **12**:67–92
layering, **12**:15, **12**:18, **12**:32, **12**:96,
 12:103, **12**:117, **12**:164, **12**:169,
 12:171
multicritical, **12**:39, **12**:56, **12**:59,
 12:84, **12**:91, **12**:124
ordinary, **12**:147
order-disorder, **12**:19, **12**:120,
 12:123, **12**:127, **12**:145, **12**:168,
 12:178
prewetting, **12**:15, **12**:17, **12**:30,
 12:75, **12**:90–91, **12**:105,
 12:108, **12**:156, **12**:163, **12**:164,
 12:171
roughening, **12**:15, **12**:103, **12**:164
second order, **2**:360
solid–liquid, **2**:271, **2**:290, **2**:323,
 2:331, **2**:358, **2**:360
tricritical wetting, **12**:17, **12**:28,
 12:49, **12**:56, **12**:90, **12**:124
wetting, **12**:6, **12**:7, **12**:15, **12**:17,
 12:18, **12**:26, **12**:28, **12**:31–35,
 12:42, **12**:60–70, **12**:100–106,
 12:144, **12**:146–151, **12**:168
Transitions ("continuous"), **9**:208–12
Transitions in synthetic polynucleotides,
 with branching structures,
 7:116–121
Transitions,
 antiferroelectric, **1**:426, **1**:430,
 1:438
 first order, **1**:3
 gas–liquid, **1**:3, **1**:183, **1**:186, **1**:232
 gas–solid, **1**:183
 liquid–gas, **1**:138
 liquid–solid, **1**:232
 magnetic, **1**:3
 order–disorder, **1**:243
 second order, **1**:3
 see Extraordinary transitions, First-
 order transitions,
 Kosterlitz–Thouless
 transitions, Liquid-gas
 transitions,
 Localization–delocalization
 transition, Ordinary transitions,

Phase transitions, Roughening
 transitions, Special transitions,
 Surface–bulk transition, Surface
 transitions, Tricritical
 transitions
 see Surface
Translation group, **1**:172
Translation invariance, **1**:113, **19**:128,
 19:291
Translation invariant, **1**:116, **1**:133,
 1:157
Translational correlation length in
 anisotropic melting, **7**:81
 measure, **7**:39
Translational invariance, **6**:46,
 17:155–158, **17**:191
Translational order, **7**:50
 phonon fluctuations and, **7**:76
 two-dimensional melting, **7**:40–45
Translational symmetry, **1**:24
Translationally invariant perturbation,
 1:40
Translationally invariant spin interaction,
 15:92
Transport anomalies, **5A**:189
Transport coefficient, **2**:444, **2**:451,
 2:452, **2**:462, **2**:478, **2**:480, **2**:486,
 2:491, **5A**:175, **5A**:185, **5A**:188,
 5A:196, **5A**:232, **5A**:236, **5A**:260,
 5A:326–329, **5A**:332, **5A**:334,
 5A:336, **5A**:340, **5A**:343, **5B**:90,
 5B:91, **9**:153, **14**:19, **14**:21, **14**:70,
 14:90
 critical anomalies, **5A**:167, **5A**:175,
 5A:185–189, **5A**:236, **5A**:265
 divergences near the critical point,
 5A:187, **5A**:189
 near the critical point, **5A**:166,
 5A:187
 renormalization, **5A**:341
Transport phenomena, **2**:450, **2**:455,
 2:461, **5B**:27
Transport processes, **2**:478
Transverse correlation length, **6**:164
Transverse correlation, **5B**:292
Transverse correlations, **10**:224
Transverse disorder *see* disorder,
 nonpotential
Transverse field, **1**:71, **6**:382

Transverse fields, **7**:173
Transverse fluctuations,
    magnetization of 2 dimensional
        systems with rotational symmetry
        and, **6**:13
Transverse Ising models one-
    dimensional, percolation fixed
    point, scaling, **7**:261
    phase boundaries, **7**:261
    quantum critical behaviour, **7**:194
    solution, **7**:182
Transverse local velocity, **5A**:214
Transverse projector, **19**:391,
    19:454–456
Transverse spin fluctuations, **6**:275
Transverse susceptibility, **5A**:129,
    5A:130
Trapping, **19**:389
Travelling salesman problem,
    18:185–6
Tree approximation, **6**:129
Tree approximation, **17**:64–67
Tree
    free, **3**:35
    rooted, **3**:22, **3**:35, **3**:56
    unrooted, **3**:34
Tree-like configurations,
    polynucleotides, **7**:121
Triangular cactus, **2**:198, **2**:210
Triangular condition, **6**:69, **6**:72
Triangular Ising solid-on-solid model
    (TISOS), **18**:256–8
    see also solid-on-solid model (SOS)
Triangular lattices, **14**:50
Triangular matrices, **6**:71
Tricritical behaviour, **6**:200, **6**:297,
    6:363, **6**:417, **6**:526
    cubic-like, **6**:398
Tricritical
    dynamics, **9**:152
    end-point, **9**:142
    exponents, **9**:32, **9**:46, **9**:49, **9**:50,
        9:52, **9**:53, **9**:55, **9**:62, **9**:70,
        9:106, **9**:137, **9**:178, **9**:199
    exponent
        classical, **9**:53, **9**:107, **9**:108, **9**:187
        in two dimensions, **9**:144
    hypothesis, **9**:31, **9**:53, **9**:96
    isotherm, **9**:58

points, **9**:2–155, **9**:188, **9**:203–204
    anomalous, **9**:55, **9**:153
    in four-component systems, **9**:192,
        9:194
    in three-component systems, **9**:191
scaling, **9**:24, **9**:25, **9**:26, **9**:50
points
    symmetrical, **9**:164, **9**:168, **9**:170,
        9:174, **9**:179, **9**:184, **9**:207–12,
        9:214, **9**:215, **9**:218, **9**:222,
        9:223
    unsymmetrical, **9**:164, **9**:168–9,
        9:171, **9**:174, **9**:178, **9**:181,
        9:204, **9**:214, **9**:223, **9**:224
    variable, **9**:105
Tricritical exponents, **6**:413
Tricritical phenomena, **5B**:69, **5B**:95,
    8:24
Tricritical point, **3**:496, **3**:497, **3**:507,
    5B:4, **5B**:68, **6**:33, **6**:98, **6**:129,
    6:170, **6**:200, **6**:235, **6**:398, **6**:400,
    6:415, **6**:539, **8**:24, **8**:33, **12**:124,
    12:152–154, **16**:8, **16**:10, **16**:15,
    16:34, **16**:*35*, **16**:37, **16**:*38*, **16**:53,
    16:*58*, **16**:59, **16**:61, **16**:92,
    16:95–6, **16**:120, **16**:151, **17**:133,
    17:140–142, **19**:259, **19**:363–371,
    19:464–466
antiferromagnetic, **8**:26
bulk, surface critical behaviour,
    8:23–25
Tricritical points, **14**:28
Tricritical
    profile, **10**:315
    end point, **10**:358
Tricritical region, **6**:202
Tricritical state, **19**:263, **19**:273
Tricritical systems, **6**:540, **8**:422–432
Tricritical transitions, **8**:43, **8**:44
    scaling relations, **8**:41
Tricritical, cross-over exponent, **11**:40
    indices (Ising), **11**:51
    Ising model, **11**:118
    $0(n)$ model, **11**:116
    point, **11**:39
    three-state Potts, **11**:42
Trilocal operator, **19**:365
Triple
    critical point, **9**:228

line, **9:**28, **9:**55, **9:**81, **9:**86, **9:**87,
    9:101, **9:**102, **9:**107, **9:**108,
    9:110
point, **9:**36
Triple point T_3, **12:**17, **12:**141
Triple point, **5B:**191, **5B:**193–195,
    11:128
Triple subgraphs, **6:**323
Triple-spin interaction model, **6:**429
Trotter's product formula, **1:**127, **1:**128
True correlation lengths (t.c.l.), **14:**49,
    14:50, **14:**58, **14:**59, **14:**87,
    14:109–10
True inverse range of correlation, **2:**434,
    2:438
Truncation of series, **19:**349, **19:**350n
TSOS (Triangular solid-on-solid) model,
    11:44, **11:**46
Tubular phase, membrane, **19:**374–377
Turbulence,
    characteristic length, **6:**2, **6:**3
Turning operator, **1:**246
Two spin exchange model, **2:**479
Two-body force, **1:**154
Two-body interaction, **19:**363, **19:**364,
    19:366, **19:**370–371
Two-component mixture, **5B:**367
Two-component order parameters, **7:**6
Two-dimensional dimer models,
    13:240–247, *see also* K dimer
    models
    3–12/1, **13:**244
    4–8/1, **13:**244–245, **13:**251, **13:**266,
    4–8/2, **13:**245, **13:**249–250,
        13:251, **13:**266–269, **13:**292–293
    4–8/4, **13:**246–247, **13:**269–270
    4–8s/2/1, **13:**245–246
    SQK models, **13:**243–244, **13:**249,
        13:270, **13:**283–285
    VH models, **13:**241–243, **13:**251–252,
        13:260–265
Two-dimensional ice, **1:**215, **1:**266
Two-dimensional model microemulsion,
    16:*43*
Two-dimensional pressure, **16:**130
Two-dimensions
    continuous symmetry, magnetic
        systems, **7:**10
    melting, **7:**8

statistical mechanics, **7:**40–66
phase transitions in, **7:**2, **7:**3
superfluidity, **7:**11, **7:**26
Two-layer model, **17:**121–126
Two-level systems (TLS), **18:**218–20
Two-loop graph, **6:**312, **6:**337
Two-loop order, **19:**259, **19:**340–347,
    19:349–350, **19:**355–356
Two-membrane contact operator, **19:**358
Two-order-parameter model, **16:**83–5
Two-particle transition probability,
    19:166, **19:**199–200
Two-phase coexistence, **9:**173, **14:**139
Two-phase region,
    analytic, **2:**97
Two-point correlation function, **5B:**235
Two-point correlation functions,
    17:30–32, **17:**53, **17:**66, **17:**154
Two-point correlation, **3:**121
Two-point correlations
    and exponential decays, **17:**32–33
    and power law decays, **17:**26–32
    and simulation studies, **17:**41–48
    singularities in, **17:**26–37
Two-point function, **6:**164, **6:**324
Two-scale factor universality, **8:**68
Two-scale-factor universality, **14:**4,
    14:10, **14:**24, **14:**26–8, **14:**34–6,
    14:39, **14:**48, **14:**52, **14:**63
Two-species models, **17:**127
    blocking transition in, **17:**128–135
    one-dimensional models, **17:**164–169
    polarized lattice gas, **17:**135–138
    see also Blume–Emery–Griffiths
        model; Potts model
Two-spin correlation function, **6:**386,
    6:388
Two-temperature model, **17:**95, **17:**96,
    17:98, **17:**171–173
    see also Multi-temperature models
Two-variable scaling form, **7:**183

U

$U(1)$ symmetry, **19:**34, **19:**35, **19:**90
Ultra-violet attraction, **6:**223
Ultra-violet divergence, **6:**11, **6:**56,
    6:121, **6:**523
Ultraviolet (UV)

convergence, **19**:294, **19**:322, **19**:334, **19**:381, **19**:423
cutoff, **19**:272, **19**:280
divergence, **19**:280, **19**:284, **19**:285, **19**:292, **19**:299, **19**:321, **19**:340, **19**:397, **19**:414, **19**:418, **19**:423, **19**:428, **19**:465
finite property, **19**:281, **19**:301, **19**:438
Ultraviolet (uv) cut-off, **11**:4
Ultraviolet
singularities, **10**:123, **10**:125, **10**:128, **10**:130, **10**:132, **10**:134, **10**:137, **10**:203, **10**:227, **10**:229, **10**:238, **10**:241, **10**:248
divergences, **10**:214, **10**:317, **10**:334
Umklapp terms, **15**:58–9
Umklapp, **12**:261, **12**:271, **12**:277, **12**:327–329
Unbinding transition, **19**:371–374
Unbinding, **14**:150, **14**:163, **14**:180
critical behaviour associated with, **14**:186
in 1 + 1 dimensions, **14**:193
in presence of frozen randomness, **14**:219–20
universitality classes for, **14**:189
via thermally excited fluctuations, **14**:193–218
Unbounded cluster, **2**:198
Uncertainty relations, **12**:249
Uncorrelated disorder, **14**:293–5
Uncorrelated randomness, dilute magnetism, **7**:156
Undulation spectrum, **16**:155
Uniaxial systems, **14**:85–6
Uniaxially anisotropic Heisenberg magnets, three-dimensional, cross over exponents, **7**:165
Unicursal, **1**:264
Uniform magnetic field, **9**:66, **9**:115
Uniform magnetization, **5A**:38–40, **9**:76, **9**:108, **9**:141
Uniformly clustering, **1**:150, **1**:170
"Union jack" model, **1**:259
Unions of closed polygons, **1**:239, **1**:240
Uniqueness theorem, **18**:43–4, **18**:76–9
Uniqueness, **19**:54–55, **19**:56
Unit cell volume, **14**:47
Unit tensor, **14**:43

Unit vector, **5B**:25
Universal amplitude combinations, **14**:9, **14**:15, **14**:17–18, **14**:26
Universal amplitude ratio, **8**:67, **8**:68, **14**:8, **14**:13, **14**:29
Universal amplitude, **14**:117
Universal behavior, **9**:9
Universal constant, **8**:65
Universal contributions, **14**:115
Universal critical behaviour, **6**:357–421, **7**:153
Universal critical-point amplitude relations, **14**:1–134
Universal factor, **14**:11
Universal function, **14**:23, **14**:46
Universal functions, **6**:373
Universal jump
disontinuity, in superfluid density, **7**:23
Kosterlitz recursion relations and, **7**:18–25
Universal properties, **14**:32, **14**:36
Universal ratio of amplitudes, **9**:73
Universal ratios, **6**:213, **10**:275, **10**:307
amplitudes, **6**:215
Universal relation, **14**:31
Universal scaling form, **14**:7
Universal surface amplitude combinations, **14**:117
Universal-amplitude, **11**:84
quantities, **11**:72
Universality class, **3**:465, **3**:473, **3**:486, **3**:583, **3**:628, **3**:642, **3**:643, **17**:15, **17**:52
for combined direct and random drives, **17**:106
for quenched random impurities, **17**:145
for repulsive interactions, **17**:141
Ising, **17**:10, **17**:94, **17**:139, **17**:141
standard model, **17**:59–72
two-layer model, **17**:126
two-temperature model, **17**:95, **17**:99, **17**:101
uniaxial magnets with dipolar interactions, **17**:95, **17**:101
Universality classes, **8**:56–57
Ising models, **8**:42
two-dimensional XY model, **8**:73

Universality
  exclusion process, **19**:199
  field theoretical formulation of
    O (N) model, **19**:414
  interface fluctuations, **19**:230–236
  large order behaviour, perturbation,
    19:437
  nonequilibrium systems, **19**:3
  physical systems, **19**:7, **19**:255
Universality Hamiltonian, **3**:487, **3**:489,
    3:492, **3**:501, **3**:502
Universality hypothesis, **3**:361, **3**:429,
    3:477, **3**:501, **3**:507, **3**:559, **3**:571,
    3:579, **3**:582, **3**:583, **5B**:24, **5B**:45,
    5B:50
Universality principle, **3**:647
Universality, **3**:321, **3**:624, **3**:627, **3**:636,
    3:642, **3**:648, **5A**:2, **5A**:16–20,
    5A:31, **6**:128, **6**:294, **6**:358, **7**:240,
    8:75, **8**:76, **9**:44, **9**:45, **9**:63, **10**:76,
    10:79, **10**:82, **10**:156, **10**:270,
    10:274, **11**:3, **11**:39, **11**:51, **11**:59,
    11:71, **11**:96, **11**:97, **11**:100,
    11:107, **12**:116, **12**:220, **12**:223,
    12:232, **12**:289, **12**:292, **12**:368,
    12:379, **14**:4–9, **14**:23, **14**:25,
    14:27, **14**:31, **14**:32, **14**:35, **14**:41,
    14:45
  class, **5A**:18, **5A**:20, **6**:420, **6**:522,
    6:526, **6**:554, **12**:42–43, **12**:117,
    12:134, **12**:148, **12**:152,
    12:154–155, **12**:157, **12**:178
  classes, **10**:80, **10**:160
  classes for delocalization, **14**:172–3
  conformational phase transitions in
    macromolecules and, **7**:102
  dilute magnets, **7**:232
  hypothesis, **5A**:17, **5A**:18, **5A**:19,
    14:30
  in folded macromolecules, **7**:122
  multi-scale-factor, **10**:165, **10**:173,
    10:235
  nonlinear theory: homogeneous
    systems, **6**:88–91
  of singular part of scaling function,
    6:119–121
  scaling and, **8**:66–69
  scaling functions, **6**:115
  statement, **5A**:19

three-scale-factor, **10**:170
van der Waals forces
  weak, **8**:74
Unnormalized moments, **14**:60
Unsolved problems, **1**:485
Unsymmetrical tricritical point, **9**:164,
    9:168, **9**:169, **9**:171
Upper critical dimension, **10**:91, **12**:30,
    12:32, **12**:39, **12**:64–66, **12**:79,
    12:110
  fractal dimensionality, **12**:469
Upper critical dimensionality, **14**:11,
    14:198
Upper marginal dimensionality, **14**:40,
    14:63
U_q [SU (2)] symmetry, **19**:108, **19**:109,
    19:119
Ursell construction, **3**:44
Ursell expansion, **6**:472
Ursell function, **5B**:206, **5B**:209,
    5B:211
  hatted, **5B**:213
Ursell functions, **1**:46, **1**:135, **3**:145,
    3:262, **9**:244, **9**:262, **9**:280, **9**:285,
    9:291, **9**:297, **11**:173, **11**:174
UV *see* ultraviolet

V

Vector spins, **8**:18
V-dimensional sphere, **15**:79
Vacancy excitation, **19**:193
Vacuum state wave functions, **1**:262
Vacuum state, **1**:261, **19**:200, **19**:202,
    19:203, **19**:441–442
Vacuum states, **5A**:240, **5A**:241
Vacuum, anomalous dimension, **6**:45,
    6:98
Vacuum-to-vacuum expectation, **1**:234,
    1:236, **1**:250, **1**:262
Vacuum–vacuum-like graphs, **6**:326
Vaks–Larkin model, **3**:488, **3**:502
Valence, **3**:138, **3**:146
  generalised, **3**:159
  g-Valence, **3**:159, **3**:160, **3**:162
van der Waals equation, **3**:444
van der Waals law, **3**:450
van der Waerden transformation,
    3:375

Van Beijeren model, **10**:41
    Eberlein construction, **10**:42
Van Beijeren–Schulman (vBS) rates,
    17:18, **17**:149, **17**:151, **17**:152,
    17:*153*
Van der Waals equation, **2**:38, **2**:41,
    2:54, **2**:474, **2**:477
Van der Waals forces, **12**:7, **12**:19–30,
    12:41–46, **12**:48, **12**:57, **12**:58,
    12:60, **12**:64, **12**:68, **12**:86–87,
    12:142, **12**:144, **12**:147, **12**:151,
    12:154, **12**:158–159, **12**:163–164,
    12:170, **12**:175, **12**:180–181,
    12:186, **12**:189, **12**:190, **19**:363
Van der Waals gas, **1**:166
Van der Waals limit, **1**:168
Van der Waals model, **2**:40, **2**:316
Van der Waals theory, **1**:3, **10**:3, **10**:60,
    10:211, **10**:237, **10**:273, **10**:292,
    10:305
Van Hove theorem, **1**:186, **1**:197,
    1:198
Van Hove theory, **11**:80
van der Waals
    binary mixture, **9**:207
    equation of state, **9**:169
    limit, **9**:97, **9**:105
    long-range interactions, **9**:66, **9**:179
van der Waals critical point, **5B**:112,
    5B:160, **5B**:170, **5B**:189
van der Waals equation, **5B**:108–112,
    5B:116, **5B**:149, **5B**:151, **5B**:156,
    5B:168, **5B**:180, **5B**:189, **5B**:251
    binary mixtures, **5B**:163
    generalized, **5B**:190
van der Waals interaction, **16**:32, **16**:53,
    16:90–1, **16**:105
van der Waals isotherm, **5B**:153
van der Waals limit, **5B**:121, **5B**:124,
    5B:128, **5B**:131, **5B**:138, **5B**:145,
    5B:189
van der Waals loop, **5B**:112
van der Waals mean field theory, **5A**:2
van der Waals theory, **5B**:157, **5B**:344
van der Waals transition, **5B**:195
van der Waals-Maxwell theory, **5B**:108,
    5B:113, **5B**:132, **5B**:136, **5B**:138,
    5B:186
Vanishing of correlations, **15**:88

Vapor pressure curve, **9**:172
Vapour pressure curve, **2**:56
Variational approximations, **19**:352–354,
    19:442–444, **19**:445–449
Variational methods, **2**:370
Variational principle, **1**:148, **1**:149,
    3:143, **2**:456, **2**:480
Vector models, **16**:28–32, **16**:59–68
Vector order-parameter field, **16**:84
Vector representation, particle (spin)
    configuration, **19**:*24*
Vector spin models, **14**:39, **14**:40
Velocity autocorrelation function,
    5A:340
Velocity
    collective, **19**:61–62, **19**:123, **19**:125,
    19:147
    pattern, **19**:388
Velocity mode, **5A**:253, **5A**:255
Velocity of sound, **5B**:359
Vertex configurations, **3**:656, **3**:658,
    3:659
Vertex deletion, **3**:137
Vertex disassembly, **3**:137
Vertex disjoint, **3**:61, **3**:66
Vertex factor, **3**:140, **3**:159
    renormalized, **3**:136
Vertex function, **5B**:215, **6**:147, **6**:310,
    6:349, **6**:554
    renormalized, **5B**:207
8-Vertex model, **6**:94, **6**:98, **6**:99
Vertex functions, **17**:60, **17**:64
Vertex models, **14**:252, **19**:51,
    19:225–229
Vertex of order, **5B**:1, **5B**:212
Vertex of valence two,
    insertion, **3**:518, **3**:519
Vertex pair disassembly, **3**:153
Vertex perimeter,
    full, **3**:83
Vertex renormalization constant,
    6:202
Vertex renormalization, **3**:3, **3**:135,
    3:136, **3**:141, **3**:142, **3**:147, **3**:155,
    3:158, **3**:165, **6**:529
    correlations, **3**:135
Vertex weight, **3**:654, **3**:655, **3**:659,
    3:660, **3**:662
Vertex, **5A**:288

Vertex, clipped, **3:**137
  coordination number, **3:**11
  degree, **3:**11
  equivalent, **3:**139
  renormalized, **3:**147
  rooted, **3:**124
  single, **3:**139
  suppression, **3:**11
  valence, **3:**11, **3:**124
  second order, insertion, **3:**11
Vertical weight theorem, **3:**590
Vesicles, **14:**365, **16:**155–61
  floppy fluid, **16:**157–61
  shape of stiff fluid, **16:**156–57,
    16:157
VH dimer models, **13:**241–243
  conservation property, **13:**251–252
  spatial anisotropy, **13:**252
  thermodynamic properties,
    13:260–265
Vicinal-surface in crystal growth, **17:**178
Villain model, **10:**40
Villani's limit theorem, **9:**260
Virasoro algebra, **11:**56, **11:**58, **11:**95,
    11:97, **11:**98, **11:**100, **11:**117
Virial coefficient, **3:**1, **3:**2
  of hard sphere gas, **3:**463
Virial coefficients, **1:**47, **2:**486
Virial expansion, **1:**47, **1:**134, **3:**118,
    3:148, **3:**371, **5B:**120, **5B:**172
Virial series, **1:**42, **1:**43, **1:**44
Virial theorem, **5B:**172
Virtual crystal approximations,
    7:210–213
Virtual processes, **12:**249, **12:**251,
    12:267, **12:**283, **12:**285, **12:**309,
    12:310, **12:**325
Virus ϕX174, single stranded DNA,
    nucleotide sequence, **7:**110
Viscosity divergence, **14:**90
Viscosity, **3:**649
  dynamics, **7:**69
  fluid-like, free disclocations and,
    7:70
  linear polymers solutions, **7:**134
  see drift velocity
Viscous fingers, **12:**392–394, **12:**472,
    12:475
Volume exclusion, **3:**219

Vorlex-antivortex correlation function,
    11:46
Voroni polygon, **2:**275, **2:**277, **2:**282,
    2:293, **2:**296, **2:**300
Voronoi construction, **7:**86
Vortex charge neutrality, **7:**83
Vortex diffusion, **7:**39
Vortex dynamics, near
    Kosterlitz–Thouless transition, **7:**31
Vortex excitations, **7:**19, **11:**2,
    12:328–329
  fugacity, **11:**26
Vortex fugacity, **7:**20
Vortex glasses, **18:**234, **18:**238–9,
    18:246–8
Vortex pair excitations in two-
    dimensional superfluids, **7:**17
Vortex rings
  in superconductors, **7:**83–84
  in superfluids, **7:**83–84
Vortex unbinding transition, third sound
    and, **7:**36
Vortices, **10:**9, **11:**22, **11:**29
  amplitude fluctuations and, **7:**17
  bound, recursion relations and, **7:**25
  in superfluids, **7:**13–14, **7:**47
  in two-dimensional XY model, **7:**15
  phase transitions and, **7:**7
  p-state clock models and, **7:**1
  superfluid density and, **7:**25
  Taylor–Green, **13:**134
  unbound isolated, **7:**18
Voter model, **19:**49, **19:**162–163
  biased, **19:**163–164, **19:**185

W

Walks, random, **8:**72
Walks, **14:**365
  self-avoiding at surfaces, **8:**107–108
  at surfaces, Monte Carlo methods,
    8:114–115
  model, polymer chain, **8:**189
Wall-fluid
  interactions, **10:**211
    long-range, **10:**213, **10:**219
  phenomena, **10:**272
  potentials, **10:**278
  perturbations (critical), **10:**332

Walls, heavy, **12:**242, **12:**245, **12:**312
  superheavy, **12:**231, **12:**242, **12:**245,
    12:312
Ward identities, **6:**509, **10:**208, **10:**289,
    10:339, **10:**351, **11:**58, **11:**93,
    11:110
  conformal, **11:**89, **11:**91, **11:**105,
    11:119
Ward identity, **17:**60, **17:**68
Water
  + ammonium sulfate + ethanol+
    benzene, **9:**170
  + benzene, **9:**203
  + ethanol, **9:**203
  + ethanol + benzene + ammonium
    sulfate, **9:**197, **9:**200, **9:**206
  + ethanol + *n*-butanol + isooctane,
    9:199
  + hexane + phenol + pyridine,
    9:192
Water–amphiphile structure function,
    16:48, **16:***50*
Water–amphiphile systems, **16:**7, **16:**20,
    16:69–74, **16:**115–28
Water–disordered phase interfacial
    tension, **16:***61*
Water–oil–amphiphile mixtures
  interfacial properties, **16:**13–16
  phase behavior, **16:**5–13
  structure, **16:**16–18
Water–water structure function,
    16:*16*, **16:**17, **16:**43–4, **16:***44*,
    16:*46*, **16:***47*, **16:**48, **16:**68,
    16:163
Water/microemulsion interface at three-
    phase coexistence, **16:**87–92,
    16:*89*, **16:***91*, **16:***92*
Water/microemulsion interfacial tension,
    16:*14*, **16:**15
Water/oil interface at three-phase
    coexistence, **16:**87–90, **16:***89*
Water/oil interfacial tension, **16:***14*,
    16:15, **16:***51*, **16:***52*, **16:**53,
    16:57, **16:**61, **16:**91, **16:**110,
    16:164
Wave function, **6:**529, **19:**37, **19:**39,
    19:84, **19:**354, **19:**439
Wave vector dependent susceptibility,
    5A:89, **5A:**92

Weiner measure, conditional, **1:**126
Weak anisotropy, **17:**42, **17:**53
Weak coupling, **9:**234
Weak embedding expansion, **3:**117,
    3:118, **3:**120, **3:**131, **3:**133,
    3:135
  for Ising model, **3:**117
Weak graph expansion, **1:**452, **1:**457
Weak long-range potential, **1:**9
Weak mean number, **2:**238
Weak mixing, **1:**173
Weak tempering, **1:**31, **1:**125
Weak-fluctuation regime, **14:**172,
    14:191, **14:**343
Weakly coupled chairs, experimental
    results, **7:**264
Weakly incommensurate phase, **12:**221,
    12:226, **12:**232, **12:**238, **12:**240,
    12:245, **12:**247, **12:**309
Weber function, **5B:**152
Wedge geometry, **11:**86, **11:**88
Weeks columnar model, **10:**64
Wegner matrices, **15:**187
Wegner model, **15:**166–7, **15:**169,
    15:186, **15:**201–7, **15:**210–16
Weierstrass functions, **15:**13
Weight factors, **6:**493
  non-linear, **6:**453
Weight functions,
  non-linear, **6:**495
Weight, bonding, **3:**384, **3:**386,
    3:387
  dynamic horizontal, **3:**632
  horizontal, **3:**587, **3:**588, **3:**600,
    3:601, **3:**602, **3:**603, **3:**605,
    3:606, **3:**608, **3:**609, **3:**610,
    3:611, **3:**613, **3:**614, **3:**615,
    3:632
  χ, **3:**386
  λ, **3:**383, **3:**384
  vertical, **3:**587, **3:**590, **3:**592, **3:**593,
    3:594, **3:**600, **3:**601, **3:**602,
    3:603, **3:**605, **3:**606, **3:**608,
    3:609, **3:**610, **3:**611, **3:**613,
    3:614, **3:**615, **3:**632
k-Weight,
  strong, **3:**89
  weak, **3:**89
Weighting function, **3:**73

Weiner integration, **1:**114, **1:**132
Weingarten equation, **16:**132
Weiss mean field equation, **5B:**251
Weiss mean field theory, **5B:**112,
    5B:170, **5B:**183
Weiss model, **1:**166, **1:**230, **2:**40, **2:**41,
    2:43, **2:**44, **2:**54
Weiss theory, **1:**3
Wetting transition, **10:**4, **10:**54, **10:**60,
    10:103, **10:**271–2
   critical point, **10:**103–4, **10:**334
   first-order, **10:**104
   temperature, **10:**103
   tricritical, **10:**105
Wetting transitions, **16:**15, **16:**53–5,
    16:61, **16:**90–6, **16:**115
Wetting, **8:**5, **8:**14, **8:**34, **8:**83–94,
    14:137, **14:**180, **14:**228–44,
    19:371
   in presence of bulk disorder,
    14:298–326
   in presence of surface disorder,
    14:326–46
   perfect, near critical point, **8:**83–89
   transition, **14:**55, **14:**143–5
   with long-range forces, **14:**244–9
Wetting, complete, **12:**11, **12:**13,
    12:18–19, **12:**31–36, **12:**39–49,
    12:125, **12:**127, **12:**134,
    12:141–144, **12:**154, **12:**171,
    12:174
   critical, **12:**13, **12:**17, **12:**24–26,
    12:51, **12:**53–56, **12:**59–66,
    12:75, **12:**78–85, **12:**100, **12:**114,
    12:125, **12:**170–174
   end point, **12:**149
   experiment, **12:**93–109
   films, **12:**l60, **12:**165, **12:**167, **12:**182,
    12:185, **12:**189
   first order, **12:**13, **12:**17, **12:**21, **12:**26,
    12:32, **12:**43, **12:**71–81,
    12:96–100, **12:**102, **12:**105,
    12:108, **12:**169–170
   helium experiment, **12:**102–104
   incomplete, **12:**11, **12:**125
   interfacial, **12:**145, **12:**166–167,
    12:187, **12:**189
   metals and semiconductors,
    12:97–98

multicritical, **12:**39, **12:**56, **12:**59,
    12:84, **12:**91, **12:**97, **12:**194
   pre, **12:**13, **12:**21, **12:**30, **12:**75,
    12:90–91, **12:**105, **12:**108
   second order, **12:**13, **12:**49, **12:**62,
    12:90, **12:**149
   transition, *see* transition
   tricritical, **12:**17, **12:**28, **12:**40, **12:**56,
    12:90, **12:**169
   triple point, **12:**18, **12:**95–98,
    12:115
Whitney polynomial, **3:**655, **11:**37
Whitney rank function, **2:**264, **2:**266
Whitney rank function, **3:**86
Wick expansion, **6:**299, **6:**303, **6:**330
Wick ordered products, **9:**249
Wick theorem, **1:**233, **1:**234, **1:**235,
    1:250, **1:**254, **19:**214
Wick's theorem, **6:**134, **6:**137, **6:**367,
    12:260
Widom function, **6:**336
Widom model, **16:**24–7, **16:**55–8,
    16:56
Widom relation, **9:**46, **10:**285
Widom scaling theory, **19:**230
Widom–Rowlinson model, **11:**167
   continuum, **18:**125–9
   lattice, **18:**20, **18:**30, **18:**70–2, **18:**77,
    18:103–4, **18:**108
Wiener integral, **1:**114, **1:**123, **1:**124,
    1:125, **1:**126, **1:**127, **1:**128
Wiener path integral, **7:**134
Wiener processes, **5B:**111
Wightman
   axioms, **9:**234, **9:**239, **9:**240
   functions, **9:**236–7, **9:**238
Wigner ensemble, **15:**98, **15:**179,
    15:183, **15:**185–9, **15:**194, **15:**202,
    15:205, **15:**206
Wigner law, **15:**172
Wigner model, **15:**171–201, **15:**203
Wigner–Seitz cell, **2:**275, **3:**574
Wilson expansion, **5B:**19, **5B:**27
Wilson formulation of critical
    phenomena, **5A:**23
Wilson functions, **10:**151, **17:**68
   see Gell-Mann–Low
Wilson modification of generalized
    Landau theory, **5A:**55

Wilson transformation, **6**:547
Wilson's Feynman graph method,
    6:305
Wilson's theory of phase transitions,
    5A:38, **5A**:54, **5A**:55, **5A**:82,
    5A:83
Wilson–Fisher fixed point, **17**:6, **17**:21,
    17:141, **17**:172
Wilsons's Recurrence Relation, **6**:73
Wilson–Fisher ϵ-expansion, **19**:446
Winding angle, **14**:98
Winding number, **15**:18, **15**:21, **15**:25,
    17:130
Wing
    coexistence surface, **9**:136
    critical lines, **9**:55, **9**:136
    critical points, **9**:101
Wired-boundary condition, **18**:52–3
Witten–Sander model, **12**:343–344,
    12:357, **12**:360
Wolf-construction, **12**:3
World line, summing over, **19**:255,
    19:408
Wulff construction, **14**:152
Wulff construction (1901), **10**:5, **10**:12,
    10:17, **10**:32, **10**:55
Wulff shape, **19**:230
Wynn's ϵ algorithm in sequence
    extrapolation, **13**:36–37
    series analysis application, **13**:42–48

X

X-ray scattering, **16**:16, **16**:153–54
X-ray structure function angular
    dependence, **7**:60
X-reference critical dimension, **12**:276,
    12:281, **12**:317, **12**:332
X-Y model, **1**:179, **1**:181, **1**:205, **1**:206,
    1:213, **3**:184, **3**:298, **3**:299, **3**:310,
    3:500, **6**:513, **6**:526
    antiferromagnetic, **3**:580, **3**:583
    classical, **3**:298, **3**:636
    dynamic properties, **3**:630
    spin-infinity, **3**:601, **3**:624, **3**:625,
        3:627
    two-dimensional, **3**:231, **3**:641
    two-dimensional, renormalization
        group equation, **6**:28

Xe, **2**:62, **2**:67
Xenon on copper, **12**:221, **12**:224,
    12:238–240, **12**:247, **12**:251,
    12:262, **12**:268, **12**:285
Xenon, **5A**:327, **5B**:197, **5B**:349,
    5B:352, **5B**:353, **5B**:363, **5B**:364,
    5B:392, **5B**:393
    initial point, **5A**:307
XH network, **12**:312–315, **12**:317
XXZ model, **12**:272–276, **12**:281,
    12:288, **12**:300, **12**:326,
    12:331–333
    antiferroelectric, **12**:303
XY chains, pure one-dimensional
    properties, **7**:178
XY magnetism, **7**:11
XY magnets, **7**:4
    See also under Classical XY model;
        Dilute magnets; Dilute XY
        model; Diluted XY model;
        Isotopic XY layer magnets;
        Quenched diluted XY models;
        Spin half diluted XY magnet;
        Spin half XY model; XY
        chains
    model, **7**:48
    diluted, **7**:191
    exact limiting slope methods,
        7:194
    magnetism, lattice vortex
        Hamiltonian, **7**:16
    specific heat, Monte Carlo
        simulation, **7**:23
    striped randomness models,
        7:181
    three-dimensions, transition
        temperatures, **7**:164
    two-dimensional, **7**:11–31
    vortices, **7**:15
    vortex pair excitations, **7**:17
    three-dimensional, specific heat,
        7:264
XY model, **8**:56, **8**:57, **11**:20, **11**:22,
    11:24, **11**:28, **11**:48, **11**:49,
    12:152, **12**:253, **12**:263–271,
    12:285, **12**:302, **12**:325, **19**:6,
    19:266
    Correlation functions, **11**:25
    critical behaviour, **8**:244

in a field, **11**:26
two-dimensional, **8**:57
   finite size scaling, **8**:193
   universality class, **8**:73
XY spin glass, **18**:239
XYZ model, **12**:299, **12**:325

Y

Yang–Mills theories, **10**:81
Yang–Lee edge singularity, **8**:250, **11**:115
Yang–Lee theorem, **1**:51, **1**:52, **1**:53,
   1:54, **1**:55, **1**:57, **1**:60, **1**:104
Yang–Lee zeros, **2**:383
Yb$\frac{1}{2}$Na$\frac{1}{2}$MoO$_4$, **3**:581
Yb$_2$O$_2$ S, **3**:581
Young diagram, **3**:292
Young equation, **14**:142
Young's equation, **12**:4, **12**:7, **12**:63
Yvon–Born–Green, **12**:66

Z

Z factors
   at one-loop order, **19**:298, **19**:301–303
   at two-loop order, **19**:342, **19**:343
   in double ϵ-expansion, **19**:366, **19**:367
   in ϵ-expansion, **19**:270
   in perturbation expansion, **19**:280,
      19:286
   in polymer modelling, **19**:417, **19**:424,
      19:426
   and **R**-operation, **19**:318
   and renormalizability, **19**:384
   and variational approximation,
      19:351–352

Z_2 symmetry, **19**:181, **19**:186
Z_4 model, *see* Ashkin-Teller
Zel'dovich theory, **19**:145
Zeolites, **19**:43, **19**:89
Zernikes' equation, **9**:225
Zero field coefficient, **3**:386, **3**:391,
   3:419, **3**:425
Zero field enthalpy, **3**:531
Zero field susceptibility series, **3**:521
Zero field susceptibility, **6**:300
   longitudinal, **6**:193
Zero normalized mass, **6**:172
Zero temperature fixed point, **14**:162
Zero temperature magnetization, site
   diluted Ising ferromagnet, **7**:158
Zero temperature transitions, **7**:178
   of low dimensional quantum systems,
   7:179
Zero-density phase, **19**:171
Zero-field
   Hamiltonian, **19**:43
   Heisenberg quantum ferromagnet,
      19:41–42
Zero-field susceptibility, **5A**:59, **5B**:264,
   5B:272, **5B**:273, **5B**:277, **5B**:295,
   5B:311–316
Zero-field symmetric vertex functions,
   6:329
Zimm model, **19**:259, **19**:385–388
   see also hydrodynamics
Zinc-aluminium alloys, spinodal
   decomposition, experimental
   studies, **8**:404
Zinn–Justin method, **13**:23–25
   series analysis application, **13**:42–48
Z_p models, *see* Clock models

ISBN 0-12-220320-8

9 780122 203206